American Imperialism and the State, 1893–1921

How did the acquisition of overseas colonies affect the development of the American state? How did the constitutional system shape the expansion and governance of the American empire? *American Imperialism and the State* offers a new perspective on these questions by recasting American imperial governance as an episode of state building. Colin Moore argues that the empire was decisively shaped by the efforts of colonial state officials to achieve greater autonomy in the face of congressional obstruction, public indifference, and limitations on administrative capacity. Drawing on extensive archival research, this book focuses principally upon four cases of imperial governance – Hawai'i, the Philippines, the Dominican Republic, and Haiti – to highlight the essential tension between American mass democracy and imperial expansion.

Colin D. Moore is an Associate Professor of Political Science at the University of Hawai'i. He has won the Walter Dean Burnham Award from the Politics and History section of the American Political Science Association for the best dissertation and the Mary Parker Follett Award for the year's best article in politics and history. His research has been published in *Perspectives on Politics, American Political Science Review*, and *Studies in American Political Development*.

American Imperialism and the State, 1893–1921

COLIN D. MOORE

University of Hawai'i

CAMBRIDGE
UNIVERSITY PRESS

CAMBRIDGE
UNIVERSITY PRESS

University Printing House, Cambridge CB2 8BS, United Kingdom

One Liberty Plaza, 20th Floor, New York, NY 10006, USA

477 Williamstown Road, Port Melbourne, VIC 3207, Australia

314-321, 3rd Floor, Plot 3, Splendor Forum, Jasola District Centre, New Delhi - 110025, India

79 Anson Road, #06-04/06, Singapore 079906

Cambridge University Press is part of the University of Cambridge.

It furthers the University's mission by disseminating knowledge in the pursuit of education, learning and research at the highest international levels of excellence.

www.cambridge.org
Information on this title: www.cambridge.org/9781316606582
DOI: 10.1017/9781316591260

© Colin D. Moore 2017

First published 2017

A catalogue record for this publication is available from the British Library

Library of Congress Cataloging in Publication data
Names: Moore, Colin D., author.
Title: American imperialism and the state, 1893-1921 / Colin D. Moore (University of Hawai'i).
Description: Cambridge, United Kingdom ; New York, NY : Cambridge University Press, 2017. | Includes bibliographical references and index.
Identifiers: LCCN 2016048279 ISBN 9781107152441 (hardback) | ISBN 9781316606582 (paperback)
Subjects: LCSH: United States—Foreign relations—1865-1921. | United States—Colonial question. | United States—Territorial expansion. | Imperialism—History. | Colonies—History. | Nation-building—United States—History. | United States—Politics and government—1865-1933. | Democracy—United States—History. | Constitutional history—United States. | BISAC: POLITICAL SCIENCE / Government / General.
Classification: LCC E713 .M84 2017 | DDC 327.73009/034—dc23 LC record available at https://lccn.loc.gov/2016048279

ISBN 978-1-107-15244-1 Hardback
ISBN 978-1-316-60658-2 Paperback

*For Cynthia Moore and
to the memory of John Moore*

Contents

Figures

Tables

Preface and Acknowledgments

In the late 1970s, the historian James A. Field, Jr. took to the pages of the *American Historical Review* to describe his frustrations with the study of American expansion at the end of the nineteenth century. His provocatively titled essay, "American Imperialism: The Worst Chapter in Almost Any Book," excoriated the profession for developing a "curious narrative" that relied on "an inverted Whig interpretation of history, differing from its predecessor primarily in that now the children of darkness triumph over the children of light."[1] Although scholars have made considerable progress since Field's witty essay appeared, much work remains to be done on the *politics* and *administration* of American expansion.

American Imperialism and the State offers a new interpretation of US expansion at the turn of the twentieth century that focuses on the institutions and structures of the nascent American empire. It argues that we must see the acquisition and governance of overseas colonies as a formative moment in American state development – one that loomed large in the minds of several presidents and the early architects of American foreign policy in the twentieth century. The concern, for many of them, was whether the American constitutional system was compatible with long-lasting formal empire.

To explore this question, this book focuses principally upon four cases of American imperial governance – Hawai'i, the Philippines, the Dominican Republic, and Haiti – to show how the American empire *developed* and *adapted* to the constraints of the American system of separated powers. Although the formal American empire of colonies, dependencies, and protectorates would largely give way to less obvious forms of imperial control, the organizational structures developed to govern the new colonies offer us a unique window into the development of the American foreign policy state, and present some more general challenges to standard stories of American state building and the development of American foreign relations. In short, a central claim of this book is that the evolution of the

---

[1] James A. Field, Jr., "American Imperialism: The Worst Chapter in Almost Any Book," *American Historical Review* 83 (June 1978): 644–5.

American empire cannot be understood without fully understanding the interplay of political institutions that governed this empire.

If the US empire was exceptional, it was not because American liberal traditions made it more benevolent than its competitors. In making this argument, I join scholars such as Julian Go who has observed that "America's national character had little to do with the forms of rule the United States enacted in its colonies."[2] Where this book departs from Go's incisive analysis is its focus on the structure of the American state and the autonomous actions of state officials. In the pages to come, I show how Congress and the American constitutional system constrained the imperial dreams of two presidents and officials in the executive branch – and would eventually lead to the empire's partial collapse by the 1920s. Yet the strategies and institutional capacities developed to overcome these congressional and constitutional restraints would also, I argue, lay the foundations for the modern executive-dominated security state.

My hope is that this book will contribute to an emerging conversation in political science about the role of territorial expansion and empire in shaping the American state. It is my view that American political development requires a clear understanding of American imperialism, but political science – a discipline where the exceptionalism of the United States is frequently taken as a starting point for analysis – has remained surprisingly silent about this period. When it is mentioned, it is too often dismissed as an aberrant or ultimately irrelevant moment in American history. Yet by focusing on the domestic state to develop their theories, scholars have missed an opportunity to apply insights from historical institutional studies of American state building to explain state action in an international context.

This book is meant to fill this gap in the literature by focusing on the development of an overseas American empire. In doing so, I intend for it to provide a historical complement to work on inter-institutional theories of American foreign policy. Second, the book is meant to offer a new analytic perspective to existing narratives of US imperialism. By adopting a state-centered view, this book diverges from accounts that view the development of US empire through the lens of power politics, American racism, indigenous resistance, and local conditions in the colonized nations. Nevertheless, I see this work as a complement, rather than a challenge, to these perspectives. I hope that the historians and sociologists who pioneered these critical studies of American imperialism will agree.

There was a time, not so long ago, when the lengthy acknowledgments that begin so many academic books puzzled me. How, I wondered, given the solitary nature of scholarship, could an author possibly have so many people to thank? I now understand. In the process of writing this book, I have managed to incur more than my fair share of debts to friends, colleagues, and institutions. And now, much to my great delight, I have the privilege to thank them.

The first thanks go to my teachers. As an undergraduate at Swarthmore College, Rick Valelly first introduced me to political science. Were it not for his inspirational teaching and enthusiasm for the study of American political development, it is unlikely that I ever would have gone to graduate school. This book began as a

---

[2] Julian Go, *Patterns of Empire: The British and American Empires, 1688 to the Present* (New York: Cambridge University Press, 2011), 25.

dissertation in the Department of Government at Harvard University. During my years as a graduate student, Eric Schickler's unrivaled knowledge of the Progressive-era Congress greatly improved my understanding of the political dynamics of American imperialism. Theda Skocpol's brilliance and deep understanding of state development and comparative historical research was matched only by her support and generosity in discussing this project from its earliest stages. My greatest debt is to my advisor, Daniel Carpenter. Throughout the process of researching and writing this book – indeed, throughout all of my time as a graduate student and a junior professor – Dan has been a patient and encouraging force. He was among the first people to see the value in this project, and he helped me shape the argument over countless cups of coffee – and even a few fly-fishing trips to western Massachusetts.

This book would not have been completed without the generous support of several institutions. I am indebted to the National Science Foundation and the Center for American Political Studies at Harvard University for financial support during my years as a graduate student. The Center for the Study of American Politics at Yale University gave me the time to finish my dissertation and to begin the process of transforming it into this book. I am particularly grateful to Stephen Skowronek for his advice and support during my time at Yale. The Robert Wood Johnson Foundation's Scholars in Health Policy Research program gave me two years away from teaching. This time allowed me to add several new sections to the manuscript under the guidance of Margaret Weir and John Ellwood at the University of California, Berkeley. Finally, my thanks go to Cambridge University Press for graciously allowing me to adapt, for Chapters 1, 4, and 5, portions of my article "State Building Through Partnership: Delegation, Public-Private Partnerships, and the Political Development of American Imperialism, 1898–1916," *Studies in American Political Development* (2011), 25: 27–55.

Over the last four years, the University of Hawai'i has proven to be an ideal place to complete this project. I owe a special debt of gratitude to Hokulani Aikau, Debora Halbert, Brien Hallett, Manfred Henningsen, Jon Goldberg-Hiller, Ehito Kimura, Neal Milner, Lawrence Nitz, Noenoe Silva, Manfred Steger, and Myungji Yang for their advice and *aloha*. They all discussed my ideas at length in the office and over long dinners in Kaimuki, barbeques on Kaimana Beach, and ridge hikes in the Ko'olau Range.

As I worked on this book over the years, I relied on a network of extraordinary friends who made the process bearable with their sound advice and good humor. Special thanks go to Scott Burns, Jonah Eaton, Dan Hopkins, Annaliesse Hyser, Doug Kriner, Ryan Moore, Dann Nassemullah, Andrew Reeves, Lizzie Rothwell, Danny Schlozman, and Spencer Strub who listened patiently as I prattled on about obscure Progressive-era figures in Cambridge, Philadelphia, and Berkeley. Bob Eaton and Wendy Batson provided me with an evening meal and a bed in Takoma Park, which made the months of archival research in Washington so much easier.

My biggest debt, of course, is to my family. My aunt, Glory Styles, knew just when I needed to take a break from work to explore the East Bay's culinary scene. Despite being occupied with their own careers, my brother and sister kept my spirits high even when they must have wondered if I was really making any progress at all. I dedicate this book to my mother, Cynthia, and to the memory of my father, John. Their love and support made it possible.

List of Abbreviations

Allen Papers	Henry T. Allen Papers, Manuscript Division, Library of Congress. Washington, DC
American Historical Collection	American Historical Collection, Rizal Library, Ateneo de Manila University. Quezon City, The Philippines
Barrows Papers	David P. Barrows Papers, The Bancroft Library, University of California. Berkeley, CA
BIA	Bureau of Insular Affairs
Bryan Papers	William Jennings Bryan Papers, Manuscript Division, Library of Congress. Washington, DC
Butler Papers	Personal Papers of Major General Smedley D. Butler, Marine Corps Research Center. Quantico, VA
Caperton Papers	William Caperton Papers, Manuscript Division, Library of Congress. Washington, DC
Cooper Papers	Henry A. Cooper Papers, Wisconsin Historical Society. Madison, WI
Dole Papers	Sanford B. Dole Papers, Hawai'i State Archives. Honolulu, HI
Edwards Papers	Clarence Edwards Papers, Massachusetts Historical Society. Boston, MA
Forbes Papers	W. Cameron Forbes Papers, Houghton Library, Harvard University. Cambridge, MA
FRUS	*Foreign Relations of the United States* (Washington, DC: Government Printing Office)
Harrison Papers	Francis Burton Harrison Papers in the Burton Norvell Harrison Family Papers, Manuscript Division, Library of Congress. Washington, DC

Hay Papers	John Hay Papers, Manuscript Division, Library of Congress. Washington, DC
Hollander Papers	Jacob Hollander Papers, National Archives and Records Administration II. College Park, MD
Jessup Papers	Philip Jessup Papers, Manuscript Division, Library of Congress. Washington, DC
Knox Papers	Philander Knox Papers, Manuscript Division, Library of Congress. Washington, DC
LeRoy Papers	James A. LeRoy Papers, Bentley Historical Library, University of Michigan. Ann Arbor, MI
Lodge Papers	Henry Cabot Lodge Papers, Massachusetts Historical Society. Boston, MA
Republic of Hawai'i Records	Republic of Hawai'i Records, Hawai'i State Archives. Honolulu, HI
RG 46	Records of the Committee on the Philippines, Senate Records, RG 46, National Archives and Records Administration I. Washington, DC
RG 59	Records of the Department of State, RG 59, National Archives and Records Administration II. College Park, MD
RG 139	Records of the Dominican Customs Receivership, RG 139, National Archives and Records Administration II. College Park, MD
RG 233	Records of the Committee on Insular Affairs, House Records, RG 233, National Archives and Records Administration I. Washington, DC
RG 284	Records of the Government of American Samoa, RG 284, National Archives and Records Administration at San Francisco. San Bruno, CA
RG 350	Records of the Bureau of Insular Affairs, RG 350, National Archives and Records Administration II. College Park, MD
Root Papers	Elihu Root Papers, Manuscript Division, Library of Congress. Washington, DC
Smith Papers	James F. Smith Papers, Washington State Historical Society. Tacoma, WA
Story Papers	Moorfield Story Papers, Manuscript Division, Library of Congress. Washington, DC
Taft Papers	William Howard Taft Papers, Manuscript Division, Library of Congress. Washington, DC
Worcester Papers	Dean C. Worcester Papers, Bentley Historical Library, University of Michigan. Ann Arbor, MI

I

Introduction

Some of the things the Senate does really work to increase the power of the Executive . . .
In this nation, as in any nation which amounts to anything, those in the end must
govern who are willing actually to do the work of governing; and in so far as the
Senate becomes a merely obstructionist body it will run the risk of seeing its power
pass into other hands.

—Theodore Roosevelt (1906)[1]

On the morning of October 12, 1898, President William McKinley rose to address
a crowd of nearly 100,000 at Omaha's Trans-Mississippi Exposition, a sprawling
fairground of monumental buildings devoted to American advances in agriculture, manufacturing, and administration.[2] Just months before, the United States
had emerged victorious from the Spanish–American War, and McKinley was on
a ten-day tour to judge the public's reaction to America's new global role. After
acknowledging the cheers that greeted his arrival on the dais, the president informed
his audience that their nation's victory over Spain came with new "international
responsibilities," which, he explained, would need to be met with the same sense
of courage and duty that prevailed during the war. "Shall we," he asked the crowd,
"deny to ourselves what the rest of the world so freely and so justly accords to us?"
"No!" came the resounding answer. "The war was no more invited by us than were
the questions which are laid at our door by its results." That these new questions
would be difficult ones, the president had no doubt. Whatever the challenges to
come, however, he remained convinced that the nation's "high and unselfish" aims
would pave the way to success. "Right action follows right purpose," he assured
his audience.[3] Months later, in return for a nominal payment of $20 million to
Spain, the United States would formally take possession of its new overseas

---

[1] Theodore Roosevelt to John St. Loe Strachey, February 12, 1906, in *The Letters of Theodore
Roosevelt*, ed. Elting E. Morison (Cambridge, MA: Harvard University Press, 1951), v. 5, 151.

[2] Robert W. Rydell, *All the World's a Fair: Visions of Empire at American International Expositions,
1876–1916* (Chicago: University of Chicago Press, 1984), 106.

[3] William McKinley, *Speeches and Addresses of William McKinley* (New York: Doubleday &
McClue Co., 1900), 101–6.

colonies, bringing the small island territories of Guam and Puerto Rico, along with the entire Philippine archipelago, under American control.

The president was not the only official who thought that "right action" followed "right purpose." For the bureaucrats charged with managing these territories, America's new colonial possessions were not only a responsibility to be borne with a sense of duty, but also an abundant opportunity to demonstrate to the world the genius of American progress. To be sure, Congress and the American public soon lost interest or grew opposed to their nation's new "responsibilities," but the officials who took up the task of governing the new possessions brought with them a belief in the transformative power of science, infrastructure, and rational administration.[4] Although colonial officials never hesitated to include rhetorical flourishes about the "republican" nature of their empire, the ability to operate outside the normal constraints of democratic politics was what they found most attractive about the colonies. For these technocratic reformers – many of whom were disgusted by the corruption and spoils politics that characterized the nineteenth-century American state – the new possessions presented an opportunity to apply the most modern theories of Progressive governance in an environment where checks on their power were minimal. There would be no political machines to dislodge, no voters to placate, and no institutional legacies to overcome in the colonial periphery. Managed by this "blessings-of-civilization trust," to borrow Mark Twain's famous (and bitterly sarcastic) characterization of the US imperial state, the colonies would become a vast billboard to advertise their nation's arrival as a world power.

Although American empire is often dismissed as a weak imitation of the more potent European form – or, more troubling, its existence simply denied – it was far more capable and its goals were far more ambitious than is often recognized.[5] In an age when the transformative power of the state was still a politically charged issue at home, American colonial administrators constructed powerful and activist colonial regimes to engage in social engineering projects that often exceeded those attempted by the domestic state.[6] They built highways and railroads. They established agriculture experimentation stations and regulated narcotics. Civil service rules were in place from the earliest days of colonial administration.[7] As a result of the colonial state's extensive education programs, English became the *lingua franca* of the Philippines.[8] Model prisons were built according to contemporary theories of criminology, and extensive public health investments reduced tropical diseases

---

[4] Michael Adas, *Dominance by Design: Technological Imperatives and America's Civilizing Mission* (Cambridge, MA: Harvard University Press, 2006), 165.

[5] This fact, of course, is hardly forgotten by the millions of people who were ruled by the United States. For an example of the generally dismissive accounts of American formal empire, see, for example, Niall Ferguson, *Colossus: The Rise and Fall of American Empire* (New York: Penguin Press, 2004). The eleven states that came directly or indirectly under American rule during this period were Hawai'i, Cuba, the Philippines, Puerto Rico, Guam, American Samoa, the Virgin Islands, the Dominican Republic, Haiti, Nicaragua, and Liberia.

[6] Alfred W. McCoy, *Policing America's Empire: The United States, the Philippines, and the Rise of the Surveillance State* (Madison, WI: University of Wisconsin Press, 2009), 37.

[7] Stanley Karnow, *In Our Image: America's Empire in the Philippines* (New York: Random House, 1989); Peter W. Stanley, *A Nation in the Making: The Philippines and the United States: 1899–1921* (Cambridge, MA: Harvard University Press, 1974); Richard E. Welch, Jr., *Response to Imperialism* (Chapel Hill, NC: University of North Carolina Press, 1979).

[8] Karnow, *In Our Image*, 202.

and infant mortality, and provided Manila with its first sewer system.[9] Yet much like domestic Progressive programs, these projects were bundled within a paradigm of white and specifically *American* cultural superiority. As one newly arrived official wrote in a passage that captures both the ambitious nature of colonial thinking and the racial lens through which the entire project was seen,

A new government is being created from the ground up, piece added to piece as the days and weeks go by. It is an interesting phenomenon, this thing of building a modern commonwealth on a foundation of medievalism – the giving to this country at one fell swoop all the innovations and discoveries which have marked centuries of Anglo-Saxon push and energy.[10]

Only seven years after McKinley's address in Omaha, Theodore Roosevelt faced another foreign policy dilemma that would have equally far-reaching consequences. The Dominican Republic, deeply in debt to European creditors, was preparing to default on its loans, and Roosevelt, fearing that German, British, or even Italian interests might intervene to force Santo Domingo to maintain payments, offered to take responsibility for the debt. Unlike McKinley, however, Roosevelt (in his inimitable style) famously conceded that he had "about the same desire to annex it as a gorged boa constrictor might have to swallow a porcupine wrong-end-to."[11] That Congress and the American public would never support such an action was, of course, the unspoken subtext. Instead of outright annexation, Roosevelt brought the Dominican Republic under American control through a unique partnership between American bureaucrats and Wall Street bankers whereby the United States arranged for a private loan to refund Dominican debt in exchange for the effective transfer of Dominican sovereignty to a US-controlled protectorate.[12] Although the policy faced fierce opposition in Congress, where Roosevelt was accused of usurping the Senate's treaty-making rights and engaging in illegal negotiations with foreign powers, this controversial neocolonial solution, later dubbed "Dollar Diplomacy" by the press, would serve as the model for subsequent colonial regimes in Haiti, Nicaragua, and Liberia during the Taft administration.

The American system of empire would change yet again a few years later – this time under the Democratic administration of Woodrow Wilson. His arguments for national self-determination in other parts of the world notwithstanding, Wilson ordered the invasion of Haiti and the Dominican Republic in 1915 and 1916,

---

[9] Stanley, *Nation in the Making*.

[10] Daniel Williams quoted in Julian Go, "Global Perspectives on the U.S. Colonial State in the Philippines," in *The American Colonial State in the Philippines: Global Perspectives*, ed. Julian Go and Anne L. Foster (Durham, NC: Duke University Press, 2003), 1. See also Julian Go, *American Empire and the Politics of Meaning: Elite Political Cultures in the Philippines and Puerto Rico during US Colonialism* (Durham, NC: Duke University Press, 2008); Julian Go, "Chains of Empire, Projects of State: Political Education and U.S. Colonial Rule in Puerto Rico and the Philippines," *Comparative Studies in Society and History* 42 (April 2000): 333–62.

[11] Theodore Roosevelt to Joseph Bucklin Bishop, February 23, 1904, in *The Letters of Theodore Roosevelt*, ed. Morison, v. IV, 734.

[12] My thinking about Dollar Diplomacy has greatly benefited from the diplomatic historian Emily S. Rosenberg's work. See, for example, her outstanding history of this era, *Financial Missionaries to the World: The Politics and Culture of Dollar Diplomacy* (Cambridge, MA: Harvard University Press, 1999).

respectively, expanding on Roosevelt's receivership and bringing the entire island of Hispaniola under direct American administration. During these "interventions," as they were euphemistically known, American officials – many of whom were transferred from the Philippines – were charged with bringing development and stability to these beleaguered nations along the model developed in the Philippines, relying yet again on Wall Street for financial support. Meanwhile, Wilson's appointees in the Philippines, although they were no less committed to "right action" than their predecessors, began a slow process of "Filipinization," which drew down the number of American officials and nationalized large parts of the colonial economy, replacing the private railroad corporations and banks with state-owned enterprises. By the 1920s, when the empire had become a political liability for both the Democratic and Republican parties, the United States began to liquidate many of its colonial possessions and protectorates, finally granting effective independence to the Philippines (1935) and ending its occupation of the Dominican Republic (1924) and Haiti (1934), but keeping Hawai'i, Puerto Rico, and several small island nations (Guam, American Samoa, and the Virgin Islands) under its control until the present day. The American age of formal empire and Progressive nation building, which had begun with so much sound and fury in 1898, would end quietly less than forty years later as the last marines steamed out of Port-au-Prince and Manuel Quezon entered Malacañang Palace as the first president of the Philippine Commonwealth.

EMPIRE AND THE AMERICAN CONSTITUTIONAL SYSTEM

Whether this well-known history of American imperialism is presented as the "first great triumph" or as the tragic social experiment that it was, it is traditionally understood as the *natural* outgrowth of structural and cultural factors such as industrialization, racism, and Manifest Destiny.[13] Lost in this decades-long quest to locate the origins of imperialism in American culture and political economy, however, are the institutional developments and interbranch politics that underlay the vigorously contested expansion of American power in the Caribbean, Latin America, and Asia in the years after the Spanish–American War. In their quest to transform the United States from a prosperous industrial republic into an imperial power, a diverse set of bureaucrats and executive officials in the emerging American foreign policy state confronted the same obstacles – conditions of mass democracy, a weak central state, and the complex constraints of the US Constitution – that earlier reformers had encountered in their efforts to rationalize the administration

---

[13] Warren Zimmermann, *The First Great Triumph: How Five Americans Made Their Country a World Power* (New York: Farrar, Straus, & Giroux, 2002). In a passage that seems to capture the general thrust of most historical scholarship, the English historian V. G. Kiernan writes of the American experience in the Philippines, "Fully committed to empire-building as the U.S. in the first years of the century might appear to be, the annexations of 1898 proved before long a deviation from the main line of advance, a passing fantasy or a specific tonic for a spell of domestic sickness." V. G. Kiernan, *America: The New Imperialism: From White Settlement to World Hegemony* (London: Zed Press, 2005 [1978]), 157. For a general overview, see Edward P. Crapol, "Coming to Terms with Empire: The Historiography of Late Nineteenth-Century American Foreign Relations," *Diplomatic History* 16 (Fall 1992): 573–98.

of the domestic American state.[14] Time and time again, the indifference of the American people to an empire that was too far and too foreign, as well as tenacious and strategic opposition from colonized people, stymied the efforts of the president and these officials.

Yet the lack of support and funding from Congress for an expansive American empire was always the most difficult obstacle to overcome. After a brief burst of pro-imperial enthusiasm (a period that generated a number of quotable, but ultimately irrelevant, speeches), Congress quickly soured on the "imperial experiment." At first, colonial bureaucrats *did* try to build public support for their imperial policies. They sponsored exhibits at fairs; they tinkered with customs laws to create favorable investment environments; and they solicited positive press coverage to advertise the good works they were doing in America's showcase of democracy. Such strategies quickly proved unsuccessful for some rather straightforward reasons: Members of Congress from both parties remained uninterested in populations that could not vote, and the American public's racism and fear of possible economic competition from their *own colonies* made them indifferent and occasionally hostile to the new American colonies. The empire, quite simply, was bad politics in a mass democracy. And, in an age before the "imperial presidency," Congress saw no reason to defer to the executive in foreign affairs. Using its formal powers over appropriations and tariffs, as well as its informal powers to mold public opinion, Congress's attempts to control and limit overseas empire were extremely effective. Such opposition could have easily spelled a quick end to American empire, but it did not.[15]

This book asks why. Accordingly, it confronts three broad, but perplexing, theoretical and substantive questions:

1. How did American executive officials engage in these ambitious nation-building projects with such limited congressional and public support?
2. Why did the United States distance itself from a policy of formal colonialism so quickly after creating institutions designed to manage its new colonial possessions?
3. How did the essential tension between American mass democracy and imperial governance shape the expansion of the American empire?[16]

---

[14] See Go, *Patterns of Empire* for a comparison of the American and British empires.

[15] For other theories of imperial expansion, see David B. Abernathy, *The Dynamics of Global Dominance: European Overseas Empires 1415–1980* (New Haven, CT: Yale University Press, 2000); Alexander Motyl, *Imperial Ends: The Decay, Collapse, and Revival of Empires* (New York: Columbia University Press, 2000); Michael Doyle, *Empires* (Ithaca, NY: Cornell University Press, 1986); Jack Snyder, *Myths of Empire: Domestic Politics and International Ambition* (Ithaca, NY: Cornell University Press, 1991). In recent years, the debate over empire has generated fierce debates in the academic and popular presses. See, for example, Robert Kagan, *Dangerous Nation: America's Place in the World from Its Earliest Days to the Dawn of the Twentieth Century* (New York: Knopf, 2006); Neil Smith, *America's Empire: Roosevelt's Geographer and the Prelude to Globalization* (Berkeley, CA: University of California Press, 2003). For two pioneering collections of essays from historians and sociologists that have focused on the state and American empire, see Go and Foster, eds., *The American Colonial State in the Philippines*; Alfred W. McCoy and Francisco A. Scarano, eds., *Colonial Crucible: Empire in the Making of the Modern American State* (Madison, WI: University of Wisconsin Press, 2009).

[16] I thank an anonymous reviewer for suggesting this phrase.

The answers, I argue, lie in understanding the systems of imperial rule and expansion not as evidence of state capture by American finance capital or the expression of deep cultural values, but rather as innovative and adaptive responses by presidents and executive officials to congressional opposition. Faced with a lack of support from Congress and an indifferent public, presidents and colonial bureaucrats shifted their strategy to one of private finance, secrecy, and extraconstitutional action. Their frustrations with the parochial concerns of Congress pushed them to consider ways to achieve their goals with less interference. In many ways, these responses were designed to "solve" the fundamental tension between democracy and empire by subverting the constitutional checks of the American system of separated powers.

As will be explained in Chapters 4–6, colonial bureaucrats gained financial support for their policies by forming partnerships with Wall Street bankers, while their manipulation and monopolization of information about the colonies and a loyal civil service protected them from congressional notice or interference. Through these sources of power, presidents and colonial officials were able to proceed with their ambitious plans for the American empire and to accomplish goals which they lacked the financial capacity and political support to achieve independently.[17] Armed with independent sources of revenue, they were able to continue their modernizing projects in the Philippines and bring the Dominican Republic, Nicaragua, Liberia, and Haiti under American control. Their efforts to build the empire also led to the creation of new governance patterns that made the executive much less reliant on domestic state capacity in foreign affairs. In short, the American external state, cast in the crucible of imperial management and given limited access to the resources of the domestic state, *developed* and *adapted* to these circumstances not as a centralized state subordinate to Congress, but largely independent of it as a system of dispersed and self-funding governing authorities.[18]

Rather than dismissing the age of formal American empire as a strange exception and one with little effect on state development, we need to understand it as the first major experience the American state had as an international actor, and one that would markedly influence how the United States confronted the world. Woodrow Wilson, writing in the preface for the fifteenth edition of *Congressional Government*, recognized this possibility as early as 1901:

Much the most important change to be noticed is the result of the war with Spain upon the lodgment and exercise of power within our federal system: the greatly increased power and opportunity for constructive statesmanship given the President, by the plunge into international politics and into the *administration of distant dependencies, which has been that war's*

[17] I am indebted to Rosenberg, *Financial Missionaries*, for insight into this process.
[18] The "low stateness" of American foreign policy has been remarked in other contexts. In a study on US policy in Latin America, for instance, Katznelson and Prewitt argue that the "low stateness" of the American policy combined with its "low classness" limits the options available to foreign policy actors. Most interestingly, they make reference to the often "covert" behavior of the American foreign policy state. As they write, "Such ideas as legislation-dominated political processes, and such doctrines as separation of powers, are in apparent contradiction with an executive-centered foreign policy process and descriptions of the 'imperial presidency' that have become fashionable in the United States." Ira Katznelson and Kenneth Prewitt, "Constitutionalism, Class, and the Limits of Choice in U.S. Foreign Policy," in *Capitalism and the State in U.S.–Latin American Relations*, ed. Richard R. Fagen (Stanford, CA: Stanford University Press, 1979), 37.

most striking and momentous consequence. When foreign affairs play a prominent part in the politics and policy of a nation, its Executive must of necessity be its guide: must utter every initial judgment, take every first step of action, supply the information upon which it is to act, suggest and in large measure control its conduct . . . *The government of dependencies must be largely in his hands. Interesting things may come out of the singular change.*[19]

Such developments are not merely of historical interest. Over the past three decades, scholars studying domestic state institutions have come to a clear consensus that state structure and development have important effects on state action.[20] Yet by focusing on the domestic state to develop these theories, researchers have missed an opportunity to apply these valuable insights to explain state action in an international context.[21] This is especially curious since scholars in all three empirical subfields of political science – comparative politics, American politics, and international relations – have suggested that there may be important policy effects that result from a state's unique external face. In a seminal volume on the state written over three decades ago, Theda Skocpol and her coauthors hint at this possibility: "For both older and newer national states," they write, "there may also be systematic differences between parts of states oriented to transnational environments and those specializing in purely domestic problems."[22] More recently, Ronald Rogowski writes that there is "good evidence" that differences in institutional forms have profound effects on "the style and relative success of [a state's] foreign policy," yet he bemoans the lack of attention to these issues in international relations.[23]

---

[19] Woodrow Wilson, *Congressional Government: A Study in American Politics*, 15th edn. (Boston: Houghton, Mifflin & Co., 1901), xi–xiii [emphasis added].

[20] See, for example, Stephen Skowronek, *Building a New American State: The Expansion of National Administrative Capacities, 1877–1920* (New York: Cambridge University Press, 1982); Theda Skocpol, *Protecting Soldiers and Mothers* (Cambridge, MA: Belknap Press of Harvard University Press, 1992); Elisabeth S. Clemens, *The People's Lobby: Organizational Innovation and the Rise of Interest Group Politics in the United States, 1890–1925* (Chicago: University of Chicago Press, 1997); Daniel P. Carpenter, *The Forging of Bureaucratic Autonomy: Reputations, Networks, and Policy Innovation in Executive Agencies, 1862–1928* (Princeton, NJ: Princeton University Press, 2001); Jacob Hacker, *The Divided Welfare State: The Battle over Public and Private Social Benefits in the United States* (New York: Cambridge University Press, 2002). From the comparative literature, see Peter A. Hall, "Policy Paradigms, Social Learning, and the State: The Case of Economic Policymaking in Britain," *Comparative Politics* 25 (April 1993): 275–96; Paul Pierson, *Dismantling the Welfare State? Reagan, Thatcher, and the Politics of Retrenchment* (New York: Cambridge University Press, 1994); Kathleen Thelen, *How Institutions Evolve: The Political Economy of Skills in Germany, Britain, the United States, and Japan* (New York: Cambridge University Press, 2006).

[21] For some of the limited APD work on the American foreign policy state, see Bartholomew H. Sparrow, *From the Outside In: World War II and the American State* (Princeton, NJ: Princeton University Press, 1996); Ira Katznelson and Martin Shefter, eds., *Shaped by War and Trade: International Influences on American Political Development* (Princeton, NJ: Princeton University Press, 2002); Amy B. Zegart, *Flawed by Design: The Evolution of the CIA, JCS, and NSC* (Stanford: Stanford University Press, 2000); and Douglas T. Stuart, *Creating the National Security State* (Princeton, NJ: Princeton University Press, 2007).

[22] Peter B. Evans, Dietrich Rueschemeyer, and Theda Skocpol, eds., *Bringing the State Back In* (Cambridge: Cambridge University Press, 1985), 360.

[23] Ronald Rogowski, "Institutions as Constraints," in *Strategic Choice and International Relations*, ed. David A. Lake and Robert Powell (Princeton, NJ: Princeton University Press, 1999), 125.

This book attempts to correct these oversights by marshaling theories of institutional development and interinstitutional politics to understand how the American state organized and governed its overseas colonies and how these actions, in turn, shaped the American foreign policy state or "external state," which I define as that portion of the state concerned with a state's projection of power outside of its domestic borders.[24] The result is an American external state that, as Stephen Krasner has argued, is both powerful abroad and strangely "weak in relation to its own society."[25] Furthermore, a focus on this interinstitutional struggle over American empire in an earlier period reveals how presidents and bureaucrats might behave when faced with a Congress whose authority over foreign affairs and whose institutional and informational resources were relatively greater than they are today. In this era, the American foreign policy state was weak and disorganized and presidents *did* fear Congress's formal powers in a way that is difficult to imagine today.

Putting institutions and ideas first, of course, means that many compelling theories of political culture[26] and gender[27] are largely pushed to the background. In positing an institutional explanation to explain the development of American empire, my purpose is not to suggest that these explanations have no merit – indeed, many provide brilliant insights into the background conditions of American imperialism – but they

---

[24] To be sure, this is not an entirely new insight. J. P. Nettl in his seminal article, "The State as Conceptual Variable," pointed this out decades ago when he described the state as a "gatekeeper between intrasociety and extrasocietal flows of action," and Peter Gourevitch has argued that state "structure itself derives from the exigencies of the international system." In *States and Social Revolutions*, Theda Skocpol famously drew attention to the destabilizing effects of international competitive pressures on states and their influence on revolutionary outcomes. Even Locke in chapter 12 of the *Second Treatise* notes the existence of a third, "natural" power, which he terms "federative," and "contains the power of war and peace, leagues and alliances, and all the transactions with all persons and communities without the commonwealth." Wildavsky's famous claim that there are two presidencies, one for domestic concerns and another, even more powerful one for foreign matters is another well-known variation. J. P. Nettl, "The State as a Conceptual Variable," *World Politics* 20 (July 1968): 564; Peter Gourevitch, "The Second Image Reversed: The International Sources of Domestic Politics," *International Organization* 323 (Autumn 1978): 881; Theda Skocpol, *States and Social Revolutions* (Cambridge: Cambridge University Press, 1979); John Locke, *Second Treatise of Government* (Indianapolis, IN: Hackett, 1980 [1690]), Ch. 12; Aaron Wildavsky, "The Two Presidencies," *Trans-Action* 4 (December 1966): 7–14.

[25] Stephen D. Krasner, "U.S. Commercial and Monetary Policy," in Peter J. Katzenstein, ed., *Between Power and Plenty: Foreign Economic Policies of Advanced Industrial States* (Madison, WI: University of Wisconsin Press, 1978), 57.

[26] As Louis Hartz noted in his classic work on American political thought, "in a liberal community the imperialist drive at the turn of the century was hamstrung by a unique nationalism: national liberalism." Louis Hartz, *The Liberal Tradition in America* (New York: Harcourt & Brace, 1991 [1955]), 292.

[27] Gender and the discourse of "manliness" was absolutely essential to the imperial project, and it is well explored in a number of recent works. See, for example, Linda Gordon, "Internal Colonialism and Gender," in *Haunted by Empire: Geographies of Intimacy in North American History*, ed. Ann Laura Stoler (Durham, NC: Duke University Press, 2006); Laura Briggs, *Reproducing Empire: Race, Sex, Science, and U.S. Imperialism in Puerto Rico* (Berkeley, CA: University of California Press, 2002); Kristin L. Hoganson, *Fighting for American Manhood: How Gender Politics Provoked the Spanish–American and Philippines–American Wars* (New Haven, CT: Yale University Press, 1998); Eileen Findlay, *Imposing Decency: The Politics of Sexuality and Race in Puerto Rico, 1870–1920* (Durham, NC: Duke University Press, 1999).

are often unable to account for the *variation* and *adaptation* of governing arrangements over time. Before I explain my own argument in more detail in the following sections, let us take a brief look at three of most prominent explanations of American empire: economic interests, race, and international relations. To be sure, none of these theoretical approaches claims to explain all aspects of American imperialism, but their dominance in the field has obscured the value of focusing on state structure and the actions of state officials. How can a state-centered, institutional account of empire enrich our understanding? Where does it depart from these traditional explanations?

American Economic Expansion and "Gentlemanly Capitalism"

Economic explanations have long been central to studies of American imperialism.[28] In the 1920s, American scholars built on earlier work by the English political economist John Hobson to criticize US interference with Caribbean nations, arguing by implication that the interests of American business were dictating American foreign policy.[29] William Appleman Williams and his students at the University of Wisconsin later expanded on these earlier themes to conclude that much of American foreign policy could be explained by a relentless quest for overseas markets.[30] Despite

---

[28] John Lewis Gaddis, "New Conceptual Approaches to the Study of American Foreign Relations: Interdisciplinary Perspectives," *Diplomatic History* 14 (Summer 1990): 407. For other, less economically driven theories of imperial expansion, see David B. Abernathy, *The Dynamics of Global Dominance: European Overseas Empires 1415–1980* (New Haven, CT: Yale University Press, 2000); Alexander Motyl, *Imperial Ends: The Decay, Collapse, and Revival of Empires* (New York: Columbia University Press, 2000); Doyle, *Empires*; Jack Snyder, *Myths of Empire: Domestic Politics and International Ambition* (Ithaca, NY: Cornell University Press, 1991); Smith, *America's Empire*.

[29] John Hobson made the connection between imperialism and capital most forcefully in his 1902 book, *Imperialism: A Study* (London: James Nisbet & Co., 1902). Hobson's work served as the basis for Lenin's famous 1916 pamphlet, "Imperialism, the Highest Stage of Capitalism," which specifically discusses US imperialism. For the application of Marxist arguments to the American case, see, for example, Scott Nearing and Joseph Freeman, *Dollar Diplomacy: A Study in American Imperialism* (New York: B.W. Huebsch and Viking Press, 1925). Charles and Mary Beard, while not Marxists, also explained American imperialism through the lens of economic interests. See, for example, *The Rise of American Civilization*, 2 vols. (New York: MacMillan, 1927); Charles A. Beard, *The Open Door at Home: A Trial Philosophy of National Interest* (New York: MacMillan, 1934); Charles A. Beard, *The Idea of National Interest: An Analytical Study in American Foreign Policy* (New York: MacMillan, 1934). The Beards, however, were never clear on the mechanisms of this connection; sometimes it was suggested that special business interests were at work, while other times they favored structural interpretations.

[30] For the classics in this tradition, see Walter LaFeber, *The New Empire: An Interpretation of American Expansion 1860–1898* (Ithaca, NY: Cornell University Press, 1963) and William Appleman Williams, *The Tragedy of American Diplomacy* (New York: Norton, 1959). See also Emily S. Rosenberg, "Economic Interest and Foreign Policy," in *American Foreign Relations Reconsidered, 1890–1993*, ed. Gordon Martel (New York: Routledge, 1994). Another variant of the economic influence thesis holds that business, while initially opposed to the war, eventually became convinced that expansion would serve its interests. "Hence business in the end," according to Julius Pratt, "welcomed the 'large policy' and exerted its share of pressure for the retention of the Spanish islands and such related policies as the annexation of Hawaii and the construction of an isthmian canal." See Julius Pratt, *Expansionists of 1898: The Acquisition of Hawaii and the Spanish Islands* (New York: Quadrangle, 1964).

TABLE I.I. *Direct and portfolio American foreign investments by region*

Region	1897 (%)	1908 (%)	1914 (%)	1919 (%)	1924 (%)
Europe	22	19	20	29	25
Canada	28	28	25	22	24
Mexico	29	27	24	13	9
Caribbean	7	9	10	9	10
Central America	3	2	3	2	1
South America	6	5	10	11	13
Asia	3	9	7	4	6
All Others	2	1	2	3	3

Source: Calculated from Celona Lewis, *America's Stake in International Investments* (Washington, DC: Brookings Institution, 1938), 606; Lance E. Davis and Robert J. Cull, *International Capital Markets and American Economic Growth, 1820–1914* (New York: Cambridge University Press, 1994), 81–2.

the theoretical dominance and intuitive appeal of the "Wisconsin School" theories of American diplomatic history, the exact connection between private economic actors and American imperialism remains unclear.[31] Although American foreign direct investments did increase significantly in this period, relatively little of that money was sent to areas under direct American control. As Table 1.1 demonstrates, investment in the Caribbean and Latin America represented but a fraction of total American foreign investments both before and after the Spanish–American War, increasing only by 3 percentage points between 1897 and 1914.

Furthermore, as Table 1.2 shows, even by 1911 most American investment in the Caribbean region was concentrated in the lucrative Cuban sugar industry, a business in which American investors had long played a central role. In contrast, American direct investment in the Dominican Republic, Haiti, and Nicaragua – all three of which saw Dollar Diplomacy interventions – was extremely modest, accounting for half of the investment in Guatemala alone, a nation that never came under direct American administration. As economic historians Lance Davis and Robert Cull argue, "[I]t is difficult to rationalize the level of intervention with the size of the American's investment stakes in those countries."[32]

To be sure, this could be due to the fact that those areas under formal American control were, first and foremost, meant to secure a global trading network – particularly to gain access to the fabled China market – and were not necessarily seen as areas of investment themselves. Yet American investment in Asia was also

---

[31] For an especially cogent analysis of Marxist theories of imperialism as applied to the US experience, see Robert Zevin, "An Interpretation of American Imperialism," *Journal of Economic History* 32 (March 1972): 316–60. For another critique, see Jeffry A. Frieden, "International Investment and Colonial Control: A New Interpretation," *International Organization* 48 (Autumn 1994): 559–93; Jeffry A. Frieden, "The Economics of Intervention: American Overseas Investments and Relations with Underdeveloped Areas, 1890–1950," *Comparative Studies in Society and History* 31 (January 1989): 55–80.

[32] Lance E. Davis and Robert J. Cull, *International Capital Markets and American Economic Growth, 1820–1914* (New York: Cambridge University Press, 1994), 106.

TABLE 1.2. *Investment in Central America, 1911*

Nation	Direct investment ($ in millions)
Cuba	220
Costa Rica	7
Guatemala	20
Honduras	3
Dominican Republic and Haiti	7.5
Nicaragua	2.5
Panama (outside Canal)	5
El Salvador	2.5

Source: Celona Lewis, *America's Stake in International Investments* (Washington, DC: Brookings Institution, 1938), 610.

quite modest. Even by 1900, trade with China *and* Japan amounted to less than 4 percent of total foreign trade.[33] American capitalists, it seems, simply saw no reason to enter fragile developing markets when there was easier money to be made in the rapidly expanding economies of Western Europe, Canada, and Mexico. Nor did they necessarily need the state's assistance to expand their markets. As one detailed study of American industrial exports in this period holds, "[f]or the most part, the larger producers had their own sources of market information and their own business employees to represent them abroad . . . Big business did not rely on the American government to further its interests in foreign markets."[34]

Nevertheless, the value of considering economic motivations cannot be dismissed. American *portfolio* investments in the sovereign debt of Central American and Caribbean nations did increase significantly during this period, growing essentially from nothing in 1897 to about $58.6 million in 1914, and this suggests the value of considering the role of financiers and the nascent American investment banking industry apart from American manufacturers.[35] During this period, American bankers were becoming increasingly interested in the sovereign debt market of Latin America, but this market presented unique challenges that did not confront manufacturers, particularly the need to be backed by a state that would provide a vigorous defense in the case of default.[36] Of course, the role of financiers

---

[33] David M. Pletcher, *The Diplomacy of Involvement: American Economic Expansion across the Pacific, 1784–1900* (Columbia, MO: University of Missouri Press, 2001). In the late 1890s, to use a well-known example, two American capitalists in China, James Harrison Wilson and James J. McCook, attempted to secure the capital necessary to extend the Trans-Siberian railroad into China. After extensive meetings with Standard Oil, a number of railroads, and even representatives from J. P. Morgan, Wilson and McCook failed to achieve anything more than the most tepid interest in their project. Pletcher, *Diplomacy of Involvement*, 217.

[34] William H. Becker, *The Dynamics of Business–Government Relations: Industry and Exports, 1893–1921* (Chicago: University of Chicago Press, 1982), 181.

[35] Calculated from Cleona Lewis, *America's Stake in International Investments* (Washington, DC: Brookings Institution Press, 1938), 606.

[36] See Charles Lipson, *Standing Guard: Protecting Foreign Capital in the Nineteenth and Twentieth Centuries* (Berkeley, CA: University of California Press, 1985); Frieden, "The Economics of Intervention."

is central to older theories of imperialism. Both Bukharin and Lenin distinguished the export of capital from the export of commodities, and both emphasized that imperialism emerged from the necessity of finding profitable investment opportunities for so-called "surplus capital."[37] Yet the search for new markets, even markets for investment capital, leaves much unexplained, including the role of the state. As a rule, classical Marxian theories of imperialism treat the state as the agent of financiers, an assumption that does not allow for the possibility that state actors may have their own set of interests – a proposition that would be much more difficult to defend today.[38]

What is needed, then, is a more nuanced interpretation which allows for the possibility that the interests of American finance capital and state actors became *aligned*; one which acknowledges these activities as a partnership rather than a relationship of capture or coercion. Indeed, recent work by historians has posited such a connection. For example, in their well-known "gentlemanly capitalism" theory of British overseas empire, Cain and Hopkins emphasized the close bond and shared worldview of British financiers and high-level state actors in shaping British imperial policy.[39] American historians have made broadly similar arguments about the United States, most notably Emily Rosenberg in her landmark analysis, *Financial Missionaries to the World.* Yet the specific causal mechanisms that led to this shared project, as well as the generalizable lessons for state development that such partnerships imply, are not always made as clear as they might be in these more descriptive works.[40]

Race and American Empire

No study of American empire can ignore the central role of race in American expansion. Americans' confidence in the racial superiority of Anglo-Saxons reached its height during the imperial age as these long-held beliefs gained the patina of objectivity through newly popular theories of social Darwinism and pseudoscientific studies of racial capacities.[41] The grotesque caricatures of Latinos and Asians that filled newspapers during the imperial era are well known to students of American history. It should come as no surprise, then, that race is found as a major

---

[37] For an elegant survey of these theories, see Anthony Brewer, *Marxist Theories of Imperialism: A Critical Survey,* 2nd edn. (London: Routledge, 1990).

[38] As Anthony Brewer argues, "[The state] may represent the *interests* of finance capital; that is not the same thing as acting as their direct *agent*." Brewer, *Marxist Theories,* 107.

[39] P. J. Cain and A. G. Hopkins, "Gentlemanly Capitalism and British Expansion Overseas I. The Old Colonial System, 1688–1850," *Economic Historical Review* 39 (November 1986): 501–25; P. J. Cain and A. G. Hopkins "Gentlemanly Capitalism and British Expansion Overseas II. New Imperialism, 1850–1945," *Economic Historical Review* 40 (February 1987): 1–26. For an updated treatment of the theory, see P. J. Cain and A. G. Hopkins, *British Imperialism, 1688–2000,* 2nd edn. (London: Routledge, 2001).

[40] For some critiques of Cain and Hopkins, see Raymond E. Dumett, ed., *Gentlemanly Capitalism and British Imperialism: The New Debate on Empire* (New York: Longman, 1999) and Shigeru Akita, ed., *Gentlemanly Capitalism, Imperialism and Global History* (New York: Palgrave, 2003).

[41] See Michael H. Hunt, *Ideology and U.S. Foreign Policy* (New Haven, CT: Yale University Press, 1987), 78.

explanatory variable in many prominent accounts of American imperialism.[42] Some historians have even connected the increasingly oppressive racial regime in the South with the advent of American imperialism. No less an authority than C. Vann Woodward, for example, wrote that by the 1890s the North "was looking to southern racial policy for national guidance in the new problems of imperialism resulting from the Spanish war."[43] Other scholars posit that the invocation of racial Anglo-Saxonism was an attempt to legitimate American colonialism by emphasizing its racial ties to the British Empire.[44]

As compelling as these accounts are, a lingering problem with theories of imperialism that use race as their primary explanatory variable is that they operate at a relatively high level of abstraction. This leaves little room to consider other important variables like political institutions and state capacity. While American beliefs in the superiority of white culture and values may have encouraged expansion, they were often checked by Americans' equally powerful aversion to the incorporation of nonwhite territories into the United States.[45] Indeed, as historian Eric Love argues, "race ideas were used most openly, aggressively, and effectively by enemies of imperialism."[46] As we will see, much of the opposition to imperialism was caused by the American public's strong antipathy to the incorporation of nonwhite citizens into the Republic.

In this work, race is included as one of several ideas that shaped thinking about American imperial administration. Particularly significant in my account are the different racial understandings of colonial state officials, which often differed from those of American soldiers. Top colonial administrators were far more likely to emphasize the behavioral or historical aspects of race over essentialist or biological theories.[47] As Julian Go has argued, race was a contested category even among the soldiers and bureaucrats charged with overseeing the empire. For some, race was a matter of biology and blood that remain fixed, while for others race was merely seen as correlated with certain behaviors or intellectual abilities.[48] For these officials, race was an inherited set of characteristics that could be overcome with the help of aggressive social engineering projects to "hustle the East," as they often described it, to a more advanced stage of development. This study, when race is

---

[42] For a more recent interpretation, see Matthew Frye Jacobson, *Barbarian Virtues: The United States Encounters Foreign Peoples at Home and Abroad, 1876–1917* (New York: Hill & Wang, 2000); Rydell, *All the World's a Fair*. On the Philippines, see Paul Kramer, *The Blood of Government: Race, Empire, the United States and the Philippines* (Chapel Hill, NC: University of North Carolina Press, 2006).

[43] Quoted in Eric T. Love, *Race over Empire: Racism and U.S. Imperialism, 1865–1900* (Chapel Hill, NC: University of North Carolina Press, 2004), 3.

[44] See Julian Go, "The Provinciality of American Empire: 'Liberal Exceptionalism' and U.S. Colonial Rule, 1898–1912," *Comparative Studies in Society and History* 49 (2007): 74–108 for the most sophisticated articulation of this view. On the connection between ideas of Anglo-Saxon racial destiny and imperialism, see Paul A. Kramer, "Empires, Exceptions, and Anglo-Saxons: Race and Rule between the British and United States Empires, 1880–1910," *Journal of American History* 88 (March 2002): 1315–53.

[45] Love, *Race over Empire*, 8.

[46] Ibid., 7.

[47] Julian Go, "'Racism' and Colonialism: Meanings of Difference and Ruling Practices in America's Pacific Empire," *Qualitative Sociology* 27 (Spring 2004): 35–58.

[48] Ibid.

considered, focuses on how racial understanding affected the concrete actions of colonial administrators themselves.[49]

Empire and International Relations

Scholars of international relations have long accounted for imperial expansion through the lens of power politics. If Thucydides is correct and "the strong do what they have the power to do," then we should expect that as its economic and military power increased, the United States would expand more aggressively.[50] According to Robert Gilpin, "A more wealthy and more powerful state (up to the point of diminishing utility) will select a larger bundle of security and welfare goals than a less wealthy and powerful state."[51] While such theories certainly help us to understand why the American state was interested in projecting more influence – particularly in the Caribbean – elements of the American case are poorly explained by traditional and defensive realism. To be sure, such accounts are primarily focused on explaining state competition and the drive for empire, rather than on the form these empires take. Much like race-based explanations, they operate at a much higher level of abstraction, which make them less useful in explaining the development of US imperialism. For instance, although the acquisition of colonies for strategic purposes fits well with realist accounts, the intensive development projects in the colonies do not. It is, for example, difficult to explain how it was in the *strategic* interests of American officials to pour millions of dollars into developing a railroad in the Philippines. Furthermore, as I explain in the following sections, the acquisition and management of colonies as strategic military assets to project US power into Asia and the Caribbean provide an adequate explanation for only the smallest colonies of American Samoa, Guam, and the Virgin Islands. The larger

[49] For histories of this era told from the perspective of colonized people, see the following: On Hawai'i, see Noenoe K. Silva, *Aloha Betrayed: Native Hawaiian Resistance to American Colonialism* (Durham, NC: Duke University Press, 2004) and Jonathan Kay Kamakawiwo'ole Osorio, *Dismembering Lahui: A History of the Hawaiian Nation to 1887* (Honolulu, HI: University of Hawai'i Press, 2002); on Nicaragua, Michel Gobat, *Confronting the American Dream: Nicaragua Under U.S. Imperial Rule* (Durham, NC: Duke University Press, 2005); on Haiti, Mary A. Renda, *Taking Haiti: Military Occupation and the Culture of U.S. Imperialism, 1915–1940* (Chapel Hill, NC: University of North Carolina Press, 2004); on Puerto Rico, José Trías Monge, *Puerto Rico: The Trials of the Oldest Colony in the World* (New Haven, CT: Yale University Press, 1997); Eileen Findlay, *Imposing Decency: The Politics of Sexuality and Race in Puerto Rico* (Durham, NC: Duke University Press, 1999); on the Philippines, see Kramer, *Blood of Government*; on the Dominican Republic, see Valentina Peguero, *The Militarization of Culture in the Dominican Republic: From the Captains General to General Trujillo* (Lincoln, NE: University of Nebraska Press, 2004). To the best of my knowledge, no comparable study of native resistance exists for Liberia – an unfortunate example of the lack of scholarship on American–Liberian relations.

[50] See, for example, Kenneth Waltz, *Man, the State, and War: A Theoretical Analysis* (New York: Columbia University Press, 1954) and Paul Kennedy, *The Rise and Fall of the Great Powers: Economic Change and Military Conflict from 1500 to the Present* (New York: Random House, 1987). Thucydides, *History of the Peloponnesian War*, trans. Rex Warner, revised edn. (New York: Penguin Books, 1972), 402; Quoted in Fareed Zakaria, *From Wealth to Power: The Unusual Origins of America's World Role* (Princeton, NJ: Princeton University Press), 19.

[51] Robert Gilpin, *War and Change in World Politics* (New York: Cambridge University Press, 1981), 94–5.

colonies – and the Philippines, in particular – were often viewed as military liabilities just years after the United States seized them.

The second problem is that classic theories of international relations are not well equipped to explain the timing and governing structures of American empire. By the 1880s, the United States was the wealthiest country in the world, unmatched in its industrial capacity by any Western European state, and yet this economic power did not translate into international leadership. Its army was smaller than Bulgaria's (the fourteenth largest in the world); its decrepit navy was full of rotting and antique ships; and its diplomatic corps consisted of party spoilsmen who lacked even rudimentary training in foreign affairs.[52]

In an attempt to account for this discrepancy, Fareed Zakaria argues that state capacity is more important than sheer economic power in explaining a state's desire to expand. Building on studies of American state development, Zakaria finds that the rise of a centralized bureaucratic state during the Progressive era led to greater American involvement in international affairs, which allowed the executive branch "to bypass Congress or coerce it into expanding American interests abroad."[53] What remains confusing in Zakaria's account, however, is why we should expect reforms in domestic state capacity to lead to changes in foreign policy capacities.[54] Moreover, if increases in state capacity lead to a more aggressive foreign policy, then why did the United States scale back its initial hunger for overseas colonies? As it turns out, how presidents and bureaucrats tried to "bypass Congress" is a far more complex story than Zakaria allows; in fact, it was the result of a particular form of state building that relied on private partnerships, independent resources, and information control.

A central claim of this book is that important dynamics of American imperialism become visible when examined from a slightly lower level of abstraction than the classic theories of economic expansion, racism, and power politics. At this level of analysis – one where state structure and bureaucratic action play a major role – we can begin to make sense of the unusual variation and development of the empire in ways that these more general theories cannot.

American Empire and Interbranch Politics in the Age of Congressional Dominance

The story of American foreign relations as it is traditionally told is the story of presidential dominance. From Aaron Wildavsky's "two-presidencies" thesis to Arthur Schlesinger's notion of the "imperial presidency," the consensus is that the president and the attendant foreign policy state have increased their dominance of American foreign affairs throughout the twentieth century.[55] Congress, meanwhile, has been left to play a supporting role, despite constitutional powers that are

[52] Zakaria, *From Wealth to Power*.

[53] Ibid., 11.

[54] A number of works point in this direction. For a review, see David R. Mayhew, "Wars and American Politics," *Perspectives on Politics* 3 (September 2005): 473–93.

[55] Wildavsky, "The Two Presidencies"; Arthur M. Schlesinger, Jr., *The Imperial Presidency* (Boston: Houghton Mifflin, 2004 [1973]); Louis Fisher, *Presidential War Power* (Lawrence, KS: University Press of Kansas, 1995); see also, Robert Dahl, *Congress and Foreign Policy* (New York: Harcourt, Brace, 1950).

arguably superior to the executive's in foreign affairs. The reasons for this are many, but among the most prominent explanations for the perceived executive dominance of foreign policy are the president's first-mover advantage and his greater access to information.[56] These informational advantages are due in large part to the president's command of the foreign policy state and its attendant bureaucracies that arose in the postwar era.

As scholars have long pointed out, bureaucrats may manipulate the policy agenda through their informational advantages.[57] Yet information control does not necessarily imply that bureaucrats need to withhold facts from policymakers. Often it is enough to merely present information in such a way that highlights a favored policy.[58] While such informational asymmetries are present in all relations between bureaucrats and policymakers, they may be particularly acute in foreign affairs. Knowledge about domestic conditions is often cheap and plentiful, and, perhaps most important, members are likely to have *independent* sources of information from concerned interest groups. Yet these conditions are much less likely to hold in a foreign policy environment when information is extremely costly and the interest group environment is weak. As Robert Dahl recognized over 50 years ago, in foreign affairs the executive holds a "quasi-monopoly over important information."[59] Many scholars have observed that in the modern era Congress has difficulty competing with this tremendous informational advantage – one provided by the multitude of foreign policy agencies and officials who report directly to the president. Electoral incentives play a role as well. Given that members of Congress represent single geographic districts, they are unlikely to get much of the credit (or the blame) for decisions made in the conduct of American foreign relations.[60]

Few doubt that the president has dominated foreign affairs in the postwar era, but new work has called into question many assumptions about Congress's supposed weakness over executive actions. William Howell and Jon Pevehouse find that Congress can yield significant influence over the *decision* to use military force, while Douglas Kriner has shown how Congress exercises a surprising degree of influence once military actions are underway.[61] Although Congress rarely uses its legislative powers to block presidential actions, much of this influence comes from presidential anticipation of congressional support or opposition. In other words,

---

[56] William Howell and Jon Pevehouse, *When Dangers Gather: Congressional Checks on Presidential War Powers* (Princeton, NJ: Princeton University Press, 2007).

[57] Edward Page, *Political Authority and Bureaucratic Power* (Knoxville, TN: University of Tennessee Press, 1985); Ezra N. Suleiman, *Politics, Power, and Bureaucracy in France: The Administrative Elite* (Princeton, NJ: Princeton University Press, 1974); Robert D. Putnam, "The Political Attitudes of Senior Civil Servants in Western Europe: A Preliminary Report," *British Journal of Political Science* 3 (July 1973): 257–90.

[58] See Junko Kato, *The Problem of Bureaucratic Rationality: Tax Politics in Japan* (Princeton, NJ: Princeton University Press, 1994).

[59] Robert Dahl, *Congress and Foreign Policy* (New York: Harcourt, Brace, 1950), 62.

[60] Thus the federated nature of the American electoral system make foreign affairs policies – imperialism in particular – a difficult "fit." For an in-depth discussion of "fit" as it relates to American public policy, see Skocpol, *Protecting Soldiers and Mothers*.

[61] William Howell and Jon Pevehouse, "Presidents, Congress, and the Use of Force," *International Organization* 59 (Winter 2005): 209–32; Howell and Pevehouse, *When Dangers Gather*. Douglas Kriner, *After the Rubicon: Congress, Presidents, and the Politics of Waging War* (Chicago: University of Chicago Press, 2010).

when presidents *know* that their policies are likely to be opposed, they are less likely to pursue an aggressive course of action. Yet as Kriner points out, presidential anticipation is not the only mechanism at work. Congress *can* raise the costs of these actions by launching high-profile debates, by appealing to public opinion through speeches and press conferences, and by engaging in a variety of other informal actions in the public sphere.[62]

One potential problem with this line of scholarship is that it tests congressional influence almost exclusively during the postwar era – a period in which the executive has undisputed informational advantages and in which Congress has rarely exercised its formal powers to limit presidential action. Naturally, showing *any* significant congressional influence in the modern era is a major finding, but the president did not always have these advantages over Congress. The "imperial presidency" is itself a historically conditioned development dependent on the growth of the postwar foreign policy state. Would the executive still dominate foreign affairs if Congress were more powerful and assertive? The American age of empire offers an opportunity to investigate this question.[63] During this period, Congress was at the height of its power and the president was in no way imperial. As is often pointed out, it was Congress, not the president, which led the charge to the Spanish–American War. It was in this environment of congressional dominance and executive fear of Congress's formal powers that the American empire took shape.

As I explain in the following sections, congressional opposition to imperial expansion profoundly influenced the development of the empire, but it did not stop it, because the executive and its emergent bureaucratic state adapted to these restrictions. Ironically, congressional power may have shaped a foreign policy state that developed in such a way to avoid congressional scrutiny and control. Nevertheless, the fragile structure of American empire also offered an opening for colonized people to resist US control by using these interinstitutional conflicts to their own advantage – a process that also shaped how colonial officials expanded the empire.

INCONSPICUOUS ACTION, STATE BUILDING THROUGH COLLABORATION, AND IDEAS AS ROAD MAPS

A principal contention of this book is that institutional theories developed in political science can illuminate the development of American imperialism, while a careful look at the development of the American empire may also improve theories of interbranch politics and state building in foreign affairs. There is no doubt, as the literature suggests, that presidents and executives do anticipate congressional opposition, but they, too, may develop ways to avoid such congressional scrutiny and sanction while still pursuing their preferred policies. Yet in an age when congressional constraints were far more threatening, and when the executive had, at best, a modest informational advantage, this required an adaptive strategy.

---

[62] Kriner, *After the Rubicon*, 57–72.
[63] For an account of the decline of empire that is sensitive to differences in political institutions, see Hendrik Spruyt, *Ending Empire: Contested Sovereignty and Territorial Partition* (Ithaca, NY: Cornell University Press, 2008).

One important way bureaucrats may gain independence, as Daniel Carpenter has shown, is by cultivating a diverse set of public constituencies through reputation-building to gain political support for their policy goals – in this way, they can develop a form of bureaucratic autonomy from Congress and even, in some cases, from the president.[64] But the mechanisms of "bureaucratic autonomy" in its strict sense do not explain executive strategies in imperial expansion. Although the preferences of presidents are clearly reflected in these actions, a new cadre of bureaucrats who were led by some uniquely entrepreneurial executive officials developed the strategies of imperial expansion that avoided congressional scrutiny and attention.

As I show in the pages to follow, the officials involved in the management and creation of American empire joined a new agency, the Bureau of Insular Affairs (BIA), that would come to govern most of the American colonies. They came from a diverse array of backgrounds – the military, law, and academia being the most common – and together they developed a commitment to a Progressive, technocratic version of US imperialism. Their interest was not in promoting their own bureau's reputation, but in bringing order, stability, and discipline to the colonies. As we will see, the diversity of their professional backgrounds also allowed them to forge partnerships with US banks and the law firms that would administer colonial loans.

In this book, I show that the systems of imperial control developed by colonial bureaucrats allowed them to exercise considerable power *without* a broad coalition of domestic constituencies, apart from a rarefied group of financiers, to form their insular empire. The autonomy that allowed colonial officials to achieve many of their objectives as the American empire expanded eventually undermined the stability of the colonial regimes – often leading to more reckless (and quasi-legal) efforts to stabilize them. As the supervisory regimes installed in the Dominican Republic and other nations began to fail in spectacular fashion by World War I, for example, the Wilson administration was forced to shore them up by extending formal imperial control, leading to another round of nation building and borrowing that would itself collapse in the 1920s, resulting in more congressional investigations. Thus, a policy designed to extend American hegemony "on the cheap" and one designed to avoid congressional scrutiny would become both expensive and highly politically visible – a bad outcome for American colonial state officials and a tragic one for the millions of people unfortunate enough to come under their rule.

At its core, this book investigates how bureaucrats may exploit politicians' lack of interest in policies that bear little on their chances for reelection and for which they have little incentive to direct their attention or oversight – even in an era when Congress was relatively more powerful than it is today. Three mechanisms are crucial to the pages that follow: (1) "inconspicuous action" as a bureaucratic strategy, (2) the formation of public–private partnerships as an alternative means of state development as well as the unique pitfalls of this approach, and (3) the role of ideas as focal points and roadmaps for actors operating under conditions of uncertainty and in decentralized organizational environments. Taking each point in turn, let me first explain the theoretical motivation for understanding the process in question and then illustrate how each process explains the development of American imperialism.

---

[64] Carpenter, *The Forging of Bureaucratic Autonomy*.

Inconspicuous Action

In a study of the relative powers of Congress and the president, Canes-Wrone et al. find that political incentives "encourage members of Congress to delegate more policymaking authority to the president in foreign than domestic affairs."[65] Delegation, then, is likely to be more common and delegated authority is likely to be broader in foreign affairs. Delegation, however, is fraught with significant risk for members of Congress. Bureaucrats, after all, often hold preferences that are at odds with those of the median member of Congress and often have far more administrative expertise than their political superiors. Consequently, the ability of a democracy to control the actions of these unelected public officials has been debated by scholars for generations.

A more recent, but no less vexing, problem concerns the limited incentives of Congress to monitor the behavior of bureaucrats.[66] With their focus on winning the next election, members are unlikely to invest the time or resources in dutifully patrolling the actions of obscure federal agencies.[67] Despite these problems, the proposition that Congress can and will design institutions to control its "agents" is well accepted in political science.[68] According to this literature, when Congress delegates responsibilities to a federal agency, it can build in *ex ante* checks through statutory controls and administrative procedure requirements that lower the costs of oversight and through *ex post* actions such as oversight hearings.[69] Empirical research supports many of these theoretical propositions through studies that demonstrate how the outputs of bureaucratic agents change as different political principals are appointed or how signals of principal preferences are communicated to the agents through budget shifts.[70]

Nevertheless, as a result of its focus on the *decision* to delegate and the politics of institutional design, this literature makes some important, yet possibly problematic, assumptions that preclude the possibility of endogenous institutional

---

[65] Brandice Canes-Wrone, William G. Howell, and David E. Lewis, "Toward a Broader Understanding of Presidential Power: A Reevaluation of the Two Presidencies Thesis," *The Journal of Politics* 69 (January 2007): 6.

[66] William A. Niskanen, *Bureaucracy and Representative Government* (Chicago: Aldine, 1971).

[67] David R. Mayhew, *Congress: The Electoral Connection* (New Haven, CT: Yale University Press).

[68] See, for example, Terry M. Moe, "The New Economics of Organization," *American Journal of Political Science* 28 (November 1984): 739–77; Matthew D. McCubbins, Roger G. Noll, and Barry R. Weingast, "Administrative Procedures as Instruments of Political Control," *Journal of Law, Economics, & Organization* 3 (Autumn 1987): 243–77; B. Dan Wood and Richard W. Waterman, "The Dynamics of Political Control of the Bureaucracy," *American Political Science Review* 85 (September 1991): 801–28; B. Dan Wood and Richard W. Waterman, "The Dynamics of Political-Bureaucratic Adaptation," *American Journal of Political Science* 37 (May 1993): 497–528; B. Dan Wood and Richard W. Waterman, *Bureaucratic Dynamics: The Role of Bureaucracy in a Democracy* (Boulder, CO: Westview Press, 1994).

[69] Mathew D. McCubbins and Thomas Schwartz, "Congressional Oversight Overlooked: Police Patrols versus Fire Alarms," *American Journal of Political Science* 28 (February 1984): 165–79.

[70] Daniel P. Carpenter, "Adaptive Signal Processing, Hierarchy, and Budgetary Control in Federal Regulation," *American Political Science Review* 90 (June 1996): 283–302; David Epstein and Sharyn O'Halloran, *Delegating Powers: A Transaction Cost Politics Approach to Policy Making under Separate Powers* (New York: Cambridge University Press, 1999).

adaptations driven by the "agents" to change the rules from within. First, the bureaucrats in such models, although always assumed to have their own divergent set of interests, are rarely accorded much agency of their own. Such models primarily focus on the ways in which bureaucrats react to a particular system or set of incentives designed to solve the problems of congressional oversight.[71] Second, the institutions designed to constrain bureaucratic behavior, once created, are assumed to remain self-reinforcing – change is expected only when some exogenous process upsets the equilibrium.[72] Finally, the salience of a particular issue is assumed to be exogenous to the agency itself. Although there is near-universal agreement that the incentives of Congress to monitor agency behavior will increase with an issue's political salience, *the ability of bureaucrats to manipulate issue salience is almost entirely neglected.*[73] In this book, I forward the concept of "inconspicuous action" to explain how bureaucrats may gain autonomy by exploiting the limited electoral incentives of members of Congress to invest in administrative oversight.

In this way, inconspicuous action represents the negative image of Carpenter's (2001) theory of reputation-building. Rather than work to build favorable constituencies and to increase the salience of their policies, inconspicuous action prevails when bureaucrats actively pursue strategies to stay *off* the political agenda. This can be accomplished in two ways. The first is through the control and monopolization of information that may draw unwanted attention from the public or concerned interest groups. The second is to avoid requesting resources from Congress. Resources invite congressional oversight, and by seeking funds from elsewhere, bureaucrats may pursue policies while minimizing attention.

In the context of American empire, this strategy of "inconspicuous action" was achieved in three ways. First, colonial officials ruthlessly enforced censorship laws in the colonies that prevented both American and indigenous journalists from reporting on the colonies. Second, executive officials rarely requested direct appropriations from Congress; indeed, the currency reserve funds, colonial tax base, and loans from private banks provided the vast majority of the funding for the empire. Third, the structure of the colonial bureaucracy itself made oversight difficult. Borrowing from insights developed in organizational economics and work by Alexander Cooley on post-Soviet Central Asia, I argue that the multidivisional form (M-form) of colonial administration facilitated this strategy by concentrating all aspects of colonial administration in one executive agency.

In his pioneering scholarship on business organization, Alfred Chandler, later followed by Oliver Williamson, noticed that large industrial enterprises tend to be

---

[71] Terry Moe, "The Politics of Bureaucratic Structure," in *Can the Government Govern?*, ed. John E. Chubb and Paul E. Peterson (Washington, DC: Brookings, 1989), 282.

[72] My thinking owes much to James Mahoney and Kathleen Thelen, "A Theory of Gradual Institutional Change," in *Explaining Institutional Change: Ambiguity, Agency, and Power*, ed. Mahoney and Thelen (New York: Cambridge University Press, 2009).

[73] Evan J. Ringquist, Jeff Worsham, and Marc Allen Eisner, "Salience, Complexity, and the Legislative Direction of Regulatory Bureaucracies," *Journal of Public Administration Research and Theory* 13 (April 2003): 141–64. Kathleen Bawn, "Political Control versus Expertise: Congressional Choices about Administrative Procedures," *American Political Science Review* 89 (March 1995): 62–73.

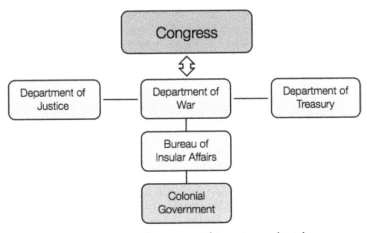

FIGURE 1.1. *Organizational structure of American colonial governance.*

governed either as unitary forms (U-form) or as multidivisional forms (M-form).[74] The U-form organization, represented in Chandler's account by the Ford Motor Company, maintains distinct administrative divisions in its peripheral divisions, while the M-Form, represented by General Motors, gives relative autonomy to its various peripheral companies. U-form hierarchies, however, have far higher governance costs that rapidly increase as firms expand, because of the overwhelming amount of information generated by separate divisions. M-form hierarchies, in contrast, are able to distill information among their separate divisions more efficiently and are more easily adaptable to local conditions, leaving the chief executive with only the most important decisions.[75]

While the management of automobile production and imperial colonies are decidedly different projects, Chandler's insights about organizational hierarchy do much to help us to make sense of colonial administration. M-form hierarchies may be more efficient organizational forms, but they tend to exhibit serious informational asymmetries, and may exacerbate the already strong principal–agent problems in foreign affairs. As will be demonstrated empirically in the following chapters, this form of organizational hierarchy resulted in a network of insular officials who were able to control information about the colonies with little interference from outside agencies or from Congress. As demonstrated in Figure 1.1, by centralizing control over the islands under one agency and further insulating it from the rest of the War Department, there were few opportunities for Congress to receive independent assessments or to prepare its own bills outside the network

---

[74] See Alfred D. Chandler, Jr., *Strategy and Structure: Chapters in the History of the American Industrial Enterprise* (Cambridge, MA: MIT Press, 1969) and Oliver Williamson, *Markets and Hierarchies: Analysis and Antitrust Implications* (New York: Free Press, 1975). Although my conclusions are slightly different, my discussion in this section draws heavily on Alexander Cooley, *Logics of Hierarchy: The Organization of Empires, States, and Military Occupations* (Ithaca, NY: Cornell University Press, 2005).

[75] See Cooley, *Logics of Hierarchy*, Ch. 3.

of the insular administration. In the United States, most aspects of colonial governance were directly overseen by the Secretary of War through the colonial clearinghouse known as the BIA. And the structure of American colonial governance was far from a typical Weberian bureaucracy; indeed, it resembled nothing so much as a classic corporate trust. What remained was an ambiguous authority structure that excluded the State Department, defied the normal organizational hierarchy of the War Department, and minimized interference from Congress and other bureaucracies.

State Building through Collaboration

How might bureaucrats make policy with low administrative capacity and weak congressional and public support? One mechanism I suggest in this book is the formation of collaborative relationships with actors *outside* formal state institutions. One point that nearly all scholars of American politics can agree on is that the American state is a "Rube Goldberg state," one with untold numbers of lacunae, veto points, conflicting institutions and, it must be added, political entrepreneurs who know how to exploit them.[76] The porous nature of the American state makes it more difficult to conduct policy from the center, but it also offers determined actors abundant opportunities to realize their goals; that is, when one path is blocked, there are often other ones available. Liberal states – the United States in particular – are likely to have rich civil societies that contain a number of strong and influential non-state actors and organizations, offering abundant opportunities for bureaucrats to harness this already-existing capacity for their own ends by collaborating with powerful private actors. Such public–private collaborations have occurred with surprising frequency throughout American history and in a wide variety of policy environments from the anti-vice crusade of Anthony Comstock to the enforcement of prohibition and equal opportunity employment laws.[77] As Brian Balogh details in a recent work, much of state building in the twentieth century follows these associational patterns of development.[78]

---

[76] For an example of entrepreneurial activity in the liberal state, see Carpenter's *Forging of Bureaucratic Autonomy*, which provides an analysis of American executive agencies during the Progressive era. Carpenter breaks apart the concept of state to examine the autonomy granted through reputation-building to certain executive agency bureaucracies. I borrow the phrase "Rube Goldberg state" from Elisabeth S. Clemens, "Lineages of the Rube Goldberg State: Building and Blurring Public Programs, 1900–1940," in *Rethinking Political Institutions: The Art of the State*, ed. Ian Shapiro, Stephen Skowronek, and Daniel Galvin (New York: New York University Press, 2007), 187–215.

[77] Nicola Beisel, *Imperiled Innocents: Anthony Comstock and Family Reproduction in Victorian America* (Princeton, NJ: Princeton University Press, 1997); Wayne E. Fuller, *Morality and the Mail in Nineteenth-Century America* (Urbana, IL: University of Illinois Press, 2003); Richard F. Hamm, *Shaping the Eighteenth Amendment: Temperance Reform, Legal Culture, and the Polity, 1880–1920* (Chapel Hill, NC: The University of North Carolina Press, 1995); K. Austin Kerr, *Organized for Prohibition: A New History of the Anti-Saloon League* (New Haven: Yale University Press, 1985). Robert C. Lieberman, *Shaping Race Policy: The United States in Comparative Perspective* (Princeton, NJ: Princeton University Press, 2005), 174–201.

[78] Brian Balogh, *The Associational State: American Governance in the Twentieth Century* (Philadelphia, PA: University of Pennsylvania Press, 2015).

Certain developments in American imperialism, I argue, constitute yet another case of borrowing capacity from private actors, and an especially clear case at that. Facing significant restrictions on their authority, colonial bureaucrats began to look to private actors for support, a process I term "state-building through collaboration." The crux of their strategy lay in the cultivation of public–private partnerships with investment bankers; partnerships that were developed and supported through a variety of crosscutting professional networks in American banking, economics, and colonial administration.[79] Although public–private partnerships have often meant delegating administrative power to private actors – a common pattern in American social policy – state building through collaboration explains how the state can also enhance its power and autonomy. Yet, much like in Carpenter's account, the creation of these partnerships relies on the entrepreneurial behavior of officials who can span boundaries between the state and private interests. These "weak ties," in other words, can be turned into the "strong ties" of collaboration.[80]

Despite its relatively common appearance in American *domestic* state development, this pattern of state building is somewhat alien to theories that account for the development of external state capacity, which still assume that state building means the creation of formal bureaucracies along traditional Weberian lines. Most scholarship equates increases in foreign policy capacity with centralization and hierarchy, an understandable bias given that the study of state building emerged from scholarship that focused on Western European state structures. State building through collaboration, however, is unlikely to follow such a traditional developmental path. After all, borrowing capacity and mobilizing outside support are not the same thing, and recognizing this requires us to complicate our understanding of liberal state development. As Elisabeth Clemens argues, these efforts to "borrow" rather than to directly build state capacity must be recognized as "expressions of power, but in the form of the exercise of government within particular institutional arrangements, rather than the cooptation of supporters or strategic pursuit of some electoral logic."[81]

My theory of state building through collaboration, then, builds on the work of scholars such as Ellis Hawley, whose concept of the associationalist state began this area of inquiry, as well as Clemens and Balogh, who have reinvigorated it. It applies these insights to the construction of external state capacity and shows how these partnerships can be used to enhance the autonomy of state agencies.[82] In other

---

[79] I mean here something different than Peter Evans's concept of "embedded autonomy," which refers to a particular set of ties between the state and industrial elites that can support a "shared project." Evans is concerned with the type of bureaucracies that are likely to develop this relationship with society, whereas I am interested in how state actors are able to "borrow" capacity from society to further their own goals. See Peter Evans, *Embedded Autonomy: States and Industrial Transformation* (Princeton, NJ: Princeton University Press, 1995).

[80] Mark Granovetter, "The Strength of Weak Ties," *American Journal of Sociology* 78 (May 1973): 1360–80. For an illustration of this concept in a very different context, see Colin D. Moore, "Innovation without Reputation: How Bureaucrats Saved the Veterans' Health Care System," *Perspectives on Politics* 13 (June 2015): 327–44.

[81] Clemens, "Lineages of the Rube Goldberg State," 193.

[82] Ellis W. Hawley, *The New Deal and the Problem of Monopoly: A Study in Economic Ambivalence* (New York: Fordham University Press, 1995); Sparrow, *From the Outside In*. See also Gerald Berk, *Louis D. Brandeis and the Making of Regulated Competition, 1900–1932* (New York: Cambridge University Press, 2012) for a discussion of the "cultivational" approach to state development.

words, state building through collaboration implies that private actors are central players in the *administration* of policies and not merely supportive constituencies used to build support for public programs. At the same time, state building through collaboration requires that bureaucrats remain independent from societal interests and retain their own irreducible preferences, which they then pursue through these partnerships. In this way, these partnerships represent something quite distinct from older theories of bureaucratic "capture." Furthermore, the shift away from the hierarchical organization of traditional state agencies to the contractual model of private agreements makes political oversight significantly more difficult as the line between public and private authority becomes blurred, which may provide important *political* gains to state actors.[83]

But how were these partnerships formed? Why would important private interests lend state actors their own capacity or resources? A number of recent and well-received studies of institutional development and adaptation argue that the answer to these questions can be found in the entrepreneurial behavior of state actors who facilitate partnerships among groups both within the state and between the state and society.[84] The political entrepreneur, defined variously as "strategic, self-activated innovators who recast political institutions" or "someone who sees a prospective cooperation dividend that is currently not being enjoyed," stitches together various interests by crafting policies or institutions that meet a variety of goals.[85] Furthermore, these entrepreneurs are likely to sit at the center of multiple crosscutting networks, which gives them access and influence with other groups.[86] Although the frequent rotation in and out of office by members of the American state has often been seen as a signal weakness, such limited tenures mean that state actors – especially high-level officials – are likely to have strong and enduring relationships with major societal interests.

[83] Oliver O. Williamson, *Markets and Hierarchies: Analysis and Antitrust Implications* (New York: Free Press, 1975).

[84] See especially Carpenter, *Forging Bureaucratic Autonomy*; Eric Schickler, *Disjointed Pluralism: Institutional Innovations and the Development of the U.S. Congress* (Princeton, NJ: Princeton University Press, 2001); Adam Sheingate, "Political Entrepreneurship, Institutional Change, and American Political Development," *Studies in American Political Development* 17 (Fall 2003): 185–203.

[85] Adam Sheingate, "The Terrain of the Political Entrepreneur," in *Formative Acts: American Politics in the Making*, ed. Stephen Skowronek and Matthew Glassman (Philadelphia, PA: University of Pennsylvania Press, 2007), 13; Kenneth A. Shepsle and Mark S. Bonchek, *Analyzing Politics: Rationality, Behavior, and Institutions* (New York: W. W. Norton, 1997), 245. See Schickler, *Disjointed Pluralism*, for the role of entrepreneurs in Congress and Carpenter, *Forging of Bureaucratic Autonomy*, for their role in executive agencies. Whether political entrepreneurs truly need to be self-consciously strategic is also a matter of debate. See Daniel P. Carpenter and Colin D. Moore, "Robust Action and the Strategic Use of Ambiguity in a Bureaucratic Cohort: FDA Officers and the Evolution of New Drug Regulations, 1950–1970," in *Formative Acts*, 341.

[86] For example, John Padgett and Christopher Ansell's study of power in fifteenth-century Florence shows that Cosimo de Medici's power came from his position at the intersection of kinship, patrimony, and financial exchange networks. John F. Padgett and Christopher K. Ansell, "Robust Action and the Rise of the Medici, 1400–1434," *American Journal of Sociology* 98 (May 1993): 1259–319. In a very different context, Carpenter's (2001) study of the USDA illustrates how chief forester Gifford Pinchot's connections to professional, scientific, and environmental organizations allowed him to push his own agenda of land regulation that many members of Congress bitterly opposed.

Yet a strategy of state building through collaboration also has a number of unique pitfalls. For one, the ability of state actors to "borrow" private capacity is dependent on the maintenance of the partnership. Should either state or private actors renege on their commitments, or should external factors dramatically alter the costs to either party, the partnership could very quickly crumble. Furthermore, the costs of exiting the partnership may increase over time. Such a situation may lead to suboptimal outcomes as state actors are forced to act in ways that are politically controversial, or at least highly visible, to meet commitments made earlier to their private partners.[87] This suggests that while state building through collaboration may offer state actors powerful short-term increases in capacity and a way around restrictions on their power, it may also prove to be less stable than traditional state building strategies.

American imperialism, I argue in this book, constitutes a case of state building through collaboration. Beginning with their efforts to develop the Philippines, colonial bureaucrats slowly began to form relationships with bankers who, in turn, floated Philippine bonds on Wall Street to fuel the railroad and infrastructure development projects in the islands. By leveraging colonial gold reserves and other resources, they offered these often-reluctant bankers financial incentives to invest in the American empire and to increase the capital available for development. These initial experiments in the Philippines with the use of private capital to fund foreign policy priorities were soon used to bring new nations under American control, beginning with the Dominican Republic in 1905 and soon spreading throughout the Caribbean and Latin America during the Taft administration. From their modest beginnings in the Philippines as a way to overcome legal and financial limitations on colonial development, the public–private distinction was further blurred as these partnerships were formalized as "Dollar Diplomacy," an arrangement that would govern America's "drive to hegemony" in the first decades of the twentieth century.[88] Indeed, as a result of its attempts to limit bureaucratic drift, Congress inadvertently encouraged colonial officials to form these partnerships with private actors. The partnerships they forged among themselves and with private organizations created new systems of governance in foreign affairs that allowed the president and colonial bureaucrats more autonomy to pursue objectives independent of congressional and democratic checks.

If the concepts of inconspicuous action and state building through partnership help us to understand the *how* of American imperial bureaucrats, they do not account for the *why*. Although bureaucratic goals can, of course, often be reduced to simple graft, budget maximization, or turf protection, bureaucratic organizations and policy communities also provide a "structured environment," which shapes individual decisions, evaluations, and goals.[89] In many cases, ideas – whether they are about safety regulations or foreign policy – lie at the heart of bureaucratic goals.

---

[87] Paul Pierson, *Politics in Time: History, Institutions, and Social Analysis* (Princeton, NJ: Princeton University Press, 2004), 149–50.
[88] I borrow the phrase from David Healy, *Drive to Hegemony: The United States in the Caribbean, 1898–1917* (Madison, WI: University of Wisconsin Press, 1988).
[89] Herbert Simon, "Rational Choice and the Structure of Environment," *Psychological Review* 63 (1956): 129–38.

The Switchmen of History: Ideas as Focal Points and Road Maps

There is no question that ideas, as opposed to interests, have occupied a particularly uncertain place in social–scientific explanation.[90] Yet for scholars of politics, it is hard to deny that ideas are often at the root of political action, and a number of recent works have criticized rational choice and historical–institutional scholars alike for their lack of attention to ideas as something more than background noise.[91] We now know a great deal about how actors behave in institutional contexts when their preferences are given, but we know much less about where these preferences come from and, perhaps more importantly, how ideas might shape concrete political action. For Weber, ideas were the "switchmen" who "determined the tracks along which action has been pushed by the dynamic of interest," while Hugh Heclo later argued that the search for ideas – what he described as a process of "puzzling" – was central to state action.[92] The challenge, as Robert Lieberman has recently written, is to take ideas seriously as a political force while also retaining the "essential strengths of institutionalism in all its varieties: its accounts of strategic behavior by purposive agents under structural constraints."[93] The question, then, might be more narrowly stated as follows: How do ideas shape the strategies and concrete actions of bureaucrats?

If we accept that actors in organizations are boundedly rational – that is, they exhibit "behavior that is rational given the perceptual and evaluational premises of subjects" – then ideas are likely to become influential through policy paradigms, which encompass "not only the goals of policy and the kind of instruments that can be used to attain them, but also the very nature of the problems they are meant to be addressing."[94] More specifically, we can identify two pathways, first discussed by Judith Goldstein and Robert Keohane, through which this process might occur: (1) ideas as focal points and (2) ideas as road maps.[95] As road maps, ideas clarify actor goals and define the means–end relationship to achieve those goals, and are thus expected to be

---

[90] By no means do all scholars see ideas as something separate from interests, and some have even argued that they are often not much more than tools to further elite interests. See, for example, Kenneth A. Shepsle, "Comment," in *Regulator Policy and the Social Sciences*, ed. Roger Noll (Berkeley, CA: University of California Press, 1985), 231–7.

[91] See Frank Dobbin, *Forging Industrial Policy: The United States, Britain, and France in the Railway Age* (New York: Cambridge University Press, 1994); Sven Steinmo, Kathleen Thelen, and Frank Longstreth, eds., *Structuring Politics: Historical Institutionalism in Comparative Analysis* (New York: Cambridge University Press, 1992); Robert C. Lieberman, "Ideas, Institutions, and Political Order: Explaining Political Change," *American Political Science Review* 96 (December 2002): 697–712. For a work that treats ideas seriously, see Margaret Weir, *Politics and Jobs: The Boundaries of Employment Policy in the United States* (Princeton, NJ: Princeton University Press, 1992).

[92] Max Weber, "Social Psychology of the World's Religions," in *From Max Weber: Essays in Sociology*, ed. H. H. Gerth and C. Wright Mills (New York: Oxford University Press, 1958), 280; Hugh Heclo, *Modern Social Politics in Britain and Sweden: From Relief to Income Maintenance* (New Haven, CT: Yale University Press, 1974).

[93] Lieberman, "Ideas, Institutions, and Political Order," 699.

[94] Peter A. Hall, "Policy Paradigms, Social Learning, and the State: The Case of Economic Policymaking in Britain," *Comparative Politics* 25 (April 1993): 279.

[95] Judith Goldstein and Robert O. Keohane, eds., *Ideas and Foreign Policy: Beliefs, Institutions, and Political Change* (Ithaca, NY: Cornell University Press, 1993). See also John L. Campbell, *Institutional Change and Globalization* (Princeton, NJ: Princeton University Press, 2004), Ch. 4.

most powerful under conditions of uncertainty when interests are ill-defined, goals are unclear, and actors remain uncertain what their interests might be.[96]

As focal points, ideas "define cooperative solutions or act as coalitional glue," which may be especially important for diffuse organizations where hierarchies are less explicit.[97] In a bureaucratic context, focal points may also reduce the likelihood of bureaucratic capture by dominant economic interests through the articulation of separate organizational goals. The logic here is quite intuitive. When faced with new tasks, particularly when given significant discretion over how to define and solve a problem, bureaucrats are likely to rely on ideas more than past practices or routines. How they select among competing ideas is a less certain process, although it is likely to reflect the background and political beliefs of the organizational leaders and the policy ideas that are currently in vogue.[98]

Once selected, however, ideas shape organizational goals and normative structures (the focal points) and the policies designed to achieve those goals (the roadmap). At times, these goals may strongly influence the evolution of the institutional arrangements themselves, particularly when the institution is created with no clearly articulated congressional mission. Or, as Krasner argued in his classic work on state autonomy, "[t]he independence of central decision-makers from particular pressures allows them to formulate objectives that could not be effectively articulated by any nonstate actors."[99]

Civil service laws, sound infrastructure and planning, improved public health, elementary education, and neutral policing were all central to the domestic agenda of Progressive reformers, and the early American imperial administrators transported these ideas to America's newly acquired colonies. Their organizational goals, which were poorly defined by Congress, came to include popular Progressive policies that were consistently applied across the American empire with little regard for local conditions or populations.

As will be emphasized in the empirical sections of this study, American colonial policy was mainly a collection of Progressive-era social policies, rather than a separately articulated "imperial" policy. In many cases, these new domestic policy prescriptions for agriculture, education, and even urban design were transported largely intact to America's overseas colonies. To give one well-known example, American architect and urban planner Daniel Burnham, famed for his design of Chicago's Outer Drive and Washington's Union Station, proposed a similar makeover for Manila in the City Beautiful style.[100] Although only parts of his design

---

[96] Goldstein and Keohane, *Ideas and Foreign Policy*.

[97] Ibid., 12.

[98] For a classic discussion of this process, see John W. Kingdon, *Agendas, Alternatives, and Public Policies*, 2nd edn. (New York: Longman, 2003).

[99] Stephen D. Krasner, *Defending the National Interest: Raw Materials Investments and U.S. Foreign Policy* (Princeton, NJ: Princeton University Press, 1978), 346.

[100] Daniel F. Doeppers, "Manila's Imperial Makeover: Security, Health, and Symbolism," in *Colonial Crucible: Empire in the Making of the Modern American State*, ed. Alfred W. McCoy and Francisco A. Scarano (Madison, WI: University of Wisconsin Press, 2009); Thomas S. Hines, "American Modernism in the Philippines: The Forgotten Architecture of William E. Parsons," *Journal of the Society of Architectural Historians* 32 (December 1973): 316–26. Jonathan Best, "Empire Builders: American City Planning in the Philippines," *The American Historical Collection Bulletin* 37 (January–March 2009): 25–34.

were ever built, the broad boulevards and neoclassical buildings of contemporary Manila remain among the most visible reminders of America's colonial occupation.

The focal points provided by these Progressive ideas also helped to coordinate action despite the distance from Washington and a diffuse organizational environment. In part this problem was alleviated by a network of lower-level administrators who served in both the Caribbean and the Philippines, but it was also due, I argue, to the relative consistency of the goals of American administrators. These Progressive policies gave colonial administrators some unique focal points that both increased the coalitional glue of "old colonial hands" and made them more resistant to capture by special interests.

Such ideological consistency was made easier by the relatively small network of colonial authorities and advisors. Until the Wilson administration, every governor-general of the Philippines came up through lower-level positions in the colonial civil government, and many went on to greater positions in the Philippines and other insular territories. The leadership of the BIA, the War Department's colonial bureau, was perhaps the most extreme example. From its creation in 1901 until 1929, only two men held the title of chief of the Bureau: Clarence Edwards (1901–12) and Frank McIntyre (1912–29), and McIntyre had served as Edwards's assistant for six years prior to his appointment.[101] Yet this pattern was not confined to the upper echelons of the colonial bureaucracy. It was repeated among most lower-level officials as well. Clerks from the Philippines were recruited to assist in Puerto Rico, and, later to run customs houses in the Dominican Republic, Nicaragua, and even Liberia. Proven service in the colonial possessions became the key criterion for advancement and recruitment to other areas of America's colonial empire.

In contrast to domestic Progressives, colonial officials exercised a virtual monopoly on state power, allowing them to engage in extensive experimentation and to implement policies in the colonies without regard to politics or organized opposition. At times, colonial policies even led, rather than followed, domestic achievements. Opium, for example, was outlawed in the Philippines well before the Harrison Narcotics Act forbade its sale at home, and Gifford Pinchot's plan for Philippine forestry management was promptly adopted in 1904, predating by several months the 1905 Transfer Act that gave control of US forests to the Division of Forestry.[102] Naturally, the metrics of success were similar to those applied in domestic reform movements. American imperial reports demonstrate the same attention to quantifiable "improvements" that were used so often by domestic Progressives – how many children were educated, how many bridges were built, and how many hospitals were constructed.[103]

---

[101] George Meikeljohn, a machine politician from Nebraska, was briefly in charge of an earlier version of the Bureau.

[102] Anne L. Foster, "Prohibiting Opium in the Philippines and the United States: The Creation of an Interventionist State," in *Colonial Crucible: Empire in the Making of the Modern American State*, ed. Alfred W. McCoy and Francisco A. Scarano (Madison, WI: University of Wisconsin Press, 2009); Greg Bankoff, "Conservation and Colonialism: Gifford Pinchot and the Birth of Tropical Forestry in the Philippines," in *Colonial Crucible*.

[103] The choice of these policies was hardly inevitable. American colonial administrators might have borrowed ideas from the Bureau of Indian Affairs or even the Freedmen's Bureau – the most prominent bureaucratic efforts to manage dependent people. As I explain in Chapter 2, however, I find little evidence to support this position.

To accept that the architects of American empire genuinely believed in their reforms as good works is not to accept they were justified. Such Progressive ideas also came with a darker agenda of social control. Much like the urban reformers who were transforming American cities at the same time, colonial administrators did not hesitate to use the power of the state to impose their will on colonial societies.[104] They conscripted laborers to build roads, demolished homes in the name of urban sanitation, and saddled colonial societies with mountains of debt to pay for infrastructure improvements.[105] In short, it is almost impossible to explain America's approach to imperialism without understanding the role of ideas in shaping the goals of the officials who created the empire.

Case Selection and Terminology

The arguments introduced earlier present an institutional explanation for the evolution of American empire and the formation of the American external state drawn from a variety of works in the social sciences; the remainder of this book will test how they hold up against the historical record. Subsequent sections proceed in a roughly chronological fashion, beginning with a discussion of the politics of American overland empire and Congress's dominance of the nascent American foreign policy state.

As I discuss in Chapter 2, the political logic of settler expansion differed considerably from the later overseas empire, in part because Congress and American settlers dominated this earlier process. As all members of Congress and the executive were keenly aware, today's settlers were destined to be tomorrow's voters. More than anything else, the politics of territorial administration were driven by this central fact. Such clear political logic left politicians with every incentive to be solicitous and accommodating to Western settlers, particularly because Western states, unlike the southern or northeastern states, remained less firmly in the control of either party. Unlike the American West, however, Congress put up legal impediments to private direct investment in America's overseas colonies – the investment that fueled expansion in the West – and these very restrictions motivated colonial officials to reach out to private partners. To explain this distinction, I focus on the unique case of Hawai'i in Chapter 2, an early case of empire that, I argue, belongs more to the earlier cases of overland expansion and reveals differences in how the later colonies were acquired and managed.

---

[104] I borrow this characterization from Paul Boyer's study, *Urban Masses and Moral Order in America, 1820–1920* (Cambridge, MA: Harvard University Press, 1978), Ch. 12.

[105] The partnerships colonial administrators formed with banks and American business interests to achieve their goals also made it possible – even likely – that American policy in its colonies would become dominated by these interests. That this did *not* happen – at least not initially – was due, in part, to the early articulation of the goals and methods of Progressive nation building. The bureaucrats who ran America's overseas empire were sensitive to criticism that they were serving at the pleasure of Wall Street, and they went to great lengths to distance themselves from American interests they considered to be rapacious or irresponsible. While the interests of American banks and colonial administrators often became aligned, the unique and often far more disruptive goals of the bureaucrats allowed them to retain their independence from these metropolitan interests.

The majority of this book focuses on the two decades between the Spanish–American War and the end of the Wilson administration in 1921, a brief period that nevertheless allows us to observe the American empire during its rise and at the height of its power, as well as the beginning of its rapid decline.[106] Several longer case studies of the governance of the Philippines, the Dominican Republic, and Haiti are nested in the broader historical analysis of the development of the American imperial state and among the larger population of cases of American imperial governance. I chose these as the principal cases because each illustrates important institutional adaptations and interinstitutional political dynamics in American imperial governance. They are also "hard" or "least likely" cases, because they faced strict limitations imposed by Congress (or a lack of congressional approval altogether) and had the least domestic public or commercial support. The Philippines was the largest (in size and in population) and most ambitious example of American formal empire, and it serves as the central case for this study. The Dominican Republic and Haiti are considered together as the first "Dollar Diplomacy" cases where the public–private receivership system of colonial control transformed the entire island of Hispaniola into a de facto colony despite never being formally annexed by the United States. The major cases that motivate this study offer illustrations of the different and evolving strategies that colonial officials employed to create autonomous and ambitious colonial regimes despite congressional restrictions. At various points, I include shorter discussions of the empire in American Samoa, Puerto Rico, and Cuba to contrast these colonies with the Philippines and bring further clarity to my analytical points.

The decision to focus on these particular cases was also motivated to avoid a regional focus. One of the difficulties in studying empire is that it lies at the intersection of some major fault lines in academia. Social scientists and historians tend to sort themselves into those who study domestic societies and those who study the relations among them. These divisions are further complicated by regional subspecialties within the disciplines; a scholar of Latin America, for instance, will likely have little familiarity with the Philippines, while a scholar of Southeast Asia may have the opposite problem. As a result, few past studies have considered the ties between the American colonial state in the Philippines and Caribbean nations.[107] Furthermore, as one of the few francophone countries in the Caribbean, Haiti is often studied in isolation, which, once again, leaves many connections between it and the rest of the American empire unexplored.[108]

Empire is a notoriously vague concept, and I borrow Michael Doyle's very useful definition of empire as "a relationship, formal or informal, in which one state

---

[106] I make this statement about formal empire with one important caveat: after World War II, the United States administered several small island nations as part of the UN Trust Territory of Pacific Islands. The Marshall Islands and the Federated States of Micronesia both became independent in 1986, while the island nation of Palau was granted independence in 1994; all three nations remain under the US security umbrella. The Northern Mariana Islands did not seek independence and have operated as a commonwealth territory of the United States since 1975.

[107] For a notable exception, see Go, *American Empire and the Politics of Meaning*.

[108] It bears noting that the most recent edited volume on American empire does not include a single essay on Haiti or the Dominican Republic. See McCoy and Scarano, eds., *Colonial Crucible*.

controls the effective political sovereignty of another political society."[109] Naturally, no book of any reasonable size can do justice to every territory that came under American occupation and control. Although I refer to these cases in passing, I leave in-depth investigations of Guam, the Virgin Islands, Liberia, and the Panama Canal Zone to other scholars.

Finally, a note on terminology: To avoid confusion, I use the term "colonial state" whenever I am referring to colony-specific governments. In the case of the Philippines, for example, the colonial government began as an arm of the BIA, but became a hybrid government controlled by American officials and a Philippine assembly. I use the terms "imperial state" or "insular state" when I am referring to the BIA and other coordinating agencies in Washington, DC. I use the terms "external state" or "foreign policy state" to mean the collection of bureaucracies that include the State Department and Department of War – the precursors to what is often described as the national security state today.

Methods: Comparative History and Archival Data

Methodologically, this book offers a series of comparative histories to assess variation over time and across cases. Although each example of American imperial rule is considered in-depth, they cannot be considered "cases" in the traditional sense; that is to say, they are *not independent and identically distributed.* As my theory of imperial rule suggests, earlier experiences with colonial government had important effects on the later colonies. Consequently, I employ a method of narrative panel analysis, which allows me to assess how these critical experiences, sequences of events, and interactions among separate authority structures affect the development of institutions – in this case, those of the American empire – over time.[110]

Any historical study primarily focused on institutional development confronts serious endogeneity problems and this work is no exception. Yet such difficulties do not mean that genuinely historical social–scientific analysis is impossible. To confront these problems, this book adopts Peter Hall's method of "systematic process analysis."[111] Hall recommends that scholars first develop "a set of theories that identify the relevant causal factors and how they operate" followed by "predictions about the patterns that will appear in observations of the world if the causal theory is valid and if it is false." The theories outlined earlier, if correct, contain a number of observable implications, and I try to test them as clearly as possible in each empirical chapter.

Interinstitutional Politics. One central claim in this work is that interinstitutional fights between Congress and the executive motivated the design and development of American empire. My claim is that executive officials were able to accomplish their goals for an expansive American empire even in an environment of relative

---

[109] Michael Doyle, *Empires*, 45.
[110] For another example of narrative panel analysis, see Carpenter, *Forging of Bureaucratic Autonomy.*
[111] Peter A. Hall, "Aligning Ontology and Methodology in Comparative Research," in *Comparative Historical Analysis in the Social Sciences*, ed. James Mahoney and Dietrich Rueschemeyer (New York: Cambridge University Press, 2003).

congressional strength. I argue that fear of congressional reprisals and ex ante anticipation of congressional actions motivated the approach to American imperial management and expansion. If this is true, then I must be able to show that the preferences of the executive and Congress diverged on the question of empire, and that the institutional developments that facilitated this empire were designed in response to congressional restrictions on executive authority, rather than as a result of other factors such as efficiency or cultural considerations.

Inconspicuous Action, State Building through Collaboration, and Ideas as Road Maps. One of the three mechanisms at work in American imperial expansion was a concerted effort by executive officials to keep the empire off the congressional agenda. Inconspicuous action requires a purposeful effort to monopolize information and to limit opportunities for Congress to receive information from independent (i.e., nonexecutive) sources. It may also involve avoiding the very sort of activities likely to attract congressional scrutiny, such as the appropriations process. At its core, this concept requires me to demonstrate a conscious and strategic effort to reduce the salience to Congress of the policy actions was pursued by executive officials.

The second mechanism, state building through collaboration, is dependent on entrepreneurial behavior. As such, the actors responsible for the initial arrangements ought to sit at the center of crosscutting networks that span the public–private divide. Furthermore, if the arrangements are genuine partnerships and not examples of coercion by public authorities or capture by private actors, we should observe gains to both parties.

Finally, my theory hinges on the ability of ideas to influence the concrete actions and policy choices of colonial bureaucrats. If this is indeed the case, I should be able to demonstrate that ideas are positively correlated with policy outcomes and that they predate these outcomes. In other words, ideas should be used to shape the policies pursued and not as post-hoc justifications for certain goals or actions.[112]

Sources. The blurring of public and private authority in the governance and expansion of American empire, as well as the fact that much of my story is designed to uncover actions and strategies that were *designed* to be hidden, necessitated that the evidence provided range far wider than government reports or congressional testimony. Relying on these more traditional sources exclusively may bias the analysis, because bureaucrats are often quite selective about the information they share with Congress. While politicians tend to make their preferences quite well known, bureaucratic opinion and strategies are more often hidden in the formulaic and neutral language of official reports, which obscures the behind-the-scenes preferences and strategies. Thus, much of the historical evidence for this study comes from primary sources: Thousands of confidential letters, internal memoranda, and telegrams gathered from more than 30 collections of personal papers, the archival records of the colonial states in the Philippines, the Dominican Republic, Haiti, Cuba, Puerto Rico, American Samoa, as well as the records of the Department of

---

[112] Sheri Berman, *The Social Democratic Moment: Ideas and Politics in the Making of Interwar Europe* (Cambridge, MA: Harvard University Press, 1998).

State, Department of War, Marine Corps, and the BIA. When appropriate, specific claims are tested using quantitative data.

Looking Ahead

Parts of my argument hinge on the complex relationship between American overland expansion and the genuinely new responsibility of overseas American empire. In Chapter 2, I discuss the early American external state and explain how the experience of American overland empire and the American conquest of Hawai'i, as well as the past management of dependent people in the Bureau of Indian Affairs, were distinct from the period of overseas imperialism. Chapter 3 investigates the institutions designed for imperial governance, and the divergent trajectories of the Philippines and Cuba. In Chapter 4, I focus on the construction of the early American colonial state in the Philippines. Chapter 5 narrates the development of the customs receivership in the Dominican Republic and the institutionalization of Dollar Diplomacy. Chapter 6 returns to the Philippines for a look at the colonial state at its most autonomous and powerful. In Chapter 7, I discuss the empire under the new, Democratic Wilson administration, the financial collapse of the Philippine colonial state, and the military invasion of the Dominican Republic and Haiti. I conclude with a discussion of how the experience of American imperial management changed American foreign relations.

2

Clerical State Colonialism and the Annexation of Hawai'i

> I shall have no difficulty in saying that it is in the direction of the external interests of society that democratic governments appear to me decidedly inferior to others.
> —Alexis de Tocqueville, *Democracy in America*[1]

Perhaps it should come as no surprise that the conduct of "external interests" was not among the many admirable qualities that Tocqueville saw in the American democratic experiment. The foreign affairs of the Jacksonian-era United States consisted mainly of managing its relations with Indian nations, preventing its own citizens – the so-called *filibusters* – from fomenting revolutions in Latin America, and dispatching party hacks to staff its few foreign ministries abroad – all policies in which Congress played a direct role.[2] These facts were not lost on Tocqueville, who charitably described American foreign policy as "eminently expectant" and concluded that "it consists much more in abstaining than in doing."[3]

What is more surprising is that very little had changed in the sixty years since Tocqueville's visit, despite the fact that the United States had fought a devastating civil war and emerged as one of the world's leading industrial powers. Later foreign observers echoed Tocqueville's concerns about the capacity of the American foreign policy state and wondered how the United States would manage its overseas colonies if it chose to become an imperial power; a possibility that many Britons, in particular, began to encourage as Anglo-American relations started to warm at the end of the nineteenth century. But how, some wondered, could a state characterized by low capacity, disorganization, and domination by Congress manage overseas colonies? British historian and jurist James Bryce described the problem in 1897:

Britain has had painful experience of these difficulties in her own colonies; yet in her monarchical system and her colonial service she possesses machinery much more flexible

---

[1] Alexis de Tocqueville, *Democracy in America*, trans. Harvey C. Mansfield and Delba Winthrop (Chicago: University of Chicago Press, 2000 [1835]), 219.
[2] American ministers to Britain and France were typically more distinguished.
[3] Tocqueville, *Democracy in America*, 219.

and more adaptable to these conditions than the far more consistently democratic system of the United States has ever possessed or seems capable of constructing. In other words, the problems which the United States would have to solve in Cuba or in Hawaii, were either of them to be annexed, would be, for the United States, perfectly new and extremely perplexing problems.[4]

Whatever the merit of Bryce's evaluation of American government, his judgment that these problems were "perfectly new" is curious. The Constitution, after all, was designed to accommodate the admission of new territories to the Union, and no less an authority than Thomas Jefferson considered it perfectly suited for "extensive empire."[5] Even if the Framers had not considered overseas territories in their plans for American government, the management of new territories and dependent peoples was, by the end of the nineteenth century, a governing responsibility with which the American state had over a century of experience. Thousands of miles of new territory stretching from the Mississippi Delta to the Pacific Slope had been added to the United States through military conquest and legal legerdemain, and these new territories had been organized and settled under the watchful eye and with the encouragement of the federal government. Nor was it the case that the management of nonwhite populations was anything new. African-Americans and American-Indians – people deemed unfit to participate in Jefferson's "empire of liberty" – had long found themselves under the heavy thumb of the American state. Certainly it would have come as news to these former slaves and indigenous people that the US federal government lacked the coercive capacity for colonialism.

Rather than lacking experience in colonialism, the American state seems to have possessed it in spades. But did these past experiences with overland expansion provide a clear blueprint for the administration of an overseas empire? Many scholars have argued that it did. For some, the Louisiana Purchase "set the basis for and legitimated overseas annexation; it also provided models for overseas governance," while others have argued that American-Indian policy "served as a precedent for imperialist domination over the Philippines."[6] These arguments are not wrong so much as incomplete. For the most part, these connections are found in the case law that granted imperialism a measure of legality and the American cultural tropes that celebrated expansion and a messianic mission of "civilization." Nevertheless, when we turn to the *politics* of territorial empire and its *administration*, the picture is somewhat less clear.[7]

---

[4] James Bryce, "The Policy of Annexation for America," *Forum* 24 (December 1897).

[5] Thomas Jefferson to James Madison, 1809, in *The Life and Writings of Thomas Jefferson*, ed. Samuel Eagle Forman (New York: Bowen-Merrill, 1900), 185. It is worth noting that Jefferson was advocating the annexation of Cuba in this letter.

[6] Julian Go, "Modes of Rule in America's Overseas Empire: The Philippines, Puerto Rico, Guam, and Samoa," in *The Louisiana Purchase and American Expansion*, ed. Sanford Levinson and Bartholomew H. Sparrow (Lanham, MD: Rowman & Littlefield, 2005), 210; Walter L. Williams, "United States Indian Policy and the Debate over Philippine Annexation: Implications for the Origins of American Imperialism," *Journal of American History* 66 (March 1980): 810. See also Lanny Thompson, "The Imperial Republic: A Comparison of the Insular Territories under U.S. Dominion after 1898," *Pacific Historical Review* 71 (November 2002): 535–74.

[7] See, for example, Gary Lawson and Guy Seidman, *The Constitution of Empire: Territorial Expansion and American Legal History* (New Haven, CT: Yale University Press, 2004);

In contrast to the executive-dominated and centrally coordinated system of colonial rule that would run the overseas empire, territorial expansion was governed by a diverse array of domestic political constituencies, and its administration was the product of the conflicting political priorities of Western settlers, ambitious territorial politicians, Christian reformers, and eastern financiers. Members of Congress, anxious to please their settler constituents and potential new voters in the territories, championed this early stage of territorial expansion, and their administration followed the familiar logic of the nineteenth-century clerical state – one dominated by party officials, and one that reflected the "paucity of planning" so characteristic of the nineteenth-century American state.[8]

Yet the fact that this process demanded little state capacity is not to deny its brutality. The politics of overland American expansion operated according to a lethal political logic: White American settlers demanded more land, and their representatives in Congress marshaled the coercive capacity of the US Army to dispossess millions of indigenous people to provide them with this land. Nevertheless, this process of dispossession and territorial expansion ran according to the administrative and political logic of the nineteenth-century American clerical state, and it provides us only limited insight into understanding what emerged later. As I describe in Chapters 3–6, the creation of an overseas American empire was one that involved significant central state planning and presidential management.

This chapter documents how the clerical state created a territorial empire and managed its foreign relations. The first section describes the institutions and inter-institutional politics that governed territorial expansion and the subsequent settler empire. With few exceptions, this process was dominated by members of Congress who saw settlers as valuable future voters – an electoral fact that left Congress with every incentive to defer in most matters to the preferences of white territorial residents. Naturally, this did not result in the development of a territorial office that could operate independently from Congress or create the state capacity to discipline settlers in anything but the most superficial ways.

This is not to suggest that the state played no role in territorial settlement: it did. As Paul Frymer has persuasively argued, the state was most directly involved in the creation of settler empire through its strategic use of land policies, variously encouraging or preventing white settlement in territorial lands seized from Indian nations.[9] The following sections show how it facilitated white settlement and provided federal jobs and subsidies. But the territorial office never developed the sort of capacity that would make it a plausible home for a future overseas colonial bureau. Even the Office of Indian Affairs (OIA), the precursor to today's Bureau of Indian Affairs, and a plausible place to look for overseas imperial precedents, became known mainly for its bumbling incompetence – a charge that, if not always

---

Mark A. Graber, "Settling the West: The Annexation of Texas, The Louisiana Purchase, and *Bush v. Gore*," in *The Louisiana Purchase and American Expansion*; Christina Duffy Burnett, "The Constitution and Deconstitution of the United States," in *The Louisiana Purchase and American Expansion*.

[8] I borrow the term "clerical state" from Carpenter, *Forging of Bureaucratic Autonomy*, Ch. 2. Richard L. McCormick, *The Party Period and Public Policy: American Politics from the Age of Jackson to the Progressive Era* (New York: Oxford University Press, 1986), 206.

[9] Paul Frymer, "'A Rush and a Push and the Land is Ours': Territorial Expansion, Land Policy, and U.S. State Formation," *Perspectives on Politics* 12 (March 2014): 119–44.

true, demonstrates the contentious politics that shaped Indian dispossession and territorial expansion.

The second section focuses on the American foreign policy state: That small set of executive agencies in the State Department charged with managing (and more often mismanaging) US foreign relations. Although control over these diplomatic and national security agencies would later become a hallmark of the president's informational advantage over Congress and helpful in leading the expansion of overseas empire, the executive had no such information monopoly in the latter half of the nineteenth century. The Senate played an active and perhaps dominant role in American foreign affairs, and the same party spoilsmen and clerks who managed American domestic affairs dominated this foreign policy state. It was this lack of a disciplined diplomatic or colonial corps that European observers like Bryce and many American elites regularly identified as a central impediment in transforming the United States into a colonial power. To understand how this set of external state agencies would later evolve, it helps to understand their status at the end of the nineteenth century.

This chapter concludes with a discussion of the annexation of Hawai'i, a case that fits uneasily into traditional stories of American territorial expansion or overseas empire. Although it was an overseas colony, its acquisition owes more to the political logic of settler expansion than to a later politics of formal empire, particularly because the descendants of white Americans controlled its government after the monarchy was overthrown. Nevertheless, its large nonwhite population and its existence as a sovereign state means that Hawai'i also fits poorly with the traditional process of American territorial expansion. As such, the hybrid nature of the Hawaiian case provides a revealing look at how the clerical state sought to grapple with an overseas possession on the eve of the Spanish–American War.

TERRITORIAL EXPANSION: THE POLITICAL LOGIC OF SETTLER EMPIRE

Senator Thomas Hart Benton, among the more vociferous proponents of Western settlement, wrote in 1843 that American expansion "was not an act of government leading the people and protecting them, but like all the other great emigrations and settlements of that race on our continents, it was the act of the people going forward without government aid or countenance, establishing their possession and compelling the Government to follow with its shield and spread it over them."[10] As historians such as Patricia Nelson Limerick, Richard White, and Brain Balogh have conclusively demonstrated, this longstanding trope of Western history conveniently ignores the many activities of the American state in overland expansion.[11]

---

[10] Thomas Hart Benton, *Thirty Years View; or, A History of the Working of the American Government for Thirty Years, from 1820 to 1850* (New York: D. Appleton, 1856), v. 2, 468–9, quoted in Richard White, *"It's Your Misfortune and None of My Own:" A New History of the American West* (Norman, OK: University of Oklahoma Press, 1993), 57.

[11] Patricia Nelson Limerick, *The Legacy of Conquest: The Unbroken Past of the American West* (New York: W. W. Norton, 1987); Brian Balogh, *A Government Out of Sight: The Mystery of National Authority in Nineteenth-Century America* (New York: Cambridge University Press, 2009); White, *It's Your Misfortune.*

For one, the federal government usually led rather than followed white settlers, and the violent subjugation of American Indians demanded significant state strength. Nevertheless, in matters of territorial administration, there is a certain truth to what Benton had to say. The federal government may have had considerably more latitude to operate in the territories than in domestic states, but aside from truly exceptional cases – most famously, the persecution of Mormons in Utah – it chose not to exercise much control. What little administrative oversight the state did provide was notable mainly for the patronage opportunities it offered to members of Congress rather than for its coercive capacity.

Much of this reluctance, I argue, can be explained by the political logic of American settler empire, whereby the United States overcame its limited capacity for imperial management by developing land policies to encourage whites to settle on territorial lands. US land policies, in other words, were designed to transform territories occupied by indigenous or nonwhite Spanish and French settlers into Anglophone territories that could be easily incorporated into the Union. Once the territories had gained a sufficient white population, Congress could consider them for statehood.[12]

When settlers arrived in these new territories, the policy also had important implications for how these territories were administered. Any inclination executive officials had to exercise power over American settlers, particularly after it had become clear that most would be Anglo-Americans, was tempered by the knowledge that the territories would soon be incorporated into the Union as states, turning those settlers into voters. The federal government, then, had considerably more constitutional latitude to operate in the territories, but such capacious legal authority did not translate into administrative capacity or an enhancement of executive power. As all members of Congress were keenly aware, today's settlers were destined to be tomorrow's voters.

More than anything else, the politics of territorial administration were driven by this fact. Such clear political logic left politicians with every incentive to be solicitous and accommodating to Western settlers, particularly because Western states, unlike the southern or northeastern states, remained less firmly in the control of either party. Congress, then, carefully supervised most aspects of territorial governance, even as it largely deferred to the popular will of white settlers in the territories.

The Northwest Ordinance and the Framework of Territorial Governance

Although the Constitution did not outline any specific policies to govern Western territories, Article IV, Section 3 clearly vested this power in Congress.[13] The Northwest Ordinance of 1787, largely designed by James Monroe, laid out a three-step process

---

[12] Frymer, "A Rush and a Push," 121.

[13] "The Congress shall have power to dispose of and make all needful rules and regulations respecting the territory or other property belonging to the United States." *Constitution of the United States*, Article IV, Section 3.

that would eventually end in statehood.[14] First, Congress would choose a governor for a three-year term and three judges (the president gained this power in 1789 after the new Constitution went into effect). Once the population of the territory had reached 5,000 free men, a bicameral legislature could be established, although the governor retained an absolute veto and the power to prorogue the territorial legislature.[15] When the population reached 60,000, the territory could apply for statehood.[16] In this period of apprenticeship, federal policymakers were interested in establishing federal control over the territory, gaining "the sentimental attachment of white residents," imposing a regime of racial exclusion, and securing republican values.[17] Depending on the background of the settlers, this district period would vary in duration, but would eventually give way to self-government.

In 1802, Ohio became the first state to enter the Union under this policy, followed by Indiana in 1816 and Illinois in 1818.[18] As it became clear by the 1820s that Anglo-Americans would form the bulk of Western settlers, the perceived need for a strong centralized territorial government began to disappear, and the first period of governor-run district government was eliminated from the territorial formula in 1823.[19] Even in this early period, Congress largely left the territories to their own devices, and it never once took action on laws in Indiana or Illinois. In part, as historian Jack Eblen has argued, this was due to the fact that Congress "had no procedure for the systematic review of territorial laws as they were received." But even more important, he argues, "was the lapse of federal concern with the territories."[20] There was simply no need, or so the thinking went, to subject these white settlers who were already well versed in the responsibilities of republican citizenship and sentimentally attached to the nation to any period of direct rule. "As a matter of practical politics," argues another student of territorial politics, "centralization could not have been conceived in the East or tolerated in the West."[21]

The major exception in antebellum America to this general process was Louisiana. Jefferson's controversial decision to purchase this massive property from Napoleon in 1803 – nearly doubling the size of the United States in the process – would put the territorial government framework to an early test. It was not so much that Louisiana was large, but that its inhabitants – French-speaking white

---

[14] For a discussion of the intellectual roots of the Northwest Ordinance, see Peter S. Onuf, *Statehood and Union: A History of the Northwest Ordinance* (Bloomington, IN: Indiana University Press, 1987).

[15] Why create such an autocratic early stage? The answer, it seems, is that the Framers were not at all certain that Anglo-American populations would be the dominant Western settlers. As historian Jack Eblen suggests, the centralized control imagined for settlement of the "Northwest by French-Canadians and other aliens unfamiliar with American political and legal institutions." Jack Ericson Eblen, *The First and Second United States Empires: Governors and Territorial Government, 1784–1912* (Pittsburgh, PA: University of Pittsburgh Press, 1968), 45.

[16] Whitney T. Perkins, *Denial of Empire: The United States and Its Dependencies* (Leyden: A. W. Sythoff, 1962), 14–15.

[17] Peter J. Kastor, *The Nation's Crucible: The Louisiana Purchase and the Creation of America* (New Haven, CT: Yale University Press, 2004), 5.

[18] Kentucky and Tennessee were directly admitted as states by Congress in 1790.

[19] Earl S. Pomeroy, *The Territories and the United States, 1861–1890* (Seattle, WA: University of Washington Press, 1969 [1947]), 3.

[20] Eblen, *First and Second*, 102.

[21] Pomeroy, *The Territories*, 107.

and mixed-race *creoles* – were foreign.[22] For American policymakers, this "foreign-ness" meant that republican culture, racial hierarchy, and attachment to the nation would need to be taught or imposed through a complex process of incorporation.[23]

W. C. C. Claiborne, who governed the Territory of Orleans (present-day Louisiana) for nearly a decade, famously opposed popular government. Soon after his arrival in the territory, he wrote to James Madison, "[until] the progress of information shall in some degree remove the mental darkness which at present so unhappily prevails, and a general knowledge of the American language, laws, and customs be understood, I do fear that a representative Government in Louisiana would be a dangerous experiment."[24] Yet even in Louisiana, a system of centrally managed territorial control – one that would more clearly resemble the colonial governments to come – proved to be short-lived. As historian Peter Kastor writes, "It was *demographic* expansion, rather than *geographic* expansion that was the subject of so much concern." Once settlers began to arrive and local elites made common cause with the American administrators, any rationale for the establishment of a coercive colonial government quickly evaporated – and, in fact, became politically costly. Although Louisiana's admission as a state was hurried along by the War of 1812, by 1820 its identity was firmly American, decidedly Southern, and completely self-governing.[25] The brief attempt by Claiborne to use his office to develop Louisiana as a colony was stillborn, and territorial governance did little to enhance executive power for the governance of overland expansion. The effect of this demographic expansion gave the United States easy control over Louisiana, but did not leave it with increased capacity for formal imperial management.

Federal Territorial Administration: Future Voters and Federal Subsidies

Territorial administration was never truly centralized at the executive level, even if, officially, there was a small territorial office housed in the executive bureaucracy. The Department of State initially served as the principal administrative body, but these responsibilities were slowly given over to the Interior Department after its creation in 1849.[26] Yet as Earl Pomeroy, the foremost student of federal–territorial relations writes, "It was an undefined jurisdiction which the department received, and an undefined jurisdiction which it passed on to the Department of the Interior in 1873."[27] In point of fact, neither the Secretary of State nor the Secretary of the Interior ever viewed territorial administration as much more than a peripheral responsibility, and no secretary made an effort to fully consolidate the functions of territorial government.[28] Consequently, they made few efforts to defend their supervision of territorial

[22] Kastor, *Nation's Crucible*, 4.
[23] See ibid. for a fascinating study of this process.
[24] Quoted in Perkins, *Denial of Empire*, 21.
[25] Kastor, *Nation's Crucible*, 226.
[26] Despite its significance, little has been written on federal management of American territories. Earl Pomeroy's study – now more than 60 years old – remains the definitive source. See Pomeroy, *The Territories*.
[27] Pomeroy, *The Territories*, 6.
[28] Ibid., 106.

affairs from the War, Justice, Post Office, and Treasury Departments, which each performed separate duties in the territories. Nearly all financial matters, for example, were handled by the Treasury Department. Officials in Interior, the ostensible territories office, did not receive information on territorial spending and had no independent funds even to pay the postal or telegraphic charges for their correspondence with territorial administrators.[29] But it was not the case that these other agencies were competing to achieve greater control over the territories. For the most part, it seems, they were loath to become involved in territorial matters at all and largely deferred to Congress in any serious matter; even the attorney general made every effort to avoid ruling on intra-territorial legal issues.[30]

Along with a lack of executive capacity, several structural factors prevented presidential dominance of territorial administration and allowed Congress to maintain its active role. In the territories, a broad array of federal bureaucracies oversaw specific governing tasks. Naturally, this often led to inefficient governance, but it did provide a number of outlets for Congress to receive information from different agencies about the state of the territories – a situation that left territorial governors with the responsibility to interpret the various (and occasionally contradictory) instructions that emanated from Washington.[31] These officials, writes Western historian Patricia Limerick, "found their supervisors reluctant to give advice; governors were often dispatched without instructions, and the Washington office was known to refuse advice on particular matters."[32] Congressional oversight followed much the same pattern. Although there were standing committees that supervised territorial affairs in both houses of Congress, this did little to stop other committees from involving themselves in territorial affairs when it suited their interests and needs; a situation that encouraged members to provide benefits to favored constituencies in the territories.

There was, after all, something in the territories that excited the interest of all members of Congress: future voters. At this time, most Western territories were not aligned with one party or the other, and leaders in Congress were anxious to ingratiate themselves with these potential voters through promises of federal jobs and territorial subsidies. This federal money, although often modest by national standards, was quite significant in less-developed territories. Federal jobs, the construction of public buildings, and government printing contracts were important routes to a secure income for territorial residents.[33] In the early days of the Dakota Territory, for example – prior to the discovery of gold in the Black Hills – historian Howard Lamar notes how "Washington was in essence subsidizing a government which had few citizens, no income, and a highly questionable future." This, he argues, instilled an "old Dakota attitude that government itself was an important paying business."[34]

The dependence of territorial settlers on Washington and the desire of politicians to court future voters led members of Congress to pay diligent attention to

[29] Ibid., 26.
[30] Ibid., 25.
[31] Eblen, *First and Second*, 300.
[32] Limerick, *Legacy of Conquest*, 81.
[33] Ibid., 82.
[34] Howard R. Lamar, *Dakota Territory, 1861–1889: A Study in Frontier Politics* (New Haven, CT: Yale University Press, 1956), 276, quoted in Limerick, *Legacy of Conquest*, 83.

politics in the territories and to zealously guard their share of federal subsidies. Zachariah Chandler of Michigan, for example, in advocating for his own candidate for the governorship of New Mexico, was perfectly blunt:

Michigan is almost without representation in Territorial appointments while Kansas is *well taken care of* . . . [If] the appointment lies between Michigan and Kansas, . . . it ought not to lie there long. Michigan never wavers *any where*. She is found at the ballot box, at conventions in the Senate, House of Representatives *everywhere* & 1,250,000 such people are not excelled even by Kansas.[35]

Politicians from states adjacent to territories often paid particular attention to the appointment of territorial officials who, they hoped, would buttress or establish regional loyalties to their party. As a supporter of one candidate for the governorship of New Mexico wrote to President Cleveland, "I do not know him personally but I find he is strongly endorsed by the leading citizens, men . . . whose influence will be felt to hold New Mexico as a Democratic ally when she assumes the dignity of a State which she will soon do."[36] The importance members of Congress assigned to these jobs is revealed in just how vociferously they demonized their opponents' appointees. Under Republican administrations, the minority Democrats decried the "carpet-bag officials who have been intriguing, blundering, and domineering in the Territories as they used to do in the South." When party rule switched during the first Cleveland administration, Republicans were only too happy to denounce Democratic officials in the territories as "broken-down politicians and needy individuals."[37]

Some scholars have argued that the standard characterization of territorial officials as incompetent party hacks is somewhat overblown.[38] While that may be true, they were generally inexperienced amateurs. Only 32 of the 424 governors, secretaries, and territorial judges appointed between 1861 and 1890 had held a previous territorial office.[39] The United States never created a specific territorial service and there were consequently few "old hands" in territorial administration. By and large, governors served relatively short terms – an average of three years from 1788 to 1912 – and nearly 40 percent were already territorial residents.[40] Settlers usually resisted "outsiders" arriving to govern them. Furthermore, the pay, as a rule, was modest, while living costs in the territories were high.

Such realities discouraged more prominent men and outsiders from taking these jobs. As the Seattle *Weekly Post-Intelligencer* noted in 1882, "The three Judges of the Supreme Court of Washington Territory, with the judicial affairs of 100,000 people in their hands, get salaries aggregating $7,800 per annum. The five Judges of British Columbia, having jurisdiction over 30,000 white people, and 20,000 Indians,

[35] Chandler to Fish, July 16, 1871, quoted in Pomeroy, *The Territories*, 68.
[36] L. R. Bacon to Cleveland, May 9, 1885, quoted in Pomeroy, *The Territories*, 71–2.
[37] "Carpet-bag officials," Ben Tillman, C. Rec. (48th Cong., 1st sess.), 2783; "needy individuals," Stewart, C. Rec. (50th Cong., 1st sess.), 6459, both quoted in Pomeroy, *The Territories*, 104.
[38] Kermit L. Hall, "Hacks and Derelicts Revisited: American Territorial Judiciary, 1789–1959," *Western Historical Quarterly* 12 (July 1981), 284.
[39] Pomeroy, *The Territories*, 63.
[40] Eblen, *First and Second*, 288–9.

receive $22,670, with not to exceed half the work done . . . on this side."[41] To support themselves on these relatively small salaries, most territorial officials, including those who had arrived from other states, tried to establish businesses in the territories. Yet as Pomeroy points out, "Non-residence was a stigma for any officer; he was suspect from the beginning . . . If they starved, they showed that they were driven west by their incompetence; if they prospered, they showed that they were dishonest."[42]

As a result of these objections, nonresident appointments were slowly phased out. The 1888 Republican platform went so far as to decree "all officers thereof should be selected from the bona fide residents and citizens of the Territories wherein they are to serve."[43] By 1893, every single territorial governor was a resident of the territory when appointed.[44] In point of fact, many of these men used their territorial positions as a springboard to national office when the territory was admitted to the Union; indeed, nearly one-third of all territorial governors in American history eventually served in the House or Senate.[45] Naturally, this combination of dependence and political ambition left territorial authorities with little discretion and little desire to implement policies that conflicted with the will of the settlers, leaving the preferences of territorial administrators entirely reducible to the preferences of the parties and the territorial residents.

Despite the relatively light federal presence in the territories, Western settlers still chafed at restrictions imposed by Washington, and most attempts to impose order from the East were complete failures. American settlers, to be sure, were quick to denounce any laws that restricted their actions as utter tyranny. For Martin Maginnis, the delegate to Congress from the Montana Territory in the 1880s, the territorial system was "the most infamous system of colonial government that was ever seen on the face of the globe." Territories, Maginnis argued, were "the colonies of your Republic, situated three thousand miles away from Washington by land, as the thirteen colonies were situated three thousand miles away from London by water."[46]

The equation of Washington with London and territorial officials with George III's agents first appeared in 1793 in the *first issue* of Cincinnati's *first newspaper* and quickly became a standard rhetorical flourish to be employed whenever the federal government did something that displeased the settlers – an event that was not infrequent.[47] Yet such melodramatic denunciations of the federal government betrayed the relative liberty Washington granted the territories. Faced with this "tyranny," territorial residents certainly showed no fear of reprisal, and, with the willing assistance of the local partisan press, proved themselves willing to heap invective on the hapless territorial administrators. In 1862, to give one example, the New Mexico legislature felt perfectly free to print the governor's message in the Santa Fe *Gazette* with a preamble decrying the "false, erroneous absurd and ill-sounding ideas therein contained."[48]

[41] Seattle *Weekly Post-Intelligencer*, March 27, 1882, quoted in Pomeroy, *The Territories*, 39.
[42] Pomeroy, *The Territories*, 101.
[43] Quoted in Pomeroy, *The Territories*, 78.
[44] Eblen, *First and Second*, 278–8.
[45] Ibid., 315.
[46] Quoted in Pomeroy, *The Territories*, 104.
[47] Eblen, *First and Second*, 302.
[48] Santa Fe *Gazette*, December 20, 1862, quoted in Pomeroy, *The Territories*, 101.

"Citizens resented the territorial status," according to one historian, "not only because they were Westerners, but also because they had been Easterners."[49] Officials in Washington understood this, too. No coercive system of territorial administration was established because none was needed. Although the fact that most settlers were formerly state residents made them more resistant to control from Washington, it also meant that federal officials could leave them in relative peace with the knowledge that US sovereignty would not be compromised and that settlers would retain their sentimental attachment to the Union.

The logic of American overland expansion also meant that these Western settlers were to gain political power once their territories entered the Union, and this fact, above all, encouraged members of Congress who hoped to count on their support in coming elections to treat them with kid gloves. The incentives were much the same for the territorial administrators, who had little reason to exercise much independent discretionary power. Most were residents of the territories themselves and had little interest in imposing unpopular projects on people whose votes they very much wanted to win when the territory became a state. Consequently, the federal government provided generous subsidies to support settlements, including the maintenance of postal routes, the construction of public buildings, and payment of official salaries, but it left these responsibilities to the relevant executive agencies like the Post Office and Treasury.

The territories, although ostensibly part of a central executive agency, were administered individually with little centralized planning or policy. Throughout the nineteenth century, territorial administration itself remained a low capacity, temporary affair, divided among a number of agencies, valuable for its patronage opportunities, and responsible mainly to the settlers themselves. It was a process loosely managed by a series of federal agencies and supervised by members of Congress who were more interested in courting future voters with promises of jobs and subsidies from Washington. The experience of managing white settlers in Jefferson's "expansive empire," then, did not produce the capacity or expertise for an overseas empire of colonies and permanent dependencies.

SETTLER EMPIRE AND THE OFFICE OF INDIAN AFFAIRS

Unlike white settlers in Western territories who were generally allowed to run their own affairs, Indian nations had long been controlled by the OIA, an agency, which by the mid-nineteenth century managed every aspect of their lives, from where they lived to how they prepared their food to the style of their clothing.[50] If we are looking for administrative precedents or a model for later overseas empire, the OIA seems like a plausible place to begin.

---

[49] Pomeroy, *The Territories*, 104.

[50] The OIA was renamed the Bureau of Indian Affairs in 1947. The literature on federal–Indian relations is vast, but the best and most comprehensive source is still Francis Paul Prucha's magisterial work, *The Great Father: The United States Government and the American Indians* (Lincoln, NE: University of Nebraska Press, 1984). Other excellent sources include Frederick E. Hoxie, *The Campaign to Assimilate the Indians, 1880–1920* (Lincoln, NE: University of Nebraska Press, 1984) and Paul Stuart, *The Indian Office: Growth and Development of an American Institution, 1865–1900* (Ann Arbor, MI: UMI Press, 1979).

The OIA developed institutions and policies for dispossessing Indian nations of their land and assimilating them into American society – and, as Stephen Rockwell makes clear in his careful study of the agency, the OIA was often brutally effective in accomplishing these reprehensible goals and at defending itself from challenges to its authority from the military.[51] Although some of this work was centrally planned and coordinated from Washington, Indian agents on the ground were charged with enforcing constantly changing social policies and managing complex land and trade negotiations among the federal government, Western settlers, and Indian nations.[52]

Founded in 1824 to manage federal–Indian relations, the OIA long reflected the weakness and inability of the American state to enforce its own Indian policy or to stem the tide of white settlers' encroachment on Indian lands. During the Jacksonian era, when federal officials still believed that a separate Indian territory could be established in the West, the OIA was charged with enforcing the 1834 Trade and Intercourse Act, which was designed to maintain boundaries between white settlers and Indian nations. This policy quickly proved to be ineffective as more settlers moved west, and as Congress showed that it had no intention of enforcing treaties that gave away such vast tracts of land to Indian nations.[53]

During the 1840s and early 1850s, a new reservation policy was proposed to push Indians onto smaller islands of land, and, it was thought, to acculturate Indians into white society. Yet as Richard White writes, "The reservations were political plums available to the party in power. National administrations doled out the offices of agent, teacher, and reservation farmer as political rewards to minor party functionaries."[54] Consequently, by the late 1860s, the OIA was widely considered to be rotten to the core. The "Indian Ring," a dark (and largely fictional) cabal of Indian Bureau officials, Western settlers, and politicians, was blamed for a host of problems by early reformers, the most acute being the constant flare-up of hostilities in Indian country.[55]

As Indian uplift became a *cause célèbre* among eastern intellectuals and Christian missionaries, one solution to the endemic corruption of the Indian office was to allow these organizations to participate directly in Indian affairs.[56] As one historian writes, "The political origin of the corruption was taken for granted; and the notion began to be advanced that an effective antidote to such corruption might be found by the participation of churches in Indian Affairs."[57] The Board of Indian Commissioners was born in 1870 to reform the Indian service by trusting the appointment of Indian superintendents as well as the general management of

[51] Stephen J. Rockwell, *Indian Affairs and the Administrative State in the Nineteenth Century* (New York: Cambridge University Press, 2010).

[52] Rockwell, *Indian Affairs*, 35.

[53] Stuart, *The Indian Office*.

[54] Richard White, *It's Your Misfortune*, 93.

[55] Prucha, *Great Father*, Ch. 23.

[56] R. Pierce Beaver, *Church, State, and American Indians: Two and a Half Centuries of Partnership in Missions between Protestant Churches and Government* (St. Louis, MO: Concordia Publishing House, 1966).

[57] Pierce, *Church, State, and American Indians*.

agencies to religious societies.[58] Yet the efforts of these Christian reformers were hampered by the continued appointment of party loyalists to the Indian service and the increasing dominance of Western politicians in Indian affairs.

In the late 1880s and 1890s, seven states with large Indian populations entered the Union – the two Dakotas, Montana, Washington, Utah, Wyoming, and Idaho – and the representatives these new states sent to Washington were keen to solve the "Indian problem" once and for all.[59] It was not until 1896 that most Indian Office employees were brought under civil service protection, merely two years before the outbreak of the Spanish–American War.

As Stephen Rockwell has documented, Indian agency officials were more disciplined and competent than is often acknowledged, and they did exercise considerable coercive power over Indian nations.[60] Nevertheless, positions in the OIA continued to go to Republican or Democratic votaries until the end of the nineteenth century, and frequent corruption scandals involving Indian agents and Western suppliers left the OIA with one of the most tarnished reputations in the executive branch. Despite its unique organizational mission, the Indian Office had earned itself an infamous reputation for corruption and mismanagement by the end of the nineteenth century. Francis Paul Prucha, the foremost historian of federal–Indian relations concludes, "The Indian service, upon which rested much of the responsibility for solving the 'Indian problem' of the post-Civil War decades, was itself a large part of the problem."[61]

The OIA's dreadful reputation was due to the complex politics of Indian affairs, which were buffeted by Western settlers, mining and railroad concerns, and humanitarians.[62] There was little the OIA could do that would not earn it the ire of at least one of these powerful constituencies. The agency's location within this complicated web of territorial politics led it to pursue policies that reflected, at first, the goals of eastern Christian reformers, and, later, the preferences of Western politicians and white settlers – and often the OIA agents were left to their own devices with few explicit instructions from Washington. Rather than gaining more autonomy over Indian affairs, the president and the OIA's authority was slowly diminished after Congress stopped the practice of making treaties with Indian nations in 1871, a move that allowed the House of Representatives significantly more involvement over Indian affairs.[63]

---

[58] The relationship between Christian reform organizations and the BIA is another well-tilled area of American Indian history. See, for example, Francis Paul Prucha, *American Indian Policy in Crisis: Reformers and the Indian, 1865–1900* (Norman, OK: University of Oklahoma Press, 1976); Francis Paul Prucha, *The Churches and the Indian Schools, 1888–1912* (Lincoln, NE: University of Nebraska Press, 1979); Clyde A. Milner II, *With Good Intentions: Quaker Work among the Pawnees, Otos, and Omahas in the 1870s* (Lincoln, NE: University of Nebraska Press, 1982); Robert H. Keller, Jr., *American Protestantism and United States Indian Policy, 1869–82* (Lincoln, NE: University of Nebraska Press, 1983); William T. Hagan, *The Indian Rights Association: The Herbert Welsh Years, 1882–1904* (Tucson, AZ: The University of Arizona Press, 1985).

[59] Hoxie, *A Final Promise*, 108.

[60] Rockwell, *Indian Affairs*.

[61] Prucha, *Great Father*, 582.

[62] Rockwell, *Indian Affairs*, 227–8.

[63] Ibid., 311.

Although many of the previous administrative practices developed during the treaty period endured, this reform made it even easier for the multiple interests concerned with Indian affairs to influence policy – and to accuse the OIA of corruption and mismanagement. As Chapter 3 will detail, the architects of America's overseas empire were well aware of the Indian Office's infamous reputation, and it became, for many, precisely the sort of model to avoid. As with territorial expansion, cultural notions of manifest destiny and some legal principles from the Indian Office did influence the design of overseas empire, but the political environment was vastly different.

CLERICAL STATE FOREIGN POLICY

American foreign policy in the late nineteenth century evinced no more state capacity or presidential leadership than did territorial administration. Prior to the 1890s, what passed for a foreign policy in the United States amounted to various isolated encounters with foreign powers and occasional standoffs with Great Britain.[64] While the United States certainly had foreign relations between the Age of Jackson and the end of the nineteenth century, it would be a stretch – with the exception of the Civil War period – to describe these encounters as a formal foreign policy.[65]

Most foreign policy actions were, in the words of one historian, "the result of the activities of individual pressure groups, enterprises and statesmen rather than the deliberate choice of the American people themselves or their representatives in Washington."[66] Given the importance foreign affairs had played in the initial decade of the Republic's existence, it likely would have shocked the Founders to see what had become of the American external state less than a century later. As Henry Cabot Lodge wrote in his 1889 biography of George Washington, "Our relations with foreign nations today fill but a slight place in American politics, and excite generally only a languid interest. We have separated ourselves so completely from the affairs of other people that it is difficult to realize how large a place they occupied when the government was founded."[67]

For Progressive Americans like Lodge, anxious to see their nation take its rightful place among the Great Powers, the incompetence of the American external state was as frustrating as the spoils-ridden domestic state. But as these American elites knew all too well, America's traditional isolationism and the increasing dominance by Congress of American foreign policy made it difficult to construct a coalition to reform the external state. Yet we should be clear that this was not a "stateless" space. As with territorial administration, the federal government played a central

---

[64] Perhaps nothing better illustrates the weakness of the American external state in the mid-nineteenth century than the scourge of American filibusters who raised private military forces to invade foreign nations for their own profit or adventure. See Robert E. May, *Manifest Destiny's Underworld: Filibustering in Antebellum America* (Chapel Hill, NC: University of North Carolina Press, 2002), xi.

[65] Robert L. Beisner, *From the Old Diplomacy to the New, 1865–1900*, 2nd edn. (Arlington Heights, IL: Harland Davidson, 1986), 29.

[66] Paul M. Kennedy, *The Samoan Tangle: A Study in Anglo-German-American Relations, 1878–1900* (Dublin: Irish University Press, 1974), 133.

[67] Henry Cabot Lodge, *George Washington*, (Boston: Houghton Mifflin, 1889), v. 2, 129.

role in the foreign affairs, as scholars such as Brian Balogh have so persuasively shown. But to suggest that the state was the major player in foreign affairs is not to concede that it conducted them effectively or well.[68] The state's essential role in managing foreign relations is why Progressives like Lodge so desperately wanted to reform the external state bureaucracies in a way that would allow for a muscular American foreign policy. Authority was not their concern; they feared that the United States would prove unable to manage an overseas empire.

Patronage, Spoils, and the Reputation of External State Bureaucracies

Nowhere was the incapacity of the American clerical state more evident than in its foreign affairs departments. The few hapless clerks employed by the State Department spent much of their time defending the rights of Americans who had, often through their own shady dealings, run into troubles abroad. Even as other areas of the American state began to modernize, the American external state stayed well within the mold of the Jacksonian clerical state and remained one of the last bastions of the spoils system.

For the second half of the nineteenth century, the American diplomatic corps, with important exceptions for men such as Charles Francis Adams, generally managed to cause more problems for their country than they solved. As historian Robert Wiebe writes, "[it] consisted of honorary ambassadors, inexperienced ministers, and underpaid subordinates, men who came and went according to the dictates of partisanship and the availability of more attractive opportunities elsewhere."[69] "If a man was making trouble," Elihu Root later wrote, "the best way to get rid of him was to get him a place as a consul – it ordinarily pleased his wife, and he could be disposed of."[70]

The nineteenth-century state could count among its distinguished foreign representatives such men as Rumsey Wing, who attempted to assassinate the British ambassador during his tenure as minister to Ecuador and later drank himself to death; James Watson Webb, whose extortionate conduct while serving in Rio de Janiero was so appalling that Congress was forced to provide monetary compensation to the Brazilian government; or Charles DeLong, the barely literate minister to Japan, who enjoyed cracking his whip at bystanders while racing his carriage through the streets of Tokyo.[71] The spoilsmen did not make for distinguished representation abroad.

While most American diplomats did not manage to be quite as colorful as Webb and DeLong, they were often amateurs who knew little about the conduct of foreign relations. Furthermore, because the United States owned few permanent embassies, the relative grandeur of the American presence depended on the personal wealth of the ambassador. For ambassadors of more modest means, this could prove embarrassing. While serving as American ambassador to Italy, one diplomat complained

---

[68] Balogh, *A Government Out of Site*, 151–218.
[69] Robert H. Wiebe, *The Search for Order, 1877–1920* (New York: Hill & Wang, 1967), 227.
[70] Philip C. Jessup, *Elihu Root* (New York: Dodd, Mead & Co., 1938), v. 2, 101.
[71] Beisner, *Old Diplomacy*, 29.

to the Secretary of State that it was "really ignominious for the representative of a Great Power to be at a local landlord's mercy – especially an Italian landlord."[72]

The consular service was in no better shape. Much as they had been in the early days of the Republic, foreign affairs were divided between the diplomatic and consular services, both of which theoretically reported to the Department of State, but rarely did so in practice. As one young consular officer would later recall, before leaving Washington he was instructed by an official in the Consular Bureau that "the really efficient consul doesn't bother the Department very much."[73] In truth, nobody bothered much with the external state bureaucracies. Congress was suspicious of creating an elite diplomatic or consular corps and had hardly increased funding for consulate and diplomatic positions between 1880 and 1900. Consequently, there was virtually the same number of American consulates (238) in 1890 as there was in 1900 (248), despite the massive expansion of American influence in the international realm in the last decade of the nineteenth century.[74] Most of the consuls working in these offices were not even Americans – of the 14 consuls in Russia in 1890, for example, only *three* were citizens. This is less surprising than it may seem: in 1900, three quarters of consuls were foreign nationals.[75]

Even when Americans occupied the consul positions, however, communication between the consulate and Washington was abysmal, and officials at the State Department rarely knew what was going on at their far-flung consulates. As one famous (and possibly apocryphal) anecdote holds, a newly appointed consul arrived at his post only to be told that "his predecessor had been insane for three years and could be found tied to a chair upstairs."[76] Others arrived to find that their new colleagues had simply left their posts or were engaged in fantastic schemes to bilk the federal government out of thousands of dollars in fees. Even the rare consul who did wish to execute his duties honorably often had little understanding of the office. In theory, newly appointed consuls were required to attend a 30-day instructional program in Washington, but in reality their instructions usually amounted to a one-day stopover to pick up a copy of the consular relations handbook. Often the new consuls did not even bother with this, and they left the country without any instructions whatsoever.[77]

Neither the consular nor the diplomatic branches of the external state were helped by their public image. If American ministers were generally seen as wealthy dilettantes in the popular mind, the less illustrious consuls were often seen as washed-up drunks – and there was, it seems, some truth to the stereotype. The American consul, wrote foreign-service reformer Wilbur Carr, could "be truthfully pictured sleeping under the proverbial palm tree with his bottle beside him."[78] Even by the relatively low standards of the American patronage state, the consuls stood out as particularly incompetent; a consequence of the fact that American political parties used these positions as a dumping ground for their most troublesome

---

[72] Quoted in Richard Hume Werking, *The Master Architects: Building the United States Foreign Service, 1890–1913* (Lexington, KY: University Press of Kentucky, 1977), 13.

[73] Ibid., 8.

[74] Ibid., 3.

[75] Ibid.

[76] Ibid., 8.

[77] Ibid., 4–5.

[78] Quoted in Ibid., 4.

members – the drunks, the debtors, and the degenerates. In the words of one Secretary of State, the consular offices were treated by both parties as a place "to shelve broken down politicians and to take care of failures in American life whose friends were looking for some way to support them at Government expense."[79]

Not that there was much motivation for consuls to remain honest or to execute their office in an efficient manner. The official salaries were low and there was almost no opportunity for advancement. By 1899 the salary scale for individual consulates had not been changed since 1874, and even that was but a minor fix to the 1856 classification. As a result, the United States remained woefully underrepresented in South America, where trade relations had greatly increased since the Civil War, and overrepresented in Europe and Canada. The lack of any rational organizational system also meant that there was no clear way to promote consuls within the service, which left most officials with little motivation for hard work. The logic of the spoils system exacerbated these problems through the constant rotation of offices. These problems were further compounded when the Pendleton Act reduced the number of positions available to politicians, putting even more pressure on the consular service to accept party hacks.[80] After McKinley took office in 1897, for example, he proceeded to replace 238 of the 272 most senior consuls with Republican loyalists.

Even as it began to disappear in other areas of the American state, the spoils system remained an essential part of the external state by the close of the nineteenth century. Consequently, when the time came for Progressive Republicans to look for an agency to manage the newly acquired colonies, the incompetent ranks of the State Department's consular and diplomatic corps did not seem particularly desirable. As domestic bureaucracies began to become more professional, centralized, and dominated by the executive after the adoption of the Pendleton Act, the American external state remained largely unchanged since the Civil War. Furthermore, the Senate, through its control of offices and its treaty power, remained an important – even dominant – force in American foreign affairs.

The Senate's Dominance and the Clerical Foreign Policy State

The disorganization of the American foreign policy state made the conduct of foreign relations difficult for nineteenth-century presidents. But state incapacity and the incompetence of the bureaucracy was only part of the problem. The period between the end of the Civil War and the Spanish–American War was also the height of senatorial dominance over foreign affairs.[81] The Senate controlled appointments to the American consular and diplomatic corps, blocked treaties, and generally intimidated executive officials and the president. Henry Adams, reflecting on John Hay's tenure as Secretary of State, described the results of the Senate's dominance accordingly:

The Secretary of State exists only to recognize the existence of a world which Congress would rather ignore; of obligations which Congress repudiates whenever it can; of bargains which

---

[79] Elihu Root quoted in Ibid., 11.
[80] Ibid., 7–11.
[81] W. Stull Holt, *Treaties Defeated by the Senate* (Gloucester, MA: Peter Smith, 1964), 121–64.

Congress distrusts and tries to turn to its advantage or to reject. Since the first day the Senate existed, it has always intrigued against the Secretary of State whenever the Secretary has been obliged to extend his functions beyond the appointment of consuls in Senators' service.[82]

At the turn of the century, this position would have seemed entirely reasonable. The Senate of Adams's day was responsible for blocking countless treaties and trade agreements, and according to historian Robert Beisner, "[m]any more accords never went beyond the negotiating table or never were submitted for ratification, because of anticipated Senate hostility."[83] Indeed, between 1871 and 1899, *the Senate did not approve one significant treaty* and it rejected 20.[84]

Among the more revealing examples of how this clerical state foreign policy and congressional dominance prevented presidential action came with President Ulysses S. Grant's aborted attempt to acquire the Dominican Republic. Following a policy originally outlined by Andrew Johnson, Grant sent American representatives to annex the Dominican Republic and to secure for the United States a stronghold in the Caribbean to protect the planned canal through Central America. Although Grant did manage to sign two treaties with Dominican representatives in 1869, the treaty hardly stood a chance in the Senate. Despite the fact that Republicans had a clear two-thirds majority and that Grant had taken the extraordinary step to lobby for it personally, the annexation treaty was easily defeated in June of 1870 on a 28–28 vote with nineteen Republicans voting against it.[85]

Democratic presidents did not fare any better. Grover Cleveland had negotiated a treaty with Great Britain to settle various issues related to northeastern fisheries after Canadian authorities seized several American fishing boats in 1885. Although the more belligerent Senate had passed a resolution giving Cleveland permission to retaliate against Canada, the president chose to pursue a peaceful course and the treaty was signed on February 15, 1888. When the treaty was submitted to the Senate, however, Senate Republicans expressed shock that the treaty's negotiators had not been picked by the Senate. In his remarks on the floor, Senator William Chandler of New Hampshire described Cleveland's actions as "a gross violation of the Constitution, willfully, recklessly, and defiantly perpetrated; and the Senate might well have refused on this ground even to consider the terms of a treaty thus first introduced into its presence."[86] So aggressive was the Senate in defending its institutional privileges that few bothered to attack the treaty on its merits.

Another example of senatorial intransigence came with the defeat of the Olney–Pauncefote Treaty of 1897. After a dispute with Great Britain over Venezuela's boundaries, both American and British officials decided that, in the future, it would be helpful to have a previously agreed upon method to resolve disputes without risking escalation. Cleveland and Olney negotiated an arbitration treaty, whereby Britain and the United States agreed to certain peaceful methods in advance to resolve any future dispute. The treaty received widespread popular support and even the newly elected Republican President William McKinley urged its passage

[82] Henry Adams, *The Education of Henry Adams* (Boston: Houghton Mifflin, 1918), 422.
[83] Beisner, *Old Diplomacy*, 6.
[84] Holt, *Treaties Defeated*.
[85] G. Pope Atkins and Larman C. Wilson, *The Dominican Republic and the United States: From Imperialism to Transnationalism* (Athens, GA: University of Georgia Press, 1998).
[86] Chandler quoted in Holt, *Treaties Defeated*, 145.

in his inaugural message. Despite strong support from the press and the president, it was defeated by a strange coalition that defies any partisan logic. Of the 26 no votes, 10 came from Republicans, 13 from Democrats, 2 from Populists, and 1 independent. Even contemporary observers were somewhat confused about what tied together the coalition. Yet the Secretary of State, Richard Olney, was convinced that the Senate's need to defend its institutional prestige was a primary factor. In a remarkably frank letter, Olney explained his reasoning:

> In the first place, it must be borne in mind that the Senate is now engaged in asserting itself as the power in the national government. It is steadily encroaching, on the one hand on the executive branch of the government, and on the other on the House of Representatives . . . the Treaty, in getting itself made by the sole act of the executive, without leave of the Senate first had and obtained, had committed the unpardonable sin. It must be either altogether defeated or so altered as to bear an unmistakable Senate stamp . . . and thus be the means of both humiliating the executive and showing to the world all greatness of the Senate.[87]

Given the amendments proposed prior to the treaty's defeat, there is every reason to believe that Olney was correct. Among the most debated of the proposed amendments was one that would require a full two-thirds majority to approve any agreement made with Britain as a result of the arbitration. A necessary addition, according to the minority report of the Committee on Foreign Relations, in order "to preserve the constant and unembarrassed action of the Senate."[88] A year later, in 1898, the same Senate that had defeated this arbitration treaty would lead the charge to war with Spain.

As the earlier examples illustrate, the Senate was not afraid to employ its formal powers to defend its prerogatives in foreign affairs, but often there was no need, because for most of the nineteenth century the Secretary of State *was* a former senator. Between Monroe's appointment in 1811 and Blaine's resignation in 1892, only four of the twenty-four Secretaries of State had not previously served in the Senate and only two of the four (Elihu Washburne and W. M. Evarts) served after the Civil War.[89] Naturally, these former senators had no desire to challenge the prestige of the Senate, especially when many hoped to return. In sum, at the turn of the century the Senate was hardly losing ground to the president in control over foreign relations – if anything, it was becoming more powerful.

SETTLER EMPIRE IN THE PACIFIC: THE ANNEXATION OF HAWAI'I

The 1893 overthrow of the Kingdom of Hawai'i has always fit uneasily into standard stories of American expansion – a difficulty reflected, in part, by the historiographical confusion over whether the Hawaiian case belongs to the history of

---

[87] Richard Olney to Henry White, May 14, 1897, quoted in Holt *Treaties Defeated*, 160.
[88] Holt, *Treaties Defeated*, 162.
[89] Schlesinger, *Imperial Presidency*, 80. The opposite is true after the 1890s. In 2009, Hillary Rodham Clinton became the first former senator to serve as Secretary of State in almost 30 years; from Blaine to Condoleezza Rice, only seven of the thirty-five Secretaries of State since 1892 had previously served a term in the Senate. They are John Sherman (1897–8), Philander Knox (1909–13), Frank Kellogg (1925–9), Cordell Hull (1933–44), James Byrnes (1945–7), John Foster Dulles (1953–9), and Edmund Muskie (1980–1).

the American West or to the history of American imperialism. Was Hawai'i the *last* case of Western expansion or the *first* case of overseas imperialism? Although this distinction is largely a matter of interpretation, the overthrow and subsequent annexation of Hawai'i provides a revealing look at how the weak American foreign policy state acquired its first overseas territory with a significant nonwhite population.

At first blush, of course, it appears that Hawai'i may have served as a model for the governance of overseas empire. For one, Hawai'i was the first major territory outside of North America to be annexed to the United States. Furthermore, its small white population and plantation economy left little chance that there would be significant Anglo-American immigration to the islands. When President McKinley signed the joint resolution to annex Hawai'i in July of 1898, there were only about 4,000 Americans out of a population of 110,000.[90]

Nevertheless, from an administrative and political perspective, Hawai'i largely resembled earlier settler territories. Although its white population – known in Hawaiian as *haoles* – was small, these descendants of American missionaries had overthrown the Hawaiian monarchy and maintained an iron grip on its economy and government. As a result, acquisition required no new institutional arrangements and followed a similar political logic to the settler empire that had reigned in the West.[91] It was overseen, much like any other territory, by the Department of the Interior, and local white residents were appointed as federal representatives in the islands. As this brief look at the politics of Hawai'i's acquisition reveals, this outcome was far from certain. As this section argues, the overthrow is not a story of an organized and aggressive imperial state's dominance of a weaker island nation, rather it is a story of how an ambitious group of American settlers took advantage of the disorganization that prevailed in American foreign policy at the time.

During the brief period of Hawai'i's existence as an independent republic – after a white-led coup to overthrow the monarchy and before its annexation by the United States – the leaders of the so-called Hawaiian Republic labored to show Congress that Hawai'i could be governed as a territory. In making these claims, the planters of Hawai'i made direct comparisons to their own rule and the regimes of racial hierarchy that prevailed in the American South.[92] The fact that it was overseas and had a small white population was not necessarily an impediment to the older system of territorial administration. In fact, the overthrow of the Hawaiian monarchy and the later annexation of Hawai'i reveals how a small group of white planters took advantage of America's bumbling foreign policy agencies and Congress's parochial concerns. Understanding the politics of the acquisition of Hawai'i, then, helps us to understand how the politics of territorial acquisition and the clerical state led to the annexation of this island kingdom – and puts into bold relief the changes in the governance and management of overseas colonies after the Spanish–American War.

---

[90] Perkins, *Denial of Empire*, 63.

[91] As historian Lanny Thompson has written, "Congress organized a territorial government for Hawai'i in 1900 following the well-established legal precedents of continental expansion established during the late nineteenth century." Thompson, "Imperial Republic," 545.

[92] William A. Russ, Jr., "The Role of Sugar in Hawaiian Annexation," *Pacific Historical Review* 12 (December 1943): 349.

Sugar, Immigration, and the Planters' Revolt

The United States and the Kingdom of Hawai'i had maintained formal diplomatic relations since 1842 when King Kamehameha III dispatched a member of his court to meet with Daniel Webster in Washington. Through these early contacts, a policy emerged that was mutually beneficial for both nations. By pledging to support Hawai'i's independence, the United States was able to discourage European powers from annexing the islands – a possibility that Americans feared because of the archipelago's strategic proximity to California.[93]

The more significant American contact with Hawai'i, however, came from the American missionaries, whalers, and adventurers who began to wash up in Honolulu with some regularity by the mid-1800s. As Americans became more established in the islands, they also began to serve in formal advisory capacities to the royal court. When Mark Twain visited the islands in the late 1860s, he was surprised to find that Hawai'i's prime minister was "a renegade American from New Hampshire," whom Twain derisively described as "all jaw, vanity, bombast and ignorance."[94] American-born lawyer John Ricord, for example, became Hawai'i's attorney general in 1844 and created a system of Hawaiian courts modeled on American and British common law.[95]

These early experiences in the islands paved the way for the establishment of a new industry that would dramatically alter Hawai'i's economy: sugar. In 1876, King David Kalakaua signed a reciprocity agreement that allowed for the free importation of Hawaiian sugar to the United States in exchange for a promise not to lease Honolulu's magnificent natural harbor, *Pu'uloa* (known today as Pearl Harbor), to any foreign power. Although reciprocity treaties had previously been signed, Louisiana sugar interests had always prevented their adoption in the Senate. By the 1870s, however, a majority was convinced that military considerations and the importance of cementing the political and economic ties of Hawai'i to the United States outweighed the small loss in national revenue that would inevitably result from free trade – a decision that sparked a sugar boom in the islands and made the white settlers some of the Hawaiian Kingdom's most powerful residents.[96]

In 1891, two events occurred that would push the white settlers to mount a revolution: Hawai'i lost its preferential trading status with the United States and a new monarch was enthroned. The McKinley Act of 1891 removed duties on all sugar imported into the United States and granted domestic producers, primarily based in Louisiana, a two-cent per pound price support.[97] This left the planters at a serious disadvantage to domestic sugar producers and stripped Hawai'i of its former advantage over other foreign sugar producers in the American market. For white sugar planters in Hawai'i who had built up their businesses to take advantage of

---

[93] Love, *Race over Empire*, 83.

[94] Mark Twain, *Roughing It* (New York: Harper & Brothers Publishers, 1913 [1871]), v. 2, 212.

[95] Merze Tate, *Hawaii: Reciprocity or Annexation* (East Lansing, MI: Michigan State University Press, 1968), 8–14.

[96] Sumner J. La Croix and Christopher Grandy, "The Political Instability of Reciprocal Trade and the Overthrow of the Hawaiian Kingdom," *Journal of Economic History* 57 (March 1997): 169.

[97] Arthur Power Dudden, *The American Pacific: From the Old China Trade to the Present* (Oxford: Oxford University Press, 1992), 67.

FIGURE 2.1. *Lowering the Hawaiian flag at the US annexation ceremony at 'Iolani Palace, Honolulu. August 12, 1898. Hawai'i State Archives.*

American reciprocity, this was a catastrophe, and the planters sustained losses estimated at nearly $12 million.[98]

Along with this economic blow, the white settlers faced the prospect of a more recalcitrant Hawaiian monarch. The kingdom's new leader, Queen Lili'uokalani, had plans for a national lottery and an opium licensing bill to raise revenue, measures that the settlers fiercely opposed. Her more radical move, however, came on January 14, 1893, when she prorogued the American-dominated legislature, and presented a new constitution that restored most of the monarchy's powers and denied the franchise to all but native Hawaiians.[99]

The Queen's actions threw the American settlers into a panic.[100] They quickly formed a Committee of Safety and began to draft plans for a provisional government. Fearing that the Queen would immediately order her royal guard to suppress

---

[98] Stevens to Foster, November 20, 1892; Reprinted in *FRUS, 1894, Appendix II*, 382.

[99] Gavan Daws, *Shoal of Time: A History of the Hawaiian Islands* (Honolulu, HI: University of Hawai'i Press, 1974), 271.

[100] It is unlikely that the Queen – by all reliable accounts an astute monarch, who was fluent in English and deeply knowledgeable about American politics – thought the planters would peacefully accept this new state of affairs. Despite these risks, she understood that the power of the monarchy and of native Hawaiians was quickly deteriorating, and that waiting would only put her in a weaker position. She also had every reason to believe that Washington would not support the overthrow of a sovereign kingdom that was well recognized by the international community.

the rebellion, they wrote to US Minister John Stevens to "pray for the protection of the United States forces."[101] Upon receipt of the Committee of Safety's request, Stevens – with no authorization from Washington – wasted no time in ordering American marines from the U.S.S. *Boston* to come ashore. Given that her own royal guard was mostly ceremonial, the Queen acquiesced to the coup – at least in the immediate term – but she registered a harsh letter of protest to Washington.[102] "I yield to the superior force of the United States of America," she wrote to President Benjamin Harrison, "until such time as the Government of the United States shall, upon the facts being presented to it, undo the action of its representatives, and reinstate me in the authority which I claim as the constitutional sovereign of the Hawaiian Islands."[103]

It all transpired with extraordinary speed. The Committee of Safety was formed on January 14, the marines landed on January 16, and the next day Stevens recognized the provisional white-led government. With the Queen deposed, the white rebels, with the willing assistance of Minister Stevens (who noted in a letter to Washington that the "Hawaiian pear is now fully ripe"), moved to offer Hawai'i to the United States.[104] By January 19, a delegation from the new "republic" was already steaming toward San Francisco.[105]

Despite the active involvement of US troops and the US minister, the overthrow of Lili'uokalani was not the result of a careful plan hatched in Washington and executed by a disciplined foreign service. In point of fact, Stevens's support of the white planters was only possible because of the disorganized and undisciplined nature of the American diplomatic corps. Lili'uokalani was well aware of this fact, and her protest letter to Washington was written with the expectation that the president would denounce the white rebels and return her kingdom. This was by no means an unrealistic request – and one that the *haole* leaders feared. If the general lack of centralization and careful command of American foreign representatives allowed this to occur, it was equally possible that the president would reverse their actions.

Upon their arrival in Washington, officials of Hawai'i's *haole* government – already armed with an annexation treaty – met with Secretary of State John Foster. Although Foster was sympathetic to their goals, his response reveals the complex politics surrounding Hawaiian annexation as well as the centrality of Congress. First, Foster advised them that, if annexed, Hawai'i was unlikely to receive the two cents per pound sugar subsidy going to domestic planters. He also had questions about Hawai'i's contract labor system and large Asian population.[106]

---

[101] Daws, *Shoal of Time*, 273.

[102] The Queen would later denounce Stevens in the harshest terms available to a proper Victorian lady as "mentally incapable of recognizing what is to be expected of a gentleman." Queen Lili'uokalani, *Hawaii's Story by Hawaii's Queen* (Boston: Lothrop, Lee & Shepard, 1898), 243.

[103] Quoted in Lili'uokalani, *Hawaii's Story*, Appendix C, 395.

[104] John L. Stevens to John W. Foster, February 1, 1893, *Papers and Documents Relating to the Hawaiian Islands* (Washington, DC: Government Printing Office, 1893), 47.

[105] Grover Cleveland to the Senate and House of Representatives, December 18, 1893, in *A Compilation of the Messages and Papers of the Presidents, 1789–1897*, ed. James Daniel Richardson (Washington, DC: Bureau of National Literature and Art, 1907), v. 9, 461.

[106] Michael J. Devine, "John W. Foster and the Struggle for the Annexation of Hawaii," *Pacific Historical Review* 46 (February 1977): 40.

Both issues, he thought, were likely to raise congressional heckles, especially because the Chinese Exclusion Act – among the most explosive issues of the day – was up for renewal in a few months.[107]

The larger difficulty, however, was the lame-duck status of the Harrison administration; Democrat Grover Cleveland had been elected the previous November and was due to be inaugurated in March. When Cleveland did take office, he withdrew the treaty and dispatched James Blount, a former Democratic Chairman of the House Committee of Foreign Affairs, to investigate. After receiving Blount's report, a scathing indictment of the actions of the planters and the US minister, the president left little doubt about where he stood: "But for the notorious predilections of the United States minister for annexation," Cleveland wrote, "the committee of safety which should be called the committee of annexation, would never have existed."[108]

The president was probably right to lay immediate responsibility at the American minister's feet. Stevens, it seems clear, was a long-time advocate of Hawaiian annexation. In November of 1892, well before Lili'uokalani had prorogued the legislature, he had written the Secretary of State to encourage the annexation of Hawai'i, dismissing the Hawaiian monarchy as "an absurd anachronism" and noting that as a territory the islands "could be as easily governed as any of the existing territories of the United States."[109] Stevens, for one, was so convinced that the new "republic" would be immediately annexed that he was already making recommendations for the form of its territorial government just weeks after the revolution. As he explained to Foster in a message that presented Hawai'i as yet another Western territory,

This plan and method of Government could be maintained as a transition Government until experience should prove it best to change it to a more popular form. In the meantime the responsible voters would rapidly increase and American ideas and interest would gain in force and volume. My private consultation with the Provisional Government since the departure of the commissioners for Washington has led us to think highly of the Jefferson act of 1804 for Louisiana as a transition expedient for Hawaii. This would cause no shock and would allow affairs to move along on safe and conservative lines until time and experience demand something better.[110]

Given time, Stevens seemed to think, enough white settlers would immigrate to "make the islands like southern California . . . bringing everything here into harmony with American life and prosperity."[111] But however much annexation agit-prop Stevens dispatched to Washington, it is unlikely that the State Department or President Harrison directed the American minister to assist with the coup.

This is not a minor distinction. The disorganization of the diplomatic corps and the lack of discipline among its appointees allowed a relatively minor official to support the overthrow of a sovereign monarch without receiving clear instructions to do so from Washington. To a degree that would seem unfathomable even a decade later, Stevens was operating independently in his support of the coup. Even if Harrison and Foster were pleased by the result, both expressed some discomfort

[107] Devine, "John W. Foster," 40.
[108] Cleveland, *Messages*, 470.
[109] Stevens quoted in Cleveland, *Messages*, 463.
[110] Stevens to Foster, February 1, 1893; *FRUS*, 1894, *Appendix II*, 400–1.
[111] Stevens quoted in Love, *Race over Empire*, 96.

in their minister's involvement. Harrison later disapproved of Stevens's use of the *Boston*'s marines, and Foster pointedly warned him that he should not "impair the independent sovereignty of that Government by substituting the flag and power of the United States," and he immediately ordered Stevens to lower the American flag which had been flying above 'Iolani palace.[112]

Although Cleveland did find the coup illegal, he refused to reinstall the Queen by force and left Congress to decide the Kingdom's fate. As he later wrote, "the Congress has . . . signified that nothing need be done touching American interference with the overthrow of the Government of the Queen."[113] Cleveland later used Stevens's questionable actions as a pretext to withdraw the treaty from Congress, but in doing so, he was also adhering to an established policy – and the balance of public opinion. This, after all, was certainly not the first time the United States had considered taking Hawai'i. In 1852, 1863, and at various points during the Civil War, annexation had been considered, but, as one historian documents, at each point Congress decided that it "was too distant, too tropical, too unknown, too strange, its population too heterogeneous."[114] In the early months of Cleveland's administration, when Hawaiian annexation was still on the table, similar arguments were made to oppose annexation in the press. The *Chicago Herald* called the very idea "ridiculous," and suggested that they would form a "pigmy state of the Union," while the *New York Evening Post* argued that "we have enough race problems on our hands already without adding the Kanaka to the negro, Indian, and Mongolian question."[115]

Carl Schurz – the legendary Civil War general, Republican US Senator, and former Secretary of Interior – used similar logic to make a forceful argument against annexation. The Constitution, he argued in an October 1893 article in *Harper's*, required that land annexed to the nation must eventually join the Union on an equal basis, and this would mean welcoming Hawai'i's nonwhite, tropical population into the "family circle."[116] Such a possibility, Schurz hardly needed to point out, was unthinkable. The entire idea of territorial administration was premised on white settlement and eventual statehood; if this process could not occur in Hawai'i, then it simply could not be annexed, whatever its strategic or economic value might be.

It was not only Cleveland's misgivings or American racism that slowed the path to annexation. One similarity between Hawai'i and later overseas colonies was the move by colonized people to use the American state's own weakness to resist occupation. The Queen herself, anticipating a strategy that would later be used in the Philippines and the Caribbean, journeyed to Washington to protest the occupation and request the return of her kingdom. As Noenoe Silva has shown, Hawaiians, working in conjunction with the Queen, organized associations in opposition to annexation, such as *Hui Hawai'i Aloha 'Aina* (Hawaiian Patriotic League), an organization that represented over half of all the enfranchised Hawaiians in the

[112] George W. Baker, Jr., "Benjamin Harrison and Hawaiian Annexation: A Reinterpretation," *Pacific Historical Review* 33 (August 1964): 304; Foster to Stevens, February 14, 1893, in *FRUS, 1894, Appendix II*, 406–7.
[113] Quoted in Silva, *Aloha Betrayed*, 171.
[114] Quoted in Love, *Race over Empire*, 101.
[115] Quoted in Love, *Race over Empire*, 101–3.
[116] Carl Schurz, "Manifest Destiny," *Harper's Weekly* (October 1893), 739; cited in Love, *Race over Empire*, 105.

islands.[117] This group presented petitions opposing annexation and a closely asso-ciated delegation visited Washington to assist the Queen's anti-annexation efforts. Resistance by the Queen and her allies exposed the lies and propaganda spread by the pro-annexationist leaders of the so-called republic, who now needed Congress to accept Hawai'i as a land fit for white settlement – and may have contributed to the defeat of an annexation treaty.[118]

The Hawaiian Republic and Annexation

The *haole* elite now faced a serious problem.[119] They had assumed that if they presented Hawaiian independence as a *fait accompli*, the islands would be imme-diately annexed to the United States. They now knew that this would not be the case – at least not immediately.[120] In the past, these men had relied on the good graces and shared economic interests of the Hawaiian monarchy to sustain their prominence and to protect their property. With the monarchy now gone, a small white oligarchy would not retain power in Hawai'i for long without access to far more coercive capacity than was available to the new state.[121]

The two men at the heart of the annexation campaign – both of American mis-sionary parentage and lifelong residents of the islands – were the Republic's pres-ident, Sanford Dole, and Lorrin Thurston, the Attorney General.[122] As Dole and Thurston were well aware, the major argument against Hawaiian annexation – that the islands could never be governed like other territories because of their large

---

[117] Silva, *Aloha Betrayed*, 130–1.

[118] Ibid., 157.

[119] Was the revolution merely to protect sugar interests? This question has generated no shortage of debate among historians of Hawai'i and the answer is complex. A number of planters were not in favor of annexation because they feared that US law would cut off their supply of cheap labor. Sugar baron Claus Spreckels, for example, held this opinion. The few holdouts, however, seem to have come around given this Hobson's choice. As William Blaisdell, a manager of the Makee Plantation on Kauai, wrote,

> When the Queen was first overthrown there were very few in favor of annexation, very few of the planters especially. I was one that did not see that we could be improved, especially in view of the contract-labor system which is our mainstay . . . After looking over the matter carefully and talking over the matter with other interested parties – that is, planters principally – we came to the conclusion that we would rather take our chances on the labor question than to take the chances of an independent government.

Quoted in Richard D. Weigle, "Sugar and the Hawaiian Revolution," *Pacific Historical Review* 16 (February 1947): 48. See also Russ, "Role of Sugar," 345.

[120] It was, however, initially suggested that the United States would support her diplomatically if she agreed to pardon the rebels. The Queen, understandably, refused to comply with this request.

[121] As a Hawaiian legislative document ominously noted, "While we believe that we can continue to maintain the control of the Government in the hands of those favorable to Annexation, it is only necessary to consider the history of the past ten years in Hawaii to demonstrate that delays are dangerous." See "Argument in Support of Enactment of the Hawaiian Legislature of an Act Effectuating Annexation," Dole Papers, Box 2.

[122] Dole's life is well chronicled in Helena G. Allen, *Sanford Ballard Dole: Hawaii's Only President, 1844–1926* (Glendale, CA: Arthur H. Clark, 1988).

nonwhite population – explained more about annexation's failure than Cleveland's misgivings over the actions of Minister Stevens or the niceties of international law.

To proceed, the white elite would have to convince Congress that Hawai'i could plausibly fit into the older model of territorial expansion. Soon after the original treaty was withdrawn, Dole had encouraged the Republic's minister in Washington, Francis Hatch, to consider any feasible form of government that would bring Hawai'i into the Union, even suggesting the development of a new, quasi-colonial status for the islands:

> It is desirable that arrangements for annexation shall not be limited by the precedents which the American law on territories furnish . . . I now suggest the word *colony* as an additional. It will be of great advantage to us if the deliberations of our friends in Congress can be free from the precedents of their territory laws. It is perhaps an occasion for them to make something of a new departure in their acquisition of new domains. The insular position and the exceptional status as to population of these islands makes such action the more easy and reasonable.[123]

This approach, however, seems to have been quickly discarded in favor of an aggressive campaign to encourage Congress to see Hawai'i as a *territory* – an Anglophone republic governed by white men. As Thurston reported to Dole, "There is nothing that will do this so effectively as the reorganization of the government on Republican [sic] lines. The more popular the *form* can be made the better, keeping in sight however the primary necessity of retaining the control for the present in the hands of those who are friends of the new order of things."[124] This strategy, as another scholar has insightfully detailed, was adopted so their congressional allies could justify "Hawaii's annexation not for the redemption of native peoples but for the sake of the island's whites."[125]

The problem they faced, however, was how to make this impression while retaining the fundamentals of white rule – a quandary about which they were perfectly candid. "In general terms," one official of the Hawaiian Republic wrote, "the problem to be solved is, how to combine an oligarchy with a representative form of government so as to meet the case."[126] Given this peculiar predicament, one provisional government official recommended that Thurston look at the 1891 Mississippi Constitutional Convention, because it had the "effect of disenfranchising a majority of the negroes of that state."[127] For further advice, Dole had written to the political scientist John Burgess of Columbia – well-known for his critical writings on Reconstruction – who recommended that they establish a strong central government and high property qualifications. In the end, the *haoles* followed this advice and, much like the Southern states they sought to emulate,

---

[123] Dole to Francis Hatch, November 29, 1895; Republic of Hawai'i Records, "President's Letters: January 18, 1893–June 18, 1900."

[124] Thurston to Dole; quoted in Paul T. Burlin, *Imperial Maine and Hawai'i: Interpretative Essays in the History of Nineteenth Century American Expansion* (Lanham, MD: Lexington Books, 2006), 220.

[125] Love, *Race over Empire*, 120.

[126] Smith quoted in Daws, *Shoal of Time*, 280.

[127] Quoted in Burlin, *Imperial Maine*, 220.

adopted a carefully crafted constitution that maintained all the trappings of republican government while effectively excluding Asians and Hawaiians with no property – a decision that decreased the number of voters from 14,217 in 1892 to 2,693 in 1897.[128]

With the establishment of this "republican" government, the *haoles* could now assert their American-ness with greater confidence – and insist on its suitability as an American territory, rather than an imperial colony. In an 1897 pamphlet, *A Handbook on the Annexation of Hawaii*, Thurston went on at great length in this vein. "The public school system is based upon that in the United States," he noted.

More than half of the teachers are Americans. English is the official language of the schools and courts, and the common language of business. The railroad cars, engines, waterworks, waterpipes, dynamos, telephones . . . are all American made. United States currency is the currency of the country . . . All American holidays, Washington's Birthday, Decoration Day, Fourth of July and Thanksgiving Day are as fully and enthusiastically celebrated in Hawaii as in any part of the United States. This is not the growth of a day, but of two generations, so that even to the native Hawaiian it appears to be the natural order of things.[129]

Hawai'i, in other words, could be annexed and administered as a territory because it was already American.

Among the members of Congress influenced by this argument was George Frisbee Hoar, the senior senator from Massachusetts and a Republican, who would later become known for his fiery denunciations of imperialism after the Spanish–American War.[130] As Hoar later detailed in his autobiography, he came to the conclusion that the islands were exceptional in their relationship to the United States. "We had sustained a peculiar relation to it," he noted, and "American missionaries had redeemed the people from barbarism and Paganism."[131] Along with these sentimental connections, the republican nature of the white-led government seemed to convince him of Hawai'i's suitability for territorial status. "It was said that the Constitution was the result of usurpation which would not have come to pass but for American aid and the presence of one of our men-of-war," he wrote. "But that Government had been maintained for six or seven years. Four of them were while Mr. Cleveland was President, who it was well known would be in full sympathy with an attempt to restore the old Government."[132] Through this line of reasoning, Hoar reached the rather dubious conclusion that "if the people had been against it, the Government under that Constitution would not have lasted an hour."[133]

[128] Perkins, *Denial of Empire*, 65–6.
[129] Lorrin Thurston, *A Handbook on the Annexation of Hawaii* (St. Joseph, MI: A.B. Morse, 1897), 31.
[130] Love, *Race over Empire*, 153.
[131] George Frisbie Hoar, *Autobiography of Seventy Years* (New York: Charles Scribner, 1905), v. 2, 306. Hawaiians, on the other hand, were "a perishing people. Their only hope and desire and expectation was that in the Providence of God they might lead a quiet, undisturbed life, fishing, bathing, supplied with tropical fruits, and be let alone." Hoar, *Autobiography*, 306.
[132] Hoar, *Autobiography*, 306.
[133] Ibid. It is difficult to believe that Hoar honestly believed this to be true, since he had earlier met with Hawaiian delegates and received petitions in opposition to annexation.

Similar arguments seem to have held sway with the newly elected Republican president, William McKinley, who wrote in his annual message of 1897,

The wisdom of Congress will see to it that, avoiding abrupt assimilation of elements perhaps hardly yet fitted to share in the highest franchises of citizenship, and having due regard to the geographical conditions, the most just provisions for self-rule in local matters with the largest political liberties as an integral part of our nation will be accorded to the Hawaiians. No less is due to a people who, after nearly five years of demonstrated capacity to fulfill the obligations of self-governing statehood, come of their own free will to merge their destinies in our body-politic.[134]

Although the final push for annexation came as a result of the Spanish–American War, the terms of its annexation broadly reflected Hoar's and McKinley's conclusion that because Hawai'i was controlled by whites, it could be admitted as a self-governing territory *without* any significant institutional innovations.[135] Whether McKinley and Hoar honestly believed these absurd claims is less important than the fact that they began to use them as the public justification for Hawai'i's annexation. In other words, while the acquisition of colonies remained politically impossible, the extension of American sovereignty for the protection of white settlers had more than a century of legal and political precedents. Nevertheless, the decision to annex Hawai'i could never gain the requisite two-thirds majority in the Senate, so McKinley, led by Roosevelt, Lodge, and other imperialist Republicans, annexed the Pacific archipelago by joint resolution, which required only a majority vote, on July 7, 1898.

The annexation of Hawai'i was considered acceptable because it fit within the well-known experiences of territorial expansion whereby white settlers slowly pushed out indigenous populations – and it would be governed as a territory. Indeed, once annexed, McKinley largely left the officers of the Hawaiian Republic in place. "I appreciate your action in continuing the personnel of the independent government," Dole, the former president of the Republic and its new territorial governor, wrote to the president in August 1898. "It is an endorsement which is very grateful to us, and it is, as well, significant of a conservative policy in regard to Hawaii which will be of great importance in our transition period."[136]

The *haoles'* view that they should be seen as a territory persisted after the war during the debates over Hawai'i's Organic Act. As Hawai'i's Supreme Court justice

[134] McKinley, quoted in Perkins, *Denial of Empire*, 68.
[135] The importance of the war in securing final annexation for Hawai'i is a complex question and the answer is inconclusive. For example, historian Thomas Bailey writes that "The argument that annexation was imperative for prosecuting the war in the Philippines carried, whatever its merits, great weight in Congress and out." Although, as Bailey points out, these arguments were generally countered by an anti-annexationists who pointed out that ships from San Francisco could refuel at the Aleutian Islands (already owned by the United States) and save 400 miles on the journey. See Thomas A. Bailey, "The United States and Hawaii during the Spanish–American War," *American Historical Review* 36 (April 1931): 557. Others have argued that "they regarded annexation and the prosecution of the war as separate matters." See Thomas J. Osborne, "Trade or War?: America's Annexation of Hawaii Reconsidered," *Pacific Historical Review* 50 (August 1981): 287. See also Allen Lee Hamilton, "Military Strategists and the Annexation of Hawaii," *Journal of the West* 15 (April 1976): 81–91.
[136] Dole to McKinley, August 15, 1898; Republic of Hawai'i Records, President's Letters: January 18, 1893–June 18, 1900.

Alfred Hartwell put the matter in an 1899 issue of the *Yale Law Journal*, "there is no occasion for classifying Hawaii as one of our 'insular possessions,' or for deferring legislation for organizing its government . . . Hawaii is no more a possession in the sense of being a dependency than are the territories of Arizona, New Mexico, Oklahoma, and Alaska."[137]

Congress broadly agreed with this assessment. As with territories lying within the continental United States, the 1900 Hawaiian Organic Act mandated that the governor and territorial judges of Hawai'i be residents of the islands, and in an attempt to ensure that Hawai'i would retain its "American" character, the Organic Act encouraged the swift disposal of public lands to encourage more immigration to the islands from Anglo-Saxon settlers.[138] The case of Hawai'i, then, at least from an administrative perspective, belongs to the older American settler empire. Its geography and population were unique, but its system of administration required no institutional innovations or expanded state capacity.

THE PROGRESSIVES AND THE END OF
CLERICAL STATE COLONIALISM

For many Progressive thinkers, the development of a respectable American foreign policy – one that would provide a clear and consistent American voice to the world – was a key part of their movement. If they were not united on how to achieve this goal, they had reached consensus that the American external state bureaucracies – the dumping ground of the spoils system – were inimical to the nation's best interests. Whether or not they desired the United States to acquire overseas colonies, the embarrassment of American representation abroad and the vindictive behavior of the Senate led many Progressives to advocate for increased efficiency and reform in American foreign relations.

Richard Olney, reflecting on his experience as Secretary of State under Grover Cleveland, made the case for reform in a March 1900 issue of the *Atlantic Monthly*:

> The isolation policy and practice have tended to belittle the national character, and have led to a species of provincialism and to narrow views of our duties and functions as a nation. They have caused us to ignore the importance of sea power and to look with equanimity upon the decay of our navy and the ruin of our merchant marine. They have made us content with a diplomatic service always inadequate and often positively detrimental to our interests.[139]

Nowhere was this connection made more explicitly than in Herbert Croly's *The Promise of American Life* in one of the most illuminating, if least read, chapters in his book. "As much in foreign affairs as in domestic affairs," Croly argued, "must the American people seek to unite national efficiency with democratic idealism."[140] European observers agreed. In the *American Commonwealth*, Lord Bryce

---

[137] Alfred Hartwell, "The Organization of a Territorial Government for Hawaii," *Yale Law Journal* 9 (December 1899): 107.

[138] Perkins, *Denial of Empire*, 74–5.

[139] Richard Olney, "Growth of Our Foreign Policy," *Atlantic Monthly* 85 (March 1900): 289–301.

[140] Herbert Croly, *The Promise of American Life* (New York: MacMillan, 1909), 293.

had argued that the United States was able to manage its unique system of foreign affairs for so long simply because it had so few foreign relations. "European states-men," Bryce wrote, "may ask . . . how a consistent attitude can be maintained if there is in the chairman of the Foreign Relations committee a sort of second foreign secretary. The answer is that America is not Europe. The problems which the State Department of the United States has had to deal with have been far fewer and usu-ally far simpler than are those of the Old World."[141] Implicit in Bryce's argument, however, was the suggestion that centralization and reform would be necessary should the United States decide to engage with the world more directly. This is exactly what many American Progressives wanted to do. "The tendency of modern times is toward consolidation," wrote Henry Cabot Lodge in a March 1895 article:

It is apparent in capital and labor alike, and it is also true of nations. Small States are of the past and have no future. The modern movement is all toward the concentration of people and territory into great nations and large dominions. The great nations are rapidly absorbing for their future expansion and their present defense all the waste places of the earth. It is a movement which makes for civilization and the advancement of the race. As one of the great nations of the world, the United States must not fall out of the line of march.[142]

For some of the more hawkish among them, especially Lodge and Roosevelt, nothing short of America's future status in the world order was at stake. To join the ranks of the Great Powers, the United States would not only need improved diplo-matic representation, but also colonies. The conclusion of the Spanish–American War would give them the chance to acquire an empire, although Congress had no intention of relinquishing its power and authority over American foreign affairs.

As we will see in Chapter 3, Congress's active involvement in colonial adminis-tration began early. There is, in fact, no better illustration of the Senate's dominance in foreign relations than the lead up to the Spanish–American War; the last war in American history where Congress, not the president, led the charge. Although the press and public opinion were increasingly in favor of war with Spain, Grover Cleveland had pushed for the United States to remain neutral.[143] Despite the change in administration after the 1896 presidential election, President McKinley was also firmly against the war from the start, and, in the assessment of Richard Hofstadter, "found himself under incredible pressures for positive action, which he resisted as long as most Presidents would have been able to do."[144] By March of 1898, there was a very real possibility that Congress would declare war without him. After the U.S.S. *Maine* mysteriously exploded off the coast of Cuba, McKinley did reluc-tantly give his approval and Congress promptly declared war on April 24, 1898. Despite the president's final acquiescence to war with Spain, it remains clear that by the close of the nineteenth century Congress had no intention of accepting a secondary role in American foreign relations.

---

[141] James Bryce, *The American Commonwealth* (Indianapolis, IN: Liberty Fund, 1995 [1888]), v. 1, 97.

[142] Henry Cabot Lodge, "Our Blundering Foreign Policy," *Forum* 19 (March 1895).

[143] Richard Gott, *Cuba: A New History* (New Haven, CT: Yale University Press, 2004), 100.

[144] Richard Hofstadter, *The Paranoid Style in American Politics and Other Essays* (New York: Vintage, 2008 [1952]), 155–6.

3

Institutional Design of the Insular Empire

The Philippines present . . . a very hard problem because we must consider it in connection with the country's needs and ideas also, and with what it is reasonable to expect as a permanent policy of this country with its alternating system of party control.

—Theodore Roosevelt (1905)[1]

When Commodore Dewey reached the Philippines on April 30, 1898, the Spanish colonial government was already under attack. In 1895, the same year revolutionary forces began to agitate for Cuban independence, Filipino revolutionaries, led by their legendary general, Emilio Aguinaldo, declared their independence from Spain. After six short months in exile, Aguinaldo returned to the Philippines aboard an American ship and was given American weapons to continue his revolution. While the revolutionaries gained control of the countryside, the Americans laid siege to Spanish forces in Manila. As it became increasingly clear that victory was imminent, Aguinaldo declared the Philippines independent and named himself president of the revolutionary state. None of this seemed to faze Dewey, who gave the revolutionaries the impression that the United States recognized Aguinaldo's government as legitimate, which may have allowed him – apparently with some difficulty – to convince Aguinaldo to delay his invasion of Manila until American reinforcements could be assembled.[2]

In the ensuing six months between the victory in Manila and the signing of the Treaty of Paris, the Philippine revolutionaries were left to establish their own independent government in nearby Malolos, where a congress was elected to draft a constitution, which included among its members a number of figures who would later become prominent officials in the American colonial government. Aguinaldo's suspicions that the Americans would not leave the Philippines peacefully were

---

[1] Quoted in William C. Widenor, *Henry Cabot Lodge and the Search for an American Foreign Policy* (Berkeley, CA: University of California Press, 1980), 151.

[2] Brian McAllister Linn, *The U.S. Army and Counterinsurgency in the Philippine War, 1899–1902* (Chapel Hill, NC: University of North Carolina Press, 1989), 7.

confirmed with the signing of the Treaty of Paris in December when American intentions to retain the Philippines as a colony were finally revealed. McKinley, it seems, tried to soften the blow by announcing through a proclamation that the Americans came "not as invaders or conquerors, but as friends, to protect the natives in their homes, in their employment, and in their personal and religious rights."[3] Such lofty sentiments, however, rang hollow for Aguinaldo and his revolutionaries.

Over the next month a series of meetings between Aguinaldo and General Elwell Otis took place, but owing to the intransigence of both parties, proved unable to quell the growing frustration of the revolutionaries or the hostility of the Americans. On February 4, 1899, Private Grayson of the Nebraska volunteer regiment fired on a Filipino, prompting General Aguinaldo in Malolos to declare war the following day.[4] The Philippine–American War, as the insurrection/war of independence came to be called, dragged on for over two years and proved to be a bloody and deeply unpopular conflict.[5] While the United States could often defeat the Filipino insurgents in clear battles, the American Army was severely hampered by the guerilla tactics employed by Aguinaldo and his generals, who planned to prolong the conflict until the US Army succumbed to disease or exhaustion.

The war continued for the next two years, as the Army chased Aguinaldo and his army throughout Luzon, finally capturing him in the spring of 1901.[6] The price of victory, however, was high by almost any measure. During the two-year insurrection, a total of 4,165 American soldiers died, while 2,911 were wounded.[7] The counterinsurgency effort also deflated popular enthusiasm for the imperial experiment, and revelations in the press about Army tactics, including the use of water torture to interrogate Filipinos, were deeply unsettling to the American public.[8]

[3] Quoted in Leonard Giesecke, *History of American Economic Policy in the Philippines during the American Colonial Period, 1900–1935* (New York: Garland, 1987), 26.

[4] Lewis Gleek, *The American Half-Century, 1898–1946* (Quezon City: New Day, 1998), 25–30.

[5] For more on the Philippine War, see Stuart Creighton Miller, *"Benevolent Assimilation": The American Conquest of the Philippines, 1899–1903* (New Haven, CT: Yale University Press, 1982).

[6] Aguinaldo was placed under house arrest in Manila and later released a statement "acknowledging and accepting the sovereignty of the United States throughout the entire Archipelago." Until his death in 1964, Aguinaldo wore a black bow tie as a symbol of the lost Philippine Republic, yet he never attempted to take up his struggle again. Indeed, during the colonial period, he remained on cordial terms with the Americans, dispensing advice over games of chess to several sets of American governors-general. His thoughts on the period are well-expressed in his fascinating autobiography: Emilio Aguinaldo and Vicente Albano Pacis, *A Second Look at America* (New York: Robert Speller, 1957). Taft later remarked to Root that Aguinaldo "was very dignified and courteous in his demeanor and cautious and reserved in his expressions as to public matters." Taft to Root, July 20, 1902; Root Papers, Box 164.

[7] Linn, *Guardians of Empire: The U.S. Army in the Pacific, 1902–1940* (Chapel Hill, NC: University of North Carolina Press, 1997), 16. This does not include the thousands of Filipinos who lost their lives in the struggle.

[8] Richard E. Welch, Jr., *Response to Imperialism: The United States and the Philippine–American War, 1899–1902* (Chapel Hill, NC: University of North Carolina Press, 1979).

THE ORIGINS OF THE PHILIPPINE COLONIAL STATE

Despite this ongoing insurgency, the Spanish–American War *officially* ended with the signing of the Treaty of Paris on December 10, 1898, giving Washington control over an overseas empire that, as contemporary newspapers proudly pointed out, stretched 10,000 miles from tip to tip. But as the ecstatic celebrations of the victory died down, more sober minds began to worry about America's ability to manage Spain's former possessions. Of the new territories, the 7,000-island Philippine archipelago was the most worrisome. Unlike Hawai'i or even Puerto Rico, it had a negligible American population – in 1889, the US consul in Manila counted a mere 23 American citizens, six of whom were members of his own family – and was 4,500 miles west of Honolulu, the closest city under American control at the time.[9] Its population not only dwarfed that of other territories and dependencies but also was more populous than any *state* but New York. How, many wondered at the time, could the American republic govern an overseas empire, especially one as large, foreign, and distant as the Philippine Islands?

The solution to the "Philippines Question," as it would come to be known, was not immediately apparent. As Frank Vanderlip, Assistant Secretary of the Treasury, frankly assessed the situation in the August 1898 edition of *The Century*, "It is a problem for the solution of which we have surprisingly little data. Neither precedent nor experience can be satisfactorily drawn on, and we see with sudden clearness that some of the most revered of our political maxims have outlived their force."[10] When the time came to solve this "problem," Congress demonstrated that it was far less concerned with managing the colonies than with pleasing its domestic constituencies. In a move that would frustrate American imperialists, Congress did not authorize a comprehensive system for colonial administration and rejected suggestions from the Department of War – there was, for example, to be no large colonial service. It appropriated little money and refused to place the Philippines – its *own colony* – behind the steep American tariff wall. Finally, in an effort to placate domestic sugar and tobacco producers, subsequent legislation placed restrictions on land sales and franchise laws to make the establishment of plantation agriculture more difficult.

These unfruitful encounters with Congress would drive members of the American insular state to manage the empire through inconspicuous action and by collaborating with US financial institutions. As I argue in Chapters 4 and 5, during these first few years of civil government, imperialists in the executive branch took advantage of Congress's relative indifference to the day-to-day operations of its colonies to lay the groundwork for a remarkably autonomous system of government and to set the agenda for the colonial state. These officials confronted congressional limitations on their authority – restrictions they universally regarded as politically motivated and short-sighted – by creating new networks and strategies of governance. In an age of congressional strength, colonial authorities developed strategies to minimize Congress's limited attention to affairs in its colonies and to take advantage of the short time horizons of most members.

Information came to be among the most valuable assets of colonial authorities.

---

[9] Frank Ninkovich, *The United States and Imperialism* (Malden, MA: Blackwell Publishers, 2001), 39.

[10] Frank A. Vanderlip, *The Century* 56 (August 1898): 555–63.

As we will see in Chapter 4, insular officials carefully guarded their near-monopoly on information about the colonies, presenting carefully planned and sometimes false or misleading reports, and dispatching their own representatives to committee hearings to advocate for the colonial government's policies. Press accounts were carefully monitored and congressional bills were written by colonial officials and sent to allies in the House and Senate. For its part, Congress had few independent sources of information about its colonies – the Philippines in particular. By monopolizing and controlling the flow of information through the restriction of negative press stories, and writing most of the colonial legislation themselves, insular officials were, at the very least, able to minimize congressional oversight and to exercise autonomy by remaining inconspicuous. Yet such information control and closed recruitment procedures were facilitated by the initial organization of the colonial state, which concentrated power in one executive agency that defied the normal organizational hierarchy of the War Department and minimized interference from Congress and other bureaucracies.[11] Driven by an unshakable belief in their power to make America's insular empire a vast advertisement for the righteousness of their nation, these executive officials attempted to wall-off the colonies from the politics of the domestic state.

This chapter describes the initial organizational design for the American colonial state, and the institutional roots of its later autonomy. It traces the first interactions between Congress and the officials of the new bureaucracies that were just beginning to take shape to manage the empire. It shows how Congress, far from taking a back seat to colonial administration, used its considerable power to restrict precisely the sort of aggressive colonial development that proponents of the Spanish–American War predicted would turn the United States into an imperial power. For the executive and colonial officials who very much wanted an expansive American empire, this presented a serious problem, and their attempts to overcome these congressional constraints would shape the development of American colonial policy. By 1902, they had formed the structural roots of a colonial state that would eventually gain significant autonomy from its congressional masters.

THE POLITICS OF ACQUISITION

American Progressives were deeply divided over the decision to acquire colonies after the Spanish–American War. On the whole, they generally favored American imperialism, but this support was by no means universal.[12] Former Secretary of State Richard Olney, for example, who had written so persuasively of the need to reform the American external state, bitterly opposed the new imperial policy. "The United States," he argued, "has come out of its shell and ceased to be a hermit among the nations, naturally and properly. What was not necessary and is certainly of the most doubtful expediency is that it should at the same time become

---

[11] The chairman of the Philippine Committee, Henry Cabot Lodge, for example, was largely frozen out of the BIA/Commission network.

[12] William E. Leuchtenburg, "Progressivism and Imperialism: The Progressive Movement and American Foreign Policy, 1898–1916," *Mississippi Valley Historical Review* 39 (December 1952): 483–504.

a colonizing Power on an immense scale."[13] The question was especially vexing because it defied normal partisan categories and deeply divided the Progressive wing of the Republican Party as well-known Republicans such as Carl Schurz, a leading mugwump and former Union general, and Senator George Frisbee Hoar (R-MA) entered a tense alliance with Democrats against the rank-and-file of the party.

The rift led Schurz to oppose his friend and protégé Theodore Roosevelt's gubernatorial campaign in New York. "I do not hesitate to express the solemn conviction that there are worse things even than free silver and Tammany," he wrote to Roosevelt, "and that one of them is the imperialism which in its effects upon the character and durability of the Republic I consider as pernicious as slavery itself was, and which we are now asked to countenance and encourage."[14] So opposed were some Progressive Republicans to the course that now seemed increasingly likely, that they were forced to reach out to William Jennings Bryan, a man they generally regarded as a dangerous demagogue. The editor of E. L. Godkin's fiercely Republican New York *Evening Post*, for example, could not hide his embarrassment in making such overtures. "You may be surprised, sir," he wrote to Bryan, "to learn that an editor of the *Evening Post* has any sympathy with your cause."[15]

Those Republicans opposed to colonialism primarily focused on the anti-republican nature of colonial rule or the unfitness of so-called "tropical people" for the rights and privileges of a democracy.[16] Carl Schurz led the latter faction, which opposed imperialism on racist grounds. In an August 19, 1898 speech in Saratoga, New York for the Civic Federation, he made this clear: "Now I challenge the advocates of annexation to show me a single instance of a tropical country in which people of that kind have shown themselves able to carry on democratic government in a manner fitting it for statehood in our Union. Show me a single one!"[17] Senator Hoar led the former faction, giving a series of speeches denouncing the McKinley administration's policies as anti-republican. "When you raise the flag over the Philippine Islands as an emblem of dominion and acquisition you take it down from Independence Hall."[18] Hoar would later declare government without the consent of the governed offensive to the spirit of the Declaration of Independence and to the memories of the Founding generation who considered such principles sacred: "They were not glittering generalities. They were blazing ubiquities," Hoar said. "Do you suppose," he asked, "it ever occurred to our fathers that these rights were to be departed from and trampled underfoot whenever the country or any people or any Congress should deceive itself and beguile itself by

---

[13] Richard Olney, "Growth of Our Foreign Policy," *Atlantic Monthly* 85 (March 1900): 289–301.

[14] Carl Schurz, "Opposition to Roosevelt for the Governorship of New York," October 21, 1898, *Evening Post*. Reprinted in Frederic Bancroft, ed., *Speeches, Correspondence and Political Papers of Carl Schurz* (New York: G. P. Putnam, 1913), 521–7.

[15] Quoted in David Healy, *U.S. Expansionism: The Imperialist Urge in the 1890s* (Madison, WI: University of Wisconsin Press, 1976), 226.

[16] For an excellent discussion of the relationship of race to the anti-expansionists, see Love, *Race over Empire*.

[17] Carl Schurz, "Our Future Foreign Policy," Address at Saratoga, NY, August 19, 1898; Reprinted in Frederic Bancroft (ed.), *Speeches, Correspondence and Political Papers of Carl Schurz* (New York: G.P. Putnam, 1913), 477–94.

[18] George F. Hoar, speech reprinted in William Jennings Bryan, ed., *Republic or Empire?: The Philippine Question* (Chicago: The Independence Company, 1899).

the specious pretense that it thought the thing it was doing was for the benefit of the victim?" Even less, he continued, would they believe that their descendants,

[W]ould depart from them and trample them under foot, that they might get a little cheap reward in the way of trade, or that they might strut among the nations of the world in the cheap and gaudy uniform of imperialism; that they would be beguiled from these sacred and awful verities that they might strut about in the cast-off clothing of pinchbeck emperors and pewter kings; that their descendants would be excited by the smell of gunpowder and the sound of the guns of a single victory as a small boy by a firecracker on some Fourth of July morning.[19]

This is not to suggest that the positions were mutually exclusive, and Schurz and Hoar worked closely together, going so far as to propose a plebiscite to decide "the question whether the citizens of the United States favor such annexation of tropical countries."[20] This unlikely coalition formally came together with the formation of the Anti-Imperialist League in late 1898. The group included among its members conservative businessmen such as Charles Francis Adams and Eastern intellectuals like Harvard President Charles Eliot Norton along with American Federation of Labor leader Samuel Gompers and Socialist provocateur Morrison I. Swift, who exclaimed that the goal of imperialism was "the expansion of billionaires."[21]

The expansionist majority of the Republican Party had little patience for these arguments. Led by Senator Henry Cabot Lodge of Massachusetts, they lashed back at the anti-imperialists, dismissing them as a combination of foolish intellectuals, isolationists, and Bryan loyalists. Imperialism, they argued, was simply the next phase of America's Manifest Destiny and its mission to bring democracy to the world. In Indianapolis, Senator Albert Beveridge delivered what would become his famous "March of the Flag" speech on September 16, 1898: "Will you affirm by your vote that you are an infidel to American power and practical sense? Or will you say that ours is the blood of government; ours the heart of domination; ours the brain and genius of administration? Will you remember that we do but what our fathers did – we but pitch the tents of liberty farther westward, farther southward – we only continue the march of the flag?"[22] For Beveridge and the expansionist Republicans, America's new empire was simply the next step of American expansion.

The fight would be played out on the floor of the Senate when the Treaty of Paris was sent for ratification in January 1899. Lodge had earlier warned Roosevelt that "[w]e are going to have trouble over the Treaty. How serious I do not know, but I confess I cannot think calmly of the rejection of that Treaty by a little more than one-third of the Senate." The Senate opposition, led by Senator George Vest of Missouri, introduced a joint resolution on December 6, 1898 – 4 days *before* it was signed with Spain – declaring the acquisition of foreign colonies unconstitutional, "except such small amount as may be necessary for coaling stations." Yet for Lodge, the Progressive

---

[19] A. P. C. Griffin, ed., *Orations of American Orators* (New York: The Fifth Avenue Press, 1900), v. 3, 76.

[20] Carl Schurz to George F. Hoar, December 1, 1898, in *Speeches, Correspondence and Political Papers of Carl Schurz*, ed. Frederic Bancroft (New York: G.P. Putnam, 1913), 530.

[21] Healy, *U.S. Expansionism*, 219–20. If this was true, one billionaire, at least, was not interested. Throughout its existence the League was given generous financial support from the world's richest man, the fiercely anti-imperialist Andrew Carnegie.

[22] Albert J. Beveridge, *The March of the Times and Other Speeches* (Indianapolis, IN: Bobbs-Merrill, 1908), 50.

intellectual who had long hoped to see his country counted among the Great Powers, more was at stake than the treaty itself. If the Senate should fail to adopt it, he wrote, it would be a "humiliation of the whole country in the eyes of the world, and would show we are unfit as a nation to enter into great questions of foreign policy."[23]

There was every reason to be fearful: The Senate had not approved one important treaty in over 25 years, and to gain the necessary two-thirds majority in the Senate, several Democrats would need to support ratification.[24] McKinley had anticipated this problem and included three senators, including one Democrat, in the American delegation to Paris. Despite this gesture to senatorial prerogative, the treaty looked doomed to fail by the middle of January. The staunch anti-imperialist, Andrew Carnegie, who had come to Washington to work for its defeat, thought his side would carry the day. "I told the President two weeks ago," he wrote, "we should beat the Treaty & he was sure I was 'away off.' He knows now."[25] Things began to look up by the beginning of February, but the administration still needed to win over senators who were on the fence. On February 6, Lodge was still trying to gain the support of one last senator, which he finally got not five minutes before the vote. Lodge, writing to Roosevelt, described it as "the closest, hardest fight I have ever known, and probably we shall not see another in our time where there was so much at stake."[26] The treaty had been ratified, but the bitter fight to see it adopted presaged the difficulty the imperialists would have in generating political support for the overseas empire. How the new colonies would be managed, and whether or not such colonial acquisitions were permissible under the Constitution, emerged as a central issue. This acrimonious debate would shape the initial legislation for colonial governance.

Legal Foundations: The Insular Cases

With the Treaty of Paris finally adopted in February of 1899, Congress next turned its attention to the establishment of civil government for the new colonies. Yet in doing so, the question that had fueled so many debates about imperialism could be avoided no longer: Did the Constitution follow the flag? Three years after the start of the Spanish–American War, in a collection of decisions dubbed the *Insular Cases*, the Court would decide the official constitutional status of the territories.[27]

---

[23] Lodge to Roosevelt, December 7, 1898, in *Selections from the Correspondence of Theodore Roosevelt and Henry Cabot Lodge, 1884–1918*, ed. Henry Cabot Lodge (New York: Charles Scribner, 1925), v. 1, 368.

[24] The last was in 1871. Holt, *Treaties Defeated*, 165.

[25] Quoted in Holt, *Treaties Defeated*, 167.

[26] Lodge to Roosevelt, February 9, 1899, in *Correspondence of Theodore Roosevelt and Henry Cabot Lodge*, 391.

[27] There is no strict list of *Insular Cases*, and scholars have listed as few as three to as many as 35 in Bartholomew Sparrow's recent study. The key cases include *DeLima v. Bidwell*, 182 U.S. 1 (1901); *Goetze v. United States*, 182 U.S. 221 (1901); *Armstrong v. United States*, 182 U.S. 243 (1901); *Downes v. Bidwell*, 182 U.S. 244 (1901); *Huus v. New York & Porto Rico S.S. Co.*, 182 U.S. 392 (1901); *Dooley v. United States*, 183 U.S. 151 (1901); *Fourteen Diamond Rings v. United States*, 183 U.S. 176 (1901); *Hawaii v. Mankichi*, 190 U.S. 197 (1903); *Kepner v. United States*, 195 U.S. 100 (1904); *Dorr v. United States*, 195 U.S. 138 (1904); *Rasmussen v. United States*, 197 U.S. 516 (1905); *Balzac v. Porto Rico* 258 U.S. 298 (1922). For the most comprehensive treatment, see Bartholomew H. Sparrow, *The Insular Cases and the Emergence of American Empire* (Lawrence, KS: University Press of Kansas, 2006).

The first constitutional test of American colonial policy would come as a dispute over customs duties. The case of *Downes v. Bidwell* concerned the firm of S.B. Downes & Co., which was charged $659.35 for importing oranges from Puerto Rico to New York. Downes, with the assistance of international lawyer Frederic Coudert, sued the New York customs collector, George Bidwell, to recover the duties on the basis of the Constitution's uniformity clause, which holds that "all duties, imposts, and excises shall be uniform throughout the United States." If, as the plaintiff argued, Puerto Rico was not a foreign country, then the Foraker Act, which established civil government in Puerto Rico and dictated customs duties, should be declared null and void.[28] At issue was whether the US Constitution applied to all territory acquired by the United States. If this were the case, then the residents of these new territories – very few of them white – would receive the same constitutional protections and rights as all other Americans.

The Court handed down its decision on May 27, 1901. Justice Henry Brown, writing for the majority, argued for the minimal view of the United States, reasoning that the Constitution extended only to states in the Union. "[T]he power to acquire territory by treaty implies, not only the power to govern such territory," the majority held, "but to prescribe upon what terms the United States shall receive its inhabitants, and what their status shall be in what Chief Justice Marshall termed the 'American Empire.'"[29] The rights guaranteed by the Constitution, in other words, would not *automatically* extend to all areas possessed by the United States. Consequently, the inhabitants of America's overseas territories would not be granted constitutional protections beyond the natural rights of life, liberty, and property that were basic and existed prior to the state. As Elihu Root – the architect of the American Empire – was later to pithily summarize the decisions, "Ye-es as near as I can make out the Constitution follows the flag – but doesn't quite catch up with it."[30]

The decision, however, did more than merely define the status of the territories under the Constitution; it also clarified the relationship the Court and Congress would have to the newly acquired colonies. By granting that Congress could govern the territories in ways that were contrary to the spirit of the Constitution, the Court largely removed itself from a position of legal oversight of American imperialism.[31] The real victor to emerge from the Insular Cases was Congress itself, which retained supreme power over the colonies unhampered by the Constitution or the Supreme Court.

CREATING A COLONIAL BUREAU: INSTITUTIONAL DESIGN FOR INFORMATION CONTROL

Now that the United States had acquired colonies, how would it govern them? For those who had supported the war and the subsequent acquisition of overseas territories, the stakes could not have been higher. War hero and recently elected governor of New York, Theodore Roosevelt, wrote to Secretary of State John Hay to express his concern that the administration might botch colonial governance,

---

[28] Sparrow, *Insular Cases*, 35.
[29] Sparrow, *Insular Cases*, 86–97.
[30] Quoted in Miller, *Benevolent Assimilation*, 157.
[31] Sparrow, *Insular Cases*, 139.

dooming the United States to several more decades of isolation. "A series of dis-
asters at the very beginning of our colonial policy would shake this administration and therefore our party," he wrote "and might produce the most serious and
far-reaching effects upon the nation as a whole, for if some political cataclysm was
the result, it might mean the definite abandonment of the course upon which we
have embarked – the only course I think fit for a really great nation."[32]

Roosevelt was right to be concerned – and he was not the only future president
who was. Woodrow Wilson, writing in *The Atlantic*, feared that the limited capacity
of the American state to take up the task of colonial governance would doom the
experiment to failure.[33] "We shall see now more clearly than ever before," Wilson
wrote, "that we lack in our domestic arrangements, above all things else, concentration, both in political leadership and in administrative organization; for the lack will
be painfully emphasized, and will embarrass us sadly in the career we have now set
out upon."[34] Whatever specific remedies they recommended, most American intellectuals believed that past methods of territorial administration would never work
for the new colonies. "To expect that the problem of the Philippines or of Cuba and
Porto Rico can be dealt with by our ordinary methods of administration," wrote
Yale historian Edward Borune, "is to live in a fool's paradise."[35]

There was no shortage of possible solutions to this problem, and most American
intellectuals advocated some combination of centralization and civil service
reform – anything that would remove the provincial interests of Congress from
the picture. The president of Stanford, David Starr Jordan, suggested that a uni-
fied colonial bureau be created. "If we have colonies, even one colony," Jordan
wrote, "there must be some sort of a colonial bureau, some concentrated power
which shall have exact knowledge of its people, its needs, and its resources."[36]
A. Lawrence Lowell, then a young professor in Harvard's Government department, recommended that the colonial service employ "only thoroughly trained
administrators, fit them for their work by long experience, and retain them in
office irrespective of party." To this end, he suggested the establishment of an academy along the lines of West Point or Annapolis to train this new class of colonial
officials.[37] "Does all this seem impracticable and Utopian?," asked Yale's Bourne,
who also advocated for a professional civil service. "Yet," he continued, "if
our colonial service is sacrificed to party interests as spoils . . . [t]he consequence
will be humiliation for ourselves and irritation and discontent among our depend-
ents."[38] Lowell, for example, singled out the OIA, which retained its dreadful

---

[32] Roosevelt to John Hay, July 1, 1899, in *Correspondence of Theodore Roosevelt and Henry Cabot Lodge*, 406.
[33] Some members of Congress did suggest that the territorial system be applied to the new territories, but they were decidedly in the minority. See *Cong. Rec.*, 56th Cong., 1st sess., (April 2, 1900), 3617.
[34] Woodrow Wilson, "Democracy and Efficiency," *The Atlantic Monthly* 87 (March 1901): 289–99.
[35] Edward Gaylord Bourne, "A Trained Colonial Civil Service," *North American Review* 169 (October 1899): 529.
[36] David Starr Jordan, *Imperial Democracy* (New York: D. Appleton, 1899), 212.
[37] David Starr Jordan, "Colonial Lessons of Alaska," *The Atlantic Monthly* 82 (November 1898); A. Lawrence Lowell, "The Government of Dependencies," *Annals of the American Academy of Political and Social Science* 13(Suppl. 12) (May 1899): 46–59.
[38] Bourne, "A Trained Colonial Civil Service," 534.

reputation for mismanagement, as one of the "painful examples" of relying on political appointees.[39]

It was not merely the corrupting influence of the spoils system that worried these intellectuals. Their primary concern was the lack of expertise in Congress about colonial administration and the limited incentives to acquire it. In his comprehensive examination of colonial policy, *The Administration of Dependencies*, Alpheus H. Snow noted that even "[w]ith the best and most honest intentions in the world, a man elected to the Senate or House of Representatives is under a pressure to protect the local interests and the interests of the whole Union, which makes it impossible for him to place the interest of the dependencies on anything like an equality with the other interests."[40] Even the president, Snow argued, was "likely to be swayed by partisan considerations."[41] Snow's proposed solution to this problem was to place the president in charge of "the habitual and daily administration of the dependencies . . . assisted by expert investigators and advisers."[42]

Yet Snow was not naïve. He also feared that such centralization of power and expertise would tempt the president "to convert his conditional and limited power into a power practically unconditioned and unlimited, and, judging from history, the temptation would not be withstood."[43] The only way to confront this additional problem was to vest "the superintendence and final control of the administration" with Congress. This would allow genuine expertise to develop in colonial administration without a concomitant increase in presidential power; it would also allow for more continuity of policy, as only one actor would be ultimately responsible for the day-to-day administration. The analogy Snow used to describe this arrangement, however, was far more revealing than the solution itself. The most effective form colonial administration could take, he argued, most closely resembled a *trust*. The president would serve as the acting trustee and Congress as the superintending trustee, an arrangement, he noted, "frequently adopted for the very purpose of more firmly fixing the responsibility for action."[44] It also resembled the system that was then being designed by Elihu Root, among the most famous corporate attorneys of the Gilded Age, who, as William Howard Taft would later recall, "initiated our Philippine policy, [and] is responsible for its success from the standpoint of statesmanship and far-sightedness."[45]

Elihu Root: Architect of the Empire Trust

As Secretary of War under McKinley and Roosevelt and Secretary of State during Roosevelt's second term, Elihu Root, perhaps more than any other person, was responsible for the formation of an American colonial policy and the foundation

---

[39] A. Lawrence Lowell, "The Colonial Expansion of the United States," *The Atlantic Monthly* (February 1899): 153–4.

[40] Alpheus H. Snow, *The Administration of Dependencies* (New York: G. P. Putnam's Sons, 1902), 579.

[41] Snow, *Administration of Dependencies*, 579.

[42] Ibid., 582.

[43] Ibid., 579.

[44] Ibid., 583.

[45] Taft quoted in W. Cameron Forbes, *The Philippine Islands* (Boston: Houghton Mifflin, 1928), v. 2, 500.

of the new American external state.[46] The son of a Hamilton College professor, Root was raised in a modest household in Clinton, New York, and moved to New York City to attend law school. By the 1870s, through his demonstrated brilliance at arranging airtight corporate trust agreements, he had risen to the heights of power and wealth available to the newly emerging class of "corporation lawyers." Well known for his biting wit and moral probity, Root quickly became a popular and well-respected member of Manhattan's social elite. He was also an indispensable guide through the rocky shoals of the emerging antitrust regulations for such captains of American industry and commerce as Frederick W. Vanderbilt, August Belmont, William C. Whitney, along with the National Cash Register Company, Standard Oil, Union Tobacco, and the Havemeyer Sugar Trust.[47] "I have had many lawyers who have told me what I cannot do," William Whitney once mused, "Mr. Root is the only lawyer who tells me how to do what I want to do."[48]

When McKinley began looking for someone to help him make sense of colonial administration, he turned to Root – a prominent citizen, a good Republican, and a lawyer with extensive experience in restructuring large organizations. At the end of the Spanish–American War, McKinley contacted Root about the possibility of becoming the next Secretary of War to replace the incompetent Russell Alger, who had spent much of the war supervising his lumber interests in Michigan.[49] Root later recalled being flattered by McKinley's interest, but told the president, "I know nothing about war. I know nothing about the army." McKinley's representative responded that the president was not "looking for anyone who knows anything about war or for anyone who knows anything about the army; he has got to have a lawyer to direct the government of these Spanish islands, and you are the lawyer he wants."[50]

Although Root had earlier turned down an offer to serve as American minister to Spain, he accepted the position of Secretary of War. Root, it seems, took the view that the War Department was simply another large organization that required his particular gift for management. As he later joked to Attorney General John W. Griggs, "I think the main feature of the change I am making is the formation of a new law firm of 'Griggs and Root, legal advisers to the President, colonial business a specialty.'"[51] Whatever he may have thought about colonial administration prior to becoming Secretary of War, Root would spend the next decade of his life

---

[46] There are two major biographies of Root, both quite old: Philip C. Jessup's authorized two-volume *Elihu Root* (New York: Dodd, Meade, 1938), which tends toward the hagiographic, and Richard Leopold's more critical *Elihu Root and the Conservative Tradition* (Boston: Little, Brown, 1954). For a more recent interpretation that pays particular attention to Root's design of US policy toward Latin America, see María del Rosario Rodríguez Díaz, *Elihu Root y la política estadounidense en América Latina y el Caribe, 1899–1908* (Morelia: UMSNH, Instituto de Investigaciones Históricas, 2006). Root was also largely responsible for reforming the organization of the Army, a topic outside the scope of this book, but one that is well treated in Skowronek, *Building a New American State* and Edward M. Coffman, *The Regulars: The American Army, 1898–1941* (Cambridge, MA: Belknap Press of Harvard University Press, 2004), 142–201.

[47] Jessup, *Elihu Root*, v. 1, 184.

[48] Ibid., 185.

[49] Zimmermann, *First Great Triumph*; Skowronek, *Building a New American State*.

[50] Root quoted in Robert Bacon and James Brown Scott, eds., *The Military and Colonial Policy of the United States: Addresses and Reports by Elihu Root* (Cambridge, MA: Harvard University Press, 1916), xiv.

[51] Quoted in Jessup, *Elihu Root*, v. 1, 219.

FIGURE 3.1. *William Howard Taft and Elihu Root in 1904. Library of Congress Prints and Photographs Division.*

designing and managing an American colonial state that would come to operate with remarkable autonomy from Congress – and from the millions of people in the Philippines and the Caribbean whose views on their own governance he rarely consulted.

Early Congressional Responses to Empire: Cuba and Puerto Rico

Root's early efforts led to the design of the Platt Amendment in Cuba. Congress had prevented the outright annexation of Cuba with the Teller Amendment – passed in response to McKinley's war message – but American military officials did everything in their power to discredit *independentismo*, the nationalist movement that had worked for decades to achieve Cuban independence.[52] In a line of argument that would become familiar in the rest of the occupied territories, Cubans

---

[52] Louis A. Pérez, Jr., *Cuba under the Platt Amendment, 1902–1934* (Pittsburgh, PA: University of Pittsburgh Press, 1991). The text of the Teller Amendment can be found in Louis A. Pérez, Jr., *Cuba and the United States: Ties of Singular Intimacy*, 3rd edn. (Athens, GA: University of Georgia Press, 2003).

were deemed unfit for self-government, and supporters of independence were discredited as dangerous radicals intent on sowing discord throughout the island. As historian Louis Pérez would later describe the conundrum as seen by American imperialists, "formal annexation was proscribed, but complete independence for Cuba was preposterous."[53]

The Cuban elite shared this dim view of *independentismo* and were anxious for Cuba to remain in the American orbit, if not as an official colony, then as a US protectorate.[54] Initially, American officials had hoped that their upper-class allies would win control of an independent Cuba, but as it became clear that this would not happen, Root began to cast around for alternative solutions. In his view, the electoral success of the independence coalition indicated that a sovereign Cuba would be hostile, or at least inappropriately deferential, to the United States. Yet the continued occupation of Cuba was both expensive and politically costly for the administration. "I am getting pretty tired of having Congress on one hand put us under independence of Cuba resolutions," he wrote to General Leonard Wood, "and resolutions of hostile inquiry and criticism, and on the other hand shirk all responsibility."[55] His solution would put Cuba on a different path than the Philippines, but leave it without full sovereignty.

Working with Senator Orville H. Platt, Root's proposal – later passed as the Platt Amendment – allowed American hegemony in the Caribbean to remain intact, but adhered to the language of the earlier Teller Amendment by giving the Cuban nation technical sovereignty. Under the Platt Amendment, Cuba's right to treat with other nations and its ability to take on public debt was restricted. The more significant change was in Article 3, which provided the United States with the right to "intervene for the preservation of Cuban independence, the maintenance of a government adequate for the protection of life, property and individual liberty." This language was accompanied by assurances to Cuban officials that "the intervention described in the third clause of the Platt Amendment is not synonymous with intermeddling or interference with the affairs of the Cuban nation."[56] Officially, the military occupation of Cuba would end on May 20, 1902, although the infamous Platt Amendment would authorize several later American occupations and keep Cuba under American hegemony for decades. Perhaps the most immediate lesson that Root and other American officials took from this experience was that Congress, which had tied their hands with the Teller Amendment, seemed unwilling to invest the resources to construct a strong colonial state.

Unlike Cuba, Puerto Rico received no congressional guarantee of sovereignty, and it came under military occupation from 1898 to 1900 as Congress debated its fate. As would occur in the Philippines, an investigative commission was dispatched from Washington to study the conditions on the island. They reported that Puerto Ricans supported American intervention and hoped to eventually be admitted as a state. The commission recommended a familiar set of policies to build schools and to support the island's agricultural industries, as well supporting

---

[53] Ibid., 43.
[54] Ibid., 37.
[55] Root quoted in ibid., 44.
[56] Ibid., 53.

free trade with the United States.[57] The Puerto Ricans had also dispatched representatives to Washington, and what they found there was unsettling. Members of Congress seemed to care very little about their new colonial possession, and were instead entirely occupied with seemingly minor matters in their home states.[58] Furthermore, it was the Philippines, with its much larger population and ongoing war, which concerned most in Congress. In comparison, as one member of Congress reported, Puerto Rico "was easily governed, its people friendly and peaceful," and, he concluded, "we all agree that no great danger to the industrial system of this country can come from the acquisition of Puerto Rico."[59] Indeed, if there was any anxiety over the establishment of civil rule in Puerto Rico, it was that it might establish a precedent for the Philippines.

The Foraker Act of 1900 was designed with these concerns in mind. Although some agricultural producers were concerned about competition from Puerto Rico, the balance of American interests supported free trade with the island. The US sugar industry, of course, was the strongest proponent of eliminating tariff barriers, but other commodity interests, such as rice farmers in Louisiana, saw Puerto Rico as a major new market for their products – and one that would become dependent on the United States as it severed ties with Spain.[60] Under the Foraker Act, a modest 15 percent duty was charged for imports from Puerto Rico, which was eliminated within two years. This quickly made sugar the most valuable of Puerto Rico's exports and stimulated massive American investments in the Puerto Rican sugar industry.[61] The Act further integrated Puerto Rico into the US economy by eliminating the peso and introducing the dollar as its currency.[62] In many ways, the McKinley administration and Congress saw the Foraker Act as a test case for the far more controversial organic act that would come to govern the Philippines. As one member of Congress put the matter, "I understand full well that the Administration does not care a fig for Puerto Rico." It was, he added, "not for the mere sake of deriving revenue from that island, but as a precedent for our future guidance in the control of the Philippines."[63]

The Bureau of Insular Affairs: A Colonial Trust

Although the Teller Amendment blocked the formal annexation of Cuba and the Foraker Act set Puerto Rico on the path to full integration with the US economy, the Philippines was another matter entirely. This archipelago would be directly managed and governed by the American state, not as an overseas settler territory like Hawai'i, but as a formal colony. Precisely how that would be done, however,

[57] Go, *Patterns of Empire*, 9; Edward J. Berbusse, *The United States in Puerto Rico, 1898–1900* (Chapel Hill, NC: University of North Carolina Press, 1966).

[58] Berbusse, *United States in Puerto Rico*, 117.

[59] Quoted in Pedro A. Cabán, *Constructing a Colonial People: Puerto Rico and the United States, 1898–1932* (Boulder, CO: Westview, 1999), 88.

[60] Quoted in Berbusse, *United States in Puerto Rico*, 155.

[61] Cabán, *Constructing a Colonial People*, 103.

[62] James L. Dietz, *Economic History of Puerto Rico: Institutional Change and Capitalist Development* (Princeton, NJ: Princeton University Press, 1987), 89.

[63] Rep. William E. William, quoted in Cabán, *Constructing a Colonial People*, 89.

was left to the new Secretary of War, who was unequivocal in his belief that the United States could legally govern the newly acquired colonies as it saw fit. In his first annual report of 1899, Root described the relationship between the United States and the colonies as one of dependency, and noted that "the people of the islands have no right to have them treated as States, or to have them treated as the territories previously held by the United States have been treated, or to assert legal right under the provision of the constitution which was established for the people of the United States themselves and to meet the conditions existing upon this continent, or to assert against the United States any legal right whatever not found in the treaty."[64] And, as previously discussed, the Supreme Court largely affirmed Root's interpretation, granting Congress total control over the Philippines and Puerto Rico, with exceptions for the protection of basic rights such as life, liberty, and property.

The greater problem was an administrative one. Although he had been appointed as Secretary of War to develop an administrative system for the colonies, it was clear, as he noted in his *Annual Report* of 1901, that the "War Department had no machinery for the purpose. No provision for any administrative machine was made by law."[65] While Root was indeed correct that the War Department had no clear machinery, it was certainly not the case that there were no precedents to follow. The United States, after all, had a rather clear system of administering territories, a fact that many members of Congress suggested be applied to the new possessions. During early debates on the status of the newly acquired colonies, Senator Shelby M. Cullom of Illinois argued, "I do not believe the Constitution of the United States puts Congress in a straitjacket and requires a particular form of government for every new acquisition of territory. We can give them a Territorial form of government, such as is our usual form . . . So far as I am concerned, I believe in the ordinary Territorial form of government; but so far as the Constitution is concerned, I do not regard the country as tied down to any particular form."[66] Yet Root dismissed such suggestions as ill-considered and inappropriate. As he argued in his 1901 *Annual Report*, "We have no precedents, save the simple and meager proceedings under the occupation of California and New Mexico, more than half a century ago, and it has been necessary to decide every question upon its own merits and to make our own precedents for the future."[67]

Naturally, Root approached the challenge of colonial administration from his perspective as a corporate attorney, and the organizational structure he developed resembled nothing so much as a corporate trust. From the beginning, Root was anxious to shield the islands from congressional interference, and to centralize their administration in the War Department, while giving significant autonomy to local administrators. What was needed, he concluded, was a clearinghouse that would manage communications between metropolitan authorities in Washington and the colonial government in Manila. To accomplish this, Root transformed an obscure

[64] US War Department, *Report of the Secretary of War, 1899* (Washington, DC: Government Printing Office, 1899), 24.

[65] US War Department, *Annual Report of the Secretary of War, 1901* (Washington, DC: Government Printing Office, 1901), 87.

[66] Howard W. Caldwell, *American Territorial Development: Source Extracts* (Chicago: J. H. Miller, 1900), 250.

[67] *Annual Report of the Secretary of War, 1901*, 87.

division of the War Department known as the Division of Customs and Insular Affairs (DCIA) from a records office into the American colonial office. The DCIA, later renamed the BIA, became the de facto colonial office of the United States and served as the clearinghouse for colonial state communications.[68]

In the beginning, it was no foregone conclusion that the management of colonial government would end up in War. As the Spanish–American War was drawing to an end, most department secretaries, including Interior, Navy, Treasury, and State, were angling to have some control over the civil government. For a short time, it seemed that McKinley seriously considered entrusting their administration to the State Department.[69] The history of American territorial administration gave all of these departments (except, perhaps, Navy) a greater claim to experience in territorial administration. As discussed in Chapter 2, until 1873 the State Department had general supervisory powers over American territories, while the Department of Treasury handled their finances, and legal concerns were sent to the Attorney General. Although Interior gained control of territorial administration in 1873, it still left Treasury and Justice to supervise financial and legal matters.[70]

Root apparently thought it prudent to avoid dividing authority among several bureaucracies. He convinced McKinley to leave colonial administration under War – and he guarded this power jealously. In his draft of the Philippines Bill of 1902, for example, Root defined the BIA's role in extremely broad language, merely noting that it had control over "all matters related to civil government in the island possessions of the United States subject to the jurisdiction of the War Department."[71] When the Department of Treasury attempted to require that the insular government submit to it revenue reports, Root quickly put a stop to it, because, as he wrote to Senator William Frye, it would create "an element of double control, which would be quite intolerable."[72] And, in the frank assessment of former BIA director Frank McIntyre, one of the BIA's chief responsibilities was preventing "other American agencies from interfering with the government of the islands."[73]

Not only was the BIA separate from other government agencies, but it also retained some autonomy from the rest of the Department of War. In the beginning, the exact relationship between the BIA and the regular military hierarchy was so unclear that the auditor of the Military Government of Cuba was uncertain as to the appropriate title of the head of the agency. "Will you please tell me," he wrote to Edwards, "how I should address communications to your Dept. from this

[68] Despite its central role in colonial administration, very little has been written about the Bureau of Insular Affairs. The two major sources that my account draws on are Earl S. Pomeroy, "The American Colonial Office," *Mississippi Valley Historical Review* 30 (March 1944): 521–32 and Romeo V. Cruz, *America's Colonial Desk and the Philippines, 1898–1934* (Quezon City: University of the Philippines Press, 1974). There are also a few works by former directors of the BIA including Clarence R. Edwards, "The Work of the Bureau of Insular Affairs," *National Geographic Magazine* 15 (June 1904): 239–55 and Frank McIntyre, "American Territorial Administration," *Foreign Affairs* 10 (January 1932). Given the lack of published sources, however, the vast records of the BIA, housed at NARA II in College Park, MD, are an indispensable resource. The agency still exists as a small division of the Department of the Interior.

[69] Cruz, *America's Colonial Desk*, 29.

[70] Pomeroy, *The Territories*.

[71] S. Doc. No. 280, 57th Cong., 1st sess., 239.

[72] Root to Senator William P. Frye, February 7, 1902, quoted in Cruz, *America's Colonial Desk*, 48.

[73] McIntyre, "American Territorial Administration," 299.

office? Should it be The Adjutant General, U.S. Army or The Chief of the Division of Customs and Insular Affairs?"[74] To solve this confusion, Root placed the BIA under the control of the Secretary, and the chief of the Bureau reported directly to him. Partly this was a result of Root's strong belief in the importance of civil government for the islands, but it also allowed him to isolate colonial administration from the rest of the Department of War, where Congress exercised far more oversight. As he wrote in his 1901 *Annual Report,*

> The policy followed by the American Executive in dealing with the government of the Philippines (and also in dealing with the government of the other islands ceded or yielded by Spain which have been under the control of the War Department) has been to determine and prescribe the framework of insular government; to lay down the rules of policy to be followed upon the great questions of government as they are foreseen or arise; to obtain the best and ablest men possible for insular officers; to distribute and define their powers; and then to hold them responsible for the conduct of government in the islands *with the least possible interference from Washington.*[75]

Perhaps the most distinct difference between the new system of colonial administration designed by Root and past forms of territorial administration was its organizational form. As discussed in Chapter 2, the administration of past American territories was divided among a number of bureaucratic agencies, and, while this often resulted in inefficient governance, it did provide a number of outlets for Congress to receive information from a variety of different agencies that had a hand in territorial administration. In contrast, the administration of the Philippines (and, later, other colonies) was concentrated in a small bureau in one executive agency, which allowed the Philippine colonial state to maintain a monopoly on colonial information. This M-form organizational hierarchy would not only prevent other agencies from gaining a foothold in colonial administration, but also make congressional oversight significantly more difficult.

For its part, Congress came to rely almost exclusively on the BIA for information about the Philippines. According to historian Romeo Cruz, "[the] insular knowledge of Congress was next to zero and whatever the Senate Committee on the Philippines and House Committee on Insular Affairs learned about the Islands had been furnished by the Compilation Division and Library of the BIA."[76] By 1907, Congressman Herbert Parsons (R-NY) could write an article about the BIA he frankly titled, "A Bureau of Information and Report for the Insular Possessions." "He who would get assured facts in regard to any matter in the Philippines," wrote Parsons, "can ascertain them from this bureau; from it he can learn the progress made on the new railroads in the Philippines; the prospects of capital being invested in the agricultural bank in the Philippines; conditions in regard to banking, currency and finance." And thus, Parsons concluded, "a great service to this, the home country, and of potent usefulness to the Philippines is the bureau of

---

[74] Office of the Auditor for the Island of Cuba to Edwards, May 6, 1900; Edwards Papers, Box 1, Folder 13.

[75] *Annual Report of the Secretary of War, 1901* [my emphasis], quoted in Edwards, "Work of the Bureau of Insular Affairs," 240.

[76] Cruz, *America's Colonial Desk,* 100.

insular affairs."[77] If this central source of information was useful to Congress, it was doubly useful to the executive branch, which was able to present a carefully curated set of facts about colonial progress and to shield the colonial governments from potential scandals.

The BIA also became the de facto lobbying and acquisitions arm of the Philippine colonial state at home. As Edwards frankly described the role of his bureau, "It may be called a clearinghouse for all questions as between the government of the Philippine Islands and the government of the United States."[78] By May of 1902, at least one clerk was charged with reading and making notes in the congressional record and with furnishing a response to any charges made against insular authorities.[79] Although the BIA remained small even by the relatively modest standards of US federal agencies in this period – in 1902, it could count only 61 employees – it produced thousands of reports and answered a steady stream of congressional inquiries.[80] As Root himself would acknowledge in 1901, "it performs with admirable and constantly increasing efficiency the great variety of duties which in other countries would be described as belonging to a colonial office, and would be performed by a much more pretentious establishment."[81]

In sum, Root considered the office essential to the administration of the empire. "It is," he later wrote, "the only thing which enables us to keep our hands at all on the government of our distant possessions, and it is admirably organized for that purpose; it is really doing the work of a colonial department."[82]

INSTITUTIONAL AND IDEOLOGICAL ORIGINS
OF THE PHILIPPINE COLONIAL STATE

In March of 1899, a month after hostilities commenced between Aguinaldo and the American Army, the First Philippine Commission arrived in Manila. Known as the Schurman Commission after its leader, Jacob Schurman (the president of Cornell), the group included Rear Admiral George Dewey, Gen. Elwell S. Otis, Charles Denby, a former US minister to China, and Professor Dean Worcester, a zoologist from the University of Michigan who had previously done research in the Philippines. The Commission made a surprisingly thorough investigation of the Islands. They traveled throughout Luzon and spoke to a number of wealthy

---

[77] Herbert Parsons, "A Bureau of Information and Report for the Insular Possessions," *Annals of the American Academy of Political and Social Science* 30 (July 1907): 123–9.

[78] Edwards, "Work of the Bureau of Insular Affairs," 244. In his retrospective on American stewardship of the Philippines, Cameron Forbes wrote of the Bureau's "active participation in the preparation of important acts of Congress affecting the insular government . . . It contributed constructively and painstakingly to all important Philippine tariff legislation until unlimited free trade between the United States and the Islands was secured in 1913." Forbes, *Philippine Islands*, v. 1, 137.

[79] Cruz, *America's Colonial Desk*, 89.

[80] *Annual Report of the Chief of the Bureau of Insular Affairs to the Secretary of War, 1902* (Washington, DC: Government Printing Office, 1902), 742. Edwards was often desperate for more staff and repeatedly requested additional employees to little avail. See Edwards to William Cary Sanger, January 4, 1902; Edwards Papers, Box 2, Folder 1.

[81] *Annual Report of the Secretary of War, 1901*, 87.

[82] Root to Cooper, January 25, 1905; Edwards Papers, Box 5, Folder 4.

and influential Filipinos, known as *ilustrados*, including Felipe G. Calderón, the principal author of the Malolos Constitution, who provided them with a description of the Filipino population that would prove to be the dominant view of most American administrators throughout the initial years of colonial governance. As Calderón testified to the commission, "The archipelago as a whole is composed of three classes of individuals: the rich and intelligent element; the poorer element of the country – the element that is willing to devote itself to work – and an element that may be called intermediate, made up of clerks and writers, who have a habit of stirring up the town."[83]

Calderón's characterization of Filipinos was reinforced in the minds of American officials as they toured the islands, and in their final report, they confidently concluded that the majority of the population was decidedly primitive and in need of a firm hand to guide them. Furthermore, the Commission held, the insurrection was largely made up of disaffected leaders who could be drawn to the American side through promises of stability and economic advancement.[84]

The Commission also took away a decidedly negative opinion of Spanish stewardship. The Catholic friars, who had long served as quasi-official representatives of the Spanish Crown throughout the Philippines, were especially hated. In rural areas, where royal officials had little to no presence, the clergy served nearly every administrative role. According to Father Juan Villegas, who testified to the second Commission, he was, among other roles, inspector of primary schools, president of the board of urban taxation, censor of municipal budgets, member of the prison board, president of the board of statistics, and censor of plays, comedies, and dramas.[85] The friars had also managed, in their nearly 400 years of rule over the islands, to amass huge tracts of land, amounting roughly to 400,000 acres by 1900. Compounding the resentment over their near-monopoly on offices and their significant wealth was clear evidence of corruption and rampant sexual abuse of the population.[86]

In the end, the Commission largely condoned the principal complaints the revolutionaries had of the Spanish regime as well as the reformers' goals, which the Commission concluded were the following:

(1) The expulsion of the friars and the restitution of the lands held by them to the townships or to the original owners; (2) the recognition of Filipino priests in filling the incumbencies vacated by the friars; (3) absolute religious toleration; (4) the equality of all persons – Filipinos as well as Spaniards – before the law; the assimilation of the laws of the archipelago to those of Spain, and the equality of Filipinos with Spaniards in the civil service; (5) the freedom of the press; (6) the establishment of representative institutions; (7) home rule; (8) abolition of deportation and other unjust measures against Filipinos; and (9) the continuance of the war as a means to coerce Spain into granting these rights.[87]

[83] Quoted in Stanley, *Nation in the Making*, 55.
[84] See United States Philippine Commission, *Report of the Philippine Commission to the President, 1900* (Washington, DC: Government Printing Office, 1900).
[85] Stanley, *Nation in the Making*, 11–12.
[86] Philippine national hero José Rizal's masterpiece, *Noli Me Tangere*, is a fierce indictment of the friars and an excellent study of negative Filipino feelings toward the clergy through a fictional lens.
[87] *Report of the Philippine Commission, 1900*, v. 1, 82–90.

What the commissioners decided unequivocally was that the Philippines could not be given independence. In their final report, presented to McKinley on December 31, 1900, they declared that the Filipinos needed "the tutelage and protection of the United States." "But," the report continued, "they need it in order that in due time they may, in their opinion, become self-governing and independent. For it would be a misrepresentation of facts not to report that ultimate independence – independence after an undefined period of American training – is the aspiration and goal of the intelligent Filipinos who to-day so strenuously oppose the suggestion of independence at the present time."[88]

The style of imperialism they envisioned, however, was to be uniquely American. "It does not appear," they argued, "that in themselves any of the British types of colonial government is susceptible of direct application to the Philippine Islands."[89] Jacob Schurman, it seems, rejected the idea of colonial autonomy as practiced in Canada and Australia, but also of the model of direct rule in India. As he wrote in a book published two years after his tenure as president of the Commission, "to reconcile the political rights and privileges of the Filipinos with the inviolable sovereignty of the United States, I turned to the congressional acts organizing the successive territories of the Union, beginning with the classic Jeffersonian measure of 1804 for the organization of the territory of Louisiana."[90] Schurman, however, was not looking for administrative models, but for historical justification for American imperialism. As the Commission noted, "[Jefferson] seems to have felt no incongruity between the principles of the Declaration of Independence of the thirteen self-governing colonies and this scheme of government of the politically inexperienced inhabitants of Louisiana."[91] What they would settle on, however, was a decidedly American, obsessively Progressive vision for the islands, where theories of scientific management would complement imperial control.

From an administrative perspective, the aspect of Filipino society that surprised the Americans most of all was the centralized nature of Spanish colonial government, which demonstrated a total "rejection of absolute home rule for their town and provinces."[92] That this was repeated in the revolutionary's Malolos Constitution surprised them even more. As Schurman later wrote, "The Constitution of the Philippine Republic expressly provides for 'intervention' of the central government in the affairs of the provincial and municipal government. This idea of 'intervention,' which is foreign to us, is fundamental to the whole political life and thought of the Filipinos."[93] For Americans accustomed to the weak federal state, such centralized government must have seemed impossibly Spanish, and they quickly recommended that the government be decentralized to allow Philippine towns and provinces to be "vested with substantially the same powers as are now enjoyed by town and counties in the United States."[94]

---

[88] Ibid., 83.
[89] Ibid., 106.
[90] Jacob Schurman, *Philippine Affairs: A Retrospective and Outlook* (New York: Charles Scribner, 1902), 32.
[91] *Report of the Philippine Commission, 1900*, v. 1, 108–9.
[92] Schurman, *Philippine Affairs*, 31.
[93] Ibid., 31–2.
[94] *Report of the Philippine Commission, 1900*, v. 1, 97. The decision to decentralize the central government would have profound effects on the trajectory of post-independence politics in the Philippines. Most significantly, it facilitated the rise of national leaders with political bases outside of Manila, most famously Sergio Osmeña and Manuel Quezon.

While McKinley had given the military full executive and legislative authority in August 1898, there was a strong push to move to civilian rule. Consequently, in the summer of 1900, a second Commission was dispatched to the islands to begin the process of transitioning from military to civil authority. At the time, there was some talk of sending members of Congress along to judge conditions for themselves. As the *New York Times* reported, "As to the question of again sending a commission to the Philippines, it has been suggested in the Congress, by both Senators and Representatives, that a joint committee of members might be named for that purpose. It would be very popular, and also very expensive, but it is insisted that it would be a better way of preparing Congress for legislative action than the plan of making up a commission outside of Congress and expecting members of both houses to read their report after it had been made in order to become more informed."[95] The second Commission, however, left the United States unaccompanied by any congressional delegation, and, as they would be forced to do for most of America's occupation of the archipelago, members of Congress were indeed left to read the Commission's report to become more informed about the islands.

William Howard Taft and Civil Government

More than any other American, William Howard Taft would become the dominant figure in US imperialism.[96] As he rose through the ranks from Governor-General of the Philippines to Secretary of War to President, he maintained an active interest in the islands, famously returning in 1905 and 1908 to make a special report to President Roosevelt. Yet he initially did not want the job.[97] By the age of 34, he was happily serving as a federal judge in Cincinnati when Senator Foraker of Ohio, who headed the recently created Committee on Porto Rico, recommended him to McKinley. Even after he arrived in Washington, however, Taft was reluctant to join the Commission, explaining to the president that he was anxious to avoid disrupting his judicial career and that he, much like Professor Schurman, had not supported retention of the islands. As he later described his meeting with the president to his brothers,

I told him that I was very much opposed to taking [the Philippines], that I did not favor expansion, but that now we were under the most sacred duty to give them a good form of government. I explained that I did not agree with Senator Hoar [R-MA] and his followers that the Filipinos were capable of self-government, or that we were violating the principles of our government, or the Declaration of Independence as far as they were concerned; that I thought we were doing them great good but that I deprecated our taking of the Philippines because of the assumption of a burden by us contrary to our traditions at a time when we had quite enough to do at home; but, being there, we must exert ourselves to construct a government which would be adapted to the needs of the people so that they might be developed into a self-governing people.[98]

95 "Philippine Junket Proposed," *New York Times*, January 12, 1900, 1.
96 Taft Avenue remains a major street in Manila.
97 As it turns out, however, Roosevelt himself was very interested in the position. While still Governor of New York, he wrote to Henry Cabot Lodge, "As you know, the thing I should really like to do would be to be the first civil Governor General of the Philippines. I believe I could do that job, and it is a job emphatically worth doing. I feel that being Vice President would cut me off definitely from all chance of doing it; whereas in my second terms as Governor, were I offered the Philippines, I could resign and accept it." Theodore Roosevelt to Henry Cabot Lodge, January 22, 1900 in *Correspondence of Theodore Roosevelt and Henry Cabot Lodge*, v. 1, 437.
98 Quoted in Herbert S. Duffy, *William Howard Taft* (New York: Minton, Balch, 1930), 74–5.

McKinley reassured him that the position would not hurt his chances for a seat on the Supreme Court. But Root, who was also in the meeting, put the matter more starkly: "This is the parting of the ways. You may go on holding the job you have in a humdrum, mediocre way. But here is something that will test you; something in the way of effort and struggle, and the question is, will you take the harder or the easier task?"[99] Taft decided on the "harder" task, but on the condition that he could be president of the Commission.[100] Writing to Senator Foraker a week later, he reflected, "The work now to be undertaken is of the most perplexing and original character and I gravely fear that I am not qualified. But the die is cast – I must accept it."[101]

Along with Taft, the Second Philippine Commission was composed of Dean Worcester, the only returning member of the First Philippine Commission; Luke Wright, a corporate lawyer and gold Democrat from Tennessee; Henry C. Ide, a former US Court judge in Samoa; and Bernard Moses, a professor of Latin American history from the University of California, Berkeley. Although they probably did not realize it upon appointment to the Commission, these men, with the exception of Moses, would dominate the Philippine civil government for the initial years of American occupation. Their instructions, as drafted by Root, were incorporated in the annual message of McKinley to Congress on December 3, 1900. And these instructions, which became one of the most remarkable, if largely unknown, statements of American foreign policy, left no doubt about America's ambition in its newly acquired colony. They are worth quoting at length:

In all the forms of government and administrative provisions which they are authorized to prescribe, the Commission should bear in mind that the government which they are establishing is designed not for our satisfaction or for the expression of our theoretical views, but for the happiness, peace, and prosperity of the people of the Philippine Islands, and the measures adopted should be made to conform to their custom, their habits, and even their prejudices, to the fullest extent consistent with the accomplishment of the indispensable requisites of just and effective government.

At the same time the commission should bear in mind, and the people of the islands should be made plainly to understand, that there are certain great principles of government which have been made the basis of our governmental system which we deem essential to the rule of law and the maintenance of individual freedom, and of which they have, unfortunately, been denied the experience possessed by us; that there are also certain practical rules of government which we have found to be essential to the preservation of these great principles of liberty and law, and that these principles and these rules of government must be established and maintained in their islands for the sake of their liberty and happiness, however much they may conflict with the customs or laws of procedure with which they are familiar.[102]

Taft called it "one of the greatest state papers ever issued" and William F. Willoughby gushed that "[it] will always occupy a leading place side by side with that of the Northwest Ordinance. Its significance lies in the fact that in its few pages

---

[99] Quoted in Stanley, *Nation in the Making*, 62.

[100] Taft to Root, February 3, 1900; Root Papers, Box 164.

[101] Taft to Foraker, February 11, 1900 in Joseph Benson Foraker, *Notes of a Busy Life* (Cincinnati, OH: Stewart & Kidd, 1916), v.-2, 2nd edn., 87.

[102] *Instructions of the President to the Taft Commission*, quoted in Charles Burke Elliott, *The Philippines to the End of Commission Government: A Study in Tropical Democracy* (Indianapolis, IN: Bobbs-Merrill, 1917), 488.

is formulated, in the most authoritative way, the whole theory of the American people in respect to the government of dependencies."[103] It would also prove to be a gross misrepresentation of the later reality of American empire.

Lofty rhetoric notwithstanding, the Commission had relatively little capacity. As Taft wrote to his friend, Assistant Attorney General Henry M. Hoyt, "You can get some idea of what we have to do if you imagine a large state like Pennsylvania or New York without any laws at all, and think of yourself as attempting to provide all the necessary legislation for the establishment of a civil government."[104] Yet by November of 1900, Taft could confidently write Root that "We have threshed out the matter of taxes and are convinced that the only adequate tax is a land tax."[105] Despite this early work on taxation, Taft's first battle was with the leadership of the US Army, which was reluctant to acknowledge the new authority of civilians in pacified areas after waging a war against the Philippine revolutionaries.[106] Back in Washington, Root was anxious to establish the clear authority of the civilian administrators, primarily to demonstrate to Congress that the war was over and that nation building could begin. The executive order he prepared for McKinley's signature (signed June 21, 1901) expanded the powers of the Commission, giving the president of the Philippine Commission "the executive authority in all civil affairs in the government of the Philippine Islands heretofore exercised by the Military Governor of the Philippines."[107]

In an act that would soon become *de rigueur*, however, Root first forwarded a draft of the order to the Commission. As he explained to Taft,

The Executive Order to be substituted for that of May 8, 1899, and the revised rules and regulations pursuant thereto, have been in fact approved by the president, but his signature to the order, and mine to the rules and regulations, are withheld until your Commission shall have had an opportunity to examine them; for two reasons: first, that you may make by cable any criticism or suggestion which occurs to you; and, second, that when finally determined upon they may be incorporated by you in the form of a statute, which has already received the approval of the president and the secretary, instead of being published as an order which might appear to overrule your action and might possibly interfere with the authority and prestige or the Commission, a thing which I am very desirous to avoid. When this has been done, inasmuch as these rules regulate the accountability of the entire Philippine Government to this Department, the Commission *will not have authority to make any change without having first secured the consent of the Department.*[108]

Before Congress had ever acted on civil government in the Philippines, then, the close relationship and lines of authority between the Commission and the War Department had already been established. Information between the Commission

[103] Taft to Root, November 30, 1900; Root Papers, Box 164; William F. Willoughby, *Territories and Dependencies of the United States: Their Government and Administration* (New York: The Century Co., 1905), 179.

[104] Taft to Henry M. Hoyt, September 8, 1900; Edwards Papers, Box 1, Folder 16.

[105] Taft to Root, November 30, 1900; Root Papers, Box 164.

[106] Kramer, *Blood of Government*, 171.

[107] Text of order from James D. Richardson, ed., *A Compilation of the Messages and Papers of the Presidents 1789–1905* (Washington, DC: Bureau of National Literature and Art, 1907), v. 10, 389.

[108] Root to Taft, January 7, 1901; Edwards Papers, Box 1, Folder 19 [my emphasis].

and War were to be freely shared, but the Commission was to report directly to the War Department through Root's new colonial bureau.

CONGRESSIONAL OPPOSITION: PROTECTIONISM AND THE EMPIRE

In what would become a pattern in US colonial government, the War Department and the colonial officials themselves wrote the bill that would eventually govern the Philippine colonial state. The "Spooner Amendment," so-named for Senator John C. Spooner of Wisconsin, who tacked it on to an Army appropriations bill, was to give congressional approval for the early acts of the Commission and statutory authority to form a new civil government. Although Senator Spooner's name became associated with the bill, Root and the Commission had been intimately involved in its preparation from the beginning. In fact, it is quite likely that Root had written most of the bill himself, including the first paragraph of the bill, which replaced civil for military governance of the islands.[109] Of crucial importance to the Commission was the original bill's proposed authorization of public land sales and the granting of corporate franchises; a policy they hoped would attract American capital and jump-start the development of the archipelago.[110] Without statutory power to begin their development projects, however, they could do very little, and so adoption of the bill by Congress quickly became a top priority of the BIA and the Department of War.

Root and the commissioners desperately wanted authority to develop the islands, and the bill as initially written gave them the authority to award franchises and sell public lands. Taft, in particular, believed that railroads were essential to the project's success. In his view, the rich natural resources of the country held the key to the colony's economic success. In that respect, the key would be railroads and a reduction of the American tariff on Filipino imports. Taft was clearly worried that Congress would take the lead, and he began to envision the worst of all possible scenarios – that Congress would not pass the Spooner Amendment, but would adopt a different bill for the Philippines written in Congress. "The report in the newspapers today is that a special session of Congress is to be called to legislate for a civil government for the Philippines," he wrote to Root. "I shall be very sorry if this results in an attempt to frame a government for the Philippines, because I do not think the conditions are ripe for the action of Congress yet, and I believe that you and the President can very much better frame a civil government than Congress, for the government by Congress would be rigid and yours could be changed as conditions require."[111]

In the fall of 1900, insular authorities were optimistic that the bill would be passed relatively quickly. "I have a letter from Senator Lodge," Taft wrote to Root in November of 1900, "in which he says he thinks the Spooner bill can be passed if the President requests it in his message." Naturally, for Taft and his colleagues on the Commission, the bill was essential. Although he had arrived in the Philippines only five months earlier, it is clear that Taft was already growing frustrated with

---

[109] Leopold, *Elihu Root and the Conservative Tradition*, 36. Jessup, *Elihu Root*, v. 1, 359.
[110] In this respect, the Commission's proposed development program was similar to American continental territories.
[111] Taft to Root, January 29, 1901; Root Papers, Box 165.

the slow pace of Congress to extend the Commission's authority. Concluding his letter to Root, he noted that if the bill was not passed, "it would be like running on one wheel to attempt to develop this country without power to offer investments to capital."[112] It did not help matters that Senator Lodge, the chairman of the Senate Committee on the Philippines, proved to be more hindrance than help. He had long been a vocal proponent of American expansion and had strongly supported the retention of the Philippines, but the patrician Lodge – "Boston incarnate" according to Henry Adams – had no intention of taking orders from the Department of War or the Philippine Commission. Lodge cared deeply about the institutional prestige of the Senate and firmly believed that it ought to play an active role in American foreign relations.[113] For Lodge, there was no reason why the Senate's role should be limited to approving or amending colonial laws written by the War Department.

Although Lodge likely thought his independence from the War Department good for public policy and American foreign relations, Taft found it merely obnoxious. Even the equanimous Root grew frustrated by Lodge's dithering, writing in an especially frank letter to Taft,

I have been unable to get the Senate to take up the Spooner resolution, or either branch of Congress to take up any measure for our relief in regard to coinage in the Philippines, or any measure which would make it possible to build the railroad into Benguet; but the Chairman of the Senate Committee on the Philippines has, without any consultation with the President, or the War Department, and without asking for any information on the subject, introduced a resolution to prohibit the importation and sale of intoxicating liquors in the Philippine Islands, and the Senate has delayed the progress of the army bill to discuss that subject seriously for several days. Of course the absurdity of attempting to legislate a subject of which they were wholly ignorant was so great that it was overwhelmingly defeated.[114]

Taft was even more blunt. "[I]t is perfectly evident . . .," he wrote to Root several months later, "that Senator Lodge is entirely useless as the head of the Committee for the Philippines. He does not seem to have much influence in the Senate and is constantly playing to the galleries."[115] Senator Spooner, both men felt, was a far more reliable ally. Yet even Spooner was pressured to push the bill through more aggressively.

For Taft, the Senate's delays and Lodge's grandstanding were costing the Commission valuable time to recruit American capital, which was the first step in the Commission's economic development plan. "[F]or Heaven's sake," he wrote to Spooner in November of 1900, "press it to a passage. It is this which we need now to assist us in the development of this country and make these people understand what it is to have American civilization about them."[116] The low opinion of Lodge's effectiveness as a result of this episode would become further solidified in the minds of colonial officials in subsequent battles with Congress.

This episode also demonstrates that the White House and particularly the architects of the imperial state saw prominent Republican members of Congress,

---

[112] Taft to Root, November 30, 1900; Root Papers, Box 164.
[113] Widenor, *Henry Cabot Lodge.*
[114] Root to Taft, January 21, 1901; Edwards Papers, Box 1, Folder 19.
[115] Taft to Root, March 17, 1901, quoted in Oscar M. Alfonso, *Theodore Roosevelt and the Philippines, 1897–1909* (New York: Oriole, 1970), 80–1.
[116] Quoted in Stanley, *Nation in the Making,* 88.

such as Lodge, as impediments to their plans. For his part, Lodge was never the reliable partner Root and Taft hoped he would be, and he and other prominent Republicans were rarely invited to craft insular legislation. As their frustration with Congress grew, insular officials moved to have less prominent, but more agreeable, members introduce their legislation.

Their difficulties with Lodge also shaped the strategy that insular authorities would begin to employ with Congress; indeed, Root's letter about Lodge is most revealing because it gives an indication of the importance he placed on information, particularly information supplied by his own bureau, in colonial lawmaking. That the Senate had attempted to legislate "without asking for any information on the subject" struck him as perfectly absurd; an experience that likely influenced his decision to mount an organized lobbying effort when it came time to pass the Philippine organic laws. For this, he would instruct the BIA to prepare – at enormous expense – thousands of pages of informational material for Congress. It may have been at this point, too, that Taft and Root decided to strengthen their relationship with the more pliable Chairman of the House Committee on Insular Affairs, Henry A. Cooper of Wisconsin, whom Taft would later describe as "much more efficient than Lodge."[117] Whether it was this event or something else, it is clear that within the first two years of Commission government, Cooper became the preferred conduit of the Commission and the BIA, and it was he, not Lodge, who would introduce the Organic Act as well as most subsequent legislation.[118]

Consequently, as it became increasingly unsatisfied with the progress of the Spooner Bill, the Commission began to lobby Congress itself – an early example of what would become standard operating procedure in its later struggles. In January of 1901, Taft cabled the War Department the Commission's thoughts on the urgency of the bill for their transmission to "proper Senators and Representatives." In the stilted English of the telegraph, the Commission warned Congress that "Sale of public lands and allowance of mining claims impossible until Spooner Bill. Hundreds of American miners on ground awaiting law to perfect claims. More coming. Good element in pacification. Urgently recommend amendment Spooner Bill so that its operation be not postponed until complete suppression of all insurrection but only until in President's judgment civil government may be safely established."[119] Although the Commission tended to paint a rosy portrait of the American adventurers who had recently arrived in the Philippines, privately, it seems, Taft was wary of them as well. Later that same year, he would dismiss them as "the rag tag and bob tail of Americans, who are not only vicious but stupid. They are most anxious to have Congress given an opportunity to open this country and develop it, but instead of facilitating a condition of peace and good feeling between

---

[117] Taft to Wright, April 11, 1902, quoted in Alfonso, *Theodore Roosevelt*, 88.

[118] My own archival investigation has confirmed Stanley's (*Nation in the Making*, n. 13, 288) claim that there is little evidence that Lodge initiated legislation or worked directly with insular authorities or the Commission to develop it. As a rule, his correspondence with Taft and Root is confined to discussions of bills that had previously been prepared by the BIA or were already introduced in the House by Rep. Cooper.

[119] Philippine Commission to Department of War, January 2, 1901; RG 350, "Correspondence of Philippine Commission," Box 1. The "hundreds of miners" the Commission predicted never arrived. Whether or not this was a deliberate fib is unknown, but it was certainly a generous interpretation of the situation.

the Americans and the Filipinos, they are constantly stirring up trouble."[120] While Taft and his fellow commissioners were anxious to develop the islands, they were insistent – and would remain so throughout the early period – that they were firmly in charge.[121]

It was not only the Senate that had concerns about possible exploitation. Root, the ever-cautious attorney, wanted the Commission government to begin on more sturdy statutory grounds than were provided by an amendment to an appropriations bill. In the near-term, as well, he wanted quick congressional authority for some of the Commission's actions, and so when it looked like Congress was becoming bogged down in debates over the planned economic development program, he decided to compromise. He wrote into the Spooner Bill certain restrictions on the Commission's power to sell or lease public lands, which were to be granted only with the president's express approval and which could not "without great public mischief" be postponed until the establishment of a permanent civil government.[122] Root's hope was that these issues could be revisited in the following session when the Philippine Organic Act would come up for a vote. Despite the acquiescence to a number of their demands, the opposition remained less than satisfied. As Senator Augustus Bacon (D-GA) would later recall, "The Spooner bill, as originally introduced in Congress, was one which had no limitation upon the power of exploitation, and that bill was not only introduced in Congress, but it was pressed under whip and spur. Everything was subordinated to it. We were threatened with extra sessions, and everything else, if it were not passed, and when it was passed, and the provision was put upon it which limited the power of exploitation, it was immediately dropped as a useless piece of furniture, and there has never been any action taken under it."[123]

In the end, the Spooner Bill, finally passed in March 1901, was a partial victory for the insular government. It created an exact separation between military and civil control in the Philippines, and gave civil authorities broad powers in their establishment of a civil government. But the Commission's plans for economic development, at least by way of traditional channels, were severely restricted. They could not sell or lease public land or develop the timber or mining industries, which they thought necessary to develop the islands. Yet Root and the BIA were clearly of the mind that this was a temporary situation. "In view of obstacles to industrial development caused by above legislation," Root cabled the Commission just days after the adoption of the Spooner Amendment, "desirable to lay before Congress

---

[120] Taft to Root, October 14, 1901; Root Papers, Box 164.

[121] The relationship between civil authorities and the "Manila Americans," most of whom had come to serve in supporting roles for the Army or were themselves former soldiers, remained tense throughout the Taft period. These Americans resented the civilian government's authority and thought they had wrongly empowered corrupt Filipinos through their policies of attraction. See Kramer, *Blood of Government*, 174–6. See also Edgar G. Bellairs, *As it is in the Philippines* (New York: Lewis, Scribner, 1902) for a sympathetic contemporary perspective on this group.

[122] Stanley, *Nation in the Making*, 88. The text of Spooner Amendment is available in Forbes, *Philippine Islands*, v. 2, Appendix 9.

[123] Cong. Rec., 57th Cong., 1st sess., 5670, quoted in Henry Parker Willis, *Our Philippine Problem: A Study of American Colonial Policy* (New York: Henry Holt & Co., 1905), 32–3, n. 1. Until his death, Sen. Bacon remained a fierce opponent of American colonization of the Philippines, but like most anti-imperialist Southern Democrats, his motivations were decidedly racist.

at opening of next session, for its approval, general railroad, land and mining laws. Begin preparation soon as possible."[124]

Congress, again, was seen as the major impediment to the development of a robust American colonial state. It simply refused to delegate broad independent authority to the colonial government to use public lands or to set its own trade policy. Consequently, the BIA now geared up to produce favorable reports and Taft prepared to journey back to Washington to present the Commission's case before Congress. If members of Congress were unwilling to acquire the information themselves, then insular authorities would inundate them with it.[125] The control of information and coordination among the Secretary's office, the BIA, and the Commission – a task eased considerably by the M-form design of colonial governance – became central to their strategy in the next round of enabling legislation.

This almost-paranoid devotion to the monopolization of the information quickly became a familiar part of the BIA's mission. Just weeks after the Spooner Amendment was adopted, Clarence Edwards, Chief of the BIA, cabled Taft to request "that all official communications to Executive Departments, Bureaus, Commissions, etcetera [sic], in addition to notifications of appointment to individuals should be sent through Division of Customs and Insular Affairs, War Department. Consider it essential to give War Department knowledge necessary for information and intelligent action."[126] Or, as one War Department official wrote to Edwards, "I understand that the Secretary has decided that hereafter this Division is to answer all the Senate Resolutions coming to the War Department . . . In other words it appears that the Insular Division will be the 'Big Gun' as regards the answering of Senate resolutions."[127] Indeed, Edwards instructed his employees to comb through the congressional record and prepare responses to any charges that were made against the colonial state.[128]

INFORMATION CONTROL AND CONGRESS

The Commission's frustration with the final form of the Spooner Amendment led it to launch a well-orchestrated public-relations campaign for the Philippine Organic Act – the law that would govern the colonial state for years. Both Root and Taft blamed Lodge for bungling the bill, and they also found fault with the lack of vigorous representation on the part of the Commission and the BIA. This time it would be different. Instead of Lodge, it would be Cooper in the House, who could be counted on to reliably introduce verbatim copies of insular legislation, with whom they would work most directly. As Clarence Edwards summed up both the goals and the strategy: "The desire in drafting this legislation is to grant the

[124] Root to Taft, March 5, 1901; RG 350, "Correspondence of Philippine Commission," Box 1.

[125] Given Root's background, that this was (and, of course, still is) a classic corporate strategy in antitrust lawsuits could hardly have been a coincidence. See Chapter 4 for a more thorough discussion of information production at the BIA.

[126] Edwards to Taft, March 20, 1901; RG 350, "Correspondence of the Philippine Commission," Box 1.

[127] War Department Official [name illegible] to Edwards, May 7, 1902; Edwards Papers, Box 2, Folder 2.

[128] Cruz, *America's Colonial Desk*, 89.

Philippine Islands the broadest powers possible, even in line with the Spooner bill, but," he conceded, "in a good many cases specific authority must be given and again we must listen to the practical prejudices of Congress."[129] To confront these practical prejudices, Taft would travel to Washington to present the case, and the BIA would busy itself in gathering favorable data.

During this period, the BIA began producing voluminous reports for Congress, usually on its own initiative. Indeed, the production of the so-called gazetteer of the Philippine Islands, designed "as a cumulative and progressive presentation of facts essential to reference upon any given subject," was among the first major tasks Root had given to the BIA.[130] Four thousand copies of the *Philippine Gazetteer* were printed at enormous expense in 1902, which, when combined with a supplementary report on the Philippines for that year, amounted to nearly 40 percent of the *entire* Senate printing bill (excluding executive and legislative documents) for the first session of the 57th Congress; 1,000 copies were sent to the Senate, 2,000 to the House, and another 1,000 to the War Department.[131] It is also clear that at this time individual members of Congress began to rely more heavily on these BIA reports. In one revealing episode, Senator Platt (R-CT) wrote to Edwards to thank him for "Magoon's [law officer of the BIA] opinion with regard to Philippine franchises." But, Platt noted, "I have not received the report on the forestry in the Philippines. I wish you would send me as published all the documents relating to the Philippine and Cuban situation issued by the Insular Division."[132] In reply, Edwards promised to send the report and noted how "very refreshing to have a Senator take such interest as do you in these two great problems."[133]

To gain the "broadest powers possible," both Root and the Commission were well aware that they needed a stronger statute than an Army appropriations act. Their authority under the Spooner Act still depended in part on the president's powers as commander-in-chief, and Root was anxious to gain independent authorization for civil governance. Writing to Taft several months after the adoption of the Spooner Act, he noted that "the form in which the present arrangements for civil government have been cast has as one of its causes a desire to continue the exercise of the President's power under the constitution, and if possible at the same time, give to what is done the sanction of Congressional authority under the Spooner amendment." To accomplish this, Root continued, "we want to do what is done in such a way that it will have behind it all the authority which the President has from any source, instead of casting loose from military power under the constitution and standing simply on the Spooner Act."[134] Taft expressed a similar opinion in his report on October 1, 1901, in which he urged Congress to "confirm the legislation of the commission already enacted, and vest Congressional enactment in the civil

---

129 Edwards to Luke Wright, December 30, 1901; Edwards Papers, Box 1, Folder 25.
130 "Gazetteer of the Philippine Islands," S. Doc. No. 461, 59th Cong., 1st sess., 3.
131 "Cost of Printing Certain Documents Ordered by the Senate," S. Rep. 1, 58th Cong., 1st sess. The *Gazetteer* proved a hit and another 1,000 copies were ordered printed in 1903. By 1906, Taft requested a concurrent resolution to produce a second edition, published once again at congressional expense.
132 Platt to Edwards, October 1, 1901; Edwards Papers, Box 1, Folder 24.
133 Edwards to Platt, October 3, 1901; Edwards Papers, Box 1, Folder 24.
134 Root to Taft, June 20, 1901, quoted in Jessup, *Elihu Root*, v. 1, 361.

governor and commission and their successors to be appointed by the President the authority heretofore exercised by them under the instructions of the President."[135]

What the insular government desired most of all, however, was the power to grant franchises, to survey and sell public lands, and to develop mining interests.[136] This, they thought, held the key to success, both to bring much-needed industrialization to the Philippines and also to provide the empire with a strong domestic constituency. The Commission recommended that Congress reduce "by at least 50 per cent the United States duty on tobacco, hemp, and other merchandise coming from the Philippine Islands into the United States," and the power to grant municipal franchises, mine laws, regulate timber, sell public land, and issue charters to railroads.[137] To attract the interest of American capital in developing the islands, the Commission immediately set to work gathering and publicizing data on the population and industries of the island; a Bureau of Statistics was established, along with a Bureau of Forestry and a Bureau of Mining to "investigate and conserve these two sources of latent wealth of the archipelago."[138]

The Commission's efforts to court members of Congress were not limited to the publication of reports; they also invited them to tour the Philippines and to see for themselves the good works the Commission was doing. Accordingly, the first of several congressional fact-finding missions visited the Philippines in the fall of 1901. The visiting members of Congress gave a number of speeches in pacified towns, where Commission authorities, working with the *ilustrados*, had arranged for appropriately patriotic displays. Towns were festooned with American flags and Filipino children were taught to sign songs (in English!) for the entertainment of the visiting dignitaries.[139]

Taft thought the visit a success in moderating the opinions of the more extreme anti-imperialists and earning the favor of moderate Republicans, yet it did little to change his negative evaluation of members of Congress and their ability to effectively govern the islands. In fact, as he later noted with some surprise, it was the Republican members of the delegation who most embarrassed the Commission. Republican Congressman Edgar Weeks of Michigan, it seems, earned the special ire of insular authorities by expressing some "rather rabid and various foolish ideas about the Filipinos" in an interview with the American-owned *Manila Times*. As Taft's private secretary, James LeRoy, later remembered the episode, "Among other things, [Weeks] estimates them to be 'little better than savages, with a thin veneer of civilization.'" That, LeRoy noted wryly, "was, of course, promptly seized on by the Spanish press, first of all by *Progreso* [a major opposition newspaper], and was run in full, with the words 'little better than savages' underscored."[140] The Commission, which desperately needed the continued support of Filipinos elites, was

[135] US War Department, *Reports of the Philippine Commission, the Civil Governor, and the Executive Departments of the Civil Government of the Philippine Islands, 1900–1903* (Washington, DC: Government Printing Office, 1904), 272.

[136] Elliott, *The Philippines to the End of Commission Government*, 6–10.

[137] *Reports of the Philippine Commission, 1900–1903*, 273.

[138] Daniel R. Williams, *The Odyssey of the Philippine Commission* (Chicago: A. C. McClurg, 1913), 94–5.

[139] LeRoy Journal, September 9, 1901; LeRoy Papers; Box 1.

[140] LeRoy Travelogue, entries for October 8 and 9, 1901; LeRoy Papers, Box 1.

horrified: "Weeks is an ass," a furious Taft wrote to Root, "but asses sometimes have great capacity for mischief."[141]

The congressional junket probably did little to change the Commission's opinion that Congress was not to be trusted with the Organic Act. In fact, no episode better conveys the increasing insularity of the colonial government than Henry Cabot Lodge's relative ignorance of the development of the legislation. If any member of Congress was expected to have intimate knowledge of the insular government's work on the Act, it was Lodge; yet he seemed to be left completely in the dark. Work on the Act had commenced just weeks after the Spooner Bill was adopted, and by the late spring hundreds of cables on the bill's progress had been exchanged between Washington and Manila.[142] By the summer, Root was in search of someone to study the currency system and Charles Magoon of the BIA was busy developing laws to govern property and business in the Philippines. Lodge, however, had no knowledge of any of these developments. In June of 1901, he wrote to Root to ask what the "idea is in regard" to the Organic legislation, "because the Philippine legislation will necessarily be in the hands of my Committee." "When any draft of a bill is made," Lodge continued, "or of any legislation, for the Philippines, if you would kindly send me a copy I should be very much indebted, for I should like to have an opportunity to study it during the summer and familiarize myself with it."[143] By late July, Lodge, who had still not seen any evidence of the bill, warned, "If the Commission have not one ready it would be impossible for Congress to frame one."[144]

To all of these pleas, Root replied that it was best for him to wait: "I do not expect to have anything for Congress to tear to pieces before the middle of October," he advised Lodge, "and if you return then you will be in ample time." He did, however, note that "there should be a series of specific acts governing the tariff, public lands, mines and corporate franchises, leaving the Commission to work out the form and machinery of government under the general rules which have been prescribed." In any case, he added, "I presume that no committee sitting in Washington would work the subject out so well as Taft and his associates can do in Manila, dealing from day to day with the practical problems as they arise."[145] In his reply several weeks later, Lodge agreed "entirely with the specific acts" Root mentioned, but thought it "best to put them all in our bill." There was, he warned, "a certain amount of fight to be met."[146] By the late fall, Lodge was still awaiting word from the Commission on the progress of the Organic Act.

The Philippine Organic Act: Restrictions on Colonial Development

The Organic Act as drafted by the War Department over the summer of 1901 and introduced to both houses on January 7, 1902 devoted large sections to mining and

---

[141] Taft to Root, October 14, 1901; Root Papers, Box 164.
[142] They are too numerous to list. See the cables in RG 350, "Correspondence of Philippine Commission," Box 1.
[143] Lodge to Root, June 7, 1901; Root Papers, Box 161.
[144] Lodge to Root, July 29, 1901; Root Papers, Box 161.
[145] Root to Lodge, July 1, 1901; Root Papers, Box 161.
[146] Lodge to Root, July 29, 1901; Root Papers, Box 161.

forestry laws, and to the creation of a new currency and banking system.[147] The Commission further recommended that Congress reduce tobacco and hemp duties by half, and grant the Commission broad powers to distribute public lands up to 5,000 acres.[148] These provisions, they knew, would encounter significant opposition from tobacco and sugar-beet interests worried about competition from the Philippines, and from Democrats and anti-imperialists opposed to encouraging investment in the islands. A marked-up version of the bill in the BIA's own records states frankly that Sections 1 through 12 (the administrative and law portion) were drafted by Charles Magoon, the BIA's law officer.[149] This was the bill that was distributed to Cooper and Lodge to introduce in the House and Senate, respectively.

By this point, Taft had arrived in Washington and was ready to personally present the Commission's case before Congress where the BIA was "night and day at work in the interests of the Philippines Government."[150] With Taft gone, the BIA stayed in constant communication with Vice Governor Luke Wright in Manila, providing him with cabled updates and copies of the Congressional Record so the Commission could stay abreast of the bill's progress. "We anticipate a terrible fight," Edwards reported to Wright. "Most of the Democrats believe you have horns," but, he assured Wright, the BIA had gained "the silent support of the biggest men in the Senate and House."[151] At this point, there was not much the Commission could do but wait. Wright (himself a Democrat) worried about the "extent of the partisan feeling developed in Congress," but he remained confident in Root's "ability to give to Congress the benefit of his knowledge and to impress his views upon them."[152]

Yet when Taft and Root arrived to testify before the Committee on the Philippines, American public opinion had already begun to sour on the imperial experiment. The Committee, which had begun an extensive investigation on military conduct during the Philippine insurrection, had created a tremendous amount of bad press for the Army, and civil authorities were eager to distance themselves from these reports

---

[147] The official title of the act announced that the Islands were to eventually gain independence: "An Act Temporarily to Provide for the Administration of the Affairs of Civil Government in the Philippine Islands, and for Other Purposes." The mining law had been prepared previously. See "Letter Transmitting Draft of a Mining Law for the Philippines," in *Report of the Philippine Commission, 1901*, 151–9.

[148] *Report of the Philippine Commission, 1901*, 149–50. The Commission also made extensive changes to the Philippines' internal tariff rules. See Philippine Commission Act No. 230 in Division of Insular Affairs, *Public Laws and Resolutions Passed by the United States Philippine Commission* (Washington, DC: Government Printing Office, 1903), 645–79. The Spooner Act had provided a 25 percent reduction in the Dingley rates. A marked-up version of the bill in the BIA's own records shows that Sections 1 through 12 (the administrative and law portion) were drafted by Charles Magoon, the BIA's law officer, while the sections concerned with banking and development were written by other officials employed by the colonial state. The draft bill is available in RG 350, "Correspondence of Philippine Commission," Box 1.

[149] A marked-up copy of the bill is available in RG 350, "Correspondence of Philippine Commission," Box 1.

[150] In late November of the previous year, the final decision was made to send Taft back to Washington. See LeRoy Travelogue, entry dated November 29, 1901, LeRoy Papers, Box 1.

[151] Edwards to Luke Wright, December 30, 1901; Edwards Papers, Box 1, Folder 25. Taft and Root could, however, count Henry Cooper, the chairman of the House Committee on Insular Affairs, as an ally.

[152] Wright to Edwards, February 20, 1902; Edwards Papers, Box 2, Folder 1.

as quickly as possible.[153] Despite the bad press, the testimony of insular authorities before Cooper's committee demonstrates their desire for more congressional discretion at every point – indeed, it is hard to read their testimony as anything less than strategic in this respect. When asked, for example, whether land purchases ought to be restricted, Root responded that he was "in favor of giving a very wide scope" to the Commission. "Although I am not much of a believer in the wisdom of having very large tracts of land owned by any one concern," he continued, "I think that you can safely put discretion in the Philippine government on the subject." During his testimony, Taft pressed Congress to liberalize American tariff rates for Philippine products, and his forceful defense of the islands reveals the Commission's increasing self-identification as professional advocates for the colonial state:

Governor TAFT. I should like to make clear the attitude of the Commission, if I may, with respect to this change of the Dingley law and its application to the products of and importations from the Philippine Islands. Our recommendations are based upon our views of the needs of the Philippine Islands and the benefit to the trade of those islands. We are asking as much as we can get, because the more we get the better we think it will be for the islands. The effect upon the policy of the United States and particular interests in the United States that will be affected we have very little knowledge of and desire to express no opinion. I hope that explanation –

Senator PATTERSON. You would not knowingly advocate any policy that would injure the industries of the United States – your own country?

Governor TAFT. I do not think I would. We do not approach it from the standpoint of those interests, however.[154]

The hearings before the Committee also reveal the increasing dependency of Congress on the BIA and War Department reports for information about the islands. Even opponents of the Act and the imperial project itself were left to combat it using the BIA's own publications, and their reliance on this strategy often left them grasping at straws, or, ironically, insisting on the veracity of the BIA's own reports. For example, consider Taft once again sparring with Colorado's Thomas Patterson:

Senator PATTERSON. In this connection I wish to call your attention to a letter from the Secretary of War transmitting an "Article on the people of the Philippines, compiled in the Division of Insular Affairs of the War Department," and transmitted to the chairman of this committee, Senator Lodge. This paper, speaking of the Tagals, uses this language:

Most of them, both men and women can read and write.

Is that a correct statement?

Governor TAFT. No, sir; it is not.

Senator PATTERSON. Further, I should like to call your attention –

Governor TAFT. If you will permit me, I gained my information from tax collectors, who have to find out.

[153] The extensive and aggressive investigation into the Army's conduct in the Philippines, particularly its use of torture to extract information from Filipino insurgents, is yet another demonstration on the active role it intended to take in foreign affairs. See Linn, *U.S. Army and Counterinsurgency*.

[154] 57th Cong., 1st sess.; S. Doc. No. 331, pt. 1, 158. This rather frank statement would come back to haunt Taft in subsequent treaty negotiations when opposition members trotted it out as evidence the Commission actively worked against the interests of the United States.

Senator PATTERSON. This document is sent to us in this way, and I should like to read some further statements made in this communication from the War Department by some officials, compiled in the Division of Insular Affairs, with reference to the Filipinos, and to ask what you have to say about it.[155]

Throughout the exchange, which goes on for some time, Patterson makes repeated references to the "official" nature of the document and its publication by the "authority of the War Department and the insular division thereof." In truth, the document Senator Patterson was quoting from was a compilation of returning officers' impressions of the Filipinos; it was published by the BIA, but the BIA did not endorse all the opinions. The point, however, is this: Even at this early stage, the lack of independent information from the islands left members of Congress at the mercy of the BIA for most of their knowledge. Increasingly, they were left to rely on Senator Patterson's strategy of sifting through official reports to find contradictory facts. While this was often effective, it left them with no choice but to concede the accuracy of the BIA's and the Commission's official reports, which left Congress increasingly dependent on insular authorities.

Despite Taft's spirited defense, when the bill was finally reported out of committee at the end of March significant compromises had been made. Republicans on the committee from sugar-beet regions worried about the development of Philippine sugar plantations that would compete with domestic supplies. As a result, Lodge's committee report recommended the reduction of individual leases from 160 to 40 acres and prohibited the lease of public land to corporations until a law regulating the disposition of the public lands was enacted.[156] Why Lodge was so willing to amend sections of his own bill is hard to explain. Lodge later justified it on paternalistic grounds, writing to a potential investor at the time that "in the long run it would be more just to the people of the islands and more for their ultimate peace, prosperity, and good government" to regulate land speculation on the islands.[157] While this may have been true, it is also likely that Lodge feared that the bill would become stalled in committee without his quick acquiescence to sugar interests. This would have given Cooper in the House, whose Committee on Insular Affairs had not yet reported a bill, the upper hand, and further diminished Lodge's position as the central legislative actor in insular affairs.

Whatever Lodge's reasons, this maneuver did not improve his standing with insular authorities who were convinced that his motivations were entirely selfish. Taft was absolutely furious about the amended bill, calling it "one of Lodge's subterfuges to avoid criticism" and Lodge himself "one of the most cowardly men I know." Writing to Luke Wright, Taft complained of Lodge, "He does not hesitate to surrender something of real interest to the Islands in order to avoid criticism provided only he can carry his bill."[158] To get around Lodge, Taft instructed Cooper

---

[155] 57th Cong., 1st sess.; S. Doc. No. 331, pt. 1, 93. The "tagals" or tagalogs were the Hispanicized population and generally considered by Americans of the time to be among the most "civilized" people of the islands.

[156] 57th Cong., 1st sess.; S. Rep. No. 915.

[157] Quoted in Glenn May, *Social Engineering in the Philippines: The Aims, Execution, and Impact of American Colonial Policy, 1900–1913* (Westport, CT: Greenwood Press, 1980), 152.

[158] Taft to Wright, June 22, 1902, quoted in Alfonso, *Theodore Roosevelt and the Philippines*, 89; May, *Social Engineering*, 152.

to prepare a substitute bill, which authorized the Commission sell up to 5,000 acres to corporations, and he asked Cooper to press House Republicans on this issue. Cooper successfully reported Taft's bill out of the House Committee on Insular Affairs, apparently using Taft's letters to influence "many members of the House."[159]

The floor debate began on April 18, 1902. In the Senate, the insular government's supporters encountered fierce opposition from anti-imperialists and Westerners with significant sugar-beet interests in their states. While most of the debate centered on the specific franchise and land grant provisions, some senators did oppose the immense delegation of administrative authority to the Commission. Senator Rawlings of Utah, among the most impassioned anti-imperialists, argued that the restrictions on land sales and franchise laws were barely restrictions at all compared to the immense powers Congress had delegated to the Commission. "[T]hese limitations upon the exercise of arbitrary power are in no degree restrictions upon the President, or upon the Secretary of War, or upon the oligarchy known as the United States Philippine Commission," he argued. "Any one of those agencies of government in the Philippine Islands is left with a free hand to violate every one of those cardinal rules, which are declared as to their subordinates, to be inviolable."[160] In other words, the minor restrictions placed on the Commission's ability to distribute lands were insignificant compared to its powers to suppress speech, pass arbitrary laws, and rule independent of democratic checks. This development was apparent even to contemporary observers. As one American touring the islands wrote in 1905, "The Commission, subject to the action of Congress, has been given a free hand to work out its plans for the Philippine Islands without obstruction."[161]

In the end, however, Congress was happy to enforce those aspects of colonial legislation that directly affected its own domestic political interests. The final bill seriously compromised the Commission's development plans. Although Root would cable Manila to congratulate the commissioners on the "continuance and enlargement of your authority," the final bill dramatically reduced the Commission's ability to attract American capital to the islands by forbidding the Commission to sell or lease more than 40 acres of land to individuals or 2,500 acres for corporations.[162] Further restrictions were applied to the timber sales and individual miners were restricted to one claim on the same mineral vein. For insular authorities, the more significant defeat was over tariff legislation. The Philippine Tariff Act of 1902 adopted on March 8 only allowed for a 25 percent reduction in Dingley tariff rates, the same provided in the Spooner Amendment. As Wright cabled Taft in Washington on hearing the news, "This is prohibitive and if expressive of ultimate policy most unfortunate."[163]

---

[159] Cooper to Taft, September 27, 1902, quoted in Alfonso, *Theodore Roosevelt and the Philippines*, 91.

[160] Cong. Rec., 57th Cong., 1st sess., 4523–5.

[161] Willis, *Our Philippine Problem*, 24.

[162] Root to Wright, June 2, 1902; Root Papers, Box 165.

[163] Wright to Taft, March 1, 1902; Root Papers, Box 165. Congress did, however, grant free trade to Puerto Rico before taking up the Philippine Tariff Act, and this may have led anti-imperialists to be even more resistant to the liberalization of Philippine trade. For an analysis of how this difference influenced the state-building trajectories of these two colonies, see Julian Go, "The Chains of Empire," in *The American Colonial State in the Philippines: Global Perspectives*, ed. Julian Go and Anne L. Foster (Durham, NC: Duke University Press, 2003).

Consider, for a moment, just how restrictive these limitations were. Congress had, for all practical purposes, *prohibited* American investment in its *own colony* by restricting land ownership and, through its refusal to significantly lower the Dingley tariffs, had made the export of raw materials from the Philippines to the United States largely unprofitable. By granting it no appropriations, by restricting its ability to attract investments, and by refusing to lower American tariff rates in any significant way, Congress had designed the Philippine colonial state to fail. This was a blow to the insular government, and it would portend the long struggle of insular authorities to fix this; indeed, just months later Taft was already cabling to the War Department the Commission's wish to put a tariff reduction before Congress yet again.[164]

Nevertheless, there were reasons to be optimistic. In their battle with Congress, colonial bureaucrats were able to gain a significant degree of autonomy to run the Philippines and, through the unique organizational form of colonial administration, to control information about the colony. Furthermore, Taft, now back in Manila, thought there was little more political hay to be made of the issues that motivated the anti-imperialists. "[W]hat little I have seen leads me to suppose that the Democrats have not found the Philippine issue, including the alleged atrocities, to be as full of successful material for them as they thought," he wrote to Root in June.[165] Naturally, the colonial government would not dare to directly flout the will of Congress, but congressional restrictions would not stop them from exploring other ways to achieve their goals for an expansive American empire.

[164] Philippine Commission to Department of War, October 4, 1902; Root Papers, Box 164.
[165] Taft to Root, June 5, 1902; Edwards Papers, Box 2, Folder 6.

4

Building a Colonial State in the Philippines

> The whole thing illustrates how foolish our representatives can be when dealing with something that does not affect their chances of reelection and concerning which they have no knowledge, nor the ambition to acquire it.
> —Daniel Williams, Secretary to the Philippine Commission[1]

On July 4, 1901, 125 years after throwing off its own colonial shackles, the United States commenced its "imperial experiment" in the Philippines as William Howard Taft took the oath of office to become the first governor-general. While serving on the Second Philippine Commission, Taft had concluded that education, improved infrastructure, sound money, and favorable tariffs would stimulate trade with the United States and transform the islands from a backwater in Spain's quickly crumbling empire into a showcase of American progress. "Nothing will civilize them so much as the introduction of American enterprise and capital here," the future governor had written to Henry Cabot Lodge the year before.[2] Honest administration, Taft thought, maintained through strong civil service laws would give necessary, but limited, support for these projects, and local elections would allow Filipinos some practical experience with democracy. Finally, American wanderlust would provide a steady stream of miners and loggers to extract the rich deposits of minerals and harvest the forests for timber.[3]

Taft never changed his mind that these Progressive Republican policies were the right ones. Despite his grandiose title, he had limited resources at his disposal to impose these modernization projects on the Philippines. Congress had appropriated no money for civil governance and American capitalists were hesitant to invest when domestic tariff rates remained so high. American public opinion had grown increasingly tepid toward America's imperial conquest in Asia due to congressional hearings on the horrific methods used to subdue Filipino revolutionaries during the war. To make matters worse, Taft was welcomed back to the islands by

---

[1] Williams, *Odyssey of the Philippine Commission*, 164.
[2] Taft to Lodge, October 17, 1900, quoted in May, *Social Engineering*, 142.
[3] For Taft's initial impressions, see the letters in RG 350, "Correspondence of Philippine Commission," Box 1.

an outbreak of cholera that threatened thousands of lives and an infestation of the rinderpest parasite, which killed off 90 percent of the carabaos, the Philippine water buffalos crucial for rice farming.[4] These two epidemics, coupled with six years of civil unrest, had so devastated rice production that the new governor-general had to confront the very real possibility of a widespread famine throughout the Philippines. Taft's dreams of Yankee capital and sugar plantations were quickly replaced by the daily reality of dead carabaos and famine conditions.

To make the Philippines the shining example of American progress that they envisioned, it became clear to Taft and to his fellow officials that they would have to play a much more active role in economic development. The Commission would need to do far more than to maintain law and order on the islands; it would need to rely on its own resources to develop the archipelago and achieve the commissioners ideological goal of creating a colony in the image of American Progressivism. Thus, the *inability* to gain robust congressional support to tap the resources from the American state shaped Taft's strategy of colonial administration from the beginning – one that would eventually increase its autonomy from Congress.

The Commission and its allies at the BIA would continue to lobby Congress for more favorable legislation and, initially, they engaged in a series of misguided publicity campaigns to increase public interest in the islands. Nevertheless, insular authorities quickly learned to rely on other strategies to "develop" the islands. This chapter traces how they coped with congressional roadblocks not by flouting the restrictions imposed on them by Congress, but by cultivating new sources of power (however unstable) that attracted little congressional attention. In a lesson that would have profound effects on the development of the American external state, insular authorities learned to take advantage of Congress's short time horizons to create their own, nearly autonomous colony in Asia by embracing a policy of inconspicuous action and forming collaborative partnerships with American bankers.

FIDELITY TO THE COLONIAL STATE: THE CIVIL SERVICE AND THE CONSTABULARY

Progressive ideas of government efficiency guided the goals of American colonial administrators from the earliest days, making American imperialism less "tutelary" than prescriptive – and the civil service became an early test of their philosophy. Given the dominance of Progressive intellectuals and attorneys on the Philippine Commission, it should come as no surprise that one of their first legislative acts was the establishment of an independent civil service. The fifth act of the Philippine Commission on September 19, 1900 mandated an examination for all civil service appointments. The reasons for this were practically axiomatic for Taft and his colleagues. As they were well aware, the American consular service had remained an incompetent mess for years as a result of Congress's predilection for filling every slot with men whose political connections were far superior to their diplomatic skills.[5] Taft, in his inaugural address as governor-general put it bluntly: "The

---

[4] This is Taft's estimate. See Taft to Root, November 15, 1902; Root Papers, Box 164.
[5] Ironically, the spoils system was later embraced by Filipino leaders. See Patricio N. Abinales, "Progressive-Machine Conflict in Early-Twentieth-Century U.S. Politics and Colonial-State

[colonial] Civil Service is the bulwark of honesty and efficiency in the government," he exclaimed. "It avoids the marked evil of American politics, the spoils system. Without it, success in solving our problem would be impossible."[6] The Commission, after all, was not interested in American government as it was, but American government as these technocratic reformers thought it ought to be. Such a policy would have been a novelty for most state-level bureaucracies in the United States; at the time, only three states had adopted such laws, and the Philippine civil service had arguably adopted the most stringent requirements for employment.[7]

Their ideological goals were not the only motivation for a technocratic colonial service, however. An independent civil service allowed for more efficient governance, but it also created a body of bureaucrats largely free of congressional control – and loyal, not to their party at home, but to the colonial administrators in the Philippines. According to the official policy, at least, qualified Filipinos were given first preference for jobs, then honorably discharged American military personnel were considered, and finally general American citizens.[8] This policy served the dual purpose of co-opting certain Filipinos, while also giving American soldiers a chance to stay in the islands. By sealing off colonial positions from congressional spoils and giving preference to former members of the military and Filipinos, the insular government simultaneously limited congressional interest by denying members patronage positions and guaranteed that the Americans in the insular service would maintain their loyalties to the colonial state, rather than to metropolitan political parties. With this decision, jobs in the colonial service, a possible source for patronage appointments, were taken off the table.

This is not to say that members of Congress made no appeals to the BIA to find jobs for party loyalists. To be sure, the archival records contain hundreds of letters requesting "special consideration" for an esteemed constituent. In most cases, the BIA answered that insular appointments were strictly governed by the rules of the Philippine civil service commission and that they could make no exceptions. "I am sorry to say that there is nothing I can personally do in the way of appointing Mr. Spratt," began a February 1902 letter from the BIA to Senator Penrose of Pennsylvania. "This Department makes no direct appointments of this nature, the same being under the sole jurisdiction of the insular authorities and embraced under the Philippine civil service."[9] The relative lack of spoils appointments became a major point of pride among the top insular officials. "No officer, high or low," Root noted in his 1901 *Annual Report*, "has been appointed upon any one's

Building in the Philippines," in *The American Colonial State in the Philippines: Global Perspectives*, ed. Julian Go and Anne L. Foster (Durham, NC: Duke University Press, 2003).

6 Quoted in Visitacion R. De La Torre, *History of the Philippine Civil Service* (Quezon City: New Day, 1986), 53.

7 Joseph Ralston Hayden, *The Philippines: A Study in National Development* (New York: Macmillan, 1942), 89.

8 US Bureau of Insular Affairs, *What Has Been Done in the Philippines: A Record of Practical Accomplishments under Civil Government* (Washington, DC: Government Printing Office, 1904).

9 BIA to Senator Penrose, February 1, 1902, RG 350, General Files, Letters Sent (bound letter books), v. 36, 417. The letter books in the BIA files have hundreds of examples of similar appeals – all denied.

request, or upon any personal, social, or political consideration. The general power of appointment was vested by the instructions of April seventh in the Commission, which is eight thousand miles removed from all American pressure for office, and which will stand or fall upon its success or failure in getting competent men."[10] So important was this policy to the insular government that Roosevelt made special mention of it in his inaugural address, insisting that in the colonial service "heed should be paid to absolutely nothing save the man's own character and capacity and the needs of the service."[11]

The adherence to civil service rules, however, did not translate into the creation of an elite corp of bureaucrats along the lines of the British India Office. The tests (given in English and Spanish) were, as a rule, fairly simple affairs designed for a solider of average education and intelligence. Consider the questions from one civil service exam given in the early days of colonial era:

Spell the words Philippines, qualify, principle, and civilization.
On April 7th a Manila merchant desires to obtain $1440. For how much must he give his note, due September 14th, without interest, to obtain the required sum when discounted at the rate of 9% per annum?
Name five American statesmen who died before 1850.[12]

This was a far cry from the famously difficult British test which required, among other things, "a general acquaintance with the works of Chaucer, Langland, Shakespeare, Milton, Dryden, Pope, Gray, Collins, Johnson, Goldsmith, Crabbe, Cowper, Campbell, Wordsworth, Scott, Byron, Keats, Shelley, Coleridge, Bacon, Sir Thomas Browne, Cowley, Bunyan, Swift, Defoe, Addison, Burke, and Macaulay," as well as a section on Sanskrit language and literature including the ability to translate Sanskrit into English and English into Sanskrit.[13]

Even top-level officials were recruited in a self-consciously nonpartisan way. In fact, social or class connections appear to have trumped partisanship, another factor that cut off the colonial government from the partisan discipline of other American bureaucracies. Both Governors Luke Wright and James Smith were (gold) Democrats, and Governor Cameron Forbes, while a nominal Republican, had a patrician's disgust for politics in general, and had never held political office. Roosevelt, it seems, had maintained it as a matter of personal pride that he had little knowledge of any colonial official's political beliefs – a fact that he apparently expounded upon at great length whenever the subject came up.[14]

---

[10] US Department of War, *Annual Report from the Secretary of War for 1901* (Washington, DC: Government Printing Office, 1902).
[11] Theodore Roosevelt, Inaugural Address, *A Compilation of the Messages and Papers of the Presidents 1789–1905*, ed. James D. Richardson (Washington, DC: Bureau of National Literature and Art, 1907), v. 10, 449.
[12] From the official Civil Service Manual, quoted in Willis, *Our Philippine Problem*, 55.
[13] Alleyne Ireland, *Outlook* (December 24, 1904), quoted in Willis, *Our Philippine Problem*, 55.
[14] Years later, as colonial governor, Cameron Forbes wrote in his journal,

> [Roosevelt] took occasion to say that there was absolutely no politics in Philippine appointments, and asked me if any political influence had been brought on me in regard to any places there. I answered, "None whatever," and turning, added low to [Roosevelt's daughter] Alice, "I wonder what your father knows about my politics."

With the exception of certain high-level appointments of Filipino elites to positions such as head of the civil service commission and chief justice of the Supreme Court, Americans filled most of the higher civil service roles during the first decade of American rule – a decision that left them firmly in control of the colonial state. The Commission was especially cautious to appoint Americans to positions in the legal system and to roles that would allow them careful supervision of provincial spending, which they justified with the questionable assertion that Filipinos were more corrupt than Americans. As early as 1900, Taft wrote to a friend, reflecting on the perceived corruption of the Filipino judicial system, "We are obliged therefore, much against our will, to fill the judicial office generally with American lawyers."[15]

Yet preferential hiring of Filipinos and American Army personnel was also a matter of necessity. The distance and supposedly dangerous conditions made it difficult to recruit qualified officials from the United States. During the height of the cholera epidemic, Edwards, who as chief of the BIA did most of the recruiting in the United States, cabled Taft, "Large number of declinations Philippine appointments probably due to cholera scare. Can we say any thing favorable; if so, what?"[16] Tellingly, the answer was not forthcoming.

The difficulty of recruiting Americans was only part of the problem. They were also significantly more expensive. Throughout the colonial period, Americans were paid much more than Filipinos for the same work, a policy justified by the dubious reasoning that Filipinos would need less money to support themselves.[17] For example, a senior Filipino clerk in the Bureau of Audits was paid ₱1,800, while a slightly more junior American was paid ₱2,800.[18] To fill professional positions, such as teachers and attorneys, the Commission was forced to pay Americans significantly more than they could make in the United States. American teachers, for instance, could earn between $75 and $125 per month, a significant improvement over the average monthly salary of $54 for men and $40 for women in rural schools back home.[19]

To be sure, there never were that many Americans employed in the Philippines, but those who did join the Philippine civil service tended to stay and to remain loyal to the American regime. The total number of American civil service employees topped out at a little over 3,000 in 1905, and began a slow decline until it stabilized at about 2,500 employees for the remainder of the Republican era. The great majority of American civil servants were teachers or officers in the colonial police force, and despite the distance and climate, many American officials remained in

Although talking to someone else, and with his head turned, he turned immediately and answered with great emphasis and much amusement, "I know nothing whatever about your politics but I suspect you of being a mugwump."

Forbes Papers, Journal, January 1906, 376–7.

[15] Taft to Henry M. Hoyt, August 16, 1900; Root Papers, Box 1, Folder 16.

[16] Edwards to Taft, October 28, 1903; Root Papers, Box 165.

[17] See US Bureau of Insular Affairs, *Report of the Philippine Bureau of Civil Service* (Washington, DC: Government Printing Office, 1903–12) for salary data. Unlike most European colonial states, however, Filipinos were placed directly in charge of lower-level American officials.

[18] Government of the Philippine Islands, Bureau of Civil Service, *Official Roster of Officers and Employees in the Civil Service of the Philippine Islands* (Manila: Bureau of Printing, 1908), 13. Note: Throughout the colonial period, the Philippine peso was pegged at 50 percent of US $1.

[19] May, *Social Engineering*, 85.

the employ of the colonial state for years. The 1908 civil service roster, for example, shows that in the American-dominated Bureau of Audits, the heads of every department but the railroad division had been members of the Philippine civil service since 1901, while the average tenure for American division chiefs in the Bureau of Customs was seven years.[20]

In large part this relatively long tenure was due to the fact that colonial civil servants were employees of the Philippine civil service, not the federal civil service, which meant that they were unable to maintain their seniority or to make a lateral transfer should they leave the islands. As a result, the BIA reported, "they find that they can not take up again their professions or occupations at home where they left off on entering the Philippine service."[21] This final restriction made it so difficult to recruit highly skilled Americans to the colonial service that the BIA had worked out an agreement with the US Civil Service Commission to allow returning employees of the colonial service to maintain their status. Nevertheless, this understanding applied "irregularly and to certain classes of employees." This put the BIA and the Commission in a difficult position. Allowing colonial civil servants to easily return home would make it easier recruit experts from the United States, but it also might begin a slow bleed of its employees as they found equivalent jobs back home. The solution to both problems, the BIA concluded, was to develop a retirement and pension system for Americans in the Philippines – a move that reveals their plans to occupy the archipelago for decades. Although never adopted during the Republican period of colonial administration, the law the BIA proposed in 1907 granted pension benefits to American members of the colonial service, but restricted access only to employees with ten or more years of service in the islands.[22] For insular officials, however, the long tenure and relative loyalty to the colonial service meant that they had at their command an experienced and disciplined bureaucratic force whose members had a direct material interest in making the colonial experiment work.[23]

---

[20] *Civil Service of the Philippine Islands*, 13–15. This is not to suggest that there were no problems with the civil employees. The treasurer of Rizal, the province surrounding Manila, was involved in a rather notorious scandal – a situation that made Taft furious. "When he came I thought I was very fortunate in being able to appoint him," he wrote to Edwards.

> It now seems that he was grossly incompetent . . . his chief clerk, who by the way had been selected through the Department Assistant examination by the United States Civil Service in Washington, was able to steal a good many thousands of dollars – how many is not yet ascertained . . . The examiners think that Sinclair is guiltless of dishonesty, but his gross incompetence is enough to make one use profanity. He seems to have been an ineffable ass, which is not punishable under our law by imprisonment, but I think it ought to be.

Taft to Edwards, March 2, 1903; Edwards Papers, Box 2, Folder 19.

[21] US Philippine Commission, *Report of the Philippine Commission to the Secretary of War, 1908* (Washington, DC: Government Printing Office, 1909), Part I, 24.

[22] Ibid., 24.

[23] A later governor, Cameron Forbes, took a great deal of pride in the independence of the colonial civil service. After Woodrow Wilson entered the White House, and before he was replaced as colonial governor, Forbes wrote the newly elected president:

> I would like to say in closing that I believe this Government very fortunate because of the men at the head of the various Bureaus. They compare favorably with men to be found in commercial enterprises and have been selected entirely on a non-partisan basis.

TABLE 4.1. *New colonial bureaus and initial funds appropriated*

Agency	Date created	Initial funding
Board of Health	July 1, 1901	$308,150
Philippine Constabulary	July 18, 1901	871,732
Bureau of Public Lands	September 2, 1901	6,052
Philippine Civil Hospital	October 1, 1901	60,512
Bureau of Non-Christian Tribes	October 2, 1901	6,434
Bureau of Agriculture	October 8, 1901	4,000
Bureau of Architecture	October 18, 1901	117,099
Bureau of Public Printing	November 7, 1901	349,320

Source: Rene R. Escalante, *The Bearer of Pax Americana: The Philippine Career of William H. Taft, 1900–1903* (Quezon City: New Day Publishers, 2007), 165.

The Philippine Constabulary

Certainly the most useful bureaucracy in maintaining coercive control over the islands was the Philippine Constabulary (PC), the paramilitary force that maintained order in the pacified regions and reported to civilian authorities in the colonial government, not to the US Army. This served both ideological and strategic goals. The PC had been recommended by the first Philippine Commission as early as 1900 and inaugurated a year later, and its budget, as Table 4.1 shows, was dramatically higher than other colonial bureaus. Americans filled most positions in the PC officer corps and nearly all came from the regular army – many personally selected by its first chief, Army Capt. Henry T. Allen – while the majority of enlisted men were Filipinos. By 1903, with an officer corps of 271 (204 Americans and 67 Filipinos), nearly 7,000 enlisted men (all Filipino), and a budget of $1.8 million, the PC constituted a fairly significant police force.[24]

The combination of American officers and Filipino soldiers was not unique; most Western imperial governments relied on native soldiers and policemen to enforce colonial order. Nevertheless, American colonial officials were well aware that a racially mixed police force might prove explosive, particularly because many American soldiers were still fighting Filipino revolutionaries. What was needed, according to PC Chief Allen, were "soldiers of no mean qualifications," specifically soldiers who could cooperate with Filipinos. Not only would an American officer need "sufficient tact to secure the cooperation of both Insular and Provincial officials," Allen wrote to Taft, "[a]bove all he should not be . . . a *nigger hater* or one who considers the Filipinos question as a *second Indian proposition*."[25]

Allen's statement reveals the emerging tension between American racial attitudes and the practical need for manpower – a tension that would be exhibited at all levels of the colonial regime. As we will see, top colonial officials would draw the

---

I personally do not know the political views of my own bureau chiefs and could not tell you today to which party three-fourths of them belong.

Cameron Forbes to Woodrow Wilson, March 5, 1913; Forbes Papers, Box 8, Folder 331.

[24] Forbes, *Philippine Islands*, v. 1, 227.
[25] Allen to Taft, October 17, 1904, quoted in McCoy, *Policing America's Empire*, 87.

line when more vicious forms of American racism began to compromise the larger mission of development and modernization. Although many of them privately held racially exclusionist beliefs, public racism was thought to undermine the colonial order and to draw unwanted attention from Congress.

The racial makeup of the PC was not its only unique quality. For Americans, the creation of a state-level police force with wide jurisdiction was something of a novelty – one that allowed the colonial regime to exercise tremendous coercive power within the islands with few checks from Washington. Although technocratic reformers at home had long favored professional police forces, these were relatively new to the United States; in fact, state police forces, aside from the Texas Rangers, did not exist in any American state.[26] For colonial officials, the creation of an independent police force had several advantages. First, it gave civilian officials the ability to suppress insurgent actions without Army interference. Second, as Alfred McCoy points out in his landmark study of this institution, through its wide-ranging powers the PC could serve in virtually any coercive capacity from spying on Americans in the islands to enforcing the colonial state's draconian health and narcotics laws.[27] "In short," Governor Cameron Forbes would later write, "the Constabulary at one time or another rendered service to practically every branch of government. It furnished guards for collectors of public revenue, disbursing officers, public land surveyors, and scientific parties on explorations, and for the transportation of lepers; it was used in the suppression of opium traffic and gambling and in the apprehension of vagrants."[28] Furthermore, its officers achieved tremendous success in their later military careers. Thirteen of the seventeen men who led the PC would later retire as generals. Allen, the PC's first commander, would later serve as US commander for Europe in World War I, while his successor, Henry H. Bandholz, would later establish the US Army's Military Police.[29]

INFORMATION CONTROL AND THE COLONIAL PRESS

The Philippine colonial state's lack of financial resources was not accompanied by a lack of civil authority. Although Congress had limited its ability to sell public lands and denied it free trade, the civil powers of the governor to pass laws, dismiss officials, or deport Americans remained virtually unchecked. Congress's interests extended, for the most part, to those aspects of colonial government that affected the metropole. For Filipinos or Americans who stood in the way of Taft's developmental goals for the islands, the consequences could be grave. The Commission's ability to present the colonial experiment as both benevolent and successful was considered essential to its viability, and Taft was not afraid to marshal his full array of civil powers to silence local residents who attempted to challenge that narrative. The control of information was always at the heart of the colonial project.[30] Their greatest fear was that scandal would lead to a congressional investigation that would further erode their tenuous political support.

[26] Forbes, *Philippine Islands*, v. I, 204.
[27] McCoy, *Policing America's Empire*, Ch. 2.
[28] Forbes, *Philippine Islands*, v. I, 204.
[29] McCoy, *Policing America's Empire*, 90.
[30] Ibid., 96.

They had good reason for such fears. Although the Army had managed to suppress most negative accounts of the Philippine–American War, by 1902 – not long after Taft had taken control of the colonial government – metropolitan journalists began to report aggressively on the atrocities committed by American soldiers. Their efforts would eventually lead to the publication of *"Marked Severities" in Philippine Warfare*, which was edited by the staunch anti-imperialists Moorfield Storey and Julian Codman.[31] Most troubling to the architects of America's empire, however, was the fact that Storey and Codman's work connected these atrocities to President Roosevelt and Secretary Root themselves.[32] In the pamphlet, Root's statements assuring the public that the war was conducted in a civilized manner, that most provinces were pacified, and that the Filipinos welcomed American troops, were juxtaposed next to Army reports that showed just the opposite. Such charges suggested two possibilities: (1) that the Secretary of War was a fool who was entirely misinformed about the situation in the Philippines or (2) that these atrocities were committed with his direct knowledge and approval. Since even his fiercest critics were quick to acknowledge Root's intelligence and competence, the latter option was supposed to suggest itself as the obvious answer.

These efforts were joined by a Senate investigation conducted by the imperialists' long-time foe, Senator Hoar of Massachusetts, who formed a special committee in January 1902 to "examine and report into the conduct of the war in the Philippine Islands, the administration of the government there, and the condition and character of the inhabitants."[33] Control of the investigation, however, was given over to Henry Cabot Lodge's Committee on the Philippines, which held hearings between January and June of 1902. Lodge made no secret of his support for the Army, but his committee did uncover disturbing facts about American conduct during the war, particularly the use of water torture to interrogate Filipino revolutionaries. Reports of the atrocities committed by American soldiers not only outraged anti-imperialists but also led many prominent Republicans to reconsider the wisdom of the "Philippine experiment." As Boston businessman Henry Lee Higginson wrote to Lodge, "A very considerable number of staunch republicans . . . who have never looked at any other ticket, would like to get out of these islands."[34]

Although these letters did little to dissuade the imperialists in the administration, they were serious enough for Roosevelt and Lodge to speak out. While condemning those who would besmirch the honor of the US Army, Lodge assured the public that individual officers who had committed barbaric acts would be punished.[35] He was joined by Roosevelt, who provided a vigorous defense of the humanity and justice of America's war in the Philippines at the unveiling of a soldiers' and sailors' monument in Arlington Cemetery. In his speech, Roosevelt condemned the lazy moral judgments of those "who sit at ease at home, who walk delicately and live in the soft places of the earth." The war, he maintained, was fought to liberate the Filipinos from their cruel and medieval system of government. Rather than

---

[31] Kramer, *Blood of Government*, 145–6.
[32] Moorefield Storey and Julian Codman, *"Marked Severities" in Philippine Warfare* (Boston: Geo. W. Ellis Co., 1902).
[33] Welch, *Response to Imperialism*, 136.
[34] Quoted in Welch, *Response to Imperialism*, 141.
[35] Welch, *Response to Imperialism*, 144.

condemn the actions of a few soldiers, Americans should applaud the fact that they were doing a "great work for civilization, a great work for the honor and the interest of this nation, and above all for the welfare of the inhabitants of the Philippine Islands."[36] In large part, Lodge and Roosevelt's counteroffensive was effective. The public remained largely indifferent to their nation's exploits in Asia; concerns about the Army's contact did not lead to dissent among the majority of Americans or the mainstream press.[37]

After the Lodge Committee's investigation, the colonial state dramatically increased its efforts to control information. Indeed, the broad restrictions on free speech and the obsessive monitoring of the local press by colonial authorities often shocked Americans who visited the islands during this period. When Professor H. Parker Willis, an economist who would later design the Philippine National Bank (PNB), first arrived in 1904, he seemed to find himself in a surveillance state.[38] "From the very outset," he later wrote, "there has been a persistent attempt to conceal the facts, and thus to muzzle public sentiment on this side [that is, the United States] of the water."[39] As Willis further observed, "Information from the Philippines . . . never comes either from the Philippine Commission or from the executive at Washington, and Congress has found itself unable to elicit much additional matter."[40]

This was by design. To protect its public image in Manila and Washington, the Commission adopted sedition and libel laws in 1901, making it illegal "for any person to advocate orally or by writing or printing or by like methods the independence of the Philippine Islands or their separation from the United States, either by peaceful or forcible means." Although the Commission could do little to manage the metropolitan American press, which tended to support or denigrate the colonial experiment according to its particular party loyalties, American reporters in the Philippines were another matter.

E. F. O'Brien, a white journalist and the editor of the *Manila Freedom*, was the first person prosecuted under the law.[41] O'Brien's editorial, entitled "A Few Hard Facts," accused the Commission of installing "notoriously corrupt and rascally" Filipinos in the highest positions and scolded the commissioners for making "fatal mistakes" in the execution of administrative duties. Three days after this editorial

---

[36] Alfred Henry Lewis, ed., *A Compilation of the Messages and Speeches of Theodore Roosevelt, 1901–1905* (Washington, DC: Bureau of National Literature and Art, 1906), v. 1, 28–34.

[37] Welch, *Response to Imperialism*.

[38] McCoy, *Policing America's Empire*, 104.

[39] Willis, *Our Philippine Problem*, 150.

[40] Ibid., 157.

[41] Kramer, *Blood of Government*, 175. See E. F. O'Brien, "A Few Hard Facts," *Manila Freedom* (April 6, 1901), reprinted in Edgar Bellairs, *As It is in the Philippines* (New York: Lewis, Scribner & Co., 1902), 45–52. O'Brien was found guilty, fined $1,000, and sentenced to six months in jail. In LeRoy's more folksy retelling,

> The Press Club affair was rather "woolly" in some respects. The personages assembled were an odd mixture. General Wright made the first speech, and, after getting the crowd into good humor, he delivered them a very pretty little lecture, not in lecture style, on the duties and responsibilities of all Americans out here, winding up with the admonition that "we are 10,000 miles from our base, all in the same boat, out in the ocean, and it is no time for anyone to rock the boat just to hear the female passengers scream."

LeRoy Journal, December 8, 1901; LeRoy Papers, Box 1.

appeared, Taft and Root directed the attorney general to bring libel charges against the *Freedom*.[42] Later, in what would become an even more notorious press scandal, the *Freedom* provided lurid details about Commissioner Legarda's personal libel suit against a Spanish-language paper, where he stood accused of seducing his own stepdaughter. Following these stories, the colonial state filed new charges of libel against O'Brien and the *Freedom*'s publisher, Fred. L. Dorr. Taft, in a furious letter to Root, explained his reasons for such aggressive prosecution:

The Dorrs and O'Brien took up the libels and circulated them. The sedition suit grew out of libels in which they sought by *the most vicious attacks on the Filipino officials and people to promote race hatred and insurrection* in order that the conditions of turmoil in which Dorr had made his money by questionable means might return . . . I do not say that all the critics of the civil government in the Islands are bad men; indeed many intelligent and honest men doubt the wisdom of our policy. But I do say that every American drunkard, every American tough, every dive keeper, every defaulting American public official, every American frequenter of brothels, every American vagrant, every dishonest American member of the Bar against whom disbarment proceedings are instituted, every American who disgraces the country whence he came, was a supporter of the *Freedom*, and is a decrier of the Civil Government, and spurns the Filipinos, calling them "niggers" and unfit to associate with Americans.[43]

The colonial state pursued its cases aggressively, eventually leading a judge to sentence the *Freedom*'s staff to a six-month prison term.[44] The *Freedom*'s accusations were threatening not only because they openly criticized the policies of the colonial government, but also because they actively insulted some of the Commission's most prominent Filipino allies. This episode reveals the Commission's obsessive efforts to control its public image, and also the complex relationship between race and American imperialism. Indeed, "race hatred," when it seemed to compromise the state's development agenda or its stability, was actively suppressed, even as beliefs about the superiority of Anglo-American culture were universally shared by the colonial elite.

As active as colonial officials were in quashing internal dissent, they were particularly aggressive in monitoring reports for a domestic American audience. In March 1902, Edgar Bellairs, an Associated Press correspondent in Manila who had long been on bad terms with the civil government, wired an article to the United States with the headline, "War Breaks Out Anew – Two Pacified Provinces Suddenly Turn Hostile." Root immediately cabled Vice Governor Wright: "Sensational Associated Press report here reports practical renewal warlike conditions in Morong, intense excitement and many inhabitants fleeing for their lives. Report immediately actual conditions by cable." Wright quickly responded, assuring both Taft and Root that Bellairs's statement had "no foundation" and described it as "grossly exaggerated."[45] Root, however, was not so easily assuaged. Days after receiving Wright's cable, he composed a furious letter to Melville E. Stone, General Agent for the Associated Press, excoriating him for printing the story. "That Bellairs should be sending dispatches

42 McCoy, *Policing America's Empire*, 113.
43 Taft to Root, February 23, 1903; RG 350, Box 102 (Serial 1744) [my emphasis].
44 McCoy, *Policing America's Empire*, 115.
45 Root to Wright, March 6, 1902; Wright to Taft, March 6, 1902; Wright to Root, March 8, 1902; Root Papers, Box 165. Taft had left Manila for Washington where he was lobbying for the Organic Act.

tending to create the impression that war was broken out anew," Root wrote, "and that the civil government is unable to maintain peace . . . seems to me very reprehensible. Such a course tends to create the very disturbance which it described, to make government more difficult, and to bring the civil administration, upon whose prestige and effectiveness our country must depend for successful government, into discredit, and contempt."[46] Stone's response to the Secretary was conciliatory and he agreed that perhaps Bellairs's article was inflammatory, but he also noted in his reporter's defense, "the point of view of the army differs from that of the civil government very distinctly in Manila."[47]

Bellairs would soon try to exact his revenge on Root and Taft. Later that year he published *As it is in the Philippines*, a report on his experience as a correspondent in Manila, in which he described the commissioners as "incompetent" and Taft himself as "a military despot but lightly veiled with a civil title" whom he compared to a Russian czar.[48] But Bellairs saved his deepest scorn for the Sedition Act itself, which, he argued, allowed members of the Commission to abuse "all those who had sent or written anything against the sacred majesty of themselves."[49] More to the point, the Act allowed the Commission to hound unfriendly reporters out of the country. Other than The Associated Press and the Laffan Press Association, Bellairs reported, "[t]here are no correspondents for newspapers in the Philippines at present," and, he continued, "it is not the province of these correspondents to touch on the political situation, but merely to record the day's happenings as they occur."[50] Nevertheless, executives at the AP had no desire to tangle with the formidable Secretary of War again.[51] Its next two correspondents, William Dinwiddie and Martin Egan, remained on good terms with the Commission, generally shying away from stories that could embarrass the colonial government at home.[52]

Did this careful control of the press matter? Was the colonial state actively trying to remain inconspicuous? Although it is difficult to assess the effects of these policies on decisions made by American newspapers, on the whole the metropolitan press ran relatively few stories about the empire. Figure 4.1 shows the number of front-page articles about the Philippines in five major American newspapers: *Chicago Tribune, New York Times, San Francisco Chronicle, Wall Street Journal,* and *Washington Post.* After the brief spike in articles during the Spanish–American War, press coverage had dwindled by 1903; an imperfect, but suggestive, measure that the public's attention had quickly waned after its jingoistic fever had broken. The attention American political parties gave to their imperial policies, at least as reflected in their party platforms, mirrored that of the press. As Figure 4.2 demonstrates, after peaking during the 1900 election, both Republican and Democratic platforms devoted relatively little attention to the colonies by 1905.

[46] Root to Melville E. Stone, March 8, 1902; Edwards Papers, Box 2, Folder 2.
[47] Melville E. Stone to Root, March 10, 1902; Edwards Papers, Box 2, Folder 2.
[48] Bellairs, *As It is,* 243–4.
[49] Ibid., 241–2.
[50] Ibid., 243.
[51] Root's letter to Stone eventually led the Associated Press to investigate Bellairs who, it was discovered, was really Charles Ballentine, a convict wanted in Florida who had managed to become an AP correspondent in Cuba and was later transferred to the Philippines.
[52] McCoy, *Policing America's Empire,* 117.

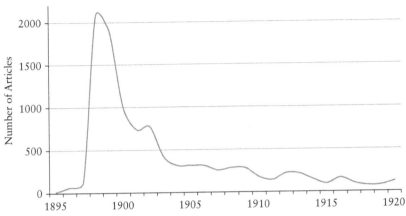

FIGURE 4.1. *Front-page articles on the Philippines in five major newspapers, 1895–1920.*
Source: Chicago Tribune, New York Times, San Francisco Chronicle, Wall Street Journal, and *Washington Post.* Collected from PROQUEST Historical Newspapers.

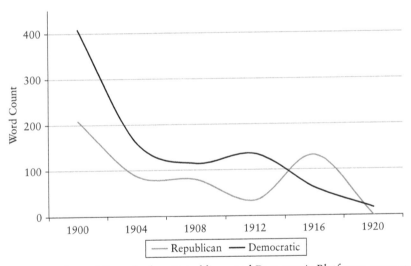

FIGURE 4.2. *Imperialism planks – Republican and Democratic Platforms, 1900–20.*
Source: American Presidency Project, "Political Party Platforms of Parties Receiving Electoral Votes: 1840–2012," http://www.presidency.ucsb.edu/platforms.p

Whether this lack of attention was due to the public's own indifference toward the colonies or the colonial state's active efforts to suppress critical stories is difficult to know. There can be little doubt, however, that just a few years after the acquisition of these new territories, the empire quickly became a minor issue in American public life. As we will see, this lack of interest from the American press would become a signal advantage for colonial officials who wished to avoid tangles with Congress.

PROMOTING THE EMPIRE

Initially, the colonial state coupled its control of information with a positive public relations campaign in the United States to attract investors and public support. Much like the Progressive-era USDA and Postal Service, colonial officials were well aware that the maintenance of good public relations was the best strategy to receive favorable treatment from Congress.[53] Unlike these bureaucracies, however, the American empire did not have a clear domestic constituency; a fact that made it more difficult to generate positive pressure in support of its goals. After all, members of Congress cared little for people who could not vote, and some of the most powerful American agricultural interests saw the Philippines as an economic threat.

This left colonial officials who represented no American voters facing off against powerful domestic lobbies who represented thousands. These circumstances, of course, allowed them to operate with relatively little congressional oversight, but they became a handicap when faced with intense and influential opposition. Originally, Root and Taft had assumed that powerful American capital interests – the backbone of the Republican Party – would step up to lobby for a favorable investment climate in the colony. But by 1904, it was already clear that American capital was far more conservative than most politicians had assumed, and that it maintained, at best, a tepid interest in the Philippines. Faced with these significant disadvantages, it became all the more important to attempt to sell members of Congress and the American public on the idea of an expansive empire.

The importance insular officials placed on this goal is demonstrated by the extraordinary number of resources – both time and money – that they poured into promotional campaigns, an effort made easier by the almost seamless coordination of War Department, BIA, and Commission efforts. For its part, the Commission did not merely try to suppress negative news, but thought of actively employing an agent to feed positive stories to the press.

James LeRoy, a Commission secretary who had earlier been a journalist in the United States, reported in his private journal that Taft approached him about just such a position. As he recounted the episode, Taft and Vice Governor Wright proposed to give him "some sort of special job as 'government press agent' and political steerer, either creating a new position for it or paying me extra money out of secret service funds, ostensibly leaving me what I am." Weeks later, LeRoy reported, Wright again asked him to take on the job: "[Wright] has gone back to his old idea of my remaining nominally as Worcester's secretary, but doing nothing for him, and having $100 a month added to my salary on the quiet, the Auditory being now engaged in studying how this can be done. My work would be to 'influence' the newspapers here and at home."[54] In the end, LeRoy decided not to take the job and it is not known if someone else was found.

Even without a dedicated press correspondent, its relative monopoly on information about the islands allowed the insular government to present itself in a very favorable light without fear that opposition groups could easily contradict its claims. The Bureau of Insular Affairs embraced public relations early. Just two

---

[53] See Carpenter, *Forging of Bureaucratic Autonomy*.
[54] LeRoy Journal, entries dated December 7 and 27, 1901; LeRoy Papers, Box 1.

years after the adoption of the Organic Act, the BIA released a pamphlet entitled, *What Has Been Done in the Philippines: A Record of Practical Accomplishments Under Civil Government*, where they falsely claimed that "[t]ranquility prevails throughout the islands" and "the Filipinos now begin to appreciate the advantages to be derived from their new situation."[55] As insular officials knew, however, reports such as these had relatively little impact. What they needed was an event that would attract the interest of all Americans. And at the turn of the century there was no bigger platform than the upcoming 1904 St. Louis World's Fair – The Louisiana Purchase Exhibition.

THE COLONIAL STATE ON DISPLAY

Plans for a Philippine exhibition at the fair were put into motion even before the Organic Act was finalized. That Taft regarded the exhibition's success as a matter "of the utmost importance" is demonstrated by the financial resources he devoted to the project.[56] In 1902, the Commission appropriated ₱500,000 ($250,000) for the exhibition – an enormous sum to spend on public relations, especially given the limited revenues available and the famine that currently plagued the islands. The Commission, after all, had collected only ₱4.5 million in internal taxes that year and was so short of money that it had begged Congress for a $3 million emergency relief fund. Their decision to put on the exhibition was nothing short of an attempt to restore the enthusiasm Americans had shown in the wake of the Spanish–American War. If they could succeed in this task, the commissioners thought, their efforts at securing funding from Congress and favorable trade legislation would be made considerably easier.

Planning for the exhibition was among the BIA's top priorities in 1903, and Edwards was anxious that no expense be spared. When commissioners in Manila began to growl about the increasing costs of the exhibition, Edwards suggested to Wright that "you tell them the character of exhibit we promised. We have simply got to make up our minds that we do not want to let money interfere with an adequate exhibit there."[57] The decision to retain as director Dr. W. P. Wilson was telling. Wilson was a professor of botany at the University of Pennsylvania, but was also the president of the Philadelphia Commercial Museum, which promoted American goods and trade around the world. Wilson's assistant, Gustavo Niederlein, had extensive experience in designing exhibitions and had worked for the French Ministry of Colonies in 1900.[58] When Niederlein traveled to the Philippines to arrange for the exhibits, Taft circulated a letter to provincial and insular officials instructing them to "assist Mr. Niederlein in every way as [a] commissioner of the insular government." To assist with this task, the colonial state exempted the exhibitors from taxes, permitted the free use of telegraphs, and provided free postage for packages related to the exhibition.[59]

55 *What Has Been Done in the Philippines*, Senate Doc. No. 304, 58th Cong, 2nd sess., 7.
56 Taft to Root, April 2, 1902; Root Papers, Box 164.
57 Edwards to Wright, March 16, 1903; Edwards Papers, Box 2, Folder 20.
58 Kramer, *Blood of Government*, 240–1.
59 Ibid., 241–2.

All of this work enabled the colonial state, in words of historian Paul Kramer, to "use the insular government's new political, technological, and informational resources, currently under construction in the Philippines, to build an immense advertisement for civilian rule in the colonies."[60] And it *was* immense even by contemporary standards. The exhibition took up 47 acres and included a miniature city with streets and parks with a central plaza for an education building (built to look like a cathedral), a commerce building, and a government building filled with relevant exhibits. Separate sections were devoted to forestry, mines, and agriculture, all "artistically placed" in the words of the exhibition report.[61] Five different villages – with their inhabitants – from around the islands were transported to St. Louis from the Philippines. In all, over 70,000 exhibits from all over the Archipelago were on display in the twenty exhibit palaces and 100 tents and lodges.[62] The BIA had 20,000 posters printed to advertise the exhibit, which opened on June 17, 1904 with a parade of 1,100 Filipinos led by the Philippine Constabulary band.[63] In his inaugural address, Taft made clear that the exhibition's purpose was to advertise the good works of the imperial state, or, in his more artful phrasing, "to make the people who come here to commemorate the vindication of one great effort of American enterprise and expansion understood the conditions which surround the beginning of another."[64]

In many respects, the exhibition was a success – ticket sales were high and many visitors considered it the highlight of the fair. As Wright wrote to Taft from Manila, "We hear from all sides that the Philippines exhibit at the St. Louis exhibition was the best part of the show, and whilst it came high – indeed, I may say 'damned high' in view of our resources – still I believe that we will ultimately more than get our money's worth out of it."[65] It would make an enormous impression on those who visited, yet it was decidedly not the impression that the colonial state had hoped to convey. Rather than focus on the economic opportunities in the islands or the good works the Commission advertised, most Americans, it seems, focused on the "savagery" and exoticism of the tribal people who had been coerced into joining the exhibition. To recoup some of its money, the exhibition organizers had pushed to include exhibitions of the "non-Christian" Filipino tribes, particularly the Igorot people whose clothes and customs, they thought, would be sure to draw a crowd and increase ticket sales.

If Americans took pride in their good works in the Philippines, the BIA reasoned, then they were likely to pressure their political representatives to pass favorable legislation. As the guidebook for the non-Christian tribal school read, "Within a trim little nipa and bamboo cottage in the rear of the Manila building 50 little savages, recruited from the various villages, gather each day and are taught to fashion English letters on big blackboards."[66] Yet these living dioramas did not have the intended effect on the American public.[67] As the *St. Louis Post-Dispatch* reported,

[60] Ibid., 237.
[61] US Bureau of Insular Affairs, *Report of the Philippines Exposition Board in the United States for the Louisiana Purchase Exposition* (Washington, DC: Government Printing Office, 1905), 4.
[62] Lewis E. Gleek, *The American Half-Century, 1898–1946* (Quezon City: New Day, 1998), 84.
[63] Kramer, *Blood of Government*, 242.
[64] Quoted in Kramer, *Blood of Government*, 253.
[65] Wright to Taft, January 2, 1905; Edwards Papers, Box 5, Folder 1.
[66] Quoted in Kramer, *Blood of Government*, 273.
[67] Kramer, *Blood of Government*, 265–6.

"The non-Christian tribes were the magnets which drew them more than anything else." Throughout the day, the article continued, "men and women were standing thick about the stockade with their faces pressed into the interstices looking at the almost naked savages."[68]

The colonial government was well aware that displays such as these could feed American racial fears and erode American support for the empire. Their attempts to shape this narrative, however, proved to be clumsy. In exhibition materials and speeches from BIA officials, the insular state emphasized that the Igorot people were no more representative of Filipino society than the Apaches were of American society.[69] They even invited *ilustrados* to be on hand to show what "civilized" Filipinos looked like. Predictably, Americans were far more interested in the "naked savages" than the more sober exhibits of Manila architecture and the commercial opportunities the BIA was so anxious to advertise.[70] Now insular officials feared that their carefully planned exhibition and "representative" displays of village life had become a circus attraction. Edwards became so worried that "the savages have been attracting more attention than the educated Filipinos who wear clothes" that he ordered the Igorotes to put on pants. This only increased interest in the exhibit among Americans who demanded to see "the natives as they are at home," and the BIA, after consulting with Roosevelt, was forced to rescind the order.[71] Nevertheless, the BIA's clumsy attempts to control its image led to a great deal of bad press. Taft was even lampooned in a *St. Louis Post-Dispatch* political cartoon that showed him running after an Igorot with a pair of pants.[72] This hugely expensive display – one intended to build public support for the empire – had backfired in a spectacular way. Rather than demonstrating the potential for investment and civilization, the exhibition only seemed to confirm that the Philippines was too foreign and its people too exotic to remain a permanent part of the white republic.

The public relations damage would prove to be lasting. If insular authorities thought they might rekindle the American public's interest in the colony before the fair, they knew by its end that they had failed. If anything, the American encounter with Filipinos at the exhibition had only increased questions about why, exactly, the United States was bothering with this distant land. Members of Congress seemed to share the public's view. "I have often heard it remarked in Congress," Edwards wrote to Taft, "that from the looks of the people in these photographs we ought not to bother much with the Philippines. When I told them the idea was merely to present the unusual types – that the great body of Filipinos are of a much higher class, they say 'one certainly would not get that idea from a casual glance at the Commission's reports,' in other words, that the representation of Igorotes, wild

---

[68] "All Roads Led to Filipinos, Thoughts of Visitors Thronged about and through the Reservation All Day," *St. Louis Post-Dispatch*, May 1, 1904, 6, quoted in Kramer, *Blood of Government*, 265.

[69] Gleek, *American Half-Century*, 83–4.

[70] Sadly, the Igorotes' popularity at the World's Fair was not lost on circus promoters. Following the exhibition, several shady operations were established to smuggle them out of the islands for use in American sideshows. See Doherty to Edwards, April 20, 1907; reprinted in Gleek, *American Half-Century*, 111.

[71] "Big Rush to See Igorotes Unclad," *St. Louis Post-Dispatch*, June 26, 1904, quoted in Kramer, *Blood of Government*, 266.

[72] Rydell, *All the World's a Fair*, 174.

Moros, etc., would give as false an impression of the people of the Philippines as would a representation of Indians and Negroes properly represent the inhabitants of the United States."[73] If insular authorities took any lesson from the St. Louis exhibition, it was that attempts to marshal public support for a robust imperial policy were expensive and ineffective.

THE 1905 CONGRESSIONAL JUNKET

If the public could not be convinced to support the colonial state, then perhaps their elected representatives could. After Roosevelt's reelection, and as the insular state began its big push for free trade legislation, Taft arranged for a three-month, all-expenses-paid trip throughout the Far East with one month in the Philippines. In part, this was designed to smooth relations with the *ilustrados*. But it was also a chance to recruit members of Congress to their side – to get the tariff passed, minds had to be changed. The tour was presented to the media as "a splendid opportunity for members of Congress to obtain first-hand information concerning affairs in the islands," and to make the trip attractive for legislators, they were invited to bring along their wives.[74] Although the *Washington Post* huffed that it was "positively objectionable" that "there should be women in the party," the Commission extended an invitation to one of America's most famous women to lend the trip some extra cachet: Theodore Roosevelt's celebrity daughter, Alice.[75] It was even reported that Speaker Cannon himself might go.[76] Some in the press saw the trip for what it was – a public relations junket – and criticized the colonial state for paying for it. "Owing to the awkward lack of law on the subject," the *Washington Post* reported, "the expenses of this trip must be borne by that puny little mendicant known as the Philippine government. IF that government has not already made an appropriation for the purpose it will do so. Laws blossom and multiply in the tropics."[77] Col. Edwards was instructed to come as well. "I really have no business to go the Islands," he wrote to General Corbin, "but the Secretary insists upon it, and thinks I will be no good if I don't go." Nevertheless, he conceded, the trip presented an opportunity to educate "our thirty Senators and Congressmen, that is, to know the facts so they will be willing to give us what we most need – the free market of the United States for Philippine products."[78]

The planning resulted in a flurry of cables sent between Manila and Washington. Prior to leaving, for example, Edwards warned the Manila government,

Kindly put your friends on to the wisdom of not unduly exploiting the resources of the Philippine Islands for the stimulated production of sugar and tobacco that the doing away of the Dingley tariff would suggest in this country. Senators Dubois and Foster and Congressman Driscoll are opponents of ours, and they are going over to look for themselves, so I would hate to see four or five arguments in support of their contention.[79]

[73] Quoted in Kramer, *Blood of Government*, 265.
[74] *Washington Post*, March 13, 1905, 6.
[75] Ibid.
[76] Ibid.
[77] *Washington Post*, March 14, 1905, 2.
[78] Edwards to Corbin, May 1, 1905; Edwards Papers, Box 5, Folder 13.
[79] Ibid.

In all, seven senators and twenty-four representatives were in the party – twenty Republicans and eleven Democrats – including some of the insular state's most prominent supporters, Sereno Payne, Charles Curtis, and Henry Cooper, as well as its most strident critics, Thomas Patterson, William Jones, and Francis Newlands.[80] In fact, nearly every member of Congress who was active in legislating for or against the colonial state decided to visit the islands, but for the conspicuous absence of Henry Cabot Lodge.[81] On August 5, 1905 the party arrived in Manila and traveled throughout the islands, with ample time for shopping and to witness frequent displays of native enthusiasm for colonial rule at the carefully arranged stops. From Manila they traveled south to Iloilo, and then to Zamboanga and Jolo.[82] Judging by the schedule, however, there can be no doubt that this trip was primarily designed to increase congressional sympathy for free trade. The congressmen held days of hearings on several different islands where they heard from a variety of Filipino planters, colonial officials, and Americans already in business. Invariably, those delivering remarks were united in their opinion of the sorry state of Philippine agriculture – a calculated effort to reduce opposition from protectionists – and the immense importance of free access to the American market.

A number of witnesses also repeated the BIA's (dubious) claim that even under free trade conditions Philippine tobacco was unlikely to make many inroads in the United States. W. S. Lyon of the Philippine Bureau of Agriculture, for example, testified that Philippine tobacco and cigars were an acquired taste and that he was unsure if they would find a market in the United States. At the very least, it would take time for Americans to "cultivate a taste for Philippine cigars." The first time he had tasted a Philippine cigar, he confessed to the visiting congressmen, "I thought it was simply vile."[83]

The trip, it seems, was largely considered a success. "All our enemies that we took with us were converted," Edwards thought, "except in the cases of Patterson, Dubois and Jones, and the two former I am quite sure will not be as virulent in their opposition as heretofore. Privately they are absolutely in accord with the Taft policy, as is everybody else. The Secretary won them all."[84] Although Taft may have concluded that the colonial government's charm offensive was effective, the public was, at best, indifferent to the "tutelary" efforts of the American colonial state.

---

[80] The following members of Congress were on the trip. Senators: Francis Warren (R-WY), Nathan Scott (R-WV), Fred Dubois (R-ID), Murphy Foster (D-LA), Thomas Patterson (D-CO), Francis Newlands (D-NV), Chester Long (R-KS). Representatives: Sereno Payne (R-NY), Charles Grosvenor (R-NY), William Hepburn (R-IA), George Smith (R-IL), David DeArmond (D-MO), William Jones (D-VA), Henry Cooper (R-WI), Frederick Gillet (D-MD), Charles Curtis (R-KS), George Foss (R-IL), Ebenezer Hill (R-CT), Theobold Otjen (R-WI), William Howard (D-GA), Michael Driscoll (R-NY), Charles Scott (R-KS), Ariosto Wiley (D-AL), Bourke Cockran (D-NY), George Loud (R-MI), Nicholas Longworth (R-OH), Swager Sherley (D-KY), Newton Gilbert (D-KY), Duncan McKinlay (R-CA), William B. McKinley (R-IL), Herbert Parsons (R-NY).

[81] Unfortunately, I have been unable to ascertain why Lodge chose not to go.

[82] Gleek, *American Half-Century*, 92–6.

[83] Government of the Philippine Islands, *Public Hearings in the Philippine Islands Upon the Proposed Reduction of the Tariff* (Manila: Bureau of Printing, 1905), quoted in Pedro E. Abelarde, *American Tariff Policy towards the Philippines, 1898–1946* (New York: King's Crown Press, 1947), 88.

[84] Edwards to General E. H. Crowder, October 9, 1905; Edwards Papers, Box 6, Folder 4.

At worst, it was beginning to fear that the colonies would compete with American agricultural producers. For the Philippine Commission, which had counted on the maintenance of robust support and favorable trade relations with the metropole, this was nothing short of a disaster.

THE PROBLEM OF COLONIAL REVENUE:
TAXES AND THE TARIFF

Congress never provided generous support to the American empire – and it had few incentives to do so. There were few voters in the colonies; there were no patronage positions; and the public at large was either hostile or deeply indifferent to the extensive empire. Aside from $3 million it gave to the Philippines to offset the effects of the rinderpest plague in 1903 and $351,000 to aid in the first census of the islands, it appropriated *no* funds for the maintenance of the colonial state. Commission authorities, naturally, did not hesitate to publish this fact. As the BIA proudly reported in one of its many promotional studies, "civil government of the islands is maintained by its own revenues and without a dollar from the Treasury of the United States."[85] Although that was technically true, it neglected the fact that Congress did pay to maintain the Army in the islands, an expense the insular government would have been wholly unable to cover itself. Independent contemporary estimates put this cost at roughly $10 million a year for the first decade of government.[86] Yet the colonial government contested even this relatively low figure. By his own reckoning, Taft put the total yearly cost of supporting the Army at half reasoning that "[t]he only additional cost therefore that the maintenance of the army can be said to entail upon the United States is the additional cost of maintaining 12,000 soldiers in the islands over what it would be to maintain the same number of soldiers in the United States."[87] Although this lack of direct financial support crippled the grandiose development plans for the Philippines, it also meant that Congress had less incentive to closely monitor the colonial state's spending.

For its own revenue, the colonial state – much like the domestic American state – relied primarily on customs duties. In a minor concession to Commission authorities, Congress had permitted the colonial government to recover duties charged to Filipino goods entering the United States, allowing it to benefit, in part, from Congress's refusal to lower tariff rates by more than 25 percent of those that applied to other nations. Thus, the Commission could collect on import and export duties for goods entering and exiting the Philippines, and on import duties from Filipino goods imported to the United States. Further complicating this already difficult situation was a stipulation in the Paris Peace Treaty that gave Spain equal treatment under the Philippine tariff with the United States until 1909. During the period of military occupation, from 1898 to

---

[85] *What Has Been Done in the Philippines*, 5.

[86] This estimate is from Frederick Chamberlin, *The Philippine Problem, 1898–1913* (New York: Little, Brown, 1913), 183–90. The biggest expense of the entire colonial experiment was the cost of the Philippine–American War from June 30, 1898 to July 1, 1902 at a cost to the American state of roughly $160 million.

[87] *Eighth Annual Report of the Philippine Commission to the Secretary of War, 1907* (Washington, DC: Government Printing Office, 1908), 309.

1901, tariffs had been left largely as they were under Spain, a complicated system of harbor improvement duties and various consumption taxes.[88]

From its earliest days, the Philippine colonial government and its allies in the Department of War desperately tried to recruit American investors by offering a variety of incentives. They passed a revised tariff schedule on September 17, 1901 designed to encourage the importation of American goods, particularly mining and agricultural machines (ostensibly to increase the mechanization of these activities), which could enter the country duty-free. The Commission, in consultation with appraisers from the New York customs house, carefully designed this tariff to avoid, in Root's words, "ambiguities which might lead to litigation." It was also published in a number of major American newspapers to invite criticism from American business interests.[89] "While no different duty in favor of American products is openly mentioned," reported the BIA's Clarence Edwards, "the articles were so described in the tariff as to allow an advantage to American goods."[90] This was both good politics and good economics for the Commission – in theory, it encouraged American manufacturers to invest in the Philippine market while maintaining their revenue base through higher tariffs on European products.[91]

Nobody thought these minor changes to the colonial tariff would lead to a radical change in colonial investments. To fully develop the islands required American capital investments and this required a dramatic reduction of tariffs with the United States. Free trade, insular authorities reasoned, could make the islands a profitable investment overnight. Without capital there would be no development, and without economic development, the reasons for annexation were seriously compromised.[92] Furthermore, a failure to make a success of its one major colonial project would lend credence to arguments that the nations of Western Europe had been making for over a century; namely, that the American Republic, while increasingly rich, was too poorly governed and chaotic to join the ranks of the Great Powers.

Free trade would also, in the estimation of insular authorities, put to rest any agitation for independence from Filipino elites by economically binding them to the American economy. Capital and good governance would demonstrate to the world the genius of the American system – a belief that colonial government authorities continued to cling to even after it became clear that such investment would not be forthcoming. Taft, speaking to the Harvard College Alumni Association in 1904, made this plain:

If we ultimately take the Philippines in behind the tariff wall . . . it will have a tendency to develop that whole country, of inviting the capital of the United States into the islands, and

---

[88] For a description of the Spanish tariff duties, see Carl C. Plehn, "Taxation in the Philippines," *Political Science Quarterly* 27 (March 1902): 125–48.

[89] *Annual Report of the Secretary of War, 1901*, 80.

[90] Quoted in William J. Pomeroy, *American Neo-Colonialism: Its Emergence in the Philippines and Asia* (New York: International Publishers, 1970), 173.

[91] While beneficial to the Commission and to American producers, these discriminatory tariff policies often had dire consequences for poor Filipinos. For example, a form of British cloth called "splits," so-named because this 52-inch-wide cloth had a thin center thread which could easily be split into two, had long provided cheap clothing for Filipino peasants. American textile producers, who wove a more expensive 25-inch cloth, demanded that tariff rates favor their own product, and this change in the law dramatically increased the price of clothing for the Filipino poor.

[92] Stanley, *Nation in the Making*, 144.

of creating a trade between the islands and this country which can not but be beneficial to both. Now . . . is it wild to suppose that the people of the islands will understand the benefit that they derive from such association with the United States and will prefer to maintain some sort of bond so that they may be within the tariff wall and enjoy the markets, rather than separate themselves and become independent and lose the valuable business such our guardianship of them and our obligation to look after them has brought to them.[93]

The connections would go both ways, however. As Root would later remark in the *New York World*,

I think that our trade will increase as the processes of civilization go on in the islands, and particularly if the tariff on Philippine goods is reduced. The Filipinos are now acquiring wants. You cannot sell hats to a bareheaded people or shoes to a barefooted people anymore than you can sell trousers to people who wear breech clouts. As the people become more advanced their wants will become greater and more varied. Civilization and trade move together.[94]

Yet a push for free trade, as the colonial administrators themselves were well aware, would put them into direct conflict with protectionist Republicans – members of their own party – and the tobacco and sugar lobby, among the most powerful interest groups in Washington.

The battle to achieve free trade did not begin auspiciously, but the Commission and War Department's efforts in this respect show, perhaps better than anything else, the ability of the various branches of the insular state to work in concert. As with the Organic Act, insular tariff bills were prepared by the BIA, with extensive input from the Commission and the Secretary's office, but this time their key point person in the House was Sereno Payne (R-NY), the powerful chairman of the House Committee on Ways and Means.

By December of 1902, the Commission had prepared a bill that lowered the tariff to 25 percent of the prevailing rates for foreign governments. Payne presented the bill to the Ways and Means Committee on December 17, 1902, and he emphasized the increasingly desperate conditions in the islands and the need to attract capital. Although the Democratic minority criticized the Republicans for the bill's "unusual haste" and mocked them for not removing trade barriers entirely, the bill easily

---

[93] Taft, 1904 Speech to the Harvard College Alumni Association, quoted in Stanley, *Nation in the Making*, 147.

[94] *New York World*, February 7, 1907, quoted in Cruz, *America's Colonial Office*, 63. Democratic opponents realized this possibility as well, and fought against increased economic ties with the islands for fear that they would forever be bound to the United States. During the later tariff battles, Forbes describes his battles with Democrats of this mind:

> Had quite an argument with Senator Newlands, who doesn't want free trade with the Filipinos because as both parties have declared for their ultimate independence we should not make the ties so strong that they will be difficult to break. I suggested to them that it was not independence we have them but an opportunity for independence if at that time they want it, and it was just as logical to give them bad economic conditions so that they wouldn't like us as it would be to give them bad political conditions or govern them badly so as to be sure that they'd want separation. This fallacy is very prevalent in the little town of Boston.

Forbes Papers, Journal, August 22, 1905.

made it out of Ways and Means and was passed by the House just one day later on December 18.[95] The colonial government had expected the House to be favorable, but the more conservative Senate presented problems. "Kindly write me full particulars as to the situation in the Senate as regards our Bills," Wright wrote to Edwards the next day. "I confess to a good deal of anxiety in regard to their fate in that august body."[96] Wright's sarcasm notwithstanding, insular authorities were not discouraged. Convinced as they were of the benefits free trade would bring to the Philippines, they were willing to work slowly. In an unusually revealing letter to Edwards, Taft reflected that free trade "cannot be brought about at once I suppose and we shall have to hammer it down and hammer it down."[97] Slow, incremental changes to tariff laws would be the strategy – one that would be achieved mainly by remaining publicly pessimistic about the possibilities for Philippine agriculture and industry, even as they privately planned to fund their lavish infrastructure projects with absurdly optimistic predictions about future productivity.

On February 20, 1903, Root reported back the unsurprising fact that the Senate "was in a snarl" and he leaned further on Lodge to push it through his committee, even enlisting Roosevelt to ask him for a "resolute effort" in seeing the bill through.[98] The bill was eventually reported favorably out of Lodge's Committee on the Philippines, but only after sugar beet and tobacco lobbyists had succeeded in raising duties to 50 percent.

Even this did not stop the most vehement opposition from Western Republicans. Senator Patterson, the Commission's long-time critic from Colorado, declared that if trade barriers were removed, "the sugar cane industry of Louisiana and the beet industry of Michigan, Colorado and other beet-sugar raising States, in ten years will be wiped out on account of the immense area of the Philippine territory that may be used for the cultivation of sugar."[99] This was a preposterous prediction given the limited sugar and tobacco production in the islands. It did not matter. As Patterson himself frankly admitted in the same debate, "as long as protection, whatever its phase may be, is the controlling economic position of this country, I propose to stand for the protection of the products of my section."[100] Such was the protectionist hysteria in the Senate, a belief that was fueled by American agricultural interests who not only were uninterested in investing in the Philippines, but also were actively working to make any investment unprofitable. The drive for development – as it would be throughout colonial rule – was championed not by business, but by the colonial state and its allies in the executive branch.

When the bill finally reached the Senate floor in the spring of 1903, no action was taken and it died with the session's end. In part, the bill's failure to come up for a vote resulted from the Senate's simultaneous consideration (and Republican filibuster) of an omnibus statehood bill for the admission of Oklahoma, New Mexico, and Arizona to the Union – a bill that many Republicans feared would

---

[95] 57th Cong., 2nd sess., H.R. Report No. 2907.
[96] Wright to Edwards, December 19, 1902; Edwards Papers, Box 2, Folder 15.
[97] Taft to Edwards, January 25, 1903; Edwards Papers, Box 2, Folder 17.
[98] Quoted in Alfonso, *Theodore Roosevelt*, 127.
[99] C. Rec. 57th Cong., 2nd sess., 2186, quoted in Abelarde, *American Tariff Policy*, 58.
[100] C. Rec. 57th Cong., 2nd sess., 2187, quoted in Abelarde, *American Tariff Policy*, 58–9.

lead to the addition of several Democrats to the Senate. Neither Taft nor Roosevelt took the defeat well. Roosevelt was "bitterly disappointed" and, as Forbes would report, "Mr. Taft took occasion to characterize some very worthy Boston people with an epithet not often heard east of the Mississippi."[101] Even the perpetually optimistic Edwards was frustrated, noting how the BIA had "slaved like dogs" to see the bill through Congress.[102] Still, the eventual outcome could hardly have been a total surprise to insular authorities or to Roosevelt. As historian Oscar Alfonso makes clear, both Root and Taft had decided that an effort to "drive many things at once" would be impossible, and they consequently devoted the majority of their resources to seeing that the currency bill was adopted.[103]

There was also an unfortunate issue of timing. Tariff legislation for Puerto Rico, which already had significant American investments and accompanying political support, came up first – and Puerto Rico had been given free trade. Having lost this battle, agricultural lobbies were more motivated than ever *not* to allow the Philippines behind the American tariff wall as well.[104] The role of American agricultural interests was hardly lost on the domestic American press, as the December 1903 cover of *Puck* (Figure 4.3) shows. Borrowing imagery from one of Charles Dickens's most famous scenes, the trusts are represented as the dreadful Mr. Bumble and the Philippines as an emaciated Oliver Twist, begging for a tariff reduction. Such (occasionally) sympathetic imagery, however, did not translate into robust political support.

After Roosevelt's 1904 reelection, the insular government made another aggressive push for lower tariffs. Neither Roosevelt nor Taft had abandoned their belief that free trade was essential for a successful colonial state. "[N]o business man will go into the Philippines unless it is to his interest to do so; and it is immensely to the interest of the islands that he should go in," Roosevelt declared in his inaugural address. "It is therefore necessary that the Congress should pass laws by which the resources of the islands can be developed."[105] There were good reasons to be optimistic. The Republicans held a large majority in both houses of Congress. Even Taft was "delightfully sanguine and optimistic" about the bill's chances.[106] The BIA, too, was arguably in a better position this time around. After four years of shepherding insular legislation through Congress, it had honed its lobbying skills and gained some powerful allies. As Edward bragged to a friend, "being so intimately associated in this legislation pertaining to Porto Rico, Cuba, and the Philippines, I naturally have come in contact with the 'powers that be' of the United States Senate, and unconsciously have made some good official friends"[107] Yet the BIA's chief remained cautious. "I know that the beet sugar people are hard at work," he warned Wright, "and have kept two or three statisticians in Washington all this

---

[101] Roosevelt to Taft, April 22, 1903, letter reprinted in Morison, ed., *The Letters of Theodore Roosevelt*, v. 3, 464–5. Forbes Papers, Journal, v. 1, 11.

[102] Edwards to Wright, January 16, 1904; Edwards Papers, Box 1.

[103] Alfonso, *Theodore Roosevelt*, 133.

[104] Go, "Chains of Empire," 197.

[105] Theodore Roosevelt, Inaugural Address, text from James D. Richardson, ed., *A Compilation of the Messages and Papers of the Presidents 1789–1905* (Washington, DC: Bureau of National Literature and Art, 1907), v. 10, 439.

[106] Edwards to Wright, September 19, 1904; Edwards Papers, Box 4, Folder 8.

[107] Edwards to friend "Hal," May 26, 1903; Edwards Papers, Box 2, Folder 24.

THE PHILIPPINE OLIVER ASKS FOR MORE.

FIGURE 4.3. *December 1903 cover of* Puck *magazine.*
Source: *Puck*, LIV (December 9, 1903), 1397.

summer getting up data to defeat the reduction of the tariff, anyway on sugars. The tobacco people are pretty active also." [108]

In part, the BIA's optimism was fueled by rumors that past opponents in the Senate had warmed (or resigned themselves) to the idea of reduced tariffs. It also helped that Roosevelt, having won reelection, was more willing to play an active role in lobbying, a task he had taken up in earnest by December. In a letter to Speaker Cannon, Roosevelt noted that he had received a telegram from Senator Platt "referring to my proposal about getting a reduction of the Philippine tariff to fifty per cent: 'Think we could pass reduction bill at 50 per cent especially if House would send it to us in that form.' It seems to me that this is a measure that ought on no account

[108] Edwards to Wright, September 19, 1904; Edwards Papers, Box 4, Folder 8.

to be allowed to fail. Can't we get the House to act upon it?"[109] The very next day, Roosevelt followed up with a letter to Payne: "I think it is of the utmost consequence that we should get the Philippine tariff reduced to fifty per cent this year," he wrote to the Chairman. "This is a compromise, as you know. Secretary Taft feels that we ought to reduce it to twenty-five per cent . . . Senator Platt, who has the great tobacco interests of the country close at heart, is content to take fifty per cent."[110]

Insular bureaucrats did have a compromise in mind, but it was not the one Roosevelt had suggested to Payne. Taft and Wright both believed that they could push through a 25 percent rate, and "[a]nything more than that," they reasoned, "will do but little good as the present Dingley tariff rates are prohibitive and were intended to be so."[111] But rather than rely on the good will of members of Congress, this time they would attempt to demonstrate that the Philippines, at least in the near future, could never produce enough of either good to put a dent in the American domestic market. They hoped this would trivialize the hysterical predictions coming from tobacco and sugar lobbies, which had resorted to dramatic measure to avoid competition with the islands. There is, in fact, good reason to think that they were behind vicious rumors about unhygienic treatments for tobacco in the islands that circulated in 1904, an effort which constituted, in Edwards's reasoned opinion, "an organized attack on the manufacturers of tobacco in the Philippine Islands."[112]

Charles Curtis of Kansas introduced a new tariff bill to the House on January 14, 1905, which called for a reduction of tariff rates to 25 percent of Dingley rates on sugar and tobacco, and for free trade on all other products. There was never any doubt about who had designed the bill. In his report for Ways and Means, Chairman Payne acknowledged that it was "the result of much investigation and labor on the part of the insular government and of the Bureau of Insular Affairs."[113] For a variety of parliamentary reasons, this particular bill (an identical one would be voted on a year later) eventually failed to secure a vote on the House floor, but the extensive public hearings held by the Ways and Means Committee give a general indication of the tone of the opposition and the insular state's defense.

Much as Edwards had predicted, tobacco and sugar interests were better mobilized now, and they led a parade of farmers and manufacturers, as well as industry lobbyists, to testify as to the dire consequences of free trade with the islands. Invariably they spoke of the rich sugar and tobacco lands in the islands and predicted how quickly production could spread once American capital arrived. "It is not for the present, but for the future that we plead," testified one representative of a Michigan sugar company.

---

[109] Roosevelt to Speaker Joseph Cannon, December 23, 1904, letter reprinted in Morison, ed., *The Letters of Theodore Roosevelt*, v. IV, 1075. Strangely, only a month before, Platt had written to Roosevelt that "a general tariff revision is unnecessary and would prove disastrous to the business interests of the country." Platt to Roosevelt, November 21, 1904, letter reprinted in Louis A. Coolidge, *An Old-Fashioned Senator: Orville H. Platt of Connecticut* (New York: G. P. Putnam, 1910), 387.

[110] Roosevelt to Sereno Payne, December 24, 1904, letter reprinted in Morison, ed., *The Letters of Theodore Roosevelt*, v. IV, 1075–6.

[111] Wright to Taft, January 2, 1905; Edwards Papers, Box 5, Folder 1.

[112] As quoted in Forbes, *The Philippine Islands*, v. 2, 184. These rumors grew so widespread that the colonial state took to stamping all tobacco exports with a label certifying the cleanliness of factory conditions.

[113] 58th Cong., 3rd sess., H.R. Doc. No. 4600.

Others relied upon more nakedly partisan appeals and threats; one witness, for example, requested that "some one of the famous leaders of the Republican Party (perhaps he now sits at this table) be delegated to clamber to the top of our falling smoke stack – the same smoke stack that furnished the text of our most effective campaign oratory – and there plant the victorious banner bearing the inscription, 'Protection and Prosperity.'" Cigar manufacturers took a slightly different tack and concentrated on the lower labor costs in the islands. Mr. A. Bijur of the National Cigar Leaf Tobacco Association, for example, explained in great detail the wage differential between American and Filipino field hands, while G. W. Perkins of the Cigar Makers' International Union wondered aloud how Congress could pass legislation that would "surely result in lowering the standard of living of such a large army of loyal American citizens."[114] The empire, in other words, was framed by American agricultural interests as deeply harmful to the domestic economy, and these groups were happy to force a split between the Republican promoters of imperialism and the remainder of the party that favored protectionism at all costs.

This time, however, the insular government was prepared. Edwards, Taft, and Col. George R. Colton, a customs collector (and later head of the Dominican Receivership and Governor of Puerto Rico), all testified for the bill. Edwards of the BIA was the key witness. He presented extensive statistics that demonstrated the relatively low production capacities for Philippine tobacco and sugar, and further noted that the growth in domestic sugar consumption in the last decade had led the United States to import 1½ million tons from abroad.[115] Taft echoed Edwards's argument that free trade would not harm domestic production, citing the fact that the same representatives had made dire predictions about free trade with Puerto Rico – predictions, he noted, that had not come to pass. While Taft acknowledged that there was indeed plenty of land in the archipelago that could produce sugar – possibly even a great deal of it – he considered these objections absurd, comparing them to a similar position taken by Mark Twain's classic character, Colonel Sellers, who "calculated the number of people in China that needed eye-water at a dollar a bottle, and he would sell it them, and he would make $400,000,000 a year."[116]

On December 4, 1905, after his return from the Philippines, Chairman Payne introduced yet another tariff bill – virtually identical to the one submitted by Curtis the previous year – in the House, and this bill, too, came with Roosevelt's vigorous endorsement. Despite opposition from 57 Republicans, it managed to pass the House with the support of free trade Democrats 258 to 72. Yet much like the earlier bills, it did not fare well in the Senate; indeed, unlike the effort in 1903, this bill did not even make it out of Lodge's Committee on the Philippines. Timing, again, played a part in the bill's defeat. A railway rate bill was also up for consideration, an act supported by Roosevelt that was bitterly opposed by corporate interests and their powerful representatives in the Senate. At the time, Lodge was trying to rescue the Philippine free trade bill from its death in committee, but Roosevelt convinced them to wait. The opposition in the Senate had grown so intense that he feared that

[114] *Hearings* before the Committee on Ways and Means, 59th Cong., 1st sess., January 23–8; quoted in Abelarde, *American Tariff Policy*, 80–3.
[115] Edwards to Corbin, May 1, 1905; Edwards Papers, Box 5, Folder 13.
[116] *Hearings* before the Committee on Ways and Means, quoted in Abelarde, *American Tariff Policy*, 86–7.

bringing the tariff bill up for debate in the toxic atmosphere would only lead to its defeat.[117] Free trade, at least in the near term, would not be achieved.

By 1905, then, with their original plans for development defeated, it was clear that the Commission would need to modify its strategy. Without free trade, the type of direct investment that had fueled the development of the domestic United States would remain small. Although the Commission still called for massive investments in colonial infrastructure, with no direct financial support from the United States and with private capital seemingly uninterested because of the high tariff barriers, it was not immediately obvious how this could be accomplished. Their efforts to gather congressional support for development had largely been greeted with derision and hostility.

To solve this problem, then, these conservative Republican bureaucrats would begin to experiment with state-led development strategies that were far more aggressive than anything attempted at home – experiments that would increase their independence from Congress and lead them to engage private money in some rather fantastic financial schemes. Their incentives to continue to push for this development, even in the face of capitalist opposition, are difficult to discern without recognizing their deep ideological commitment to American imperialism. The prestige of the United States as a modern power was at stake, as well as their theories of scientific government and development. As Governor Luke Wright put it, "our job just now is to make the Philippines worth something to the Filipinos."[118] Such ideas, of course, were justified as benevolent and tutelary, even as they were designed to demonstrate to the world the genius of American power and progress – regardless of the desires of Filipinos, Congress, or large parts of the American public.

The American imperialists' hope was that after the Commission government had provided a stable currency and, in particular, improved railroad access to the rich interior of the islands, private industry would take over. To prime the pump, however, the commissioners would need access to more money, and the most immediate way to increase revenue was to improve the efficiency of internal taxation. But increasing domestic taxes was not without its own difficulties. While the Commission did not need further congressional authorization to change internal tax laws, pursuing this revenue-enhancing strategy would put colonial authorities in conflict with Filipino elites; the wealthy *ilustrado* class whose support the colonial administration had cultivated from the very first days of civil government and who filled the ranks of the friendly *Partido Federal*.[119]

CO-OPTING LOCAL ELITES: RACE, TAXATION, AND THE *ILUSTRADOS*

From the very earliest days of American administration, there was near-universal agreement among colonial officials that metropolitan and provincial Filipino elites would need to be incorporated into the colonial state. Although these decisions were often accompanied by self-congratulatory democratic rhetoric, there were

---

[117] Alfonso, *Theodore Roosevelt*, 138–9.
[118] Quoted in Forbes, *Philippine Islands*, v. I, 147.
[119] See Abinales, "Progressive-Machine Conflict."

more pragmatic reasons for including Filipinos after Congress had proved itself uninterested in robust support for American imperialism. Simply put, the ambitious developmental goals – the new roads, capital investments, and schools – that were supposed to jump start the Philippine economy could only be achieved if peace and relative order prevailed.[120]

At its highest levels, the Commission government was designed to *minimize* conflict between Filipinos and Americans. The *ilustrados* – wealthy and educated members of Manila society, many of whom had been involved in the formation of the revolutionary government – were thought to provide two resources to the colonial state: (1) their knowledge of the islands and influence on important sections of the population and (2) their inclusion at the highest level of governance made criticism from American anti-imperialists more difficult.[121] One decision made early on to reduce possible conflict was to include the governor-general as a member of the Commission, so that, in Taft's words, "he should not be brought by the exercise of the veto power in natural opposition."[122]

The Commission itself was to consist of eight members, with five seats reserved for Americans and three for Filipinos, so that the American majority would be large enough to survive the absence of one commissioner. Taft developed close personal relationships with several of the *Federalistas* and chose the Filipino members of the Philippine commission from its ranks. These wealthy *ilustrados*, such as Pedro Paterno, Trinidad Pardo de Tavera, Felipe Buencamino, and Cayetano Arellano, to name a few of the most prominent, would dominate Filipino politics for the first decade of American rule. Arellano, for example, was appointed the Chief Justice of the Supreme Court, Pardo was appointed to the Philippine Commission, and Buencamino became the first director of the civil service.

Surely, however, the most dramatic move of the early colonial government – one that Taft insisted upon – was an Assembly of Filipinos. Although Root was initially skeptical, the addition of this body was perfectly in keeping with Taft's policy of attracting the Filipino elite to the American colonial state and neutralizing criticism at home. Taft, it seems, had thought this provision important enough to insist that it be added to the Organic Act, despite the fact that it opened up the bill to attacks on the right.[123] The arch imperialist, Senator Albert Beveridge (R-IN), one of the Commission's most reliable supporters, fiercely opposed this particular measure.[124] Taft, however, would not budge, and he urged Lodge not to strike it in committee.

---

[120] Michael Cullinane, "Playing the Game: The Rise of Sergio Osmeña, 1898–1907," *Philippine Colonial Democracy*, ed. Ruby Paredes (Quezon City: Ateneo de Manila University Press, 1989), 73.

[121] Stanley, *Nation in the Making*, 80.

[122] Quoted in Stanley, *Nation in the Making*, 77. Indeed, the Commission voted to deny the governor-general veto power.

[123] As he later recalled in a speech he gave at the inaugural session of the Assembly in 1907, "I can remember when that section was drafted in the private office of Mr. Root in his house in Washington. Only he and I were present. I urged the wisdom of the concession, and he yielded to my arguments and the section as then drafted differed but little from the form it has to-day." Taft's speech is reprinted in US Philippine Commission, *Eighth Annual Report of the Philippine Commission to the Secretary of War, 1907* (Washington, DC: Government Printing Office, 1908), pt. 1, 214–28.

[124] Lodge to Taft, March 22, 1902; Root Papers, Box 164.

"If Congress shall withhold the provision now," he wrote to Lodge, "I very much fear discouragement on the part of our friends in the Islands."[125]

The policy of attraction was coupled with one of official decentralization. The Spanish colonial state was highly centralized and based almost entirely in Manila, while the provinces were largely left in control of the Catholic Church, which had served Spain in a quasi-official capacity. The Americans, partially due to their experience with US federalism and also due to the great variety of tribes and languages that made up the archipelago, decided early on that the governance structure would be decentralized, and that provincial and municipal governments would be vested with some independent powers and responsibilities.[126] Furthermore, given the number of civilian officials and the civil government's desire to remain independent of the American military, the Commission had no choice but to include large numbers of Filipinos in local administration. Thus, the Provincial Government Code, enacted on February 6, 1901, provided for the indirect election of a provincial governor by members of the provincial municipal councils. The American governor-general would then appoint the other two members of the provincial board, a provincial treasurer and supervisor of public works.[127] Municipal authority, it was decided, would be given to a president, vice president, and council who would be chosen by popular local election. A treasurer and secretary would be appointed by the provincial president with the council's consent, but only the president, secretary, and treasurer would draw a salary. Finally, suffrage was limited to males aged 23 or more who had held office under Spanish rule, owned property with a value of at least 500 pesos, or paid an annual tax of 30 pesos, or who were literate in Spanish or English.[128]

Nevertheless, much of this local power proved illusory. First, local governments were overseen by an Executive Bureau housed in the Office of the Governor, which kept a watchful eye on provincial governments. Before the first municipal elections could be held in 1902, the colonial state was already increasing its scrutiny of these local governments, as charges of corruption reached the Executive Bureau. Yet as historian Michael Cullinane argues, "What concerned them the most was not so much the 'abnormal' political behavior of the Filipinos, but rather their mishandling of public funds, which prevented them from carrying out many important functions; in short, local governments were accomplishing nothing."[129] Tutelary democracy, in other words, was valuable only to the extent it enabled the colonial state's development agenda. Beginning in 1903, municipal treasurers became civil service appointees, while further regulations increased the supervision of spending at the provincial level.[130]

---

[125] Taft to Lodge, March 26, 1902; Root Papers, Box 164.
[126] Stanley, *Nation in the Making*, 76.
[127] In 1906, the supervisor position was replaced by the division superintendent of schools, but the superintendent position was shortly replaced by an elected third member of the board.
[128] Williams, *Odyssey of the Philippine Commission*, 141.
[129] Michael Cullinane, "Implementing the 'New Order': The Structure and Supervision of Local Government during the Taft Era," in *Compadre Colonialism: Studies on the Philippines under American Rule*, ed. Norman G. Owen (Ann Arbor, MI: University of Michigan, Center for South and Southeast Asian Studies, 1971), 20–1. See *Special report of the Secretary of War, William H. Taft* (January 27, 1908), S. Doc. 200, 60th Cong., 1st sess., 1908, 24.
[130] Cullinane, "Implementing the 'New Order,'" 21.

In one unusual move, Taft went so far as to endorse the *Partido Federal*, a political party largely made up of wealthy *ilustrados*. As early as January 1901, he cabled Root for permission to give them official recognition: "Party is composed of best men in Islands," he wrote, "main object peace and civil government under sovereignty of United States. Approval of organization does not involve approval of all its aspirations after that."[131] A month later, on February 22, 1901 – George Washington's birthday – the party celebrated its official inauguration. The president of the newly formed party, Trinidad Pardo de Tavera, a wealthy *ilustrado* educated in Paris and ostensibly a personal friend of Taft's, gave the keynote address, a florid speech that left no doubt as to the *Federalistas'* support of Americanization. "I see the day near at hand," he exclaimed, "when it shall transpire that George Washington will not simply be the glory of the American continent but also our glory, because he will be the father of the American world, in which we shall feel ourselves completely united and assimilated."[132]

By May of 1901 the Federal party could claim 150,000 members and 290 local committees, including most of the Filipino elite. And Taft's support extended beyond official sanction to financial support; he gave $6,000 from Commission accounts to the party's newspaper, *La Democracia*, and even made an unsuccessful attempt to secure $20,000 from the US Republican Executive Committee for their use.[133] Taft further recruited most Filipino employees of the colonial state from the party. As he later testified to Congress, "In the appointment of natives the fact that a man was a member of the Federal party was always a good recommendation for him for appointment, for the reason that we regarded the Federal party as one of the great elements in bringing about pacification, and if a man was in the Federal party it was fairly good evidence that he was interested in the government which we were establishing, and would do as well as he could."[134]

Along with these more material forms of support, Taft mixed socially with the *ilustrados*, pointedly dancing with their wives at Filipino–American balls – a shocking display to many of his fellow Americans. As the Commission's secretary, the ever-observant James LeRoy, wrote in a 1901 letter to a friend back home, "[The Federalist Party] has had from the first the warmest support from the Commission, has been patted on the back in little 'bouquets' in public sessions, has been strengthened by little dinners and receptions and otherwise nursed along."[135] Despite his good public relations with the Filipino elite, Taft's private opinion was less rosy. He found in the *ilustrados* a "certain tendency to venality" and thought them "born politicians, as ambitious as Satan and as jealous as possible of each other's preferment."[136] Yet Taft understood that good social relations were crucial to the success of the colonial state. His successor Luke Wright did not.

The circumstances surrounding Wright's eventual dismissal illustrate just how the ambitious developmental agenda shaped the experience of race in the islands, and are worth exploring at some length. Although Governor Wright had great

[131] Taft to Root, Jan. 9, 1901; RG 350, "Correspondence of Philippine Commission," Box 1.
[132] Karnow, *In Our Image*, 176.
[133] Stanley, *Nation in the Making*, 73.
[134] S. Doc. No. 331, pt. 1, p. 67; 57th Congress, 1st sess.
[135] LeRoy to unnamed friend, February 8, 1901; LeRoy Papers, Box 1.
[136] Karnow, *In Our Image*, 174.

personal charm – described by all white officials as a true Southern gentleman – he and his wife rarely mixed socially with prominent Filipinos.[137] For *ilustrados* who had grown accustomed to the gregarious Taft (whatever his private feelings), this was deeply offensive. As a result of these apparent indignities, there were rumors that Pardo would resign from the Commission, or, even worse, that the Federal Party would change its platform to call for independence. In part, the *ilustrado*'s anger had to do with the internal revenue law that the Commission was trying to enact (discussed below), but Wright's inability to defuse the situation seems to have convinced the BIA that changes had to be made. Taft, now Secretary of War, decided to personally visit the Philippines to calm the situation before rumors could spread to the domestic press and give congressional opponents further ammunition.[138] Indeed, just before Taft's visit, Pardo wrote to Congressman Cooper, the insular government's central ally in the House and Chair of the House Committee on Insular Affairs, to complain of his treatment under Wright's administration.[139]

Whatever Taft's personal feelings about the justice of these charges, they threatened the carefully constructed portrait of American colonization efforts, the BIA's monopolization of information, and its close relations with key members of Congress. If Wright could let things unravel to this point, Taft thought, then he would simply have to go. Reflecting privately to his wife, Helen Taft, he concluded that Wright had "managed now to get the government into a condition where it is supported by no party and where the Filipinos of Manila having social aspirations are setting their faces like flint against him."[140] Without the support of the *ilustrados*, the Commission would never be able to raise the necessary funds to develop the islands.

Repairing relations, however, would mean that the Wrights would need to be publicly snubbed – something Taft was perfectly willing to do, if it meant regaining the support of Filipino elites. As LeRoy later recorded,

I drove to the Limpjap house, to attend the ball given to Miss Roosevelt by the Filipino ladies (more or less pure-blooded and Chinese mestizos). It had been arranged since Taft got here, and partly at his interference, Mrs. Wright having shown a disposition to give these people to understand their participation in the reception to Miss Roosevelt was not wanted . . . Taft, arriving late, at once organized a rigodon and took out Sra. Limpjap . . . [he] danced several round dances, once with the little American wife of young Torres, this purpose of course, to show that he disapproved of the race prejudice now being displayed here more strongly even than in the full days of military rule.[141]

Privately, both Taft and Roosevelt admitted that Wright's personal racism was at the root of the problem. Upon his return to the United States, Taft asked LeRoy to meet with Roosevelt to give him an independent assessment of problems in the

---

[137] Wright had served as an officer in the Confederate Army as a young man, which may have fueled suspicions about his private beliefs.
[138] To transform what could have been a dull diplomatic visit into a public relations coup, Taft invited Alice Roosevelt – "Princess Alice" – to accompany him, which would ensure positive press coverage back in the United States and greatly please the *ilustrados*.
[139] Quoted in Stanley, *Nation in the Making*, 127.
[140] Quoted in Ibid., 127.
[141] LeRoy Journal, entry of August 10, 1905; LeRoy Papers, Box 1.

Philippines. As LeRoy later recorded the episode in his journal, the damage Wright's racism had done was the major topic on the president's mind:

> He blurted out squarely the question, as I was again trying to tell him the situation we found:
> The whole truth of the matter is, is it not, that General Wright will not do for the place?
> I had to say directly that he would not.
> The chief trouble with him, is it not, is that he is prejudiced on the matter of race?
> "General Wright tries not to be," I said, "and he would doubtless resent it if he were called so; but he is unable to help his general attitude and feeling as to the superiority of one race from affecting all his underlying views on the Philippine question, and thus occasionally influencing his overt acts, in small ways at least."[142]

Roosevelt, it seems, left the interview convinced that Wright would need to be removed. He soon asked for his resignation and offered him the face-saving appointment of American minister to Japan. In the end, Taft's visit did convince the *ilustrados* to remain supportive of the Commission government, but this support was likely given in exchange for the understanding that Wright would resign. If the Wright episode illustrates anything, it is the extent to which insular authorities valued the cooperation of local Filipino elites – at least in the near term.[143] With access to few resources, any colonial development goals would be simply impossible without their support. Not only did they rely on their local prestige to ease the acceptance of American authority, but also their support gave credence to the insular state's carefully constructed narrative of American good works in the islands. Public dissent from highly placed Filipinos was likely to stir up anti-imperial sentiment in Congress and make the adoption of favorable legislation all the more difficult. It is clear that Taft and Roosevelt would do whatever it took to avoid this, including the dismissal of the colonial governor himself.

TAXING THE *ILUSTRADOS*: THE PROBLEMS OF INTERNAL TAXATION

During the Spanish colonial era, internal taxes were limited and highly regressive, but they were also a significant source of revenue, providing some ₱12 million in 1897.[144] The most important insular tax was the *cédula*, a general tax imposed on the

---

[142] LeRoy Journal, entry dated October 10, 1905; LeRoy Papers, Box 1.

[143] As Julian Go points out, however, the new taxation strategies that relied upon the colonial state's reach outside Manila led colonial administrators to turn "their attention to the provincial elite, cultivating new ties with them and offering them numerous concessions to enlist their support for the new strategy." Go, "Chains of Empire," 199. See also Michael Cullinane, *Ilustrado Politics: Filipino Elite Responses to American Rule, 1898–1908* (Quezon City: Ateneo de Manila University Press, 2003). Or, as Paul Kramer writes, "In the longer term, the crisis ushered in a shift in American clientelist strategies away from the sponsorship of Manila-based *ilustrados*, the backbone of the Federalista Party, who had been instrumental in ending the war, toward the recognition of a younger generation of emerging provincial politicians." Kramer, *Blood of Government*, 299.

[144] Stanley, *Nation in the Making*, 118. See also Carl C. Plehn, "Taxation in the Philippines, I," *Political Science Quarterly*, 16 (December 1901): 680–711; and "Taxation in the Philippines, II," *Political Science Quarterly*, 17 (March 1902): 125–48.

heads of household of between ½ and 37 pesos, which amounted to over half of all internal revenue.[145] Along with the *cédula*, there was a lucrative Chinese poll tax, an omnibus tax for primitive tribes in outlying areas, a state lottery, and an opium tax.[146] The Commission found these taxes, along with others, to be confusing and illogical – rather than tax a business's revenue, for example, the tax was assessed on the size of a shop.[147] As the Commission's whilom secretary Daniel Williams noted, "[A]s in other Spanish colonies, the laws were made by the landed proprietors and people of wealth, and they saw to it that few of the burdens of government fell to them . . . There was and is today no tax upon land, while luxuries of every kind are admitted at a nominal duty."[148]

During the spring of 1903 while resting at home in Vermont, Commissioner Ide and a young colonial administrator named John Horde, who had assisted in the development of taxation policies for Puerto Rico, worked on a new system of internal taxation for the Philippines. Their new tax code incorporated many of the Progressive ideas about taxation that were currently in vogue in the United States, including a tax on corporations and an inheritance tax.[149] It also provided for a business sales tax of 0.33 percent and an increase in excise taxes on alcohol and tobacco. The state lottery that had thrived during the Spanish period was abolished as well. The lucrative tax on opium, however, was a more difficult matter.[150] During Spanish administration, the colonial state's opium monopoly had proven to be a significant source of funds, accounting for almost 7 percent of total revenue during 1894–5. Although the Americans quickly worked to eliminate the state's monopoly on the narcotic, they allowed the opium trade with China to continue – the drug, after all, remained perfectly legal in the United States at this time, subject only to import tax provisions.[151] By 1906, however, the Commission attempted to tax it out of existence after facing pressure from American missionary groups.[152]

---

[145] The *cédula* grew out of a vassalage tax that had been in place since the earliest days of Spanish rule. By the nineteenth century, all Filipinos except for the Chinese (who faced a separate and more onerous tax) and inhabitants of Palawan and Balabac (among the most undeveloped regions) were required to carry a *cédula personal* or identification certificate. Luton, "American Internal Revenue Policy," 134.

[146] Harry Luton, "American Internal Revenue Policy in the Philippines to 1916," in *Comprade Colonialism: Studies on the Philippines under American Rule*, ed. Norman G. Owen (Ann Arbor, MI: University of Michigan, Center for South and Southeast Asian Studies, 1971).

[147] Stanley, *Nation in the Making*, 118.

[148] Williams, *Odyssey of the Philippine Commission*, 84.

[149] Luton, "American Internal Revenue Policy," 129–55.

[150] Opium remained legal in the United States until the 1914 Harrison Narcotic Act.

[151] See Anne L. Foster, "Models for Governing: Opium and Colonial Policies in Southeast Asia, 1891–1910," in *The American Colonial State in the Philippines: Global Perspectives*, ed. Julian Go and Anne L. Foster (Durham, NC: Duke University Press, 2003). Foster's essay draws attention to the fact that American administrators paid particularly close attention to the opium policies of other European colonies in Asia when forming their own policies. The pressure to ban opium in the Philippines is one of the few examples of a colonial policy that was dictated by Washington; as Foster writes, "U.S. officials in the Philippines tended to accept, and even approve of, continued legal and taxed sale of opium. Their questioning of that policy grew out of criticism from officials in Washington, D.C., and missionaries." Foster, "Models for Governing," 93.

[152] There is some debate about how effective the law was in restricting opium use, and given the drug's long presence in the Philippines as well as its highly addictive nature, there are reasons

Overall, the new American tax plan as proposed by Ide and Horde was a slightly more progressive version of the Spanish system. It shifted the highest taxes from basic clothing and food to luxury items, especially alcohol and tobacco.[153] Despite this shift in the tax burden, the colonial state continued to rely on the *cédula* and excise taxes on alcohol and tobacco, and both of these regressive taxes continued to make up nearly half of all internal revenue receipts throughout the Republican era.[154] Still, colonial officials thought they had designed a revenue-neutral proposal well in keeping with many of the latest Progressive theories of proper taxation – it spread the burden more equally and reserved the highest taxes for such "sinful" items as alcohol, tobacco, and opium.[155] As Cameron Forbes, the new head of the Department of Commerce and Police, which would administer the tax, noted in his journal, "The system of taxation here was so arranged to bear most heavily on the poor. The little fellow always paid, the big fish escaped. Our government has changed this and now the big fellow pays his proportion."[156]

Yet the move to a more progressive form of taxation stirred up a hornet's nest among these "big fish" – the Filipino *ilustrados* whom the Commission had attempted to co-opt with its policy of attraction. And none of them "had a good word to say for the bill."[157] In public sessions with the Commission, they argued that the tax would be ruinous to their business interests and that the Americans had gravely misunderstood the importance of tobacco and alcohol in Filipino culture. These drugs, they claimed, were not luxuries but necessities – a position, Horde noted sarcastically in his report, "[that] they maintained in all seriousness."[158] American colonial authorities greeted these complaints with a collective frustration that they made no attempt to hide in their letters back to Washington. "As originally drafted it was intended as a comprehensive scheme of taxation which would raise an amount of revenue equal to that now derived from our customs receipts," Governor Luke Wright wrote to Taft (now Secretary of War) in the summer of 1904. "When this bill was sprung on our constituency," he continued, "you can imagine the howl it created. We have been flooded with reclamas, petition, etc."[159] Others were even more blunt: "The taxes are extremely moderate but the rich people are squealing like stuck pigs . . . It is pitiable to have a revenue so small that

---

to be skeptical that it did much at all. It is, however, clear that the changes in the law ended the opium tax as a significant source of revenue. Under the Opium Law of 1906 (Act. No. 1761 of the Philippine Commission), opium tax revenues declined from 4.6 percent of total revenues in 1907 to 0.2 percent of total revenues by 1914. Luton, "American Internal Revenue Policy," 142.

[153] John S. Horde, *Internal Taxation in the Philippines* (Baltimore, MD: The Johns Hopkins Press, 1907), 33.

[154] Luton, "American Internal Revenue Policy," Appendix II, 148. The taxes were 40 cents per gallon of distilled liquor, 8 cents per gallon on fermented liquor, and 12 cents per pound of smoking or chewing tobacco. Forbes, *The Philippine Islands*, v. 1, 252.

[155] Originally, the internal revenue policy called for taxes to be collected and deposited in provincial accounts. But tax policy shifted again with the Commission's Reorganization Act of 1905, which centralized control over revenue policy in the Bureau of Internal Revenue and funds were deposited in the insular treasury.

[156] Forbes Papers, Journal, v. 1, August 25, 1904, 52–3.

[157] Luton, "American Internal Revenue Policy," 137; Horde, *Internal Taxation*, 20.

[158] Horde, *Internal Taxation*, 22.

[159] Wright to Taft, June 15, 1904; Edwards Papers, Box 3, Folder 20.

we cannot give these people the improvements they ask for."[160] As the perennially unpopular Commissioner Cameron Forbes wrote in his journal, "The opposition to this has caused the big onslaught against the Commission, a part of which has been leveled at me."[161]

Now worried that opposition from the *ilustrados* could defeat the measure, Wright encouraged Ide and Horde to moderate the taxes, which led to substantial reduction in all the new taxes but those on liquor and alcohol, including the elimination of both the tax on corporations and the inheritance tax entirely.[162] A proposed tax on land was also suspended for three years. This decision Horde later justified on the grounds that inheritance taxes would force the division of large plantation estates "and also for other weighty reasons," one of which must have been the fierce opposition this measure faced from Filipino elites.[163] But even these concessions did not resolve all of the colonial state's substantial problems. Indeed, two of the most vocal opponents of the Act were the Filipino members of the Commission; Trinidad Pardo de Tavera, who had significant investments in tobacco, and Benito Legarda, the biggest producer of alcohol in the islands.[164] From Washington, Taft cabled the Commission to urge them to remain steadfast on this more moderate internal revenue law. The law, after all, called for taxes only one-third as high as in Puerto Rico, and the proposed excise taxes were substantially less than alcohol and tobacco taxes in the United States.[165] In the end, the majority of the Commission did hold firm on the excise tax provisions, and the final internal revenue bill was adopted in July of 1904, conveniently passed when Pardo and Legarda were visiting the United States.[166]

Privately, Taft sought to intervene on behalf of the Commission with the Filipino elites. The Secretary of War, who continued to have close personal relations with many of the top *ilustrados*, urged Legarda to give the tax a chance, reasoning that these new taxes would benefit him in the long run by eliminating "fraudulent and unsubstantial" competition.[167] Legarda, in turn, promised Taft that he would hold off on further protestations until he had a chance to look into the issue himself. He did not change his mind. Upon returning to the islands, Legarda and Pardo renewed their opposition to the Act, both convinced that the new internal revenue policies would cripple the development of nascent Filipino industries. The situation was made worse when a private letter from Wright to Roosevelt was leaked to the opposition press in which Wright called into question the value of the Commission's relationship with the Federal Party – a great embarrassment to Legarda and Pardo, the leaders of the *Federalistas*.[168] In the end, the internal revenue bill was passed with only minor concessions to the *ilustrados*, and contributed, in part, to the increase in colonial revenues between 1903 and 1904 – a necessary component of the colonial state's development strategy.

[160] Forbes Papers, Journal, August, 25 1904, 52–3.
[161] Forbes Papers, Journal, October 30, 1905, 349.
[162] Luton, "American Internal Revenue Policy," 137; Horde, *Internal Taxation*, 20.
[163] Horde, *Internal Taxation*, 23.
[164] Stanley, *Nation in the Making*, 119.
[165] Forbes Papers, Journal, October 30, 1905, 349.
[166] Stanley, *Nation in the Making*, 120.
[167] Ibid., 121.
[168] Ibid., 122.

With this victory in hand, insular authorities were already planning other ways to increase their tax base. On his journey back to the United States in September of 1905, LeRoy proposed to Taft that the insular government begin studying land use in each province to develop an appropriate land tax:

[W]hen it comes time for the expiration of the three-year suspension of the present land tax, we shall have the data upon which to evolve a *scientific system of land taxation*, making it, as it should be, one of the chief sources of revenue, and perhaps planning to make it, as time goes by, the chief source of revenue. This would open the way for the abolition or great reduction of the customs tariff, and for the *scientific revision of the internal revenue imposts*. We have been legislating thus far over there for temporary exigencies, and it is *time we began to evolve a scientific and permanent fiscal system*.[169]

As LeRoy's proposal reveals, colonial authorities were not merely interested in increasing revenue, but doing so in a supposedly more *scientific* manner. Their focus on effective and "modern" government made charges of corruption or mismanagement from home all the more offensive.

Yet charges of "excessive" taxation continued to dog the Commission throughout the Republican period – accusations that insular authorities went to great lengths to dispel, particularly because it drew attention from the US Congress to colonial spending. Nearly every year, the annual reports displayed extensive comparative statistics on the per capita tax revenues, per capita expenditures, and per capita debts of various nations.[170] And every year the Philippines appeared near the bottom of these tables. The 1908 *Report of the Philippine Commission*, for example, showed the rate of per capita taxation at $1.82, which compared favorably to Japan at $6.30, the United States at $7.45, and Great Britain at $17.57.[171] In a November address before the Brooklyn Institute of Arts, Taft acknowledged the "persistent misstatement that the Philippines are a great expense to the United States. The only expense they constitute for the United States is the expense of maintaining the regular United States forces in the islands . . . Beyond this there is no expense to the United States. Every other expenditure is paid for out of the treasury of the islands, raised by taxation from other sources."[172] The administrators appear to have taken great pride in their belief that American imperialism was not only benevolent, but also offered great value for the dollar.[173] Perhaps most important, however, was the argument that the empire did not *cost* anything, thereby limiting the interest of Congress.

Nevertheless, until the reduction in tariff rates for most goods entering the United States provided by the 1909 Payne–Aldrich tariff (discussed below), both revenue and expenditure remained relatively low. As Figure 4.4 shows, the dramatically low revenues of the first three years Commission government were largely due to the famine and aftermath of the Philippine–American War. In 1904, when trade had

[169] LeRoy Journal, entry dated September 22, 1905. LeRoy Papers, Box 1 [my emphasis].
[170] Frank H. Golay, "The Search for Revenues," in *Reappraising an Empire: New Perspectives on Philippine–American History*, ed. Peter W. Stanley (Cambridge, MA: Harvard University Press, 1984), 259.
[171] *Report of the Philippine Commission, 1908*, part 1, 45; Forbes, *Philippine Islands*, v. 1, 261.
[172] Taft quoted in Forbes, v. 2, *Philippine Islands*, 503.
[173] Golay, "Search for Revenues," 259.

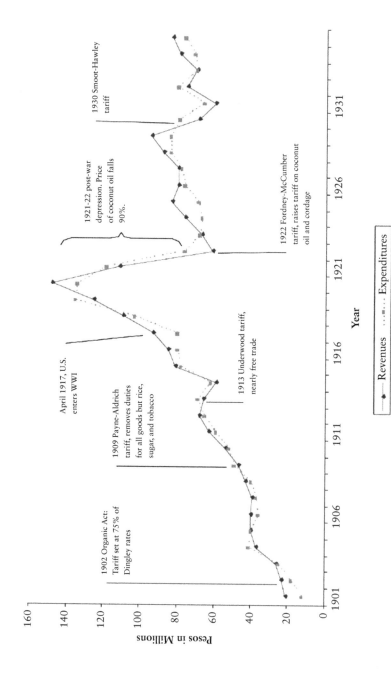

FIGURE 4.4. *Government expenditures and revenues in the Philippines.*
Source: Historical Statistics of the United States, Colonial Times to 1970.

increased, the Commission collected a little over ₱35 million (about $17.5 million) in revenue, but this remained a paltry sum to fund the roads, schools, and railways that the Commission had planned. Further increases in internal taxation would only anger the colonial state's Filipino allies, and give further ammunition to domestic critics who criticized their tax system. With direct investment hampered because of tariff barriers and political opposition to higher taxation, the colonial state would soon turn to Wall Street to fund its infrastructure projects through borrowed money – a move that granted it a nearly free hand to run the islands according to the commissioners' Progressive vision.

STATE BUILDING THROUGH COLLABORATION: COLONIAL STATE DEVELOPMENT ON WALL STREET

Taft had earlier warned Root that it would be "like running on one wheel to develop this country without power to offer investments to capital."[174] Now, it seemed, the Commission would be forced to do just that. Congress had limited its ability to attract capital through high tariff laws and public lands restrictions – the very sort of micromanaging that the colonial government found so objectionable. Even capitalists were uninterested in the islands and were willing to invest only reluctantly. "The truth is," Taft acknowledged, "that capital finds itself so profitable employed in [the United States] that it is only after the greatest effort that it can be induced to go as far as the Philippine Islands."[175]

In a lesson that would have profound effects on the development of American imperialism, insular authorities learned to adapt to these restrictions by forging private partnerships.[176] With little hope of gaining financial assistance from Congress, but with an understandable fear of flouting its wishes, the Commission began to borrow money for development, a move that would begin a process of collaborative state-building for American empire.

The Rise of American Investment Banks

Among the many dramatic changes to occur in the American system of capitalism following the Civil War was the remarkable rise in the power and international stature of American investment banks, which grew throughout the Gilded Age in response to the need for vast amounts of new capital to finance railroad construction.[177] To raise this capital, banks began to develop the infrastructure necessary

---

[174] Taft to Root, November 30, 1900; Root Papers, Box 164.

[175] Quoted in Stanley, *A Nation in the Making*, 227.

[176] Another strategy to raise capital involved the reformation of internal taxes in the islands, including the Spanish *cédula*, a general tax imposed on the heads of household of between one-half and 37 pesos. See Luton, "American Internal Revenue Policy"; Horde, *Internal Taxation in the Philippines*.

[177] Rosenberg, *Financial Missionaries*. For a more in-depth discussion of the rise of managerial capitalism in this period, see Alfred Chandler, *The Visible Hand: The Managerial Revolution in American Business* (Cambridge, MA: Harvard University Press, 1977).

to market these securities directly to the public. As the American railroads grew in power and importance, so too did the banks that provided their financing.[178] By 1900 the American banking profession had transformed itself, in the words of one financial historian, from "the passive, relatively detached merchandiser of securities typical of the pre-railroad era" into an "active investment banker, the central figure in a more integrated stage of capitalist development."[179] Between 1900 and 1913, for example, 250 separate loans with a value of nearly $1.1 billion were placed with American banks, and the very top year was 1905, when a total of $175 million issues were floated.[180]

The massive growth of American investment banks and the domestic market for securities also put New York City on the map as a major center of international finance. Although American banks still dealt primarily with domestic securities, by the end of the nineteenth century the strongest Wall Street banking houses of J. P. Morgan, Speyer & Company, J. and W. Seligman, Kidder Peabody, and Kuhn, Loeb, as well as large commercial banks like the National City Bank, began to look for international investment opportunities. In 1899, as part of a consortium of British and German banks that were arranging a £22.7 million loan to Mexico, J. P. Morgan became the first American firm to comanage a large international loan. That an American firm was involved in international lending for the first time did not escape the notice of the English press. "The strangest fact of all," noted London's *Daily Mail*, "is the appearance for the first time of an American banking house on a foreign loan prospect."[181] For American empire builders, the timing could not have been more fortuitous. Just as they began looking for money to finance their imperial policies, New York was beginning to look for more international investment opportunities.

Trading Currency and Floating Bonds

To facilitate American investment, the Commission planned to put the Philippines on a solid financial footing, preferably a gold standard, which could easily be exchanged for dollars. Given the financial chaos in the islands, however, this was no small task. During the Spanish colonial period, Madrid had maintained an official gold standard for the Philippines, but had also permitted the exchange at parity of Filipino gold coins with the more commonly circulated Mexican silver coins. As the price of silver began to decline in the 1870s, Filipino gold coins were routinely traded for Mexican silver and shipped out of the country at substantial profits. As a result, by the time the Americans arrived, the Filipino gold coin existed mainly in theory, and the day-to-day currency of the Philippines was a confusing mix of Mexican silver and various of

---

[178] These investment banks were part of a broader movement in the American economy – what Martin Sklar terms the "corporate reconstruction of American capitalism." Martin J. Sklar, *The Corporate Reconstruction of American Capitalism, 1890–1916* (New York: Cambridge University Press, 1988). See especially 1–40.

[179] Vincent P. Carosso, *Investment Banking in America: A History* (Cambridge, MA: Harvard University Press, 1970), 80–2. Carosso's account remains the definitive study of banking in this period.

[180] Carosso, *Investment Banking in America*, 81.

[181] Vincent P. Carosso, *The Morgans: Private International Bankers 1854–1913* (Cambridge, MA: Harvard University Press, 1987), 420.

the other silver-based currencies that circulated throughout Asia.[182] This was much to the advantage of exporters, who sold their goods abroad for gold and paid their workers in silver, but crippled importers who were forced to do the opposite.

In the eyes of the Republican colonial authorities, such financial chaos was completely unacceptable; in Root's estimation, the currency was "in as bad a condition as is possible."[183] Yet they were well aware of the need for caution given the combustible nature of currency issues back in the United States. The last thing the Philippine colonial government wanted to do was to make further enemies in Washington. The insular authorities needed someone to study the issue who had familiarity with the financial system of East Asia and also currency politics at home. On the recommendation of Secretary of the Treasury Lyman Gage, Root had retained Charles A. Conant, a well-known business journalist and vocal proponent of imperialism, whose book, *The United States and the Orient*, had established him as an authority on monetary issues.[184]

Conant's argument (decidedly Leninist in its formulation if not its intent) was that industrialized countries ought to secure colonies in which to invest their surplus capital, which, he reasoned, would provide an opportunity for profit while also developing the colonies. The acquisition of colonies was necessary not merely for profit, however, but also for national prestige. The great struggle of the future would, according to Conant, be between rival national trusts. "It is," he wrote, "this struggle between the great political powers of the world for bolstering up national economic power which constitutes the cardinal fact of modern diplomacy."[185] The new aim for leaders was to be "the creation of national trusts vested with the power of taxation and with military and naval force for the object of seeking and holding exclusive markets on the one hand, and of increasing competing power in free markets on the other."[186]

Conant, who would later become known for his currency reforms in Puerto Rico, Cuba, and the Dominican Republic (see Chapter 5), spent nearly a month in the Philippines studying the currency issues, eventually submitting his "Special Report on Coinage and Banking in the Philippine Islands" to Root in November of 1901. Although, as expected, he recommended a gold standard for the islands, his report was sensitive to local conditions. He noted the attachment of Filipino workers to silver coins, which he thought made the introduction of a gold-standard currency or US dollars too radical a change. His ingenious solution was a dual currency. The Philippines would have a silver peso pegged to the dollar, thus easing trade between the United States and the Islands, and also avoiding any shock that might accompany the introduction of a foreign currency.[187] Such a dual currency, it was also thought,

---

[182] Stanley, *Nation in the Making*, 92–3.
[183] *Annual Report of the Secretary of War*, 1902, 79.
[184] Healy, *U.S. Expansionism*, 194–209.
[185] Charles A. Conant, *The United States in the Orient: The Nature of the Economic Problem* (New York: Houghton, Mifflin, 1900), 175. See Chapters 6 and 7 for a discussion of Conant's work in the Dominican Republic. Conant also argued for the supremacy of the executive in foreign affairs and a professional foreign service.
[186] Conant, *United States in the Orient*, 176.
[187] Healy, *U.S. Expansionism*, 207. When it was adopted, the new currency became known locally as "conants" to distinguish it from the old "mex" currency.

had the added advantage of minimizing opposition from silver-state representatives whose constituents stood to profit from the coinage of the new currency.

The Commission, which was shown an early copy of the report, agreed with Conant's recommendations, and Conant himself was put in charge of drafting his currency plan into the Organic Act. Still, Root and the Commission worried about the reception the dual currency would receive in Congress. "[T]here are rumors," LeRoy reflected in his journal, "of Hanna and certain westerners, among them Senator Clark, being interested in seeing that Congressional action this winter shall be such as to allow the western mines a nice output for their silver."[188] Conant apparently shared these worries, too, because he recommended to Taft that he stay on as a consultant to shepherd the bill through Congress. Although this must have been an extremely unusual proposal for the time, Taft was receptive to the suggestion. "I have no doubt," he wrote to Root "that he [Conant] would be exceedingly useful with respect to the financial and banking legislation and that he would be very efficient in giving us information in respect to other legislation." Yet, he added, "how much influence he has with the prominent members of the House and Senate, I do not know."[189] Despite Taft's lingering doubts, Root approved of the plan, and Conant set to work lobbying members of Congress.

While Taft may have been correct that Conant had limited influence with members of Congress, as a former reporter and analyst for the *Journal of Commerce*, he did have influence with the New York financial community. During the debate over the Organic Act, Conant mobilized support from the financial press and wrote several articles himself for such Wall Street publications as *Bankers' Magazine*, as well as more mainstream outlets like the *Atlantic Monthly*.[190] Although Taft could have hardly appreciated it at the time, these connections between insular authorities and Wall Street would prove to be crucial in the development and expansion of American empire.

On December 3, 1902, Lodge reintroduced the currency act as a separate bill in the Senate, although the bill's prospects as a separate measure did not look much better. Conant's measure, it will be recalled, recommended the creation of a separate circulating silver peso backed up by the US gold dollar at a ratio of 2:1. This would allow for the limited circulation of silver pesos and paper currency that would be backed by a gold reserve fund in New York. Predictably, the law became caught up in the intense monetary-policy debates of Washington. In many respects, Conant and the Commissioners had anticipated this difficulty, and muted the opposition somewhat by allowing for the circulating currency to be silver, thus ensuring that the silver mines of the American West could turn a profit on the new coins. Still, there was a considerable amount of fight to be met.

Roosevelt made a valiant effort to push the legislation forward through a special message to both houses on January 7 imploring members to enact "the measure already pending in your body for the betterment of the Philippines Islands," and

[188] LeRoy Journal, entry dated September 25, 1901; LeRoy Papers, Box 1.
[189] Taft to Root, October 14, 1901; Root Papers, Box 164.
[190] C. A. Conant, "Coinage and banking in the Philippine Islands," *Bankers' Magazine*, 64 (January 1902): 89–102; Charles A. Conant, "The economic future of the Philippines," *Atlantic Monthly* 89 (March 1902): 366–71; Charles A. Conant, "Our work in the Philippines," *International Monthly*, 5 (March 1902): 358–72.

warning that "serious calamities may come from failure to enact them."[191] The president, it seems, even began to lobby members of Congress himself to ensure passage.[192] Even with Roosevelt's vigorous endorsement, however, the bill faced significant opposition, particularly in the Senate. Taft, writing to Edwards from the Philippines, observed "that Brother Aldrich [Senator Nelson Aldrich, R-RI] . . . is leading a rubber-shoe attack upon the proposed legislation. I suppose if he cannot prevent legislation he will emasculate it. It will be an immense disappointment to all the people if the coinage matter is not remedied, and I should much prefer even to have the radical introduction of the United States Currency here to the present system."[193]

For its part, the Commission arranged for the Manila Chamber of Commerce, along with the English, Spanish, and American banks in Manila, to petition Congress in support of the gold-standard currency. Insular authorities, however, feared that more direct lobbying would be necessary to carry the bill through the Senate. As a nervous Edwards cabled Governor Wright, "I am going to telegraph Professor Jenks, Conant, and perhaps Mr. Peabody, to come back here. We are certainly up to the danger line in my personal opinion."[194] Conant, now employed by the Morton Trust Company of New York, sent word to silver interests in financial circles that with the value of silver bullion in decline, their interests would be hurt by delaying the passage of the bill.[195] It is not known how much influence Conant's lobbying had on the effort to pass the bill through the Senate, although the deadlock seems to have been cleared up fairly quickly, and the final measure authorizing the dual currency was adopted in March of 1903.

As usual, insular authorities saw the Senate's actions as foolish and remained less than impressed with members of their own party, particularly Senator Aldrich. In point of fact, they were convinced that their own efforts were the primary reason the legislation was adopted.[196] "It was an immense relief to me, as I know it was to you," Root wrote to Taft, "to get the Coinage Bill through at the last session of Congress. I can assure you it was not done without an immense amount of hard work."[197]

Lodge, however, took a different view, writing to Roosevelt, "I did a good piece of work yesterday in getting through the Philippine Currency Bill. Aldrich and I managed it, and I think it did credit to our head and hearts."[198] Taft's relatively public griping about Aldrich and Lodge earned him a stern rebuke from Roosevelt. Senator Aldrich, the president wrote to Taft, "was at the end an immense help in the currency business and he made a strong and loyal fight for the reduction of the Philippine tariff."[199] Although it is doubtful that Taft agreed with the president,

[191] Message to the Senate and House of Representatives, January 7, 1903, text from James D. Richardson, ed., *A Compilation of the Messages and Papers of the Presidents 1789–1905*, (Washington, DC: Bureau of National Literature and Art, 1907), v. 10, 439, 6732.

[192] Roosevelt to Root, February 16, 1903, letter reprinted in Morrison, ed., *The Letters of Theodore Roosevelt*, v. 3, 428.

[193] Taft to Edwards, January 25, 1903; Edwards Papers, Box 2, Folder 17.

[194] Edwards to Wright, February 17, 1903; Edwards Papers, Box 2, Folder 18.

[195] Stanley, *Nation in the Making*, 96.

[196] Taft to Edwards, January 25, 1903; Edwards Papers, Box 2, Folder 17.

[197] Root to Taft, April 1, 1903; Root Papers, Box 165a.

[198] Lodge to Roosevelt, February 17, 1903, letter reprinted in Lodge, ed., *Selections from the Correspondence of Theodore Roosevelt and Henry Cabot Lodge*, v. 2, 2.

[199] Roosevelt to Taft, March 19, 1903, letter reprinted in Morrison, ed., *The Letters of Theodore Roosevelt*, v. 3, 450–1.

he composed a conciliatory letter, noting that "I did not intend to do Senator Aldrich an injustice in what I wrote you." Still, he did not let the issue drop. "My experience," he continued, "when I was in Washington was that he was especially sensitive upon any subject that affected either sugar or tobacco or silver."[200]

Conant meanwhile had been busy lobbying members for his currency bill, and had already discussed it with Speaker Henderson and Cooper, neither of whom saw any reason why it should have difficulty passing through the House.[201] In December of 1901, he finally met with Lodge, who, it seems, had begun to lose his patience with the insular government. As Conant described the encounter to Root,

I saw Senator Lodge to-day and told him that it was your desire to secure prompt action on the coinage bill and that, if agreeable to him, I would have the bill ready for introduction on Thursday, with a proper statement of its contents to be given to the press, with the statement that it had been prepared by him and Mr. Cooper in consultation with the officials of the War Department. This plan did not meet with the approval of the Senator. He stated that he had stood aside in reference to the Philippine tariff bill and that he would not stand aside in favor of Mr. Cooper in reference to other legislation. He said that he had offered to take charge of Philippine legislation and objected to its being divided up and given to other members. Among his close words, which I promptly jotted down after leaving him, were these:

"If they (referring to the War Department) want it introduced bit by bit in the House, let them do it. I will take care of it when it comes over here, but if I am to have charge of Philippine legislation I want to have charge of it."

This and other statements conveyed the very plain suggestion that House legislation would not fare well at his hands under these conditions, even if originating in the War Department. He was sufficiently courteous in manner, but did not mince the fact that he wanted the credit of handling the legislation.[202]

In the end, it may have benefited the Commission that the debate in both houses of Congress was mainly a proxy war for domestic monetary debates. That, at least, took the focus away from what was actually going on in the Philippines. Congress had given an executive agency permission to coin its own money and to develop its own monetary system, a power expressly forbidden to any state in the Union. It is important to be clear on this point: The Philippine currency was not US currency with slightly different markings – it was a separate currency backed by its own gold reserve fund.[203] The circulating coins were silver with a silver content worth less than their face value, and they were backed by a theoretical Philippine gold peso with one-tenth of the gold as a US$5 gold piece, thus fixing the pesos at exactly one-half of US$1 and allowing its value to fluctuate with other gold-standard currencies.[204] The Commission was additionally authorized to distribute paper money backed by silver pesos. But this modest delegation of authority would soon become a tool for the Philippine colonial state to finance

[200] Taft to Roosevelt, May 9, 1903; Root Papers, Box 165a.
[201] Conant to Root, December 14, 1901; Root Papers, Box 16.
[202] Conant to Root, December 17, 1901; Root Papers, Box 16.
[203] Although, as will be discussed later, it seems that members of Congress themselves did not completely understand this provision when the bill was passed.
[204] As the price of silver continued to rise after 1905, the Philippine coin became worth more as bullion, and the Commission returned to Congress to gain permission to recoin the Philippine peso with less silver.

its imperial dreams in the islands that drew little attention from Congress or the American public.

Insular Bonds Sales

Now authorized by Congress to develop a separate currency for the islands, insular authorities had to figure out how exactly to do this. At this time, there were no professional consultants in monetary policy and currency design, and no prominent member of the insular government had the knowledge to arrange such a complex system himself. Conant had anticipated this problem nearly a year before: "It seems to me that after the Filipino bill is passed, if it provides for a coinage and banking system, some official of thorough, theoretical training and practical experience will be required at Manila to attend to such matter. Would it not be well to ascertain if Professor Hollander would be willing to accept such a position? It will very likely be desirable to prepare some explanation of the law and what could be accomplished under it by the Philippine government after Congress has taken action."[205]

Unfortunately, Conant, Jenks, and Hollander, all of whom had been instrumental in economic planning for the Philippines, declined the insular government's offers of employment. Eventually, however, on the recommendation of Jenks, Edwin W. Kemmerer, an assistant professor of political economy at Cornell, was given the job. To provide the gold reserves for this new currency, the act authorized the Commission to issue and sell $10,000,000 in bonds on Wall Street, and this task was given to Col. Edwards at the BIA.[206] The idea was that the bonds would raise sufficient funds for the purchase of silver bullion to coin the Philippine peso, as well as for a Gold Standard Fund to be held in New York. But insular authorities were not entirely sure how Wall Street would react to these new Philippine bonds. The colonial government, after all, had no credit history, and failure to make a full bond sale would contribute to the already tenuous financial position of the colonial state.

Fortunately for the BIA and its allies in Manila, the sale was a success. Working through the Guaranty Trust Company, Edwards managed to easily offer $6 million worth of bonds at a favorable rate. "I am told by financial men," Edwards gloated, "that it was as successful an advertised bond issue as they have ever seen."[207] The importance of Edwards's ability to negotiate Wall Street bond markets was not lost on his superiors. "I think Edwards has done very good work in getting 3½ per cent interest on balances with the Guarantee [sic] Trust Company," Root wrote to Taft, "and if, as I hope, we can sell the certificates of indebtedness at a little premium, we will be borrowing the money to carry the operation through without its costing anything at all."[208] In all, 3 million silver certificates were successfully floated, giving the colonial state sufficient funds to carry out its currency operations.

---

[205] Conant to Root, May 6, 1902; Root Papers, Box 25.
[206] Leonard F. Giesecke, *History of American Economic Policy in the Philippines during the American Colonial Period, 1900–1935* (New York: Garland Publishers, 1987), 97.
[207] Edwards to Wright, January 1, 1904; Edwards Papers, Box 3, Folder 14.
[208] Root to Taft; Library of Congress, Root Papers, Box 165a.

Following the success of their first bond offering, BIA and Commission officials again returned to Wall Street to float $7 million worth of bonds for the purchase of a Catholic monastic order's extensive land holdings in the islands.[209] Yet for cash-strapped insular officials, the successful sale of bonds on Wall Street indicated something more – that development funds could be successfully raised from private sources. "It seems to me," Taft wrote to Edwards following the currency bond sale, "that the premium which you obtained is marvelous and indicates that the credit of the Philippine Government is such that we shall not have much difficulty in floating the bonds in more important matters." And this, Taft concluded, meant that "the idea that we are to remain in the islands for an indefinite time in the future is deeply fixed," a perception that would be sure to improve the colonial state's credit among the bankers.[210]

The insular government's success on Wall Street was remarkable – at the time, the prevailing interest rate in the islands on the best commercial security was 12 percent – and it requires some explanation.[211] While Edwards's careful planning and Conant's many connections on Wall Street likely contributed to the successful offering, these personal factors alone surely do not explain why some 3 million certificates could be sold at a good rate by an entity with no previously established credit.

A further answer lies in an ambiguity easily exploited by Edwards, namely, the official status of Philippine government bonds. Few investors would normally purchase bonds from a fragile Asian government, but they would be willing to buy them if they thought the US Treasury backed them, an impression that colonial officials were anxious to encourage. Indeed, as a result of BIA pressure, both the Secretary of Treasury and the Postmaster General had ruled that the Philippine government bonds were acceptable as security for deposits of public money.[212] As a matter of law, however, the US government did not guarantee these bonds, but the savvy investor could reasonably expect that the US Treasury would bail out the colonial government if it ever reached the point of default. Governor Taft, testifying before the House Committee on Insular Affairs in 1903 on the friar land bonds offering, admitted as much:

I suppose that investors have assumed that fact would lead Congress to assume the obligation of them if the government ever became bankrupt. I only know that banking houses are entirely willing to take the bonds without a guaranty by the Government, and the rate at which the bonds sold is an indication that the shadow of the United States in the background is very valuable.[213]

Later that year, Attorney General Philander Knox attempted to add a penumbra of legal authority to the issue. "Although the loan is not legally guaranteed by the

---

[209] Taft had visited the Vatican in 1902 to directly negotiate the price. This authorization was granted in the Organic Act. See Act of Congress, July 1, 1902, Sections 63–5.

[210] Taft to Edwards, June 5, 1903; Edwards Papers, Box 3, Folder 1.

[211] Forbes, *Philippine Islands*, v. 1, 269.

[212] Ibid., 270. The many letters in the archival records inquiring as to the legal status of the Philippine bonds show that this issue was left somewhat ambiguous by colonial authorities. See, for example, Edmund Seymour to Edwards, January 5, 1903; American National Bank to Edwards, April 3, 1906; RG 350 (Serial 9436), Box 548.

[213] Taft quoted in C. Rec, 58th Cong., 2nd sess., H.R. Rep. 2227, Part 2.

United States," he held, "the issue is obviously made over its faith and credit and by its aid and recognition." At the most basic level, he concluded, "The interest and credit of the United States are deeply and essentially concerned in these matters."[214] Opinions like these could only improve the insular government's credit on Wall Street.[215]

Whatever the justice of these claims, congressional Democrats and anti-imperialists were not the only ones concerned about the status of these bonds. As it became clear that insular bond sales would become more frequent, and that insular officials wanted to use them to leverage more capital for development projects, the ambiguity of the official status of these bonds began to worry other Roosevelt administration officials, especially Leslie Shaw, Secretary of the Treasury. Naturally, Shaw was anxious to maintain a clear separation between the Philippine colonial state's bonds and US Treasury bonds, and the speed at which the colonial state had embraced Wall Street bond markets concerned him.

He had good reason to be worried. Edwards, encouraged by his success in the first bond sale, was planning to leverage the bonds to raise yet more money. "I don't see why," he asked Wright, "we can't get up some scheme and invite those banks that are holders of the temporary certificates, which are not in the Treasury Department covering deposits, to continue them at 1% or possible 2% interest."[216] For Shaw, schemes of this nature were unacceptable, and his concern soon turned to outright obstruction, creating a power struggle between the War Department and Treasury – precisely the sort of situation that the BIA had long worked to avoid.

Never easily discouraged, Edwards had first arranged a meeting between the secretary and Roosevelt to smooth things over, and to have the president press upon Shaw the War Department's need to squeeze more capital from the bonds. But even this, it seems, was not enough. The BIA decided that its next move would need to be more subtle. As Edwards wrote to Wright on New Year Day 1904,

Secretary Shaw wouldn't give us the treatment we wanted – so we had to go at it again, and I finally [went] to former Assistant Secretary Ailes, now Vice President of the Riggs National Bank, and representing in that bank the National City Bank of New York, to happen in on Secretary Shaw and tell him why he could do as we wanted to have him. We were in the midst of an easy money market and a very soft bond market with every prospect of government bonds going down, and after careful consultation with New Yorkers and others we came to the conclusion that the best time to sell was right after the first of the year when New Yorkers and capitalists were cutting coupons and looking around for good investments.[217]

---

[214] This early decision became the operating assumption of the BIA through the 1920s. As Edwards's successor at the BIA, Frank McIntyre, explained in 1926, "Congress has not specifically pledged the good faith of the United States to the payment of the principal and interest of Philippine Government bonds, but as all bonds have been issued pursuant to its specific authorization, the Department of Justice and the War Department have invariably held that such bonds constitute a moral obligation of the United States." Letter reprinted in C. Rec, 58th Cong., 2nd sess., H.R. Rep. 2227, Part 2.

[215] Such opinions did raise objections from a small minority in Congress, who charged them with orchestrating the profits of bankers on the backs of Filipino taxpayers. See opposition report, 58th Cong., 2nd sess., H.R. Rep. 2227, Part 2.

[216] Edwards to Wright, January 1, 1904; Edwards Papers, Box 3, Folder 14.

[217] Ibid.

Even this, however, apparently did not sway the secretary. Four months later Edwards wrote again to Wright, acknowledging, "[c]onfidentially we are having a dickens of a time here to make Secretary Shaw look through the same glasses that the Bureau of Insular Affairs and our honored Chief uses."[218] The Commission argued that, as an independent government entity with financial independence from the US Treasury, it should be able to play the bond markets as it saw fit, without interference from another agency. Their logic did not prevail on the Treasury, and insular authorities had little choice but to accept the decision; after all, without the endorsement of the secretary, their bonds would not fetch nearly so favorable a rate. Nevertheless, insular authorities remained supremely confident in their ability to exploit Wall Street's investment capital to develop the islands – especially Edwards, who boasted that he was "on intimate terms now with all the hydra-headed capitalists in New York."[219]

By 1904, after the initial bond sales were concluded, colonial bureaucrats decided to cement their relationship with the Wall Street banks by employing one of their own. This, it seems clear, was a primary consideration for encouraging W. Cameron Forbes, a scion of the legendary Forbes banking family – one of America's wealthiest – to join the Commission. Forbes was not being considered because of his political connections, but because of his experience in finance and, perhaps even more important, his social connections on Wall Street. As one colonial state official wrote to Taft, "He is evidently a man of affairs and will be most valuable as a member of the Commission at a point where it is weakest, because of his practical knowledge of corporate affairs and American capitalists. I am inclined to think he is just the man to 'hustle the East,' if anybody can?"[220]

Thus, after its initial two successful bond sales, and more convinced than ever that private financing would be instrumental in the islands' development, insular officials returned to Congress to gain broad authority to take out more development bonds. And the Commission's need for revenue was becoming all the more urgent. In a plaintive letter to Taft, Wright explained, "If you succeed in getting authority from Congress to allow us to issue bonds to an amount not exceeding ten million dollars for internal improvements, or even a less amount, it will be a considerable relief. While I think we can skin through without it by practicing small economies, we may find ourselves a good deal embarrassed in completing public works."[221]

The Commission, after all, had already begun construction on a number of public works, including an ambitious and enormously expensive project to improve the breakwater in Manila harbor. A lack of money at this point would prove a great embarrassment. Money had, in fact, become so scarce, that the Commission appropriated $250,000 from the famine relief fund to the harbor project as a stop-gap. Although the friar land bonds and currency bonds were made exempt, an

---

[218] Edwards to Wright, April 6, 1904; Edwards Papers, Box 3, Folder 16.

[219] Edwards to Wright, March 25, 1904; Edwards Papers, Box 3, Folder 15. A further strategy employed by the insular state was to use its gold reserve fund deposits as an incentive for banks to provide capital; i.e., helpful banks received larger deposits. See Conant to Edwards, January 25, 1906; Conant to McIntyre, May 1, 1906; Taft to McIntyre, April 27, 1906; RG 350 (Series 14077), Box 707.

[220] Wright to Taft, April 1, 1904; Edwards Papers, Box 3, Folder 16.

[221] Wright to Taft, April 13, 1904; Edwards Papers, Box 3, Folder 16.

authorized $4,000,000 bond sale for Manila's sewer and water system was still subject to state and municipal taxation. As Taft testified before the Committee on the Philippines, "[O]ur theory is that as this is an experiment of the United States Government, and as all bonds which are issued are to effect a purpose of the United States, the right to exempt them on the part of Congress is very clear under decision of the Supreme Court, and that being an agency of the Government of the United States, the Congress may properly say to States, counties, and municipalities that you can not impose a burden on this agency of the Government."[222] In the chapters to follow, we will see how these bond sales and the independent colonial currency were used to raise yet more funds for internal development, and how the collaborative relationship between the BIA and Wall Street would shape the later development of the empire.

Relative Autonomy for the Philippines

The Senate hearing in 1906, much like the hearings the previous year in Ways and Means, saw the insular state clash with domestic sugar and tobacco interests over the effects of free trade on domestic agriculture – a "veritable war of figures" in the words of one historian.[223] Although the arguments were largely a repeat of the earlier debate, the more statistically driven nature of the Senate hearing reveals the extent to which opposition interests, too, had to rely on official insular reports for their information, and this gave the BIA a significant advantage.

Consider, for example, a lengthy brief entitled "Facts which Should be Considered Before Acting on the Philippine Tariff Bill" prepared by Truman G. Palmer, secretary of the American Beet Sugar Association. The facts cited by Palmer, although presented to support the sugar beet lobby's position, nearly all came from official Commission reports or statements made by insular state officials. In one illustrative section – "Secretary Taft's Statements Disproved by the Records of His Own Department" – Palmer's report picked apart Taft's public speeches in support of the tariff by pointing out discrepancies between the secretary's statements and the Commission's official figures.[224] The truth was the sugar lobby had little choice but to adopt this strategy – there were very few independent experts who could speak authoritatively on the islands who were not in the employment of the Commission itself. And this left the industry lobbyists in a significantly weaker position than they were in domestic tariff battles, where they could present data from their own reports.[225] And with their greater knowledge and access to information, the BIA could dismiss the opposition's data as simply outdated or improperly presented.[226]

---

[222] "Civil Government in the Philippine Islands," C. Rec, 5th Cong., 2nd sess., S. Report No. 1898, 8.

[223] Abelarde, *American Tariff Policy*, 89.

[224] *Hearings Before the Committee on the Philippines*, 59th Cong., 1st sess., S. Doc. No. 277, 590–600.

[225] The Philippine tariff battles also differed from traditional tariff battles in that there was virtually no industry lobby on the other side. In this case, state officials (Commission and BIA bureaucrats) faced off against industry.

[226] Throughout this process, the BIA was continually hampered by its laughably small staff. As late as 1909, Edwards complained that he had to share office space with his assistant and two stenographers, leaving him no space to conduct meetings. "The other day," he wrote to

Although the bill was again defeated in 1906, the opposition was weakening – finally, Taft's plan to "hammer it down and hammer it down" was beginning to work.[227] Even H. S. Frye, president of the New England Tobacco Growers' Association, admitted privately to Senator Platt that the insular government was probably right; a reduction in tariff duties on tobacco would not adversely effect the American tobacco growers and, repeating the statement made by W. S. Lyon during congressional tour, further doubted that Americans would ever develop a taste for Philippine cigars. Although he continued to publicly oppose the measure, he confessed that he had tried without success to convince his organization to drop its opposition.[228]

By this point, insular bureaucrats had been repeating the same message for three years – to wit, that Philippine sugar and tobacco production was too small to adversely affect the American market. By 1906, Roosevelt himself echoed this talking point in his annual address: "I most earnestly hope that the bill to provide a lower tariff for or else absolute free trade in Philippine products will become a law. No harm will come to any American industry; and while there will be some small but real material benefit to the Filipinos, the main benefit will come by the showing made as to our purpose to do all in our power for their welfare."[229] In report after report, the Commission took pains to show that in the last eight years there had been little increase in Philippine sugar or tobacco production and that there was no evidence that it would increase soon.[230]

By 1908, as it was beginning to gain the upper hand – it did not hurt that Taft looked likely to win the presidency – the insular state brokered a compromise with Democrats and the sugar and tobacco lobbies. Taft, who in 1906 opposed any quota for sugar or tobacco, now went on record to support it. As Representative Fordney, one of the sugar beet industry's most consistent defenders, told the House, "Our present good President, Mr. Taft, agreed in my presence that during his administration he will not permit . . . any further reduction in the sugar schedule if we will accept this agreement and let 300-000 tons come in free from the Philippines."[231] To gain Democratic support for the measure, Edwards, in consultation with top Democrats, agreed to let the agreement fail in 1908 (an election year), if they would agree to end their opposition in 1909.[232]

In the end, the compromise permitted the free entry of 300,000 tons of sugar, 150 million cigars, 1 million pounds of filler tobacco, and 300,000 pounds of wrapper tobacco. In truth, these limitations on sugar and tobacco were largely symbolic.[233] At the time, Filipino producers could not produce even close to that

---

the Secretary of War, "when a delegation of rice growers came to have a conference about the adjustment of the Philippine tariff, I was mortified by not having chairs enough for them, and a Senator and a Congressman had to remain standing." Edwards to Secretary of War, March 25, 1909, quoted in Cruz, *America's Colonial Office*, 218–9.

[227] Taft to Edwards, January 25, 1903; Edwards Papers, Box 2, Folder 17.

[228] May, *Social Engineering*, 158.

[229] Theodore Roosevelt, "Sixth Annual Message," December 3, 1906, *FRUS*, 1909, pt. 1, 38.

[230] *Report of the Philippine Commission*, 1908, Part II, 590–2; quoted in Abelarde, *American Tariff Policy*, 95.

[231] C. Rec. 61st Cong., 1st sess., p. 333; quoted in Alberalde, 97.

[232] Stanley, *Nation in the Making*, 152.

[233] Philippine rice was subject to the same restriction as rice from any other foreign country, but, as all parties knew, restrictions on rice importation meant nothing because the Philippines could not produce enough rice even to satisfy its domestic needs.

amount of sugar or tobacco; for all intents and purposes, trade between the United States and the Philippines became completely free. The victory must have been especially sweet for the recently elected President Taft – the first governor of the Philippines and its most tireless promoter – as he signed the Payne–Aldrich Act into law on August 5, 1909.

Insular authorities were thrilled. As Edwards triumphantly noted in his 1909 annual report, "This legislation was the result of a continuous effort of the department and bureau extending through several years."[234] When word of the act's passage reached Manila, Forbes, now acting governor, reported, "Sugar jumped like mad today, and orders for many millions of cigars are crowding in." Seven months later things looked even better: "From all over the Islands comes the same story – better crops, more cultivation, better feelings, and more prosperity."[235]

Forbes's early reaction was probably overly optimistic, but free trade did significantly increase Philippine trade with the United States as well as the insular state's tax revenues. Nevertheless, there is, perhaps, no other episode that so reveals just how far the insular state had come from its humble origins less than a decade before. Indeed, as this section has argued, free trade could hardly have occurred were it not for the efforts of the colonial authorities. Their control of colonial data, their ability to tap independent sources of revenue, and the ease with which they could coordinate a political strategy were crucial to their success in getting the Philippines behind the tariff wall.[236]

By 1909, then, after just eight years of civil government, the American insular state had developed a remarkable collection of resources to run the Philippines with significant independence from Congress and with little assistance from the domestic American state. It had, among other things, established a civil service, a state police force, a new tariff system, a new currency, and a taxation system. The Philippine civil service, protected by civil service laws and largely made up of Filipinos and discharged American Army personnel, had few allegiances to members of Congress or the American spoils system. In their earlier battles with Congress, most insular officials had come to the conclusion that Congress and the American people would never fund the colonial experiment, at least not to the level that insular officials thought appropriate.

To increase revenues and achieve their development goals for the islands, Commission officials developed a new internal tax (a move that very nearly lost their support among local elites), secured permission to raise money privately through bond offerings on Wall Street, and stabilized the Archipelago's money supply to attract American capital. As Chapter 6 will show, these efforts allowed insular officials to realize large parts of their vision for the islands. Having failed to "sell" imperialism as a policy to Congress and the American public, they now sought to achieve their objectives through borrowed capacity and clandestine action.

---

[234] *Report of the Chief of the Bureau of Insular Affairs*, October 31, 1909, in War Department, *Annual Reports 1909* (Washington, DC: Government Printing Office, 1910), v. 7, 5.

[235] Forbes quoted in Stanley, *Nation in the Making*, 152.

[236] In this respect, the insular state had something in common with the efforts of other Progressive-era executive agencies to sell their programs. See, for example, Carpenter, *The Forging of Bureaucratic Autonomy*, chapter 6.

COMPARATIVE ASSESSMENT: PUERTO RICO
AND AMERICAN SAMOA

The Philippine colonial state was not the only pattern that formal American empire took, and it is worth highlighting how American colonial rule unfolded in different ways in two additional US colonies during this period: Puerto Rico and American Samoa. Like the Philippines, both were formally annexed as American territories, but variations in their initial governing arrangements led to rather different outcomes than in the Philippines. For one, neither spent its early period of colonial control under the jurisdiction of the Bureau of Insular Affairs. Congress never passed an organic law for American Samoa during this period, leaving it as an unorganized possession run directly by the Navy.[237] Through a quirk of the Foraker Act, the BIA also lost control of Puerto Rico for nearly a decade; its governing arrangements more closely resembled American territorial government on the continent. A brief look at Puerto Rico and American Samoa offers us an opportunity to comparatively assess some of the governing dynamics of the Philippines.

Puerto Rico: Economic Integration without
Centralized Federal Control

As in the Philippines, American investment and capital were promoted as a way to bind Puerto Rico to the United States and to improve the material conditions of Puerto Ricans. The Foraker Act granted Puerto Rico two concessions that were not provided to the Philippines: (1) a low tariff that eventually led to free trade and (2) full integration with the US monetary system. In a nod to anti-imperialists, it did include some restrictions, such as a 500-acre limit on corporate landholdings, but these laws were so flawed that most American corporations quickly invented creative organizational arrangements that allowed them to acquire vast amounts of land.[238]

As a result of the tariff decisions and the much closer distance to the US mainland, capital quickly flowed into Puerto Rico as American sugar refiners made massive investments in the island. Between 1900 and 1917, sugar production grew from 100,000 tons to more than 500,000 tons, becoming the most important export crop for the colony.[239] The early and full economic integration of Puerto Rico with the United States made capital far easier to attract, leaving Puerto Rico's economic relationship with the metropole similar to Hawai'i's.

---

[237] The Panama Canal Zone presents a variation of the military dictatorship that governed American Samoa and Guam. After a few false starts, the Zone was managed by a three-member Isthmian Canal Commission consisting of a governor, chief engineer, and chairman who all reported directly to the Secretary of War. Major George Washington Goethals of the Corps of Engineers eventually dominated all three posts. Indeed, he would come to possess, in his own words, "dictatorial powers so far as consistent with existing law." John Major, *Prize Possession: The United States and the Panama Canal, 1903–1979* (New York: Cambridge University Press, 1993), 68–70.

[238] Cabán, *Constructing a Colonial People*, 112–13.

[239] Dietz, *Economic History of Puerto Rico*, 104–5.

The relative ease of gaining congressional approval to open the American economy to Puerto Rican exports was not the only difference between it and the Philippines. Although Puerto Rico, like the Philippines, was under military rule during its initial years of occupation, the Foraker Act withdrew the Department of War's jurisdiction when it created a civil government. The result was that until the BIA regained control in 1909 no single executive agency had exclusive control over the Caribbean territory. In this way, the island more closely followed the traditional territorial model, where the governor and the three other major department heads – the attorney general, the auditor, and the commission of education – were appointed directly by the president.[240]

Consequently, unlike in the Philippines, where the governor-general appointed members of the Philippine Commission, in Puerto Rico each department head retained his own Washington connections, leaving the colonial government without a single reporting agency in the metropole.[241] In more practical terms, this meant that each department head was accountable only to the president and not to the governor. As William Willoughby wrote in 1905, in one of the first academic analyses of American colonial government, "As they are not appointed by [the governor], and there are no provisions giving to the governor any direct authority over them, they are under no legal obligation to make their action conform to his wishes."[242] This meant that the auditors and attorneys general, who tended to stay on the island for only a short period of time, often pursued their own interests and operated through their own Washington contacts, and there was very little that the governor could do to stop them.[243]

In short, without any centralized agency overseeing their actions in Washington and with little incentive to take orders from the colonial governor, the Puerto Rican government lacked the tight discipline of the Philippine colonial state where members of the Commission served at the pleasure of the governor-general. The result, as one former attorney general of Puerto Rico described the situation, was that some governors "would spend a good deal of energy trying to jump over the variety of bureaucratic hurdles set up by their supposedly subordinate executive colleagues."[244]

Unsurprisingly, the BIA found Puerto Rico's "orphan" status wholly unacceptable, and BIA chief Edwards was tasked with bringing the island under its jurisdiction with President Roosevelt's early and enthusiastic assistance.[245] By 1905, Governor Beekman Winthrop of Puerto Rico, who had earlier served in the Philippine colonial

---

[240] Willoughby, *Territories and Dependencies of the United States*, 86.

[241] An eleven-member Executive Council made up of six American department heads and five Puerto Ricans was the primary organ of government. The Foraker Act also created a House of Delegates that consisted of 35 elected members, but with little independent power over the Executive Council that retained control over taxation and budget matters, and the governor retained the power to veto any act of legislation. The auditor, for example, served as Congress's fiscal agent and was there to ensure that the colonial government followed its budget. See Cabán, *Constructing a Colonial People* for a more detailed description.

[242] Willoughby, *Territories and Dependencies of the United States*, 90.

[243] Trías Monge, *Puerto Rico*, 54.

[244] Quoted in Trías Monge, *Puerto Rico*, 55.

[245] Cruz, *America's Colonial Office*, 133. McIntyre, "American Territorial Administration, 293–303."

government – and was therefore familiar with taking orders from BIA officials – included a plea to bring the government in San Juan under BIA control:

> The Insular Government feels greatly the need of some bureau or division of the Central Government in Washington which could act as a representative in its relations to the Federal Government and the outside public, and which could furnish information and data without delay to officials and others interested in Porto Rico and its resources. In dealing in the United States the Insular Government frequently requires the aid of trained representatives with knowledge of the conditions and needs of the Island, and, on the other hand, members of Congress and others have been too often put to the delay of writing to the Island authorities for information which was imperatively needed at the time.[246]

Winthrop repeated this request the following year, this time suggesting that some central agency "be designated as the representative of the Insular Government in the same way that the Bureau of Insular Affairs at the present time represents the Philippine administration."[247] If the BIA's claim that it could provide "facts" to Congress in a more expeditious manner was almost certainly true, its motivation for doing so was not necessarily to provide Congress with more useful information. With centralized control over colonial communications, the BIA could send the same disciplined, carefully curated information about Puerto Rico to Congress as it had for the Philippines.

The second rationale for BIA control was to provide it access to the same networks of capital that had been used to offer bonds for the Philippines. This was a curious justification; after all, unlike the Philippines, Puerto Rico did not lack for interested or able investors. By quickly granting it free trade with the United States and integrating it into the US monetary system, Puerto Rico was far more integrated into the metropolitan economy than the Philippines. Furthermore, it had little difficulty attracting investors to its sugar industry. Finally, unlike the Philippines, the Puerto Rican colonial government had only borrowed the relatively modest sum of $1 million for road improvements during its first years under colonial rule.[248]

Nevertheless, the BIA made a case to expand its jurisdiction over Puerto Rico, in part, through claims that the Philippines was getting a better deal in the bond markets. As the BIA labored to point out, the 1905 BIA bond offering for the Philippine colonial government received a more favorable rate than a similar 1907 bond offering in Puerto Rico. This, Edwards explained, "was notoriously not due to the better credit of the Philippine Government," but rather to the fact that the BIA's imprimatur – and its close relationship to the US Treasury – made the bonds more valuable to investors.[249]

What Edwards neglected to mention, however, is that Puerto Rico did not require the large bond offerings that the BIA claimed were necessary to encourage economic

[246] US War Department, *Fifth Annual Report of the Governor of Porto Rico* (Washington, DC: Government Printing Office, 1905), 42.

[247] US War Department, *Sixth Annual Report of the Governor of Porto Rico* (Washington, DC: Government Printing Office, 1906), 40.

[248] Victor S. Clark, *Porto Rico and Its Problems* (Washington, DC: Brookings Institution, 1930), 315.

[249] McIntyre, "American Territorial Administration," 299–300.

development in the Philippines. American investors had already made significant investments in the Puerto Rican sugar industry, and private colonial financial institutions were already set up to favor American plantation agriculture. The American Colonial Bank, for example, which served as the primary bank for American sugar interests, became the largest bank on the island in 1910. It restricted qualified borrowers to those with the significant collateral that could only be produced by American sugar companies – a fact that, as one economic historian notes, "contribut[ed] further to a decline in local control of land and production which took place at a rapid pace during the first decade of U.S. control."[250]

Nevertheless, the BIA believed that further investments in roads, irrigation, and other infrastructure improvements would speed along Puerto Rico's economic development. As we will see in Chapter 6, once the BIA gained control over Puerto Rico, the colonial government quickly embraced the high-debt strategy to stimulate development that it had pioneered in the Philippines.

American Samoa: Naval Administration and Economic Isolation

Compared to the full integration of Puerto Rico into the American economy, American Samoa was almost entirely isolated. Despite requests at various points to replace naval administration with a civil government, Congress never acted, leaving the islands governed by an American naval officer with the power to run them as he would a ship – that is to say, with total control and with no input from Samoans or the small number of American settlers.[251]

The United States had maintained a presence on the Samoan island of Tutuila and its valuable harbor in Pago Pago since the Treaty of Berlin divided Samoa among Germany, Britain, and the United States in 1889. The harbor in Pago Pago was meant to be a naval coaling station, but Tutuila (and, later, the neighbor island of Manu'a) came under American control in 1900 when the chiefs of Tutuila ceded their island to the United States.[252] The terms of the treaty turned American Samoa entirely over to the Navy, which guaranteed that there would be no outside interference from other nations or commercial interests, and provided that the islands would be governed essentially as a large, unsinkable collier.[253]

The first colonial governor, Commander Benjamin Tilley, was given few instructions from Washington aside from a vague order from President McKinley: "While your position as commandant will invest you with authority over the islands in the group embraced within the limits of the station, you will at all times exercise care to conciliate and cultivate friendly relations with the natives."[254] The hope, it seems, was that the Navy would receive access to a valuable port and coaling station, but do

---

[250] Dietz, *Economic History of Puerto Rico*, 91.

[251] Go, *Patterns of Empire*, 57.

[252] Theodore Roosevelt accepted this "gift" from the Samoans without submitting the treaty to Congress. The annexation was later ratified by a joint congressional resolution in February 1929. Julius W. Pratt, *America's Colonial Experiment* (New York: Prentice-Hall, 1951).

[253] Pratt, *America's Colonial Experiment*, 223.

[254] Joseph Kennedy, *The Tropical Frontier: America's South Sea Colony* (Mangilao, GU: Micronesian Area Research Center, 2009), 68.

little to arouse the attention of Congress or commercial interests. Unlike Puerto Rico or the Philippines, the Progressive zeal to remake colonized people did not extend to Samoa, in large part because, as Julian Go has suggested, Samoans (and the peoples of Oceania more generally) were seen as uniquely content with their simple lifestyle. Instead, colonial forces should focus on preservation rather than on uplift.[255] In part, this was because the potential for American investment seemed limited. Furthermore, the Samoans were deemed peaceable and primitive, and were to be largely left to govern their own internal affairs.

For its part, Congress paid almost no attention to its new possession in the Pacific, and would not pass an act to bring it under civil authority for decades. This, it seems, was partly Root's doing, who hoped that Congress would leave the Navy in charge. As he explained in a 1908 memo to Roosevelt, he saw no reason to push for a government:

If left alone Congress will probably do nothing about providing a form of government for the Islands. There are few members of either House who are competent to devise a form of government and they are otherwise occupied . . . the inactivity of Congress must be deemed to be an approval of the continuance of the existing government. It is very desirable that this should be so. It is quite improbable that if Congress were to undertake to provide a form of government it would be as good as the one which now exists. They usually make a mess of it when they undertake anything of that kind.[256]

This meant that American Samoa was seen primarily as a naval station rather than as a colony – a policy that, as one historian of Samoa has remarked, "was a very effective way for the United States to hold fast to the place while at the same time being afforded the comfort of essentially forgetting about it."[257] In large part, Tilley's design for the Navy's administration of American Samoa conformed to this vision. Aside from a provision that guaranteed him veto rights over all decisions and laws, Tilley did not interfere in most Samoan affairs and he retained the traditional Samoan chiefs as district governors.[258]

American naval governors had relatively short terms of eighteen months to two years, and they did little to develop the islands. In point of fact, the Navy cared very little about the Commandant of Samoa or how he governed the islands. Washington almost never reviewed his regulations or orders.[259] Nor did the Navy show any interest in engaging in the sort of Progressive nation-building projects that so occupied their civilian counterparts in Manila. Until 1920 there was only one state-funded school, despite the fact that several of the naval governors did request further funding for infrastructure projects.[260] In 1900 Tilley himself requested Navy funding for medical supplies, which was denied. Twelve years later another naval governor eventually received permission to construct a hospital on the island, but was only given approval after he demonstrated that American

---

[255] Go, *Patterns of Empire*, 85–7.
[256] Root to Roosevelt, April 2, 1908; quoted in Jessup, *Elihu Root*, v. 1, 349.
[257] Kennedy, *The Tropical Frontier*, 69.
[258] Ibid., 72.
[259] T. F. Darden, *Historical Sketch of the Naval Administration of the Government of American Samoa, April 17, 1900–July 1, 1951* (Washington, DC: Government Printing Office, 1952), 3.
[260] Go, *Patterns of Empire*, 81.

Samoan funds could pay for its entire construction.[261] Even education was rarely approved. Tilley could not receive Navy approval to establish a school or to provide books for students – a situation that often frustrated the naval governors, but which, as one Navy governor remarked in 1911, was because, "The islands are so far away from the United States and so isolated that the public does not know or care."[262] For the Navy, the annexation of Tutuila served a single purpose: to provide coal to American military and commercial ships. Until the 1920s, the Navy rarely interfered with the internal affairs of Samoans – a policy that ended up protecting Samoan language and customs, but left the island undeveloped and with few schools or resources.[263]

From a comparative perspective, the most distinctive Navy policy may have been its careful efforts to keep American commercial interests out of Samoa. For the most part, the Navy itself managed copra production, Tutuila's one export product, and sold products through its own Naval commissary. This policy infuriated the small number of American traders who arrived in Samoa. Fred Wilson, a former Navy clerk who stayed in Samoa after his discharge, condemned the American administration in a letter to the Secretary of the Navy as "an absolute, arrogant despotism," and accused the Naval governor himself of being an "autocratic snob." Wilson's main concern, however, seems to have been the Navy's establishment of its own commissary – which competed with his own business – and the supposed wastefulness of taxes collected by the Navy administration.[264]

American Samoa was seen – at least for the first 20 years of American administration – as a coaling depot rather than as a colony of the United States. Congress left the islands entirely in the hands of the Navy, and the Navy granted the Samoans wide latitude to manage their internal affairs. In contrast, Puerto Rico was closely integrated into the US economy and commercial investors quickly dominated the export sugar industry. If Samoa was so far, so small, and so foreign as to barely be thought a colony, Puerto Rico was so closely integrated into the American economy that it was considered a permanent acquisition of the United States.

---

[261] Kennedy, *The Tropical Frontier*.
[262] Ibid., 90.
[263] Ibid., 93.
[264] F. R. Wilson to Secretary of the Navy, November 12, 1915; RG 284, Records of the Office of the Governor, Box 5.

5

Dollar Diplomacy as Inconspicuous Action

> Our San Domingo solution has worked so well that the public is now paying no heed to the matter whatever.
>
> —Theodore Roosevelt (1905)[1]

In the years following the Spanish–American War, Theodore Roosevelt began to sour on formal imperialism. American colonial officials had met nothing but congressional intransigence in their efforts to develop the Philippines, and there was little reason to believe that this would change in the near future. A state that would not even grant its own colonies unfettered access to metropolitan markets did not seem likely to become a great imperial power. But Roosevelt, Taft, and Root, who had made it their quest to see the United States achieve a level of international influence and prestige commensurate with its economic power, were not about to give up on American power. Their goals remained the same, but they had begun to conclude that formal imperialism might not be the best way to achieve them.

How could the United States continue to expand its global reach in the face of congressional obstruction and public indifference? How could America become a great nation when its principal governing body cared nothing for international affairs? The small Caribbean nation of the Dominican Republic would serve as the testing ground for their new answer to that question, and would, in Roosevelt's later evaluation, "serve as a precedent for American action in all similar cases."[2] In his annual message to Congress of December 1904, Roosevelt laid out an aggressive new principle to govern US foreign relations. Later dubbed the Roosevelt Corollary to the Monroe Doctrine, the president announced that in "flagrant" cases of "wrongdoing or impotence" the United States may be forced "to the exercise of an international police power."[3] In effect, Roosevelt had declared to

---

[1] Theodore Roosevelt to Henry Cabot Lodge, May 15, 1905, in Lodge, ed., *Selections from the Correspondence of Theodore Roosevelt*, 123.
[2] Theodore Roosevelt, *An Autobiography* (New York: MacMillan, 1913), 548.
[3] Theodore Roosevelt, *Fourth Annual Message*, 1904. The American Presidency Project, www.presidency.ucsb.edu/ws/?pid=29545

European powers that the United States would now take responsibility for stability in the Western Hemisphere. In this case, American state officials would gain effective control over Santo Domingo in exchange for arranging a *private* loan through their partners on Wall Street. What later became known as the "Santo Domingo solution" was the first application of a more robust form of collaboration that was already in place in the Philippines – and one that would give executive officials even more autonomy from Congress.

To understand the receivership, it is necessary to understand how the American external state had matured in seven years following the Spanish–American War. The small, closed networks of officials in the Bureau of Insular Affairs, the Department of War, and parts of the State Department could now be drawn on to assist with the Dominican Republic. Largely for reasons of geographic specialization, scholars have often missed the connections between formal US colonialism in the Philippines and the advent of the Dominican Customs Receivership; yet, the officials who manned the receivership often had experience in the Philippines, and the large bond offerings that made these new arrangements possible were arranged through the same networks that had made such private financing possible in the Philippines.[4] The insular state had already conducted a number of successful bond sales on Wall Street, including the sale of bonds for its gold standard fund and for the purchase of some public lands. These same officials could draw on the extensive contacts they had made in the American financial community to fund new imperial projects.

As I argue in this chapter, the Dollar Diplomacy receiverships were supported by a more radical collaboration with banking interests that was already at work in the Philippines. Congress played an even more minor (and in some cases non-existent) role in their operation and establishment. The receiverships were deliberately designed to be inconspicuous and avoid congressional attention, a goal that was accomplished through the use of private money and the byzantine authority structures under which they operated. These new models of colonial control were seen as a panacea for the cycles of disorder, revolution, and default that seemed to plague nations in Latin America and the Caribbean.

As in the Philippines, the goals were less economic than they were strategic and ideological. Accomplishing the strategic goals of stability required the application of a particular brand of colonial Progressivism, one that had already been applied to the Philippines: sound money and infrastructure projects to boost economic development and tie the islands to the American economy. These ideas were the guiding force that united the disparate group of officials who were dispatched to bring American order to the Caribbean. The bankers, for their part – although reluctant partners in the beginning – benefited from the increasing American involvement in the Caribbean by taking advantage of the safer investment market. This strategy, however, was premised on the commitment that colonial state officials had made to the bankers that their investments would remain safe. When the promised order could not be achieved and the supervisory agreements began to fail, the instability of this form of state building would be revealed, as the receiverships were replaced

---

4 See also Rosenberg, *Financial Missionaries*.

by military occupations that would themselves become political liabilities for the ostensibly anti-imperial Wilson administration.

DOMINICAN MODEL: DOLLAR DIPLOMACY IN THE CARIBBEAN

The Dominican Republic was in a state of near-constant turmoil for the entirety of the nineteenth century. Ruled at various points by France and Spain, and suffering from repeated invasions by Haiti, its more powerful and populous neighbor to the west, it finally achieved a measure of stability under the dictatorial rule of Ulises Heureaux between 1882 and 1899.[5] But Heureaux's rule came at a heavy price – namely, crushing loads of debt. To buy off opposition leaders and provide some minimal level of public services to the population, the Dominican Republic became trapped in a spiraling debt that soon reached catastrophic proportions, while revolutionary outbreaks crippled the government's ability to collect revenues.

In 1888, the Dominican Republic under Heureaux had borrowed £770,000 from the Dutch firm of Westendorp at 6 percent interest, offering its customs houses as collateral. In 1890, Heureaux again received a loan from Westendorp for £900,000 to fund the construction of the Central Dominican Railroad from Santiago to Puerto Plata, and this loan, along with its previous obligations, left it with payments amounting to 40 percent of its monthly revenue, leaving it a mere $57,000 to cover all other needs.[6] In 1892, the Santo Domingo Improvement Company (SDIC), a private American corporation with longstanding ties to the Heureaux regime, agreed to take over the Westendorp debt in exchange for the operation of Dominican customs houses.

The SDIC did little to improve the country's finances. Between 1893 and 1897, Dominican debts increased from $5 to $35 million, but with the exception of the poorly constructed Central Dominican Railroad there was little to show for the money.[7] Finally, in 1897, after the near failure of a $21 million loan, Heureaux and the SDIC realized that any remaining credit was gone. By 1903 the debt totaled $33 million and the duties on various export commodities had already been promised to other creditors, leaving the government completely broke and with no prospects for future income. As Dominican Foreign Minister Manuel Galván announced, "we do not have one cent."[8] The situation went from bad to worse when a new revolution broke out under the leadership of Carlos Morales and toppled the ruling regime.

In the wake of the revolution, an arbitration commission was established to sort through the debts. In its decision, announced on July 14, 1904, the Dominican Republic was ordered to pay $450,000 a year to its creditors and further authorized the United States to take control of the Puerto Plata customs house in case of default. On November 1, 1905, Santo Domingo, as expected, failed to make its first payment to its European creditors, leading to demands and threats from

---

[5] Perkins, *Constraint of Empire*, 40.
[6] Cyrus Veeser, *A World Safe for Capitalism: Dollar Diplomacy and America's Rise to Global Power* (New York: Columbia University Press, 2002), 56.
[7] Veeser, *World Safe for Capitalism*, 76.
[8] Richard Collin, *Theodore Roosevelt's Caribbean: The Panama Canal, the Monroe Doctrine, and the Latin American Context* (Baton Rouge, LA: Louisiana State University Press, 1990), 384–5.

French, Belgian, and Italian bondholders.[9] Roosevelt administration officials began to fear that European powers would intervene to force payment to their creditors, which, according to contemporary international law, they were well within their rights to do. Among Roosevelt's many concerns was securing unimpeded American access to the future Panama Canal.

The Dominican default now presented itself as the first test of Roosevelt's recently articulated Corollary. Giving European powers a foothold in the Western Hemisphere so near the Panama Canal was anathema to Washington, but to prevent this, the administration needed to devise a solution that satisfied European creditors and also avoided domestic opposition to the acquisition of further American colonies. At the very least, Washington would need to take emergency control of Dominican finances to buy some time.

Roosevelt and Secretary of State John Hay were already aware that US intervention in the matter was going to be likely – at the very least to avoid European involvement. Furthermore, Roosevelt suspected that the shady dealings of the SDIC had contributed to the instability of Dominican finances, and he dispatched Assistant Secretary of State Francis B. Loomis to investigate the situation and to propose the possibility of making the Dominican Republic a US protectorate. These entreaties were met with fierce opposition from Dominican officials, and so the strategy was moderated somewhat to merely ask for US control over Dominican customs houses. Hay instructed US minister Thomas Dawson to "ascertain whether the Government of Santo Domingo would be disposed to request the United States to take charge of the collection of duties," an arrangement that Dominican President Carlos Morales readily agreed to, telling Dawson that "he had long been of the opinion that the best solution was for the United States to take charge of the collection of the revenues, guaranteeing to the Dominican Government enough to live on and arranging with the creditors."[10]

A formal agreement was quickly reached on January 20, 1905 and a treaty signed on February 7, giving the United States full authority to collect the customs revenues of the Dominican Republic, to appoint the collection personnel, and to pay any surplus funds beyond that needed to pay the national debt to the Dominican government at the end of the year. Furthermore, no changes in the tariff or port duties were to be made without the consent of the United States. For its part, the United States would take responsibility for the debt and negotiate terms with European creditors. To further allay Dominican fears that the United States might be trying to add the Dominican Republic to its collection of colonies, Hay instructed Dawson to add the words "agreeing to respect the complete territorial integrity of the Dominican Republic" to the treaty's preamble.[11]

Since the situation called for immediate action, and the United States would be unable to intervene until the treaty had gained Senate approval, President Morales was worried that if the Senate rejected the treaty his government would fall. At the very least, he would need some money to run his government for a few weeks. To give the Morales government access to some limited funds, Dawson arranged

[9] Dana G. Munro, *Intervention and Dollar Diplomacy in the Caribbean, 1900–1910* (Princeton, NJ: Princeton University Press, 1964).

[10] Hay to Dawson, December 30, 1904; *FRUS*, 1905; Dawson to Hay, January 2, 1905; *FRUS*, 1905.

[11] Hay to Dawson; February 6, 1905; *FRUS*, 1905, 322.

for Santiago Michelena, a wealthy Puerto Rican with American citizenship, to collect customs on all ports in the interim, giving the Dominican government $75,000 per month, while directing the remainder of the balance to be held in an account until the treaty could be finalized.[12] Roosevelt himself appeared to be somewhat surprised by this development. "There has been a rather comic development in the Santo Domingo case," he wrote to Hay, who was ill and away from Washington.

> Morales asked us to take over the custom houses pending action by the Senate. I decided to do so, but first of all consulted Spooner, Foraker, Lodge and Knox. All heartily agreed that it was necessary for me to take this action. Rather to my horror Taft genially chaffed them about going back on their principles as to the "usurpation of the executive." But they evidently took the view that it was not a time to be overparticular about trifles.[13]

Clearly, the president was under no illusions that the treaty would find a warm reception in the Senate. It did not help matters that word of the January agreement reached the United States before Roosevelt had announced his intention to submit the agreement as a treaty. In an aptly titled editorial, "President vs. Senate," the *New York Times* reported that "the Secretary of State is running around the Senatorial end with the Santo Domingo ball, and depositing it, as a 'fait accompli,' behind the Senatorial goal. It is a beautiful quarrel as it stands."[14]

Predictably, Senate charges of executive usurpation of senatorial powers were raised. "I deny," Senator Henry Teller (D-CO) exclaimed, "the right of the executive department of the Government to make any contract, any treaty, any protocol, or anything of that character which will bind the United States."[15] Republicans in the Senate were anxious, too. Roosevelt had negotiated the agreement with Dominican authorities without seeking the advice of the Senate and there was some uncertainty about whether he thought it necessary to seek Senate approval at all. Publicly, at least, even the Republicans felt obliged to defend their institutional prestige, and most tried to dismiss press accounts as mistaken rumors. "I do not imagine," Senator Foraker said, "the President has undertaken to exercise the treaty-making power without consulting the Senate of the United States."

In truth, there is every reason to believe that Roosevelt *did* intend to begin the Receivership without seeking Senate approval. The original January 20 agreement was scheduled to go into effect on February 1, and it was only when Senate heckles were raised that a new agreement was signed and drafted on February 7, which required Senate approval before it could begin. Although the treaty was successfully reported out of the Foreign Affairs Committee on March 10, Republican leaders informed Roosevelt that the treaty would fail and no vote was taken. Roosevelt was furious, but not surprised. Indeed, the defeat over the Dominican treaty may have finally convinced Roosevelt that executive authority would need to be exercised unilaterally

---

[12] Dawson to Loomis February 13, 1905; *FRUS*, 1905, 317–18.
[13] Roosevelt to John Hay, March 30, 1905, in Morison, ed., *Letters of Theodore Roosevelt*, v. 4, 1150–1.
[14] "President vs. Senate," *New York Times*, January 26, 1905, 6.
[15] Teller quoted in Holt, *Treaties Defeated by the Senate*, 215–6.

if the United States were to have a coherent foreign policy. In a long letter to Joseph Bishop, but one that is worth quoting at length, he explained his frustrations:

I do not much admire the Senate, because it is such a helpless body when efficient work for good is to be done . . . This feeling is in effect that the Senate should exercise the chief part in dealing with foreign affairs. Now, as a matter of fact the Senate is wholly incompetent to take such part. Creatures like Bacon, Morgan, et cetera, backed by the average yahoo among the Democratic Senators, are wholly indifferent to national honor or national welfare. They are primarily concerned in getting a little cheap reputation among ignorant people, and in addition it is but fair to say that they are perhaps themselves too ignorant and too silly to realize the damage they are doing . . . Meanwhile I have to take all the steps and have to spend an industrious summer engaged in the pleasant task of making diplomatic bricks without straw.[16]

For Roosevelt, as for Root and Taft, the Senate's attempts to shore up its institutional prestige were preventing the United States from taking its rightful place among world powers. "Apparently the Senators in question felt that in some way they had upheld their dignity," he later wrote in his *Autobiography*. "All that they had really done was to shirk their duty."[17]

Nevertheless, even Roosevelt was cautious when it came to directly flouting the will of Congress. As in the Philippines, the Senate's refusal to support the executive's aggressive goals for the expansion of American power would motivate a new, quasi-legal solution to the problem – one that would expand executive power and make it more difficult to oversee.

THE *MODUS VIVENDI* AND TREATY

With the treaty's failure, the Dominican Republic would have no access to funds and would be unable to settle with its creditors, a situation that, Roosevelt feared, might end with the intervention of European powers in the Caribbean. Refusing to back down, Roosevelt declared a *modus vivendi*, dispatched several experienced colonial hands from the Philippines to take charge of Dominican customs, and continued with his plans to bring the Dominican Republic under the aegis of the American empire.[18] Until the situation could be stabilized, Roosevelt ordered that revenue collected in Dominican customs ports was to be deposited in the United States at the National City Bank of New York, the same bank that held most of the Philippine Commission's gold reserve fund. As he informed Secretary of the Navy, Charles Bonaparte, "I intend to keep the island *in status quo* until the Senate has had time to act on the treaty, and I shall treat any revolutionary movement as an effort to upset the *modus vivendi*. That this is ethically right I am dead sure, even though there may be some technical or red tape difficulty."[19]

---

[16] Roosevelt to Joseph Bucklin Bishop, March 23, 1905, in Morison, ed., *The Letters of Theodore Roosevelt*, v. 4, 1144–5 [my emphasis].
[17] Roosevelt, *Autobiography*, 552.
[18] George Colton and William Pulliam, both of whom had previously served in the Philippines, became the first and second general receivers.
[19] Roosevelt to Charles Joseph Bonaparte, September 4, 1905, in Morison, ed., *The Letters of Theodore Roosevelt*, v. 5, 10.

The president's actions were greeted with shock and fury among his congressional opponents. As the *Washington Post* reported, "The President's action is construed sure to cause a revival of criticism of his Dominican policy when the Senate reassembles. Senator Morgan, of Alabama . . . declared last night that the President's course was unconstitutional; that it established a protectorate over Santo Domingo, and was merely an application of the original protocol, which the Senate declined to sanction."[20]

Although Roosevelt would insist to critics that these were emergency measures to give the Senate further time to consider the treaty, the *modus vivendi* appeared to operate almost exactly as the proposed and rejected convention had outlined. Under the *modus vivendi*, the United States would not officially take over Dominican customs houses, but it would nominate men to do so who were to be subsequently appointed by the President of the Dominican Republic. He subsequently directed Minister Dawson in the Dominican Republic that "no change shall take place in the situation which would render useless its consummation or bring complications into its enforcement . . . All the moneys collected from both the northern and southern ports, not turned over to the Dominican Governor, will be deposited in some New York bank to be designated by the Secretary of War and will there be kept until the Senate has acted."[21] Before the Senate could meet again, however, Roosevelt had bought himself some time to act. He must have initially feared just what the reaction would be, but after several months, he felt confident, as he wrote to Hay, that "everybody has acquiesced in what I have done in Santo Domingo." "[B]ut," he added, "of course there will be a storm over it when Congress meets."[22] Still, if he feared congressional retribution, at least he was confident that the American public remained relatively indifferent to the situation. As he wrote to Lodge, "Our San [sic] Domingo solution has worked so well that the public is now paying no heed to the matter whatever."[23]

The Receivership, however, had to be set up, and so Roosevelt turned to Root, now back in private life, for help. Returning to Washington as Secretary of State on July 19, 1905, Root found a note waiting for him on his desk: "Welcome back," wrote Roosevelt, "I shall now cheerfully unload . . . Santo Domingo on you."[24] The appointment was, on the whole, greeted with general approval. Even hostile papers, such as William Randolph Hearst's New York *American* approved:

It is a matter of common notoriety that he is tied closely to the practitioners of high finance, who, through banks, insurance companies, trust companies or any other device for taking the money of all the people and investing it for the profit of the few, are becoming rich. No man can break affiliations of this sort in a moment.

---

[20] *Washington Post,* March 29, 1905.

[21] Roosevelt to Alvey Adee, March 28, 1905 in Morison, ed., *The Letters of Theodore Roosevelt,* v. 4, 1148–9.

[22] Roosevelt to John Hay, May 6, 1905 in Morison, ed., *The Letters of Theodore Roosevelt,* v. 4, 1168.

[23] Theodore Roosevelt to Henry Cabot Lodge, May 15, 1905 in Lodge, ed., *Correspondence of Theodore Roosevelt,* v. 2, 123.

[24] Roosevelt quoted in Lars Schoultz, *Beneath the United States: A History of U.S. Policy toward Latin America* (Cambridge, MA: Harvard University Press, 1998), 191.

Yet, the editorial continued, "The *American* is not inclined to ascribe to Elihu Root any lack of devotion to the public cause."[25] In its attempt to besmirch Root's reputation, however, the *American* had noted his important ties to American finance capital; ties which would become all the more essential in Root's efforts to bring the Dominican Republic under US control.

Once again, Root and Taft would be the key figures in the extension of America's empire, a fact that only increased the insularity of America's external state. It also had the added advantage of nearly eliminating the bureaucratic competition that might result from the complicated dual jurisdiction that both State and War would end up exercising over the Dominican Receivership, thus allowing Root and Taft to exercise seamless authority between the two agencies. The attitude is well reflected in an unusual letter Taft sent to Roosevelt just prior to Root's appointment. "Would it not be well to transfer to [Root] the Panama Canal," asked Taft?

He has much more constructive and executive ability than I in such a matter and while the reorganization of the State Department is essential, I do not think his time will be so much taken up with the duties of the Department but that he can give you and the country the benefit of his remarkable powers in the great work for which your administration is so responsible. The separation between the canal construction and the War Department is easy. Edwards is the only common bond and we can arrange a dissolution there upon our return.[26]

Among the challenges Root had to confront immediately upon taking office as Secretary of State was to smooth things over with the Senate before the receivership treaty was resubmitted. Roosevelt's unilateral actions, it seems, had further damaged his already poor relationship with the Senate, and it was left to Root, whose relations were rather good, to patch things up. He reassured Senator Cullom, Chairman of the Foreign Relations Committee, that the "so-called modus vivendi . . . consists merely in a plan or way of getting along, pursued by the Government of San Domingo on its own responsibility, but with the acquiescence and unofficial good offices of the President."[27] Yet Root had to confront the very real possibility that the Senate would never pass the treaty. What then? Would the *modus vivendi* continue to operate indefinitely?

The evidence here is conflicting. Root initially appears to have resisted any such scheme for continuing to operate the Receivership in the event of outright Senate rejection of the treaty. "I strongly disapprove of the proposition," he wrote to Taft. "If the Senate refuses to give the President the legal right to act officially in regard to Dominican finances, I do not think that we should go on as we are now."[28] Months later, however, Drew Carrel, the private secretary for Dominican General Receiver George Colton, reported that

[Root], like everyone else in authority here who are trying to keep in touch with matters in Santo Domingo, cannot say what will happen to the Treaty . . . Mr. Root told me that I would be perfectly justified in saying to you, unofficially, that the original policy of the United States toward Dominican affairs is unchanged and as strong as ever.[29]

[25] Quoted in Jessup, *Elihu Root*, v. 1, 451.

[26] Taft to Roosevelt, February 1904; Root Papers, Box 166.

[27] Root to Cullom, November 23, 1905; Quoted in Jessup, *Elihu Root*, v. 1, 543.

[28] Root to Taft, November 16, 1905; RG 350, Dominican Receivership Records, Box 1.

[29] Drew Carrel to Colton, May 23, 1906; RG 350, Personal Correspondence of General Receiver George R. Colton, Box 1.

Whatever Root's intentions, the fact that the Senate had not approved a treaty left the status of the Dominican Receivership in legal limbo. Although the quasi-official status of the Receivership allowed it to operate without congressional oversight, it also left its architects unable to use American money or credit to refinance the Dominican debt and thereby keep it under American supervision – the very point of the entire project.

COLONIAL NETWORKS AND THE RECEIVERSHIP

With his declaration of a *modus vivendi* on April 1, 1905, Roosevelt created the Dominican Receivership. Officially, the General Receiver of the Dominican customs service was to be nominated by the president and commissioned by the President of the Dominican Republic. According to the terms of the agreement, the General Receiver had the ability to collect and hold all Dominican customs duties, to distribute 45 percent back to the government of the Dominican Republic, and to deposit the remainder, after subtracting the costs of running the Receivership, into an account at the National City Bank of New York. At the time a treaty was established, or the Dominican debt situation settled, that money would then be used to pay off its debts. This, at least, was how it worked on paper.

But how did it work in practice? The Receivership was a new administrative obligation for the American state and it could not be established through the force of Roosevelt's edicts alone. Had a president demanded such an arrangement in the 1890s, it is unclear who would have operated it. Unlike his predecessors, however, Roosevelt could draw on the experience and personnel of the colonial governments in the Philippines and Puerto Rico to staff this new part of the empire.

Despite the fact that the negotiations for the Receivership had been through the State Department, it would be overseen by the Bureau of Insular Affairs (see Figure 5.1) and staffed by personnel from the Philippines, Puerto Rico, and the BIA's Washington office. The employees of the colonial state were the only Americans who had extensive experience administering customs in a foreign land, and the Bureau of Insular Affairs could easily recruit them. After Roosevelt declared the *modus vivendi*, Taft began to assemble the staff for the new Receivership.

In consultation with Edwards at the BIA, it was decided that the staff should be comprised of a chief collector, four assistant collectors, a statistical expert, an accountant, and a typewriter. Taft sent Acting Secretary of State Alvey Adee a cable, asking him to "recommend" the appointment of George Colton to Dominican President Morales. "Colonel Colton is still an officer in the Philippine Government," Taft wrote, "and is here enjoying a well-earned leave of absence."[30] Colton came as close as it was possible to come in the recently established American empire to a career colonial officer. He had served in the Army in the Philippines and remained there after he was discharged, and he had served as a high-ranking customs collector in the Philippine civil service since 1901. Colton also appointed his own assistants, many of whom he brought directly from the Philippines. Indeed, by 1906, of the twenty-three Americans working for the Dominican customs service, fifteen had

---

[30] Taft to Adee, April 7, 1905; RG 139, Personal Correspondence of General Receiver George R. Colton, Box 1.

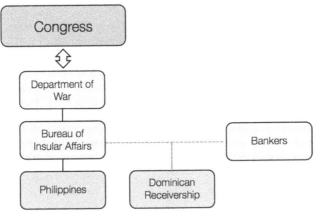

FIGURE 5.1. *Organizational structure of Dominican Customs Receivership.*

previous experience in Puerto Rico or in the Philippines.[31] When Colton later left the Receivership to become chief collector of customs in the Philippines, W. E. Pulliman, who had worked under him in the Philippines, was installed as the new General Receiver. And Pulliman, too, brought along members of his staff from the archipelago.

There was, however, a further complication. Since the *modus vivendi* was technically an informal agreement with the Dominicans, Roosevelt could not legally dispatch American civil servants to staff it. Any employee of the Receivership, at least until the treaty was signed, would need to voluntarily become an employee of the Dominican government, and the resulting authority structure was almost comically convoluted. As Taft explained to Colton prior to his departure,

> You will observe that in the duties which you discharge you are acting as an Agent of the Dominican Government and the President thereof, and not as a subordinate of either the State or War Department, or of the President of the United States; and yet, as your appointment is the outgrowth of a desire by Santo Domingo to maintain the status quo pending the ratification of the treaty, in which the United States has an interest, and the President of the United States has suggested you as a proper person to collect the revenues, the government of the United States is naturally anxious that you shall be successful in the discharge of your duties . . . Should you find time, I shall be glad to receive an unofficial account of the transactions of your office, so that I may be advised of the current events.[32]

There was, of course, nothing voluntary at all about these "unofficial" reports. As Colton knew, he was expected to run the new Receivership just as he had run the Philippine customs service, and he would report directly to the Edwards at the BIA.

[31] RG 139, "Review of the transactions of the Customs Receivership of Santo Domingo during the second year of its operation" (April 1, 1906–March 31, 1907).
[32] Taft to Colton, April 8, 1905; RG 139, Personal Correspondence of General Receiver George R. Colton, Box 1.

Recruiting lower-level officials was a more delicate matter. Once again, any employee of the Receivership could not be simultaneously employed by the US government, and this meant that they, much like Colton, would need to volunteer for the position. In his introductory letter to new appointees, Colton reminded them,

You are Dominican officials, and working in the interest of Dominicans, and therefore should endeavor to gain the good opinion and confidence of native people and officials . . . Learn and report all you can, talk frankly to natives about what *they* are interested in, but *never* about your own business, or that of the Receivership. You will make no reports, nor give any information concerning your work, except to this office, and your immediate chief.[33]

As Colton made clear in his report, all employees of the Receivership were "either members of the American or Philippine Civil Service on leave of absence, or granted leave through the courtesy of Colonel C. R. Edwards, from the Bureau of Insular Affairs, War Department, for that purpose."[34]

To preserve their status on the American or Philippine Civil Service rolls, the BIA engaged in a number of creative schemes almost too confusing to piece together from the archival record. The idea, it seems, was that Receivership employees would be placed on unpaid, indefinite leave from their regular positions, but would be subsequently transferred to a separate, temporary role so that they could maintain their seniority in the War Department or Philippine Civil Service hierarchy. The following memo contained in the personnel folder of M. E. Beall, a customs collector for the Receivership, gives an idea of the arrangement:

MEMORANDUM, re status of American employees of the Receivership on leave of absence without pay from the Bureau of Insular Affairs, War Department.
  As explained to me, those employees of the Bureau of Insular Affairs, War Department, who were given a leave of absence for an indefinite period, without pay, in order that they might be in a position to accept positions under the Dominican Government, were transferred from the regular War Department pay roll (in order to preserve their civil service status in the Department) to an existing roll established by a temporary appropriation . . . In order to provide for the employees thus left on the temporary roll Congress was asked to authorize two more positions in the Bureau at $1800.00 per annum, which was done. The situation now is that in case Mr. Beall or myself wish our leave of absence continued indefinitely, the two positions created will be given to the next persons in line of promotion, and will have to take our chances with regard to some provision being made to continue our status when the temporary appropriation mentioned is used up, and I understand that it is a small one. But if we can be spared here now we will get the new places.[35]

The legal fiction that the BIA did not employ Receivership employees, however, was often even forgotten by top American officials in the Dominican Republic. In an October 1905 letter to the Secretary of the Navy, Root took care to correct a

[33] George Colton, undated memorandum; RG 139, Personal Correspondence of General Receiver George R. Colton, Box 2.
[34] George Colton, "Review of the organizations and transactions of the Customs Receivership of Santo Domingo," typescript dated March 31, 1906; RG 139, Personal Correspondence of General Receiver George R. Colton, Box 1.
[35] Memorandum, June 21, 1905; RG 139, Personal Correspondence of General Receiver George R. Colton, Box 1 (M.E. Beall Folder).

careless statement by the American Minister to the Dominican Republic, Thomas Dawson:

This Department has just received the following dispatch from the American Minister to Santo Domingo: "American customs official Morris wounded and Dominican customs guard killed by smugglers 21st near Neyba fifty soldiers sent from here 23rd to pursue murders . . ." *In describing Mr. Morris as an American customs official Mr. Dawson, of course, means that Mr. Morris is an American who is an official in the Dominican customs service.* The whole system of revenue collection in Santo Domingo at the present time exists under Dominican authority solely, and the officers engaged in administering it are executing the laws of the Dominican Government, and are in no sense American officers, or acting under American authority. It seems important to see that this distinction is understood by all officials and representatives of our Government.[36]

The point of drawing attention to this unique employment relationship is not simply to highlight the fact that the Receivership was on shaky legal ground. That much is obvious. The central point is that the closed network of insular state authorities allowed them to exercise control over the colonial state even when the official lines of authority remained ambiguous.

This pattern is evident even after the Receivership gained Senate approval, and Americans could officially become employees. The regulations that were to govern the operation of the Receivership under the treaty were drawn up by Edwards in the BIA, and his initial proposal left things exactly as they had operated under the *modus vivendi*, which lodged control of the Receivership in the BIA. This troubled Root, who insisted that the lines official hierarchy had to leave the State Department in charge, as an archival copy of the order, which shows Root's handwritten amendments, makes clear:

In accordance with the provisions of Article 4 of the Treaty, the accounts of the General Receiver shall be rendered to the Contaduria General of the Dominican Republic, and to the State Department of the United States, and ~~submitted~~ *referred* for examination and verification to the Bureau of Insular Affairs, which shall have immediate supervision and control of the Receivership, *pursuant and subject to such directions in regard thereto as shall be received from the President directly or through the Secretary of State.*[37]

As Root explained his reasoning to Assistant Secretary of State Bacon,

[This] avoids a possible inference that it is transferred to the War Department making the Secretary of War responsible for it . . . All formal communications to and from them regarding the business will have to be through the State Department, and we cannot ask them to recognize that any other Department of our Government has any authority under the treaty, especially one the title of which connotes the use of force.[38]

There was no doubt that this was a formality, much like the status of employees under the *modus vivendi*. In practice, the BIA would remain firmly in charge.

---

[36] Root to Secretary of the Navy, October 25, 1905; RG 139, Personal Correspondence of General Receiver George R. Colton, Box 1 [my emphasis].

[37] Root's amendments in italics. Typescript. RG 139, SD-1, Box 2.

[38] Root to Bacon, July 23, 1907; RG 139, SD-1, Box 2.

In a letter communicating Root's changes back to Edwards, Bacon made this much perfectly clear: "In article 9, might it not be well, in order to conform to the language of the treaty, to provide that the reports should be made to the State Department through the Bureau of Insular Affairs. God knows I haven't the slightest desire to incur any responsibility for the State Department, but it may be of little consequence."[39] Indeed, McIntyre, Edwards's assistant at the BIA, instructed the Receivership that "all official communications should be addressed to the Bureau of Insular Affairs." As he explained his decision,

It seem to me that this is the way we would be certain to get them, and then we could submit to the State Department such papers as they called for, or such as we thought necessary, to a full understanding of the situation. I have in looking over the matter, thought it well to call on the National City Bank for a monthly statement of the account of the Santo Domingo funds, in accordance with the custom which we now follow with Philippine funds. We could not, without this, check the statements received from the General Receiver from time to time.[40]

Given the fact that nearly all the employees were former members of the BIA or the colonial service, the BIA could maintain its unofficial oversight rather easily. Employees who expected to return to their positions in either service after serving in the Dominican Republic were unlikely to mistake who their actual superiors were.

BUREAUCRATS AND BANKS: SECURING THE DOMINICAN LOAN

Among the Senate's central objections to the treaty was a provision that put the United States in charge of refunding the Dominican loan. But without congressional authorization, Root could not obtain funds from the American treasury to refinance the debt. What was needed was a way to confine American responsibility only to debt collection, not to the payment of creditors. Root's solution was to employ a third private party to take on this responsibility:

The question has arisen in my mind whether the two questions could not be separated, the debt being adjusted on a fair and reasonable basis by someone acting under the authority of Santo Domingo, and making the adjustment conditional upon the United States ensuring the service of the debt substantially as provided by the pending treaty. We would then have a different proposition to present to the Senate; that is, the single proposition of ensuring the service of a debt already adjusted.[41]

What Root had in mind was essentially this: A private investment bank would refinance the Dominican debt and settle with creditors, while a US customs receiver appointed by the American president would supervise debt collection. The United States would get out of the business of debt settlement, thus pleasing the Senate opposition, but its presence in the island would reassure a private bank that such an investment was sound. That Root had overseen the successful bond sales for

---

[39] Bacon to Edwards, July 26, 1907; RG 139, SD-1-105, Box 2.
[40] McIntyre to Edwards, September 4, 1907; Edwards Papers, Box 7, Folder 1.
[41] Root to Hollander, May 7, 1906, quoted in Jessup, *Elihu Root*, v. 1, 547.

American colonial state projects in the Philippines – projects that were also not guaranteed by the US Treasury – likely reassured him that this would work.

Before any loan could be made, however, someone would first need to sort through the web of Dominican creditors and ascertain who owed what to whom, much like any bankrupt corporation. In 1905, while the treaty was still being debated in the Senate, Jacob Hollander, a Johns Hopkins economist who had organized the conversion of Puerto Rico to the gold standard, was appointed as the president's confidential agent to study the debts and to examine "the amount actually received by Santo Domingo, the amount of indebtedness nominally incurred, the circumstances so far as they are known under which the various debts were incurred, and so forth."[42] As he began to dig into the records, Hollander became convinced that a great deal of the debt was fraudulent or the result of terrible financial decisions made by past corrupt regimes. Loans that were in default for decades had now, through the effects of compound interest, reached ludicrous amounts.[43]

In all, Hollander found that the Dominican Republic owed more than $40 million to its creditors – an impossible sum given that its annual income had never exceeded $2 million. To settle the debt, Hollander began to negotiate general reductions, and he managed to get French and Belgian bondholders to agree to accept a 50 percent reduction on the principal, while other creditors agreed to reductions of between 10 and 90 percent. Even the American-owned SDIC, the republic's largest creditor, was not immune from Hollander's audit. In his final report of October 1905, he concluded that the SDIC's "presence and activity in Santo Domingo have been a continuous embarrassment and impediment to the course of orderly and economical government," and later referred to the SDIC-owned Santo Domingo Railway as "40 miles of old junk."[44] Other members of the Roosevelt administration shared Hollander's negative reaction to the SDIC's claims. Indeed, Roosevelt himself had written to Hollander that if negative reports on SDIC practices proved to be true, "we must take sharp measures to disassociate the Government from all responsibility for the debt."[45]

The administration's hostility to the SDIC belies the notion that the receivership was merely a scheme to defend America business. For Root, the political importance of keeping the Receivership politically inconspicuous was far more important than any modest benefit it might bring to American investors. In fact, it seems that administration officials were worried that the very appearance of impropriety would draw the attention of muckraking journalists or Congress. To further

---

[42] Quoted in Dana G. Munroe, *Intervention and Dollar Diplomacy in the Caribbean, 1900–1921* (Princeton, NJ: Princeton University Press, 1964), 105. Hollander's employment status was somewhat ambiguous. Although he received $1,000 a month from the United States, he was also paid $100,000 by the Dominicans. This strange arrangement led to a congressional investigation three years later. Veeser, *A World Safe for Capitalism*, 154; Rosenberg, *Financial Missionaries*, 44.

[43] For instance, a German claim that amounted to $15,970.24 in 1889 had grown to $102,361.49 by 1902. Munro, *Intervention*, 118.

[44] Hollander quoted in Veeser, *World Safe for Capitalism*, 149–52. Veeser provides an in-depth discussion of the colonial officials' efforts to distance themselves from the SDIC. The drafts of Hollander's Report as well as a revealing "Confidential Memoranda" to Roosevelt can be found in Hollander Papers, Box 2.

[45] Roosevelt to Hollander, July 3, 1905; Quoted in Veeser, *World Safe for Capitalism*, 149.

combat such charges during the final loan agreements, Root insisted that the white shoe law firm of Stetson, Jennings, and Russell, the same firm used by J. P. Morgan and other major Wall Street financiers, represent Dominican interests.[46]

Hollander's familiarity with the Dominican situation led Roosevelt to ask him to work out the refunding negotiations with private bankers. The problem they confronted, however, was convincing banks to lend to the Dominican Republic. Reacting to what he considered the dishonorable conduct of the SDIC, Hollander reached out to prominent and well-established American banks, some of which had also been involved in financing operations in the Philippines.[47] In June of 1906, he wrote to Charles Allen, head of the prominent Morton Trust and former Governor of Puerto Rico, to encourage him to make the loan:

I think the opportunity is here presented for some high class financial institution to render a great public good, at a fair compensation for the immediate services and with ultimate advantages of some magnitude. Why should not the Morton Trust Company, under your guidance become the instrument for the fiscal reorganization first of San Domingo, and thereafter for other Latin–American governments that – if we should only turn the trick well – will surely have recourse to the United States to have done for them what we have already done for Cuba and are now asked to do for San Domingo.[48]

While the proposition was "worthwhile of anybody's attention," Allen responded, he could not commit to anything in specific.[49] Allen's reaction was typical of many bankers who were somewhat reluctant to sink their money into this new venture. Days later, Hollander received J. P. Morgan's response, illustrating another wrinkle in the scheme. "[T]he whole value of the bonds," Morgan wrote, "would depend entirely upon the form of interference contemplated by the United States Government in case of repudiation by the San Domingo Government . . . [U]nless the public are quite convinced that the American control will in future be absolute and in proper form so that no change of administration will affect the policy, the price is very high for the bonds."[50] What the House of Morgan wanted, however, was the exact thing that had held up the earlier treaty: a US guarantee of the bonds. In the Philippines, after all, the colonial state had managed to maintain a certain ambiguity about this issue, but bankers were taking a much more significant risk in floating these Dominican bonds.

Hollander must have been relieved, then, when Jacob Schiff, the legendary financier and senior partner of Kuhn, Loeb, agreed to entertain a Dominican offer.

[46] See Jessup interview with Jacob Hollander, April 7, 1934, Jessup Papers, Box A231. Archival evidence indicates that the firm did represent the interests of the Dominican Republic aggressively throughout the negotiations; a large number of letters between Jennings and Hollander can be found in Hollander Papers, Boxes 1–9. See also correspondence in RG 139, "Personal Correspondence of George Colton," Box 2.

[47] As historian Emily Rosenberg writes, "The original Dominican fiscal protectorate, then, was not a rescue mission for U.S. capitalists already on the island. Like domestic urban progressivism, dollar diplomacy emerged within a rhetoric of reform, replacing graft with efficiency and substituting corrupt interests with government-directed purpose." Rosenberg, *Financial Missionaries*, 56.

[48] Hollander to Charles Allen, June 28, 1906, Hollander Papers, Box 3.

[49] Charles Allen to Hollander, July 9, 1906, Hollander Papers, Box 3.

[50] J. P. Morgan to Hollander, July 11, 1906, Hollander Papers, Box 3.

It is not entirely clear why Schiff agreed to proceed, although Hollander later claimed that he had agreed in part as an idealistic proposition, because, as he noted, "it was such a picayune profit that it would not interest them as a business proposition."[51] Even Schiff, however, had his initial doubts. As he wrote to Assistant Secretary of State Robert Bacon a few days after acknowledging his interest,

[N]o one, I believe, will touch the proposed new Bonds unless the United States will undertake to look to the sufficiency of the customs tariff, to its proper collection and application to the service of the debt, and unless the Bondholders can look to the United States for this, no bankers, who value their reputation should undertake to sell the Proposed bonds to the public.[52]

In other words, if the government could not formally guarantee the loan, then it must administer the receivership itself. This was, of course, an easier challenge to surmount, particularly because American officials were already running Dominican finances under the *modus vivendi*.

Root and Hollander now could take advantage of the new strength of American investment banks in refinancing the Dominican loan. There was, however, one additional complication. Because the *modus vivendi* was technically an informal agreement, the Dominicans had to lead the negotiations themselves. The Dominican representative, Federico Velasquez, came to New York to negotiate the loan with Hollander's help, and he seemed likely to engage Jacob Schiff's firm of Kuhn, Loeb. Although they were not engaged in the loan purchases, this was carefully monitored by the BIA. As McIntyre reported to Edwards,

Velasquez, who is Secretary of Finance and Commerce of Santo Domingo, has been in the United States for some time. His object seems to be to float a loan of about $20,000,000, with which he can pay off the former debts to the Republic. He seems to have been dickering with Speyer & Company and Kuhn, Loeb, & Company (Jacob Schiff). It seems that the latter company has the better of the deal so far, and have practically arranged for the loan, contingent on the ratification of the present United States Dominican treaty . . . I think Speyer & Company were very much disappointed at letting this matter slip through their hands as they had been interested in this Dominican business for some time.[53]

On July 20, 1906, the Dominican representative signed an agreement with Kuhn, Loeb for the sale of $20 million in gold bonds at a rate of 5 percent for fifty years and with the Morton Trust Company, where Root had previously been general counsel and Conant was treasurer, to serve as the depository for payments.[54] Furthermore, as a result of Hollander's efforts with the Dominican creditors, the debt was cut in half, leaving $5 million of the expected bond sale for the use of public works.[55] The agreement with Kuhn, Loeb, however, was conditional on the

51 Transcript of 1934 interview of Jacob Hollander, Jessup Papers, Box A231.
52 Jacob Schiff to Robert Bacon, August 13, 1906, Hollander Papers, Box 3.
53 McIntyre to Edwards, August 1, 1906; Edwards Papers, Box 6, Folder 11. It is also worth noting that Speyer & Co. was the firm engaged in extensive capital investments in the Philippine railway system.
54 Collin, *Theodore Roosevelt's Caribbean*, 450.
55 When the Dominican Congress finally approved the convention, the panic of 1907 was underway and the loans had to be renegotiated with Kuhn, Loeb and Morton Trust, and a complicated financial renegotiation ensued that need not be rehashed here.

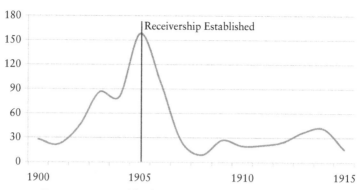

FIGURE 5.2. *Dominican Republic front-page articles in five newspapers, 1900–15.*
Source: Chicago Tribune, New York Times, San Francisco Chronicle, Wall Street Journal, and
Washington Post. PROQUEST Historical Newspapers.

approval of the American–Dominican treaty, which would allow American control
of Dominican customs houses and supervision of its finances.

The new agreement met with the approval of the Senate, and a new convention was signed with Dominican officials and sent to the Senate on February 8,
1907. The clause that obligated the United States to guarantee the integrity of the
Dominican Republic was eliminated as was the original proposal that the United
States would take over its debt. Now the only US obligation was to collect the
customs revenues. Further stipulations prevented the Dominicans from taking on
more debt or changing their duties without American consent. These amendments
were enough to secure the support of two-thirds of the Senate and the treaty was
adopted on February 25, on a 43 to 19 vote, and was subsequently signed by
Roosevelt on June 22. Yet the Senate, in approving this treaty, had been asked
for very little. No money was appropriated. No official guarantees were provided.
Whatever oversight might be necessary if US funds were used was significantly
reduced with what appeared to be – at least superficially – a relatively minor diplomatic agreement. Santo Domingo remained officially sovereign even as it came
under the control of a tiny force of Americans who reported to the Bureau of
Insular Affairs. It also had the added effect of limiting attention to the executive's
actions in the Caribbean. As Figure 5.2 shows, the Dominican Republic received
very little metropolitan press coverage after the establishment of the Receivership.

American goals in operating the Dominican Receivership, of course, were far
more modest than those in the Philippines, but the American customs officials did
manage to settle the Dominican debt situation and to provide the Dominican government with a stable supply of revenue for the first ten years of its operation.
Under American administration, trade increased dramatically with exports nearly
doubling in five years.[56] Furthermore, as Table 5.1 shows, total Dominican revenues went from $1.8 to $3.5 million in just four years, and by 1911, the Republic

---

[56] General Receiver of Dominican Customs, *Report of the Dominican Customs Receivership*
(Washington, DC: Government Printing Office, 1917).

TABLE 5.1. *Dominican Receivership: revenues and loan payments*

	Funds to Dominican Receivership ($ in millions)	Loan payment ($ in millions)	Total revenue ($ in millions)
1904	N/A	N/A	1.8
1905–7	2.9	3.1	6.8
1908	1.4	1.6	3.5
1909	1.8	1.1	3.4
1910	1.4	1.3	2.9
1911	2.0	1.3	3.4
1912	2.0	1.4	3.6
1913	1.7	1.6	4.1

Source: General Receiver of Dominican Customs, *Report of the Dominican Customs Receivership* (Washington, DC: Government Printing Office, 1914).

was receiving more money than it had in 1904 even *after* payments had been made to its creditors.[57]

The lessons American executive officials drew from this was simple: their solution worked. Through Dominican-style arrangements they could project power into Latin America and keep the Europeans out, while also avoiding the ire of the Senate. By moving to market arrangements facilitated by the state, American executive officials were able to further expand the public–private partnership that was already at work in the Philippines.

WHAT DID BANKERS WANT?: EVIDENCE FROM SOVEREIGN BOND PRICES

Although Hollander attributed Jacob Schiff's interest in refunding the Dominican debt to be based partly on idealism, no investor as talented as Schiff would have pledged his bank to an unprofitable proposition. Furthermore, the bond sale itself, while significant, was hardly a massive prize, given that Kuhn, Loeb had sold $75 million worth of Japanese bonds the year before. What, then, was in it for the bankers? In part, the bankers' enthusiasm stemmed from the fact that these foreign loans commanded a higher interest rate and were becoming increasingly attractive as the market for domestic securities began to decline in the latter half of the decade.[58] A more significant gain, however, may have come from the financial stability American intervention provided to the region.

For years, the Caribbean market for sovereign debt had suffered as state after state defaulted on massive obligations. According to a 1901 edition of *The Investor's Monthly Manual*, a major English securities publication, "The Guatemalan Government continues to trample upon every obligation undertaken by them

---

[57] For a report on general improvements made under the Receivership government, see Pulliam to Edwards, July 5, 1909; RG 139, SD-1-227, Box 3.

[58] Rosenberg, *Financial Missionaries*, 47–52.

towards their external creditors, while finding £110,000 for the payment of a junior and more favoured creditor. Honduras has, in its 28 years' default, piled up its arrears until, with the principal, they amount to nearly £19,000,000."[59] Along with Guatemala and Honduras, by 1904 Colombia, Costa Rica, and Venezuela had all defaulted on their debt obligations, leaving creditors to trade these so-called "rubbish stocks" on speculation that they might begin to service their debt again someday. If, then, bankers assumed that the *entire* Caribbean region would become a substantially better place to invest after an American intervention as the cost to default or revolution among Caribbean nations increased, they might be far more willing to encourage such actions by the government by providing it with the necessary capital. If indeed this is the case, we should see a response in prices paid for Latin American debt following the announcement of the Corollary and especially after the threat was made credible with the establishment of the Dominican Receivership. Bankers, naturally, would be willing to pay far more for debt – even in default – if they thought it stood a reasonable chance of being collected.

This notion of empire as a provider of "public goods" through stability is well established in the economics literature, which has shown significant positive effects to trade and lending under imperialism.[60] Following these suggestive results, in particular work by economists Kris Mitchener and Marc Weidenmier, I created an original dataset of monthly bond prices on the London Stock Exchange from 1900 to 1912 gathered from *The Investor's Monthly Manual*.[61] The results are striking. As Figure 5.3 shows, bond prices for Costa Rica and Guatemala (both in default at the time) rose dramatically following the announcement of Roosevelt's Corollary and continued to rise after the formation of the Dominican Receivership in 1905.[62] After trading for merely £18 in February of 1904, the price of Costa Rican debt had rocketed to £57 by May of 1905, an increase of 217 percent. In Figure 5.4, we see similar results for Venezuela and Colombia (also in default), where, for example, bond prices jumped from £20 in May of 1904 to £45 in July of 1905.[63] None of this was lost on the banking community. As *The Investors Monthly Manual* noted in January of 1905, "a feature of the month's business has been the speculation in 'rubbish'

---

[59] *The Investor's Monthly Manual* (August 1901), 449–50.

[60] Charles P. Kindleberger, "Dominance and Leadership in the International Economy: Exploitation, Public Goods, and Free Rides," *International Studies Quarterly* 25 (June 1981): 242–54. Niall Ferguson and Moritz Schularick, "The Empire Effect: The Determinants of Country Risk in the First Age of Globalization, 1880–1913," *The Journal of Economic History* 66 (June 2006): 283–312. I stress that I present this as an empirical finding and not as a normative judgment on the supposed virtues of imperialism. For an important critique of this body of literature, see Christopher J. Coyne and Steven Davies, "Empire: Public Goods and Bads," *Econ Journal Watch* 4 (January 2007): 3–45.

[61] Kris James Mitchener and Marc Weidenmier, "Empire, Public Goods, and the Roosevelt Corollary," *The Journal of Economic History* 65 (September 2005): 658–92. Although my data are drawn from a different source, my results confirm those of Mitchener and Weidenmier who also found significant effects on sovereign bond prices after the establishment of the Dominican Receivership. For making available digital copies of *The Investors Monthly Manual*, I gratefully acknowledge William N. Goetzmann and K. Geert Rouwenhorst's London Stock Exchange Project at the International Center for Finance, Yale School of Management. http://icf.som.yale.edu/imm/index.shtml. Par value for all bonds for which I gathered data was 100 pounds sterling.

[62] Costa Rican bonds are 5 percent A-series; Guatemala 4 percent.

[63] Colombia 3 percent; Venezuela 3 percent.

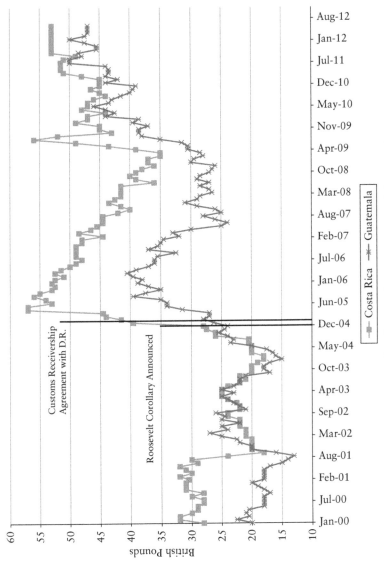

FIGURE 5.3. *Sovereign bond prices for Costa Rica and Guatemala, 1900–12.*
Source: The Investor's Monthly Manual (1900–12)

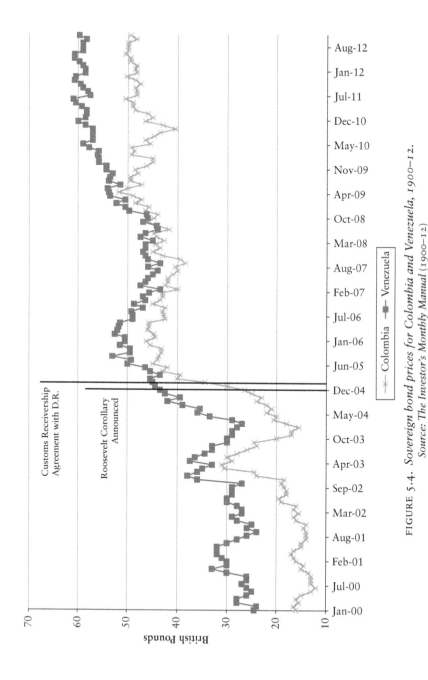

FIGURE 5.4. *Sovereign bond prices for Colombia and Venezuela, 1900–12.*
Source: The Investor's Monthly Manual (1900–12)

South American stocks."[64] Although the bonds decreased somewhat after the initial speculative fever wore off, in all four cases their value remained significantly higher in the years following the establishment of the Receivership than before.

Although these results seem to support the notion that bankers were responding to the Dominican intervention, perhaps they merely reflect a worldwide rally on the bond markets. To test for this, I created an index of Caribbean bonds by averaging the monthly bond prices from five Caribbean nations: Colombia, Costa Rica, Guatemala, Honduras, and Venezuela. At the time, all five nations had defaulted on their debt. I compared these results to a European sovereign bond index, which was constructed by calculating the average monthly sovereign bond price for Britain, Germany, and France. In Figure 5.5, I also include Mexican sovereign bond prices to measure the effect of this announcement on a relatively wealthy, and, at this point in history, fairly stable nation in Latin America.[65] As Figure 5.5 shows, the Caribbean rally was not repeated in Europe or Mexico. While the Caribbean index increased by over 160 percent between May 1904 and January 1906, Mexican bond prices increased by a mere 1 percent and European bonds showed almost no movement at all. Furthermore, the Caribbean index remained relatively stable after this period; indeed, after having never traded *above* £30 before 1905, it never dropped *below* £30 after 1905. It is important to emphasize, too, that the nations in this sample were *not* under the control of American officials – investors were simply reacting to America's new commitment to stability in the Caribbean. American intervention in the Dominican Republic improved the market for *all* Caribbean securities.

Although the data reported here are from London (few sovereign bonds were traded in New York at this point), the news would have hardly been lost on American bankers. By risking a small amount of money to assure that the United States would be able to commit to Roosevelt's new policy, they *bought*, in effect, a remarkably more stable investment market. It was not the Dominican Republic that bankers were interested in; it was the US commitment to stability in Latin America. Furthermore, bankers appear to have been willing to grant this loan without the official backing of the US Treasury – something to which the Senate would have never consented.

THE SPREAD AND INSTABILITY OF DOLLAR DIPLOMACY UNDER TAFT

When William Howard Taft was sworn in as president on March 4, 1909, he entered office with nearly a decade of experience in colonial administration, first as Governor of the Philippines and later as Secretary of War. Other officials who had experience in insular affairs joined him, including his new Secretary of State, Philander Knox, who had served as Attorney General under McKinley and Roosevelt where he had

---

[64] *The Investors Monthly Manual* (January 1905), 5.

[65] Although the countries I include in my index are different, my results here again confirm those of Mitchener and Weidenmier, "Empire, Public Goods." Colombia, Costa Rica, Guatemala, and Venezuela data came from the previously noted bonds with the addition of 6 percent Nicaragua bonds and 10 percent Honduras bonds. All have a par value of 100 pounds sterling. European bonds are as follows: Britain, 2.75 Consol; France, Retes 3 percent; Germany, Imperial 3 percent. Mexico, 5 percent Consolidated 1899 bonds. All data are from *The Investors Monthly Manual*, 1900–12.

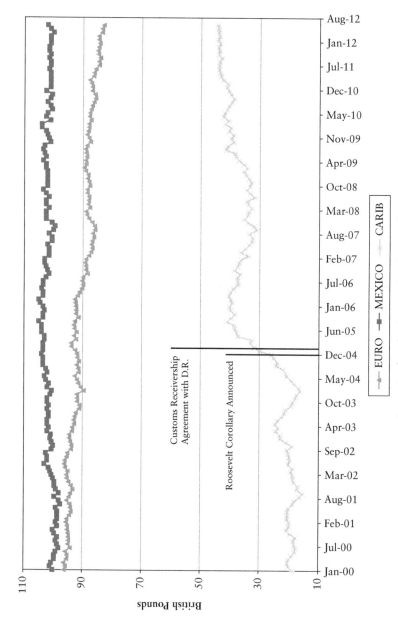

FIGURE 5.5. *Sovereign bond prices on London Exchange, 1900–12.*
Source: Calculated from data in *The Investor's Monthly Manual* (1900–12)

endorsed the use of private bond sales to develop the Philippines.[66] The incoming administration arrived convinced of the virtues of "Dollar Diplomacy," and began to view the Dominican experiment as a panacea for political instability in Latin America and as a symbol of American honor and good intentions.[67] It was, according to Knox, "a signal success" and "a bright example to all the Americas and to the world."[68] By 1909, after all, Dominican finances had improved significantly; loan payments were made on time; and the Republic appeared to be politically stable. In a commencement speech at the University of Pennsylvania entitled, "The Spirit and Purpose of American Diplomacy," Knox described the brilliant success of the Dominican solution to the graduating class of 1910:

[T]he assistance of the United States has enabled the Republic of Santo Domingo to reduce by half the face value of its debt, to furnish unquestioned security, and to have a customs administration so efficient that, after caring for the liquidation of a relatively enormous debt, it has supplied ample funds for all governmental purposes, the surplus for such purposes being actually greater in amount than the total revenues which entered the Dominican treasury prior to the present customs administration. On its political side it has freed Santo Domingo from apprehension of intervention on the part of creditor nations, and has contributed immensely to domestic tranquility and prosperity, unaccompanied by violent repression, to a degree never before known in the Republic.[69]

As Knox continued to extol the virtues of the Dominican Receivership, the phrase "Dollar Diplomacy" itself began to take on a new meaning. Originally a pejorative term employed by anti-imperialists, Knox and Taft embraced it as a broad description of their benevolent foreign policy.[70] Dollar Diplomacy, which had begun as an adaptive response to Congress's refusal to grant generous funding to America's formal colonies or to take responsibility for Dominican debt, now became a central tool of American foreign policy. Taft administration officials even began to *think* about it in this way. In one revealing interview, Knox referred to the United States as "armed with dollar diplomacy," and noted how "'Dollar Diplomacy' has substituted peace and prosperity for bloodshed in Santo Domingo."[71]

---

[66] Although Knox did not lack administrative experience, he had a low opinion of Latin Americans and Latin–American culture in general, a fact that he felt no need to hide. Root later noted that he was "absolutely antipathetic to all Spanish–American modes of thought and feeling and action, and pretty much everything he did with them was like mixing a Seidlitz powder." Jessup, *Root*, v. 1, 251.

[67] Munro, *Intervention*, 163; Rosenberg, *Financial Missionaries*, 58.

[68] "Signal success": Philander Knox, "The Spirit and Purpose of American Diplomacy," University of Pennsylvania, June 15, 1910. Knox Papers, Box 45. "Bright example": Knox quoted in Rosenberg, *Financial Missionaries*, 60.

[69] Philander Knox, "The Spirit and Purpose of American Diplomacy," University of Pennsylvania, June 15, 1910; Knox Papers, Box 45.

[70] See, for example, Oscar S. Straus, "American Commercial Diplomacy," *Report of the Seventeenth Annual Lake Mohonk Conference on International Arbitration* (May 1911), 171. Straus refers to it as "a diplomacy of exploitation."

[71] Interview with the Honorable Philander G. Knox, 1912. The draft of the statement with penciled edits demonstrates Knox's attempt to put a positive spin on the phrase "Dollar Diplomacy." One sentence, for example, is edited as follows: "The meaning of the somewhat unfortunate phrase 'Dollar Diplomacy . . .' Tellingly, 'somewhat unfortunate' is crossed out." The edited typescript of this statement is available in Knox Papers, Box 29.

It also had the signal advantage of attracting little notice from Congress. Taft, for example, emphasized the *private* aspects of the policy in his 1912 message to Congress, where he lauded the American bankers "who were willing to lend a help-ing hand" to troubled countries "because this financial rehabilitation and the pro-tection of their customhouses from being the prey of would-be dictators would remove at one stoke the menace of foreign creditors and the menace of revolution-ary disorder."[72] American investment bankers became more willing partners as well. In July of 1909, J. P. Morgan, Kuhn, Loeb, National City, and other banks wrote to the Secretary to tell him that they had joined to form a North American Group "for the purpose of obtaining information and considering South American finan-cial propositions." Knox wrote them back to commend their "laudable" enterprise and promised them the administration's help "in every proper way."[73] Now with Dollar Diplomacy recognized as a successful tool of American foreign policy and a low-cost way to bring stability and American hegemony to the Caribbean, Taft and Knox looked to apply it elsewhere, and Honduras emerged as a likely candidate.

Honduras and Dollar Diplomacy's Failure

Not every proposed extension of Dollar Diplomacy was successful. American bankers were not fools. Despite the profits that stood to be made in the sovereign bond market, there were limits to the amount of risk they considered acceptable, and mere assur-ances from bureaucrats were not enough to force an investment. In the Philippines and Puerto Rico, the formal colonial status of those nations was enough to convince them to extend credit even if the Treasury did not technically guarantee the bonds. In the Dominican Republic, the American-run customs receiver backed by a treaty, while admittedly less solid, provided enough security for Jacob Schiff to proceed with a loan. The problem, of course, was that a formal treaty – the most credible commitment the American state could make – required congressional approval. Naturally, this require-ment dramatically increased the *political* costs of Dollar Diplomacy, because Congress objected to precisely what the bankers demanded – a guarantee that the American state would defend their investments in the case of default. As Taft administration officials looked to expand the Dollar Diplomacy partnership into even more unstable nations, then, they were caught between the Senate's hostility to formal guarantees of bankers' debt and the bankers' desire for some credible signal that the American state would do precisely that. In Honduras, these obstacles would prove insurmountable, but they would also pave the way for more creative arrangements that pushed the partnership even further from congressional sanction.

Honduras, much like the Dominican Republic, entered the twentieth century in desperate financial straits. After defaulting on a British loan in 1873, its debt, in arrears for nearly 40 years, amounted to $120 million by 1909, an especially regrettable situation given the fact that, as one diplomatic memo noted, the nation had "little to show in return but a very few miles of railway."[74] For officials in the State Department, this seemed to offer a clear opportunity for another Dollar Diplomacy intervention, which, it was confidently predicted, would stabilize

---

[72] "Message of the President," December 3, 1912, *FRUS*, 1912, xii.
[73] Carosso, *The Morgans*, 591–2.
[74] State Department Memorandum, September 1909, in *FRUS*, 1912, 549.

Honduras and increase American influence in the Caribbean by replacing British with American banks. In London, the Council of Foreign Bondholders had made an attempt to settle the debt, but an internal State Department memo dismissed their proposal as an irresponsible "scheme" and observed with studied contempt that it involved "the raising of the customs duties and the mortgaging of nearly everything in sight to the detriment of commerce and future enterprise."[75]

To provide an alternative American option for refunding the debt, Assistant Secretary of State Francis Huntington Wilson set to work trying to attract J. P. Morgan, who was sought out specifically because of his good relationships with the British Council of Foreign Bondholders.[76] As in the negotiations for the resettlement of the Dominican debt, however, Morgan proved more cautious than the Taft administration would have liked. At the very least, Morgan wrote to Huntington Wilson, his bank would not extend credit in the absence of a formal treaty.[77] Although Morgan himself thought the administration was unlikely to deliver on this requirement, he agreed to proceed because the project was so strongly endorsed by both Taft and Knox.[78]

The bankers were not the only ones who greeted this further extension of Dollar Diplomacy with skepticism. In Honduras, President Dávila was understandably reluctant to sign over management of his country's finances to the Americans. But after a great deal of arm-twisting by Huntington Wilson, and faced with few other options, he agreed to send representatives to New York for discussions. After two years of negotiations, a loan convention was signed on January 1911, which provided Honduras with a $10 million loan of which $7.5 million would be immediately issued. Nearly all of this money, however, would go to settling the Republic's old British debt, making the arrangement an especially bitter pill for the Honduran government to swallow. Furthermore, the bankers would only take the bonds at a price of 88 percent of par, a rather generous 12-point profit spread, which would net them $529,900.[79] Nevertheless, Charles Conant, who had been so instrumental in establishing the credit of the Philippines and Puerto Rico and who was hired to review the contract, concluded that terms were as good as could be expected given Honduras's history of default.[80]

Taft dispatched the convention to the Senate with a note assuring the senators that the arrangement's success was "a self-evident proposition."[81] Yet what concerned the Senate Foreign Relations Committee more than its probable success in stabilizing Honduras was the American state's implied responsibility for collecting the debt. In an attempt to defend the convention from its critics on the committee, Knox provided a clear articulation of the convoluted logic that underlay the entire Dollar Diplomacy partnership:

[T]*he more this plan of assistance to some of the more backward republics is extended, the less becomes the degree of intimacy established between the Government of the United States*

---

[75] Ibid., 550.
[76] Ibid., 553.
[77] Carosso, *The Morgans*, 590.
[78] Ibid., 591.
[79] Munro, *Intervention*, 225.
[80] Charles Conant to Philander Knox, February 6, 1911, *FRUS*, 1912, 565.
[81] William Howard Taft, "Message to the Senate," January 26, 1911, *FRUS*, 1912, 559.

and that of the country to which the aid is given. I refer in particular to the fact that the provision in the Dominican convention made the general receiver of customs an appointee of the President of the United States, whereas the Honduras convention makes the collector of customs an appointee of the Government of the Republic of Honduras, the degree of intimacy in connection therefore being to that extent lessened . . . *In other words, the intimacy decreases in proportion as the ability and readiness of the country to meet its obligations increases.* This, therefore, is not a policy of which the end can not be seen. The adoption of this convention is not setting such a precedent as might be desired to apply subsequently to all of the Caribbean Republics.[82]

In short, Knox's point was that the borrowed money would *increase* stability, thereby *decreasing* the likelihood of an American intervention. "Prior to the Dominican convention this Government was constantly having to interpose between clamorous foreign claimants and the Dominican Government and to use its naval forces for the protection of United States property," Knox explained to the Committee. "Since the Dominican convention no such necessity has arisen."[83] Senators who were concerned about the US state's responsibility for the debt, then, were missing the entire point of the receivership – its "self-evident" success led to more stability, not less. The system's success, as Knox saw it, was the debt's real guarantee, and nobody in the Taft administration seriously entertained the idea that these arrangements would fail.

Yet whether the customs receiver was appointed directly by the president, as was the case in the Dominican Republic, or from a list submitted to the government, as was proposed for Honduras, did not change the fact that the American state remained responsible for the debt's ultimate collection. This distinction was nothing more than a legal technicality, although one designed to disguise just how involved the American state was in these arrangements. Furthermore, Knox's claim that the treaty's adoption did not set a precedent for the entire Caribbean was, at best, a creative manipulation of the truth; at worst, it was a clear deception. Earlier that year, Huntington Wilson had described the Honduran case to a State Department colleague "as a test case of utmost importance because . . . the principle we seek to act upon in Honduras is one we are bound to have to resort to in still other cases," and Knox himself had proposed similar arrangements for Liberia, Guatemala, and Costa Rica.[84]

In the meantime, however, a revolution had broken out in Honduras, which eventually doomed the Honduran receivership proposal. Although it was favorably reported out of the Foreign Relations Committee in 1912, the intense Democratic opposition kept it off the floor. Finally, in February 1912, with little possibility that the treaty would be approved, J. P. Morgan withdrew from the convention, leaving Knox with no private bankers who were willing to refinance Honduras's debt.[85] Not that this failure led the Taft administration to abandon Dollar Diplomacy. What was needed was a way to remove the Senate from the

---

[82] Philander Knox, Testimony before the Senate Committee on Foreign Relations, May 24, 1911, *FRUS*, 1912, 589 [my emphasis].

[83] Ibid., 586.

[84] Assistant Secretary of State to Alvey A. Adee, January 13, 1911, quoted in Rosenberg, *Financial Missionaries*, 66.

[85] Carosso, *The Morgans*, 591.

picture altogether, yet still signal to the bankers that their investments would remain safe.

Nicaragua, Dollar Diplomacy, and the Private Contract

American–Nicaraguan relations had declined precipitously after the United States shifted the transoceanic canal route to Panama in 1903. Nicaraguan President José Santos Zelaya made no secret of his dim view of this bit of Yankee treachery, and by 1909 the *Diario de Nicaragua*, Zelaya's official mouthpiece, was calling for a Nicaraguan–Japanese alliance to keep the United States in check. In Washington, Zelaya was widely blamed for fomenting instability in neighboring Central American nations.[86] In particular, Taft administration officials feared that he might attempt to sell Nicaragua's canal rights to a foreign power. In 1909 a revolution broke out in Bluefields, the American-dominated commercial center on Nicaragua's Mosquito Coast, and Zelaya was forced to flee the country after Knox ordered American marines to the region on the pretext of protecting American lives and property.[87]

To fill the power vacuum created in the wake of Zelaya's departure, Knox ordered Thomas Dawson, who had earlier negotiated the Dominican customs agreement, to Managua to work out a similar arrangement for Nicaragua. Knox also arranged for the investment houses of Brown Brothers and J. and W. Seligman & Company to send representatives for loan negotiations. Brown Brothers had earlier indicated their interest in providing such a loan, writing to Knox several months earlier to inquire if the "Government of Nicaragua is desirous of enlisting the good offices of our own Government and of entering into engagements with it which shall furnish a satisfactory basis for such security as may be required."[88] Unlike the Dominican Republic, however, Nicaragua had never defaulted on its debt, and could possibly have obtained a loan without the receivership. Earlier in 1911, Speyer & Co. (the same firm that had funded the Philippine Railway) had offered to make a $15 million loan on less favorable terms and Brown Brothers and Seligman had signaled that they would also consider making an offer before a receivership was in place. Officials in the State Department, however, had no interest in such arrangements; after all, the creation of a receivership, which they believed would have a stabilizing effect on the country, was the purpose behind all the negotiations.[89]

On June 6, 1911, the Knox–Castrillo Convention was signed providing for a $15 million loan in exchange for control of customs receipts and the appointment of an American general receiver.[90] The contract, however, was contingent on the US Senate's approval of a Dominican-style convention, but this proved impossible

[86] David Healy, *Drive to Hegemony: The United States in the Caribbean, 1898–1917* (Madison, WI: University of Wisconsin Press, 1988), 153.

[87] Zelaya, who lived out his later years in New York City, later claimed that the State Department had encouraged the Bluefields revolution, although there is little hard evidence for this claim.

[88] US Senate Foreign Relations Committee, "The Convention between the United States and Nicaragua," Hearings, 63rd Cong., 2nd sess. (Washington, DC: Government Printing Office, 1914), pt. 4, 170–1.

[89] The loan would go to pay off Zelaya's opponents who had granted themselves lavish awards for supposed damages under Zelaya's rule. Munro, *Intervention*, 195; Rosenberg, *Financial Missionaries*, 67; Healy, *Drive to Hegemony*, 157.

[90] The text of the treaty can be found in *FRUS*, 1912, 1074.

to get when the Senate adjourned before considering the treaty. When the Senate again took up the Nicaraguan treaty in early 1912, Knox worked tirelessly to have the Committee on Foreign Relations consider it. Among other things, he sent to the members a copy of a speech he had made earlier in the year in which he explained in glowing terms the success of the Dominican Receivership. In the speech, given before the New York Bar Association, he described the success of the Dominican Receivership as "brilliant" and noted that it was "the best possible guaranty of the good effects to be expected from the Nicaragua" convention. More importantly, "[i]nstead of producing foreign entanglements," he argued, "they have precisely the opposite effect because they do away with the present discontent and clamor of foreign creditors, because they insure prosperity, and because they make for peace."[91] Knox's arguments, however, did little to sway to the Senate, and the treaty never made it out of the Foreign Relations Committee.[92]

Without Senate approval and after the Honduran loan negotiations had collapsed, Taft and Knox now had a serious problem on their hands; one that placed the entire institution of Dollar Diplomacy in jeopardy. The solution was not to abandon what had become a cornerstone of American foreign policy, but rather to move even further in the direction of market-based contractual relationships.[93] While waiting for Senate approval, they had negotiated with Brown Brothers and Seligman a smaller loan of $1.5 million, and though this arrangement was originally intended to provide Nicaragua with some much-needed short-term cash, they now moved to make it permanent. A receivership along the lines of the original Dominican *modus vivendi* was thus arranged using an entirely *private* contract between the Nicaraguan government and Brown Brothers, with a customs collector to be appointed by the State Department.[94]

Why were bankers willing to take on this risk with no formal treaty? In part, of course, they were not. The $1.5 million loan was far smaller than loans in the Dominican Republic. But State Department officials moved to construct a contract that placed control of Nicaragua's assets in the hands of bankers who were given control of Nicaragua's national bank. To secure an additional $750,000 loan, the State Department next pressured the Nicaraguans to give Brown Brothers a 51 percent stake in the national railroad. For most practical purposes, then, the Nicaraguan receivership operated exactly as the Dominican Receivership had earlier. Yet, this newer arrangement had the virtue of cutting Congress out of the picture altogether, and as a technically private contract between the Nicaraguan government and the investment bank, it aroused little attention from the Senate.[95]

In point of fact, the agreement rested on the same implied guarantees that had supported the use of private capital in the Dominican Republic and even in the Philippines. In each case, whether it was the formal colonial status of the Philippines, the employment of American officials in the Dominican customs houses, or the use of Nicaragua's national bank as collateral, the bankers were left with little doubt that

---

[91] Philander Knox, "Speech before the New York State Bar Association," New York City, January 19, 1912; Knox Papers, Box 46.

[92] Munro, *Intervention*, 203.

[93] Rosenberg, *Financial Missionaries*, 73.

[94] The customs collector, Col. Clifford D. Ham, was at the time employed as a customs collector in the Philippines. *FRUS*, 1912, 1080.

[95] Rosenberg, *Financial Missionaries*, 75–7.

they could call upon the American state to defend their investments. The increasingly private appearance of these contracts was necessary only to avoid the ire of the Senate. For their part, colonial officials had supreme faith that sound American leadership under these agreements would lead to increased stability, and nobody in the Taft administration seems to have considered that this assumption might prove incorrect.

INSTABILITY IN THE DOMINICAN REPUBLIC:
THREATS TO DOLLAR DIPLOMACY

As the details of the Nicaraguan receivership were being finalized in 1912, the peace and political stability achieved in the Dominican Republic began to collapse. The long-serving president, Ramón Cáceres was fatally shot in November of 1911, leading to the rise of feuding leaders throughout the island and putting the much-heralded Dominican Receivership in jeopardy.[96] Yet evidence of the increasingly unstable political situation in the Dominican Republic did little to stop Knox's public celebrations of the receivership system's successes. On a 1911 tour of the Caribbean, the Secretary addressed the Dominican Congress to express his pleasure that the "dark cloud" surrounding Cáceres's assassination had not interrupted "the normal march of your people in the orderly path of self control." He continued to lecture in this vein in Nicaragua, where he noted that the receivership had "cured almost century-old evils" in Santo Domingo.[97] The frantic dispatches from the State Department, however, painted a very different picture. In one of the first acknowledgments of the fragility of the entire receivership system, Assistant Secretary of State Huntington Wilson warned Taft of the dire consequences should they allow Santo Domingo to collapse:

I am sure that you feel, as Mr. Knox does, and as I do most strongly, that if the situation in the Dominican Republic should go from bad to worse . . . the whole policy concerned would be seriously discredited. I am sure that you will agree that such an eventuality, involving also a disastrous setback to the somewhat similar policy the administration has pursued in Nicaragua . . . would, indeed, be a very severe blow to American diplomacy.[98]

Taft and Knox hardly needed to be reminded of this fact. If the receivership system could not be made to work, the American state would be responsible for the implicit promises to guarantee the bankers' investments they had made for years; the promises on which the entire partnership was founded. To shore up the Dominican Receivership, at least in the short term, Huntington Wilson recommended that the president adopt "such measures as the breaking of diplomatic relations, the forcible protection of the customhouses, and perhaps the withholding of the customs revenues."[99] In response, Taft dispatched a special commission headed by the new BIA chief Frank McIntyre and a detachment of 750 marines to Santo Domingo.

[96] Healy, *Drive to Hegemony*, 161. The rising conflict between the Receivership and the Dominican government can be traced in RG 139 (SD-1-261-351), Box 4.
[97] *FRUS, 1911*, 1091, quoted in Whitney, *Constraint of Empire*, 46.
[98] Huntington Wilson to Taft, September 19, 1912, RG 139, Box 5.
[99] Quoted in Munro, *Intervention*, 263.

The commission's report was brutally frank. They found "a very hard situation." The only permanent remedy, McIntyre wrote, "would require prolonged intervention and controls," but such an action, he wisely concluded, was "practically impossible."[100] By this, of course, McIntyre meant that it was politically impossible, or at least highly undesirable. Direct intervention, after all, undermined the entire point of Dollar Diplomacy. Not only would it demonstrate the inherent instability of this system, but it would also confirm the Senate's original fears that the United States was ultimately responsible for the bankers' investments. As a stopgap measure, the commission forced the ouster of the newly elected president, and replaced him with the archbishop of Santo Domingo, but nobody at the State Department fooled himself into thinking that this was a permanent solution to the problem. Indeed, the beleaguered clergyman would threaten to resign merely two weeks after assuming office, and he would agree to remain only after the personal appeal of Secretary Knox.[101]

Months later, Taft was out of office, and the festering problems in the Dominican Receivership were now left for the Wilson administration to solve. Dollar Diplomacy, built on years of partnership between the American foreign policy state and Wall Street, and billed as a peaceful solution to Caribbean instability and a way to achieve hegemony without congressional sanction, was failing in a spectacular fashion.

In the Dominican Republic and Nicaragua, private money was used to refinance sovereign debt and to bring these nations under informal American control. Yet the order that the receivership system promised proved illusory. Stability would come not from attentive financial management by colonial state bureaucrats, but from the marines ordered in by Woodrow Wilson. Ironically, a policy designed to extend American hegemony "on the cheap" and to avoid congressional scrutiny would become both expensive and highly politically visible. Yet Congress's actions came well after the damage had been done. Although both Republican and Democratic Congresses had opposed any suggestion that bankers' bonds were guaranteed by the state (even in the Philippines and Puerto Rico), colonial bureaucrats were able to develop creative institutional arrangements that effectively provided the same assurances. Congress's attempts to limit further extensions of the American Empire by refusing to approve even moderate treaties, however, only motivated foreign policy bureaucrats to rely on their private partners all the more. Congress's oversight failures in these cases were due, in part, to its general indifference toward America's overseas empire, and also from its lack of independent information. What little information members did receive about the receiverships came almost entirely from the very bankers and bureaucrats who had every interest in their establishment.[102]

---

[100] Quoted in Perkins, *Constraint of Empire*, 47.

[101] Perkins, *Constraint of Empire*, 48.

[102] For bankers, however, the collapse of the receivership system did little to temper their enthusiasm for securities in Latin America. In the 1920s, as the speculative fever in financial circles spread, they sold hundreds of millions of dollars of sovereign bonds to American investors. The increased stability of the Latin–American bond market that was due, in part, to Dollar Diplomacy contributed to this speculation, which itself would contribute to the onset of the Great Depression as the investor confidence in sovereign bond offerings began to evaporate at the close of the decade.

6

The Colonial State at the Height
of Progressive Imperialism

[T]he policy of the administration is, and has been ever since I assumed control, that of developing the material resources of the Islands as rapidly as possible . . . To build up a country one must have, first of all, money, and money in great quantities.

—W. Cameron Forbes (1913)[1]

The high-water mark of American ambitions in the Philippines would come during the administration of W. Cameron Forbes, the grandson of Ralph Waldo Emerson and the scion of one of Boston's wealthiest families. His paternal grandfather, John Murray Forbes, had made a fortune through his management of the Michigan Central and Burlington and Quincy railroads, and his father, William Forbes, was a founder of the Bell Telephone Company.[2] Forbes himself had been a successful investment banker before arriving in Manila, and he brought a businessman's focus on material investment to the colonial state, serving first as Secretary of Commerce and Police (1904–9) and later, until 1913, as governor-general. During his administration, Forbes would shift the emphasis of colonial state policy even further in the direction of economic development, emphasizing investments in infrastructure, public health, and practical education over legal reforms or democratic tutelage. He built a network of highways, new marketplaces and schools, and a modest railroad system, and he attempted to stimulate agricultural investments for export crops. To be sure, Forbes's goals remained ideological as well as practical, and during his administration the Philippines actually led the United States in implementing a variety of favored Progressive programs, including the development of a postal savings bank system and the creation of a self-governing penal colony.[3]

Yet the governor's development projects were always in the service of political goals. Perhaps even more so than his predecessors, Forbes believed that the United

[1] Forbes to Manuel de Yriarte [Second Assistant Executive Secretary], January 30, 1913; Forbes Papers, Confidential Letters, v. 2.
[2] May, *Social Engineering*, 21.
[3] Forbes Papers, Journal, v. 5, March 23, 1912.

States should remain in the Philippines well into the future, and many of his administration's policies were designed to prime the pump of colonial economic development in the hope that improved infrastructure would make the islands a more attractive market for American capitalists and that Filipinos would somehow learn to appreciate their subjugation by a foreign power. Nevertheless, despite his personal connections to the heights of American commerce and capital, Forbes would face the familiar problem of attracting capital to the islands; the consequence of congressional restrictions on landholding and investment included in the Organic Act.

Congress's continued restrictions checked the colonial government's initial plans for the islands, but it showed relatively little interest in its Asian colony. Despite the insular state's expensive efforts to interest Americans in colonialism and the expansion of American power, it could not convince Congress that such activities were deserving of its support. Instead, colonial officials began to double-down on their strategy of using the Philippine colonial state's own tax base and credit to borrow money in ways that would not attract congressional scrutiny.

In this chapter, I discuss the economic development policies of the colonial state and show how administrators built upon sources of capacity they had been given to govern the islands to achieve large parts of their developmental agenda. In some respects, their prescriptions for the Philippines were not especially novel. After all, the development of roads and railways, the sale of public lands for homesteading, and state-led assistance in agricultural development were all policies that had been used to great effect in the United States.[4] Yet the unique colonial context, the restrictions placed on development by Congress, and their inability to attract capital forced them to adopt a state-led development strategy in the Philippines, which represented a far more radical intervention into the economy than anything that had been attempted domestically – and one that they embraced with enthusiasm.

Under Forbes, colonial officials would doggedly pursue a development strategy that relied on state-assisted private loans as well as a series of creative financial arrangements involving its own gold reserve fund, the centralization of administration in Manila, and sales of public lands. Such aggressive economic development was ultimately seen as a way to cement the Philippines to the United States through the creation of domestic economic interests and to trade material prosperity for the support of elite Filipinos. Eventually, these efforts would run up against the colonial state's inability to cultivate a domestic constituency and the deterioration of its relationship with Filipino elites who would learn to use their own information to embarrass the colonial regime and to undermine its limited support in Congress. The colonial government's ability to remain inconspicuous and to avoid raising congressional hackles would become a victim of its own ambition.

THE PHILIPPINE ASSEMBLY, ELITE NETWORKS, AND THE CENTRALIZATION OF FINANCIAL CONTROL

The election of the first Philippine Assembly in July 1907 would add another level of complexity to imperial administration and play a key role in colonial politics during the remainder of American rule. The creation of the Assembly, however, was

---

[4] May, *Social Engineering*, 140.

never motivated by altruistic goals. The quest for relative autonomy was a game the colonial state played with Congress and with local Filipino politicians. The Assembly would both facilitate and later disrupt the goals of American bureaucrats. Like most imperial powers, American officials in the Philippines sought to cultivate elite support for their regime. With but a few thousand American civilian officials in the islands, there was never any doubt that local alliances were essential to the taxation, infrastructure, and development projects.

As Chapter 4 detailed, the colonial government itself – not members of Congress – had pushed for the inclusion of this institution in the original Organic Act. Along with the support given to the *Federalista* party, it was seen as a way to gain the support of Filipino elites and to deflect the criticism of anti-imperialists at home. As we will see, however, it was never a toothless or purely ceremonial organization. To gain elite support for parts of their developmental agenda, American officials were forced to cede real power to the Assembly and to cultivate a set of Filipino politicians with strong ties to the imperial regime.

The election results of 1907, which gave the pro-independence *Nacionalista* party a clear majority of 58 seats and left Taft's favored *Federalistas* out of power, reveal the complexity of these relationships.[5] Although property and literacy qualifications limited electoral activity to the Filipino elite (just 1.4 percent of the country could register), historians have long interpreted these results as a repudiation of the collaborationist *Federalistas* and the creation of a more popular Filipino politics.[6] Nevertheless, more recent research has called these conclusions into question.[7] Indeed, if American officials felt threatened by election results that seemed to undermine the power base of their *Federalista* allies, it was not obvious. Taft, who returned to Manila to open the Assembly in October 1907, tried to put the best spin on these election results:

It has been reported in the Islands that I was coming here for the purpose of expressing in bitter and threatening words my disappointment at the result of the election. *Nothing could be further from my purpose*; nothing could be less truly descriptive of my condition of mind. I am here, filled with a spirit of friendship and *encouragement* for these members.[8]

What explains the surprising equanimity with which American colonial officials greeted the *Nationalista* victory? In part, it was because these newly elected men were far less radical than their campaign materials suggested. As Forbes explained to a relative before the elections, he had questioned the *Nationalista* leadership and found that "what they wanted was office, not independence; that they understood very clearly that the present existing condition of affairs would not change and that we need have very little anxiety about what they would do when they got in; that they would be friendly to the government and not attempt to start any waves."[9] A more revealing explanation, however, comes from a shift in the structure of the Philippine local and provincial

[5] Ruby Paredes, "The Origins of National Politics: Taft and the Partido Federal," in *Philippine Colonial Democracy*, ed. Ruby Paredes (Quezon City: Ateneo de Manila University Press, 1989), 44.
[6] See, for example, Teodoro Agoncillo, *Filipino Nationalism, 1872–1970* (Quezon City: R. P. Garcia, 1974).
[7] Cullinane, "Playing the Game," 70; Paredes, "The Origins of National Politics," 41.
[8] Quoted in Paredes, "Origins of National Politics," 47 [emphasis in original].
[9] Forbes to Ralph Forbes, August 14, 1907; quoted in May, *Social Engineering*, 36.

governments, which allowed for the emergence of a new set of Filipino elites, many of whom had already developed close working relationships with American bureaucrats. American democratic "tutelage" through the new Assembly became a way for provincial elites to consolidate their dominance over Philippine society and a way for American officials to rise to higher levels in the colonial bureaucracy.[10]

Forging a Partnership: Provincial Elites and Colonial Administrators

Under the more centralized Spanish system, provincial governorships had been reserved for Spaniards. The Americans not only appointed Filipinos to serve in these roles, but also quickly made them elected positions. Beginning in 1902, the provincial governor was selected by a province's municipal councilors, making it essential for gubernatorial candidates to have a strong base of support in the provinces.[11] Consequently, the Manila-based elites gradually gave way to a new set of local politicians who could then use the patronage resources of the provincial governor's office to shore up their political support.

If the Americans had not intended this outcome, they certainly understood the consequences of this very familiar form of spoils politics. By 1904, it was clear that these new provincial politicians would soon dominate local governments. Whatever sentimental attachments Taft and other officials may have felt to the older class of Filipinos were quickly overcome by the realization that these men would soon be less useful to the colonial regime; after all, Manila itself would command only two of the eighty Assembly delegates.[12] Since the early days of American colonial government, of course, cordial relations with local elites were seen as an essential criterion for advancement in the colonial service. Even the governor-general, as Taft proved when he dismissed Wright, was expected to balance the cultivation of Filipino support with the goals of the regime.[13] And as the balance of power among Filipinos shifted, American officials discovered that cultivating ties with the new provincial politicians would prove to be more important for their own careers than catering to the Manila-based elite. As historian Michael Cullinane – a close student of early national politics in the Philippines – has shown, the benefits flowed both ways: Filipino provincial politicians could advance their careers through the support of American bureaucrats, and Americans could rise to higher positions in the insular government through their proven friendships with local elites.[14]

No development illustrates the importance of these ties more clearly than the mutually beneficial relationship Sergio Osmeña and Cameron Forbes forged in their respective rise to Speaker of the Philippine Assembly and governor-general. The episode is particularly revealing because Forbes, as Secretary of Commerce and Police, had initially seen his role in the Philippines as a sole matter of technocratic management.

---

[10] Cullinane, "Playing the Game," 105.

[11] Ibid., 75.

[12] Ibid., 99.

[13] Michael Cullinane, "The Politics of Collaboration in Tayabas Province: The Early Political Career of Manuel Luis Quezon, 1903–1906," in *Reappraising an Empire: New Perspectives on Philippine–American History*, ed. Peter W. Stanley (Cambridge, MA: Harvard University Press, 1984), 62–3.

[14] See Paredes, "Origins of National Politics"; Cullinane, *Ilustrado Politics*.

During Taft's visit in the summer of 1905, Forbes chose to forgo a lunch with a provincial governor in order to inspect a jail, leading the Secretary of War to chastise him for not considering the ramifications of this social snub.[15] Indeed, Forbes's failure to demonstrate these ties led Taft to consider his dismissal. "I thought he had made a great mistake in not cultivating the Filipinos," he later wrote to his wife, "I had told him to do so, [but] he had given no attention to them at all."[16] By 1906, however, Forbes had clearly received the message and he dramatically changed his approach. At the October 1906 Governor's Conference, he made a point to meet with Osmeña, a new provincial governor, who was widely considered a rising star of Philippine politics.[17] Osmeña himself had forged strong relations with American officials in his province of Cebu, and had been presented to Taft during his visit in 1905, leading Taft's private secretary to note that he had evidently "been groomed by the American officials here as a candidate for provincial governor."[18]

A similar pattern can be seen in the rise of Manuel Quezon, a provincial lawyer, who was also considered a future leader of the new crop of provincial politicians and had forged similarly close ties with Col. Harry Bandholtz, the local director of the Philippine Constabulary.[19] By 1906, both Forbes and Bandholtz were openly championing the careers of Quezon and Osmeña, not only because they genuinely considered them more receptive to the developmental goals of the colonial state, but also because their personal ties to these new Filipino leaders were beneficial for their own careers. In Forbes's 1906 and 1907 reports on the constabulary as head of the Bureau of Commerce and Police, Quezon and Osmeña were the only officials mentioned by name and both were singled out as being particularly good administrators.[20] Thus, when Osmeña was elected as Speaker of the Assembly in 1907, Forbes greeted the news with great satisfaction: "Osmeña elected, as I expected, and will be Speaker, I think. It means that I shall have great power with the Assembly, if signs do not fail."[21]

Both Bandholtz and Forbes would be rewarded by Taft for cultivating these ties. In 1907, Bandholtz became head of the constabulary and Forbes was elevated to governor-general two years later.[22] For the Americans administrators, the Assembly dramatically lowered the chance of open rebellion against the colonial regime – a situation that would virtually guarantee negative press at home and reduced investment in the islands. And for a new generation of Filipino provincial elites, cooperation with the Americans gave them access to the resources and power of the national government.

The American-controlled Commission made a point of imbuing the new post of Speaker with significant prestige, allowing Osmeña the use of the ornate former

---

[15] Cullinane, *Ilustrado Politics*, 248.
[16] Taft to Helen Herron Taft, September 24, 1905, quoted in Paredes, "Origins of National Politics," 58.
[17] Cullinane, *Ilustrado Politics*, 255.
[18] LeRoy quoted in Cullinane, "Playing the Game," 97.
[19] Cullinane, "Politics of Collaboration," 71.
[20] Cullinane, *Ilustrado Politics*, 283.
[21] Forbes Journal II, 269–70; Quoted by Paredes, "Origins of National Politics," 65.
[22] Cullinane, *Ilustrado Politics*, 283.

office of the Spanish governor-general and paying him a large salary.[23] Osmeña and the leaders of the Philippine Assembly certainly understood that these benefits came with obligations, but they should not be seen as clients of the colonial regime. Throughout the rest of the Republican era, Osmeña shrewdly balanced the nationalistic sentiments and political slogans that secured his own political power with the need to avoid embarrassing the American colonial government whose patronage he needed to maintain his political coalition. Just after Osmeña was elected Speaker, he moved to silence a fiery independence speech by one delegate, and during the remainder of the first legislative session he obstructed efforts by other members to propose bills for independence.[24] Furthermore, Osmeña proved willing to champion the colonial state's cherished public works and economic development bills, as long as the Commission was willing to grant certain concessions. As Forbes recorded in his journal, recounting a recent legislative battle,

I had kept in touch with Osmeña through the day, and several times I offered him concessions to help carry the important measures along. The construction of some public work to please a deputy here or there, the work in itself necessary, and a good use of money of course. We extended the time of payment of the land tax – a very pernicious thing to do but popular with the Assembly . . . By these means I was able to keep the Assembly in the frame of mind of approving our measures.[25]

None of this is to suggest that the relationship between the American colonial regime and the Assembly was always harmonious. Although Osmeña did not permit the Assembly to openly advocate for independence during this period, he did allow the adoption of bills that challenged the colonial regime's authority. During the first and second legislatures, the American commissioners vetoed a variety measures that threatened their control over revenue or their supervision of development projects. Among them were proposals to abolish imprisonment as a punishment for failure to pay the *cédula* tax and a bill to transfer control over public works from the Manila-based Bureau of Public Works to a provincial office.[26] For American colonial officials, the Assembly's existence was acceptable only insofar as it did not jeopardize its developmental goals or embarrass it in Washington.

Local Politics and Fiscal Centralization

At the heart of the maturing relationship between the Assembly and the colonial regime were two developments that secured the power base of native politicians and gave the colonial state greater control over its economic development projects and finances. First, although Filipinos were largely excluded from the upper reaches of colonial administration, the Americans were happy to cede to them control over

---

[23] Elliott, *Philippines to the End of Commission Government*, 124–5.
[24] Cullinane, *Ilustrado Politics*, 327.
[25] Forbes Journal, May 22 1909, quoted in May, *Social Engineering*, 62.
[26] Frank Jenista, Jr., "Conflict in the Philippine Legislature: The Commission and the Assembly from 1907 to 1913," in *Compadre Colonialism: Studies on the Philippines under American Rule*, ed. Norman G. Owen (Ann Arbor, MI: University of Michigan, Center for South and Southeast Asian Studies, 1971), Appendix II.

TABLE 6.1. *Provincial treasurers, 1907–13*

Year	Filipino	American
1907	1	30
1908	5	26
1909	7	26
1910	10	21
1911	11	20
1912	11	20
1913	13	18

Source: Bonifacio S. Salamanca, *The Filipino Reaction to American Rule, 1901–1913* (Hamden, CT: Shoe String Press, 1968), 56.

local politics, and Filipinos staffed nearly all of the local municipal and lower-level provincial government posts. Yet as the Americans granted more *political* posts to Filipinos, they made the very un-American decision to remove any significant powers from local governments by centralizing control over economic development and revenue.[27]

Second, the highest administrative posts of the insular government were reserved for Americans. By 1913, for example, only four Filipinos were in charge of executive departments, and even these were the relatively unimportant bureaus of Weather, Archives, Patents, and Copyrights.[28] Further evidence for these developments comes from a seemingly minor change to provincial administration made in 1904 when the office of the provincial secretary – a position appointed by the Commission and often filled by an American – was replaced by a third elected member to serve with the governor and treasurer. Although this virtually guaranteed a Filipino majority on the provincial governing boards – a change that pleased the Assembly – many of the provincial governments' independent powers had already been taken away. By 1905, colonial finances, most public works, education, control of the constabulary, and public health were all centralized under the Commission's Manila-based bureaus, and the provincial governor became a prestigious but not particularly powerful post, useful mainly as a platform for ambitious politicians on their way to the Assembly.[29] The one provincial post that did retain significant authority was the office of provincial treasurer, which, until 1907, was always filled by an American. Indeed, even after this period, as Table 6.1 illustrates, the clear majority of provincial treasurers remained Americans.

The tension between the colonial state's need to control its economic development projects and the need to maintain the support of the Philippine Assembly is further revealed in the way that corruption cases involving local officials were managed. At the municipal level, charges could be brought against municipal officials through the Commission's Executive Bureau. Yet, as American officials in Manila were well aware, the most frequent charges – neglect of duty, abuse of authority,

---

[27] Cullinane, "Implementing the 'New Order,'" 40.

[28] Bonifacio S. Salamanca, *The Filipino Reaction to American Rule, 1901–1913* (Hamden, CT: Shoe String Press, 1968), 69.

[29] Cullinane, *Ilustrado Politics,* 279.

TABLE 6.2. *Cases against and removals of municipal officers, 1904–13*

	Presidents	Vice presidents	Treasurers
1904	58 (22)	10 (4)	11 (6)
1905	51 (23)	15 (8)	0
1906	55 (10)	13 (2)	0
1907–8, no data			
1909	64 (20)	18 (9)	4 (3)
1910	67 (12)	14 (4)	7 (5)
1911	54 (9)	14 (5)	1 (1)
1912	51 (19)	15 (8)	2 (1)
1913	50 (13)	14 (3)	0
Totals:	450 (128)	113 (43)	25 (16)
Percent removed:	28%	38%	64%

Source: Adapted from Cullinane, "Implementing the 'New Order,'" 54.

and violation of election laws – were often politically motivated. Furthermore, provincial governors, who were responsible for investigating such charges, could use their office to remove political enemies and to protect friends.[30] As Table 6.2 shows, such charges were not infrequent, nor did their frequency decline for municipal presidents and vice presidents during the first decade of American rule.

The most obvious exception to this rule was the apparent honesty of municipal treasurers who were brought up on charges at a dramatically lower rate than their political counterparts. In part, this was because municipal treasurers (although Filipino) were brought under the civil service and directly overseen by the American provincial treasurer. At the same time, however, the data reveal the seriousness of such charges when they did occur. Although municipal presidents and vice presidents were often not removed from office once charged, treasurers were considerably more likely to be removed. There are many ways to interpret these data, but one implication seems to be that the colonial state cared far less about stamping out corruption in local Filipino politics than protecting its own revenue and development projects. Their rhetoric about democratic "tutelage" notwithstanding, the American colonial officials were willing to turn a blind eye to local corruption as long as it did not infringe upon the insular government's goals or rob it of revenue. As we will see, once the Assembly did begin to exert more control over these areas of colonial administration, its relations with the American regime significantly deteriorated.

COLONIAL INFRASTRUCTURE: HIGHWAYS, RAILROADS, AND PRIVATE MONEY

Despite their later disagreements over control of national revenues, US officials and Filipino elites were in agreement about the importance of public works projects. As discussed in Chapter 4, the colonial administrators, led by Taft, were

---

[30] Cullinane, "Implementing the 'New Order,'" 56.

certain that improved infrastructure held the key to developing the Philippines even before they had set foot in Manila. Opening up the islands' rich interior to development required the construction of new roads and, more importantly, a system of railroads. For Americans who had come of age during America's own railway boom, their faith in railroads as a key part of economic development is unsurprising. If railroads could lead to the development of the United States, insular bureaucrats reasoned, they could also lead to development in the Philippines. Given the reluctance of American business to enter the colonial market and Congress's refusal to appropriate funds or even guarantee colonial bonds, however, these officials would need the support of American investment firms, and these private partnerships would be forged in the service of the colonial state's developmental ideology.

Roads and Highways

Spanish neglect had left the Philippines with terrible roads that were practically impassable during the long rainy season, an unfortunate problem that dramatically increased the costs of agricultural exports. Because of this, an extensive network of new roads connecting agricultural regions to railways and ports was seen as essential to the success of the colonial government. Without roads, the colonial officials' dreams of attracting large-scale agricultural plantations and stimulating Philippine exports – developments that were all seen as essential to the material prosperity of the colony – would be impossible. Forbes, in particular, accorded the highway projects the highest priority. "It is my magnum opus," he wrote of his 1906 road-building proposal,

And if I should fail in everything else here, and this go into effect, I should not have been here in vain. It means the difference between good roads and bad, between prosperity and failure. It spells progress . . . of the most absolutely vital sort that will increase the wealth of the country annually anywhere from ten to twenty times the amount spent.[31]

Yet, as Forbes himself asked an assembly of provincial governors, "How are we going to get them?"[32] As usual, a lack of revenue was the principal problem.

Forbes's solution, which would prove to be deeply unpopular, was the resurrection of the hated Spanish corvée system, which required all able-bodied men to devote five days to roadwork or pay a tax. The adoption of the bill was contingent on its acceptance by provincial governors, but with the 1907 elections approaching, not a single governor was willing to risk the political fallout that would surely have accompanied this controversial measure. A new act, passed in May 1907, proved more palatable. The so-called double *cédula* law allowed provincial governors to double the local tax and to add the extra money to a road and bridge fund. As an extra inducement to secure passage of this measure, the Commission agreed to provide a 10 percent bonus to a province's road account and a 5 percent increase

[31] Forbes Papers, Journal, v. 2, July 13, 1906.
[32] October 18, 1906 – "Address of the Honorable W. Cameron Forbes delivered before the Provincial Governors at Manila." Forbes Papers, US Philippine commission, 1900–16, Philippine commission railway records.

in its school budget that would be paid out of a newly created ₱1.2 million fund.[33] Within a year, 27 of the 31 provinces had adopted the measure. Finally, in exchange for Forbes's assistance in fending off an attack from the *Federalistas* – now operating as the *Progresistas* – Osmeña had secured its adoption as a permanent feature of the colonial revenue system in 1910.[34]

Unlike many of the colonial state's development projects, road construction gained the wide support of Filipino legislators who were more than happy to take credit for money pumped into their constituencies, especially when the investments came in the form of state-owned highways and not from private American capitalists. Indeed, during the second Philippine legislature over 10 percent of the bills passed were for local public works projects, and some provincial governors and municipal authorities went so far as to secure "voluntary" labor to speed the construction of local roads. Unlike their supervision of revenue matters, however, American colonial authorities were less concerned with involving themselves in local politics or with understanding why, exactly, local citizens might want to freely contribute time on the road gangs. "We always suspect their 'voluntary' labor is brought about by a somewhat free use of the municipal police," Forbes noted, "but as the result is roads, it is not necessary to analyze too closely all the steps leading up to them."[35]

Through these new measures, provincial governments spent more than ₱2 million between 1908 and 1913, which, when combined with the annual appropriations from the insular state that ranged from ₱1.5 to ₱2.2 million, provided for the funds to begin construction of the new road system.[36] And it was in road construction that the colonial state excelled. As Figure 6.1 shows, the mileage of all improved roads grew dramatically during the colonial period, growing from fewer than 500 miles of first-class highways in 1908 to more than 1,500 miles just six years later (Figure 6.2).

In choosing where to build the new roads, colonial officials at the Bureau of Public Works went to get lengths to demonstrate that their methods for allocating funds were "scientific." As Forbes later recalled:

[I]n order to ascertain what roads were most urgently needed *computers were engaged to count the number of wheels which passed over each road in each province and report the result.* The road carrying the greatest traffic received the first attention of the bureau . . . The Bureau of Public Works went into the consideration of the proposed road improvement with *scientific thoroughness.* The value of the services to be performed by the road was computed, the cost of the road estimated, and the two figures compared, and the bureau was soon able to estimate with reasonable accuracy what projects were most urgently needed.[37]

By basing their road-building decisions on these calculations, roads that already were heavily traveled were the first to be improved and developed into highways. In practice this meant that shorter roads, many of which served to connect the major

[33] Elliott, *Philippines to the End of Commission Government*, 284.
[34] Stanley, *Nation in the Making*, 155.
[35] Forbes Papers, Journal, v. II, October 25, 1907.
[36] May, *Social Engineering*, 145.
[37] Forbes, *Philippine Islands*, v. I, 375–6 [my emphasis].

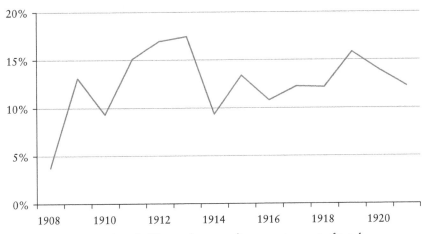

FIGURE 6.1. *Public works expenditures as percent of total.*
Source: Expenditure for public works as percent of total insular revenue. Adapted from Forbes, *Philippine Islands,* v. I, 244. Does not include money from bond sales or companies owned by the government through stock.

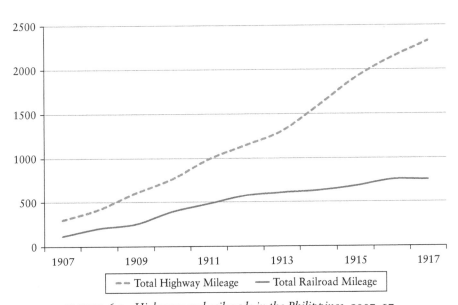

FIGURE 6.2. *Highways and railroads in the Philippines, 1907–17.*
Source: Railroad miles are the combined total of the Manila Railroad Company and the Philippine Railway Company. Highways are first-class roads. Figure for 1907 is an estimate. Data adapted from Forbes, *Philippine Islands,* v. 1, 1907.

agricultural centers to harbors, were built first.[38] This, of course, was perfectly in keeping with the colonial state's economic development goals. But the road-building project was also meant to open up new areas for investment, and so considerable resources were devoted to long highways that could serve as commercial arteries.[39] Road maintenance was approached in a similarly "scientific" manner of which Forbes was particularly proud. Roads were first divided into sections and a local laborer, known as a *caminero*, was paid to care for each section. "It was found that it cost about one-third as much to keep the road in good condition by having the *caminero* constantly at work on it," Forbes wrote, "as it had to let the road go wholly unattended – as was at that time the custom in these backward United States."[40] These roads, however, were seen as only one part of a larger transportation network that would also involve a new network of railroads.

Railroads and Collaboration

Unlike highways, the colonial state had neither the resources nor the ability to build railroads itself. But railroads, they thought, held the key to stimulating colonial exports and investments by linking the various agricultural regions to the newly improved harbors for export; indeed, the importance they placed on railroad development can hardly be exaggerated. "If we can possibly get a crowd of strong Americans to build a comprehensive railroad system for Luzon," Wright wrote to Taft in 1904, "it would be of more benefit for this people than anything we could possibly do."[41] In another cable, sent months later to Senator Edward Carmack (D-TN), Wright was even more enthusiastic:

Will open up and furnish market to large areas of Luzon now practically inaccessible. More valuable in educating people even than schools. Will increase taxable values and thus enable us to reduce rate of taxation. At the same time will furnish increased revenues and enable us to reduce if not completely break down tariff barriers to trade between United States and the Philippine Island which we earnestly desire. Will furnish needed employment at fair wages.[42]

To a surprising degree, however, Americans saw railway development as a key process of "civilization" as much as a way to facilitate economic activity. In a later letter to Root, for example, Taft went out of his way to distinguish the purpose of the new American railway from the older Spanish one. The distinction he drew was between a parasitic colonial state and a developmental one, "the sole motive of which is to furnish a great civilizing and prosperity-giving instrumentality to the people and to increase and expand its benefits to the public by offering a reasonable compensation to the private capital employed, proportioned to the risk, and without hope or expectation of substantial profit to the treasury."[43] As with

---

[38] Stanly, *Nation in the Making*, 103.
[39] May, *Social Engineering*, 145.
[40] Forbes, *Philippine Islands*, v. I, 375–6.
[41] Wright to Taft, February 15, 1904; Edwards Papers, Box 3, Folder 15.
[42] Wright to Carmack, April 26, 1904; quoted in Stanley, *Nation in the Making*, 104.
[43] Taft to Root, June 22, 1906; quoted in Elliott, *Philippines to the End of Commission Government*, 305, n. 6.

modern highways, hygiene, and a civil service, railroads were seen as essential to the modern nation they hoped to construct.

Despite the difficulties involved in railroad construction throughout much of the Philippines, Commission authorities dreamed of an extensive railway system running the length of Luzon linked with connecting lines in the Visayan Islands by a ferry system. At the time, however, the Philippines had only one narrow-gauge railroad that ran from Manila to Dagupan, which was managed by the British-owned Manila Railroad Company (MRC). The Americans considered it a joke – "absurd English engines, little forty pound rails, English and American coaches, and ponderous cement stations," Forbes contemptuously reported in his journal. "Truly Spanish, ponderous stations and light rails."[44] Yet finding American investors willing to sink their capital into a railway venture in the Philippines proved even more difficult than expected. Initially, a number of groups expressed interest, including top railroad magnates such as Charles Swift, who had already purchased the Manila street railway franchise, E. H. Harriman of the Union Pacific, James Hill of the Great Northern, and J. P. Morgan. Edwards noted to Wright that he was

Quite delighted at something I heard sub-rose, that is, that Hill will probably head the syndicate. I have always felt that to make the Philippine railroads a success, it would be necessary to have some such interest as Hill or Harriman at the head of the syndicate, because the only way to make it profitable is for the trans-continental and trans-pacific and Philippine Railway system, with inter-island steamboats touching railway points, to be all under one management.[45]

Yet these early reports proved to be overly optimistic, and insular authorities soon realized that some sort of financial inducement was necessary to attract capital. This, at least, is what the Commission took from its extensive meetings with American industrialists.[46] Although there would be little success in attracting robust financial support from the United States, the colonial government tried hard. In a remarkably frank statement that seems to capture the philosophy behind the entire project, Forbes concluded, "My idea was that we should jealously guard the interests of people who came out to the Philippines and put up money, and make sure they made money if we possibly could, with the idea of giving Manila a good name among capitalists."[47]

As a result, the ability to guarantee a certain percentage return on investment was soon deemed essential to the entire project. Initially, colonial officials were unsure if they would need congressional permission to guarantee the debt – a significant obstacle because nobody involved in the colonial bureaucracy was anxious to involve Congress in much of anything.[48] For its part, Congress retained the

---

[44] Forbes Papers, Journal, v. 1, September 10, 1904.

[45] Edwards to Wright, January 1, 1904; Edwards Papers, Box 3, Folder 14.

[46] See, for example, Edwards Papers, Edwards to Wright, September 19, 1904, Box 4, Folder 8. Edwards Papers, Taft to Root, January 13, 1903.

[47] Quoted in Stanley, *Nation in the Making*, 227.

[48] Another proposed solution was to grant lands to the railroad, but Cooper's House Committee objected to this. "There are two ways in which the Philippine government might aid in the building of railroads," the Committee's report read.

ability to micro-manage the islands, and its restrictions shaped the colonial state's infrastructure projects significantly. In 1903, Edwards met with a railroad engineer and reported back to Taft,

I told him how important, even essential, we thought the Trunk Line Railway system was for the Philippines, and stated, though I couldn't speak authoritatively, that I felt it was important enough to guarantee a small percent, probably three on the total investment to interest capitalists . . . The next was the power of the government to guarantee. The Secretary's personal letter on this subject, in answer to your last, will advise you of his views on that matter. This point hasn't been gone into extensively here, but informal, Judge Magoon and the rest of us are quite clear that you have that right, in fact, as I recollect it, you believed so.[49]

Years later, Forbes wrote that Root had actually concluded that congressional approval was unnecessary – a dubious legal conclusion indeed, but one that Root insisted upon for strategic reasons. It seems that Root was reluctant to seek approval because it might actually undermine the colonial government's autonomy. As Forbes later recalled,

[I]t was Mr. Root who pointed out to me the strategic advantage in not giving the law expressly this power, as when Congress passed such a law it indicated that the implied power did not exist, and thus by presumption lessened other implied powers, as it might be held that powers to do similar things were not implied if this power was not implied.[50]

As Forbes revealed, the real reason colonial officials would eventually return to Congress to request direct authorization was not because they had any legal qualms about independently offering the guarantee, but rather because the railroad companies refused to bid on the contracts without it.[51]

The "Cooper Act," so-named for the ever-helpful Chairman of the House Committee on Insular Affairs, was proposed to allow the Commission to guarantee an income of 5 percent on capital invested in Philippine railroads and permission to exempt from taxes the raw materials imported to construct them. Predictably, however, the proposed guarantee proved a flashpoint for the opposition. The usual objections of government handouts to corporate interests were buttressed by a new challenge that picked up on the increasingly ambiguous relationship the colonial government maintained with Washington.

As discussed in Chapter 4, insular authorities had already argued for increased financial independence, reasoning that the Commission government was an independent, albeit congressional-authorized, arm of the national state. The guarantees

---

One by the grants of lands; the other by a guaranty upon capital invested. Your committee believe, with the Secretary of War and the Commission, that for the Philippine Islands it will be much better to have the railroads constructed under a guaranty upon actual investment, and to have the lands held for the people of the Archipelago.

See "Administration of Civil Government in the Philippine Islands, Etc.," C. Rec., 58th Cong, 2nd sess., H. Report No. 2227, 10.

[49] Edwards to Taft, April 7, 1903; Edwards Papers, Box 2, Folder 22.
[50] April 5, 1910, Forbes to Dickinson; Forbes Papers, Confidential Letters, v. 1.
[51] Ibid.

to be given, after all, were from the Commission government, and not from the United States. Yet the opposition charged the Commission with trying to have it both ways. In an accusation laced with some irony, the opposition now argued that the Commission was so close to the War Department as to be nearly indistinguishable from it – a fact, the opposition asserted, that made the Commission's guarantees really guarantees by the US government:

As showing how completely the Philippine Commission, upon which is conferred the nominal authority to make these guaranties of interest, is dominated by the War Department, we call attention to the following telegram sent by Secretary Root to Governor Wright in connection with legislation had upon another subject, but directed from Washington. It strongly enforces, we think, the contention that the legislative acts of the Philippine Commission are little else than the acts of the War Department. If this be true, then it would seem to follow that the moral obligation of the Philippine Islands, to pay interest on an indebtedness such as that proposed in this section, is, to say the least, no greater than that of the United States.

Wright, Manila (January 30, 1904)

Recommendation Philippine Commission, that Bates agreement with Moros be declared no longer in force, upon grounds referred to in report of the civil governor, is approved in principle. A statute declaring and containing the legislation necessary in consequence of this abrogation, and having recitals carefully drawn, should be prepared and passed to third reading by Commission and then forwarded to the Secretary of War for his approval in advance of its enactment.

Root[52]

This, the opposition may have reasoned, would be an argument that would find favor even among members who were not opposed to the American presence in the Philippines.

Insular authorities, however, were in a much better position to defend their legislation than they were a few years before. The bill was successfully reported out of committee, but not without a great deal of arm-twisting and promises from Secretary Taft. As Edwards reported to Wright back in Manila,

Secretary Taft and myself are duplicating your experience with Congress when you were here last, except the Secretary has got them mollified. He is allowing Culberson to pick out a man to send over to West Point on the Board of Visitors; tickled Carmack, patted Patterson the back, and I shouldn't wonder, if Tillman wasn't sick in bed, but what he would have him to.[53]

The floor of the House, however, would not be so easy to cajole, and Taft and Edwards knew that they would need to amend Section 4, the controversial section that guaranteed a 5 percent return on capital investments. But in order to break the compromise, they would need to learn just what would be acceptable to New York.

By this point, the relationship between the BIA and Wall Street had become decidedly cozy. The addition of Forbes, who was enlisted to accompany Root on

---

[52] "Views of the Minority," C. Rec. 58th Cong, 2nd sess., H.R. Rep. 2227, Part 2.
[53] Edwards to Wright, March 25, 1904; Edwards Papers, Box 3, Folder 15.

his meeting with J. P. Morgan even before he left for Manila, to the Commission helped. But after the large bond sales and early negotiations for railway investment, Edwards, too, had become a familiar face on Wall Street. Indeed, as he bragged to Wright,

One or two of the ambitious financial concerns who think they are going to get the franchises for the trunk line railroads are flattering me by asking me if I won't resign, and at a big salary and manage the proposition in the Philippines. I wonder if I could get along with the Commission if I should take them up?[54]

By the fall of 1904, Edwards's letters back to Manila about the railway negotiations make him sound more like an investment banker than a colonel in the US Army:

Forbes has undoubtedly told you of Mr. Root's and his talk with J. P. Morgan, but as far as I can find out, the man who is more actively interested in the venture is Mr. Perkins, Mr. Morgan's partner. They maintain here, or at least I am told they do, an agent – Mr. William C. Seer. He tells me he is a direct agent of Mr. Perkins. I spoke to Mr. Forbes about this man, but young Jack Morgan didn't seem to know who he was . . . However, Mr. Beer I knew at West Point. He was there a couple of years with me, but didn't get through, and now has gone out and done very well in New York. He represents McCall of the New York Life and Mr. Perkins of J. P. Morgan & Company.[55]

To know what compromise on the Cooper Act would be acceptable to Wall Street, the Commission first had to generate interest among American capitalists in backing the railway. Under the advice of Sir William Van Horne, the builder of the Canadian Pacific, the Commission had earlier commissioned a survey of the Luzon lines, and this report was now privately sent to a number of top Wall Street firms. Initially J. P. Morgan & Co., James J. Hill, the Guaranty Trust, and Lee, Higginson & Company had all expressed some interest, but Speyer Brothers eventually emerged as the most likely partner.[56] This was fine with Edwards who thought Speyer's interest would signal to the rest of Wall Street that the Philippines was a sound investment. As he reported back to Wright, "Speyer, as Commissioner Forbes will tell you, is about as clever a chap as they have on Wall Street. He don't miss any opportunities, and his relation with London capital allows him to command financial situations."[57]

The insular state now had two problems. Given the opposition Section 4 had generated in Congress, they would be unable to guarantee the original 5 percent. Speyer & Co. would need to accept a lower rate, and this would involve some difficult, but relatively straightforward, negotiations. The second problem was of a more delicate nature, but one that demonstrates just how autonomous the colonial state was becoming. The Commission, it seems, had received an offer from Belgian inventors to build the Luzon lines with no guarantee at all. In pure business terms, of course, this was a good thing, because it gave them a credible counteroffer to use

[54] Ibid.
[55] Edwards to Wright, September 19, 1904; Edwards Papers, Box 4, Folder 8.
[56] Stanley, *Nation in the Making*, 105.
[57] Edwards to Wright, September 19, 1904; Edwards Papers, Box 4, Folder 8.

when negotiating with the American firm. From a political perspective, however, it was positively toxic. To accept the Belgian offer would mean that the opposition in Congress was right – firms would invest without a government guarantee. It would also mean giving over a lucrative contract to a foreign firm, an act that would diminish their reputation even among their strongest backers in Congress and almost certainly cause the Cooper Act to die, making congressional authorization less likely for future bond offerings.

In the end, they decided to threaten Speyer with the Belgian offer, presumably on the assumption that their bluff would not be called, but to otherwise remain silent. Writing from Manila, Wright told Edwards to offer Speyer 3 percent, a proposition that Edwards thought very "business-like." "Speyer & Company will cavil much about that," Edwards admitted, "because when we had that conference in New York they thought the least charter authority that should be given immediately by Congress should be 5%, but at the same time, much use can be made of the Belgian proposition to build the roads without a guaranty." Still, Edwards nervously admitted, "I am rather hopeful that this won't be known to Congress, because it will aid the opposition in their fight, if any serious fight is made, against the passage of the Cooper bill through the Senate, so I am talking nothing about it."[58]

The BIA's gambit proved successful; indeed, they had to give up less than they expected. On February 6, 1905, Congress passed the Cooper Law with a 4 percent guarantee on railway investments from the Philippine state, and allowed the insular government, with the president's approval, to fund the further construction of roads, bridges, and various municipal buildings through future bond offerings.[59] Eventually, however, the risks proved too much for some of the more cautious capitalists. J. P. Morgan backed out after the compromise over the Cooper Bill led to the reduction in the guaranteed return to 4 percent and Harriman decided not to bid after hearing from his investigators that railways in the islands would never turn a profit (a prediction that would later prove accurate). Even with a guaranteed 4 percent return on capital investment, it was difficult to find investors. As the president of the PRC would testify 30 years later, White & Co.'s initial investment was made "at the earnest request of the United States government through Mr. Taft, then Secretary of War" (that this was the same year the BIA was also engaged in recruiting capitalists to take over the debt in the Dominican Republic was hardly a coincidence).[60]

In the end, only three bids were submitted, one for each franchise: Speyer & Company bid on the Luzon line, Swift and J. G. White & Company bid on lines proposed for the Visayas, and a Seattle group bid on the lines in Albay. The Luzon line was the real prize, and Speyer, at the BIA's suggestion, had placed himself in an excellent position to win the concession by gaining control of the Manila Railway Company in 1904 – the Philippines's only existing railroad.[61] In 1906, the Commission granted concessions to Speyer's MRC without any investment guarantees for 428 miles on Luzon and to Swift and J. G. White's Philippine

[58] Edwards to Wright, September 19, 1904 and Edwards to Taft, September 20, 1904; Edwards Papers, Box 4, Folder 8.
[59] Elliott, *Philippines to the End of Commission Government*, 71.
[60] 72nd Cong., 1st sess., 330, quoted in Cruz, *Colonial Office*, 108.
[61] May, *Social Engineering*, 163.

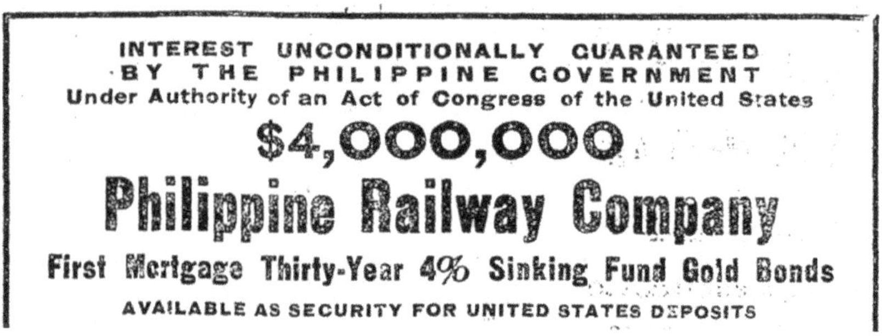

FIGURE 6.3. *Bond advertisement for the Philippine Railway Company.*
Source: New York Times, November 17, 1908, 11.

Railway Company (PRC) for 295 miles on the Visayan Islands of Panay, Negros, and Cebu. The interest guarantee with its (false) implication of federal backing made the bonds considerably easier to sell. Indeed, as Figure 6.3 shows, the PRC bond advertisement made every effort to present the US government as the clear backer of the project, emphasizing the Philippine government's guarantee by "Act of Congress."

Failure and Public Financing: Railroads and the Gold Reserve Fund

Construction on the new railroad began in earnest in 1907, but the insular state's capital problems did not end there. The Panic of 1907 made the bonds difficult to sell, leaving the banking consortiums that had sponsored the railroad bond issues in increasingly desperate straits. Speyer, whose bonds had not originally been guaranteed by the colonial state, now told the Commission that he *would* need a 4 percent guarantee to sell the bonds. Fears of a Japanese invasion along with the still unsettled status of the Philippines left investors in the United States feeling skittish, and Speyer soon ordered all work on the railroad stopped. At first, colonial authorities were hesitant to extend more loan guarantees, so Speyer transferred the MRC to a separate corporation that had no funds and threatened bankruptcy, "in which case we could sue and much good it would do us," Forbes sarcastically noted. Faced with these problems, Taft and Forbes agreed to extend the guarantees under the condition that Speyer would also build a 22-mile line to the Commission's summer capital in Baguio, along with a 135-mile line in southern Luzon linking its existing lines in Albay to the rest of the Luzon system.[62] Even this guarantee did not end the MRC's financial difficulties, and Speyer's constant lack of funds hampered the railway's progress.

The PRC did not fare much better. Although their loans had been guaranteed by the Commission, they, too, proved a difficult sell on Wall Street, and by 1908, Forbes wrote, "[t]he situation was fairly desperate."[63] Swift and his partners now owned $2 million of their own bonds that they could not seem to sell, and were on

[62] Forbes Papers, Journal, v. 3, December 25, 1908.
[63] Ibid.

the hook for a government contract that demanded they build six times more track. Rather than let the railroad fail, however, the colonial state agreed to shoulder more and more of the risk so that progress could continue. They first began to buy the PRC's bonds from their own revenues and to invest the resources of the Philippine Postal Savings Bank in the bonds. Swift and his partners, however, demanded even more help, and they requested that the BIA be authorized to *directly* receive bond bids, making it appear that the US government itself was a direct partner in the deal – a move that was deceptive and probably illegal. This change, they thought, would make the bonds more valuable on Wall Street. Both Forbes and Taft initially balked at this proposal, yet they eventually proved willing "to stretch the point" when faced with the possible collapse of the PRC.[64] Furthermore, in what must surely have been a highly unusual move for a government agency, the Philippine Commission dispatched Forbes to directly lobby large American banks to buy shares of the railroad. Cooperative banks, it seems, were to receive large deposits of the colonial state's gold reserve fund. As he recounted the episode,

I visited the presidents of the National Chase, National City Bank, and First National of New York and urged on them the assistance to the Philippine Railway loan. Vanderlip of the City Bank was particularly cordial and told me he'd see the thing through if the government wanted him to, and I told him we most certainly did. General Edwards was sent immediately to New York to arrange about deposits of government funds with the banks that helped. The bankers were highly elated and the sale went off very well and 9,000,000 of subscriptions were received for 4,000,000 of bonds, so that some of the subscribers had to be reduced.[65]

Such direct interventions, as Forbes later noted, "just about saved Swift's bacon."[66] But although the BIA did manage to keep the company afloat, it still remained insecure. Year after year, the PRC cost the Commission hundreds of thousands of dollars to cover interest payments on the guaranteed bonds.

Despite these rising costs, Commission authorities went out of their way to defend the PRC, especially when criticism seemed likely to make its way back to Washington. In one case, a new insular auditor arrived to track the PRC's progress for the Secretary of War and produced a scathing report, which implied in muted bureaucratic language that the PRC was hopelessly mismanaged and possibly corrupt – both statements were almost certainly true. By 1911, the auditor noted, it was charging $60,000 per mile of track – an astronomical sum when compared to the more reasonable $25,000 per mile charged by the MRC.

Such cost overruns were, of course, all the more disturbing because the Philippine government was obliged to pay 4 percent interest on the PRC's bonded indebtedness, which amounted to nearly $2,500 in annual interest payments for *every mile of track constructed*! Furthermore, the reported noted, the PRC's main Cebu line "runs along a narrow coast of land and there is hardly a mile of it but what you are so close to the sea that you could throw a stone from the car window into the water." This seemed to call into question the entire point of the railroad, not only because sea travel was often cheaper, but also because it ran parallel to "a fine

---

[64] Ibid.
[65] Ibid.
[66] Ibid.

public road, built at great expense to the Government."[67] Yet rather than sanction the PRC, the BIA and Philippine Commission came to its defense. Frank McIntyre, the second-in-command at the BIA, composed a furious reply to the auditor's report and ordered him back to Washington. "This road has not shown up well in earnings," McIntyre conceded, "but neither has the Philippines progressed as rapidly as it is hoped these islands will progress. It is only reasonable to believe that with reasonable progress, a railroad running through the densely settled east coast of Cebu will pay."[68] Nevertheless, by 1911, with no end to the financial difficulties in sight, the Commission agreed to let the White syndicate postpone the construction on the planned lines in Negros and Panay.[69]

Clearly, even these more aggressive forms of assistance were not enough to speed along the development of the railroad projects, and by 1911 insular officials were looking for ways to extract even more money from their limited resources. The largest previously untapped source of revenue was the colonial state's gold reserve fund, which had been set up by Charles Conant when the Philippine peso was converted into a gold standard currency. As discussed earlier, the gold reserve fund had already been used as an inducement to private bankers to buy the bonds of favored development companies. But colonial officials now began to wonder if they could leverage these funds to offer even more aggressive financial support to the railroad and other public works projects. Indeed, use of the gold reserve fund seemed to solve two problems. First, it would not require permission from Congress, which would save the Philippine Commission from engaging in costly lobbying efforts. Second, it seemed to offer a more robust form of support to the private railroad companies whose bonds had not sold as well as expected.

In December 1911, the Commission, with the consent of the Philippine Assembly, passed a radical change in the law (Act. No. 2083) governing its own gold reserve fund. In the future, the Fund would be fixed at 35 percent of the circulating currency, causing any money over that limit to be transferred directly into the Philippine Treasury. As Forbes noted in a letter to the Secretary of War, "[t]his liberates immediately the amount of ₱2,751,897.73, which has enabled me to release ₱800,000 for roads, ₱400,000 for port works, and some other money for important public improvements."[70] In a more controversial move, however, the Act authorized the Commission to *lend* up to 50 percent of the remaining gold deposits to the railroads and other public works projects.[71] Now the Commission could use the money pledged to support its currency to fund its development projects.

In part, the urgency of the loan served to protect Forbes's cherished railway route to the Baguio summer capital, which was seen as an essential addition if Americans were to remain in the islands.[72] With the use of its gold reserve fund, the colonial state could lend money to the railroads directly without the need for further bond authorizations or congressional approval to guarantee interest.

---

[67] Insular Auditor, M. Phipps to Secretary of War, November 14, 1911; RG 350, Box 711 (Serial 14221).

[68] Frank McIntyre, Memorandum [for Clarence Edwards], January 2, 1912; RG 350, Box 711 (Serial 14221).

[69] May, *Social Engineering*, 164–5.

[70] Forbes to Stimson, December 14, 1911; Forbes Papers, Confidential Letters, v. 1.

[71] May, *Social Engineering*, 163.

[72] Elliott, *Philippines to the End of Commission Government*, 310, n. 18.

Other improvements received gold reserve money, too, including municipal markets and water works systems, although as the Cebu *Advertiser* noted, "the policy of the Insular government to give decided preference at this time to revenue producing projects."[73] Thus, Forbes noted, "there was no chance of failure on the part of the municipality to repay. The policy was admirable and worked out perfectly."[74] As we will see in Chapter 7, such confidence would lead the colonial government to a state of near-collapse in the future.

Despite the difficulties in securing capital, the railroads were a moderate success, albeit hardly on the scale of the more grandiose schemes that had first been proposed. As Figure 6.2 shows, between 1907 and 1913, railroad mileage did grow from 122 to 608. That these railway extensions were built at all was due to the work of the BIA in enticing American capital to the islands; there were certainly no calls from Congress for a network for railroads in the Philippines. Yet rather than serving at the pleasure of American capitalists, these Republican officials began a process that required more and more state intervention into the colonial economy.

Understanding their actions requires us to remember that the development of the Philippines represented far more than an economic endeavor. Far from trying to *make* money on the railroad as colonial governor, Forbes was anonymously donating funds from his vast personal fortune to assure that it remained viable. In one 1912 letter to the insular auditor, he enclosed a $5,000 *personal* check (well over a year's salary for most Americans) to be deposited to the credit of the PRC itself! But he was hardly anxious for it to become known that the railroad was in such desperate financial straits that it was now receiving charitable contributions from the governor-general himself. Thus, as he noted in his letter, "It is my desire that nobody know the source of this subscription."[75] It represented, for them, a test of modern theories of government and economic development, as well as a broader test of American ingenuity. That certain tenets of market capitalism would need to be sacrificed in order to make it succeed was justified as a short-term stimulus for future development. Yet as we will see in Chapter 7, the decision to invest colonial funds directly into the failing railroads would leave the colonial government further dependent on borrowing and currency manipulation to achieve its goals. The regime's autonomy and its ideological commitment to infrastructure and development – one that would approach near-hysterical levels – would soon come at the expense of its own stability.

STIMULATING PRODUCTION: PLANTATION AGRICULTURE AND THE FRIAR LANDS INVESTIGATION

Forbes's elevation in 1909 to governor-general coincided with the passage of the Payne–Aldrich Act, which, as discussed in Chapter 4, removed most tariffs on trade between the Philippines and the United States. Although this was ultimately seen as beneficial to the Philippine economy (the government had

---

[73] July 12, 1912 – Cebu *Advertiser*, clipping in Forbes Papers, Executive Data, v. 3.

[74] Note next to clipping; Forbes Papers, Executive Data, v. 3.

[75] Forbes to Insular Auditor, February 2, 1912; Forbes Papers, Confidential Letters, v. 1.

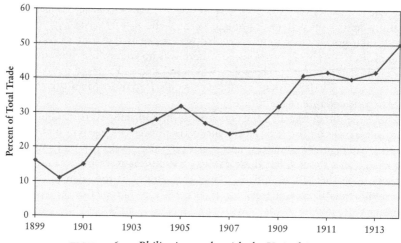

FIGURE 6.4. *Philippine trade with the United States.*
Source: Adapted from Abelarde, *American Tariff Policy*, 215.

strenuously lobbied for it, after all), its most immediate effect was to threaten insular customs revenues that had previously been collected on imports from the United States.[76] "We are entering upon a period which can only be regarded as experimental," Forbes wrote to Edwards, in a letter that also noted that the expected annual loss to the insular treasury would be somewhere between $1.5 and $2.5 million.[77] The fear was that such revenue losses would threaten the public works projects, many of which were still in their planning stages, and Forbes proposed borrowing another $5 million to prop them up.[78] In the end, this did not prove necessary.

The elimination of the tariffs led almost immediately to a dramatic increase in trade. "I am happy to be able to inform the Legislature that the expected reduction in revenues has not taken place," Forbes reported in the spring of 1910, "and that I have been able to authorize the construction of the various public works."[79] As Figure 6.4 shows, trade with the United States as a percentage of total trade had remained relatively flat since the passage of the Organic Act, hovering around 25 percent. But one year after the Payne–Aldrich tariff was adopted, it topped 40 percent. Furthermore, the feared drop in customs receipts had not damaged the Commission's revenues, and the collection of duties actually increased as imports from the United States jumped 13 percent. As the Commission reported,

This gives us a fair reason to hope that the increased purchasing power of the people, as a result of the stimulus to production and trade arising from the new tariff with the

[76] Golay, "The Search for Revenues," 249.
[77] Forbes to Edwards, June 18, 1910; Forbes Papers, Confidential Letters, v. 1.
[78] Ibid.
[79] March 30, 1910 – *Manila Times* "Finances of the Government"; Clippings in Forbes Papers, Executive Data, v. 1.

United States and the better prices for our products, will enable the people to purchase enough more foreign goods to greatly increase the imports from the United States without cutting of very greatly the duty-paying imports from foreign countries, thus leaving us with a respectable revenue from customs.[80]

Despite this welcome increase in trade and revenues, insular officials remained concerned that these trade increases would not play well politically. Although they had managed to compromise with the domestic sugar and tobacco interests in 1909, they were anxious to present the islands as an economic complement to the United States, not as a competitor. In public statements and reports, they continued to put the most emphasis on the archipelago's potential as a producer of copra (the source of coconut oil) and hemp, two products that were not grown domestically. This strategy is made clear in a revealing letter sent to Edwards by his deputy at the BIA, Major Frank McIntyre:

I think it would be well this year if in our report we should lay great stress on the efforts which are being made in the Philippine Islands to encourage the production of Manila hemp and copra, emphasizing the poor quality of hemp which has recently been produced due to careless methods and the steps which the Agricultural Department of the Islands is taking to improve the quality of hemp, both in the matter of cultivation and in preparation for the market . . . Won't you find out if the Agriculture Department has been doing these things, because they are the most important things that it could do, and it is certainly important that we should show the people that we are not devoting our entire energy to sugar and tobacco.[81]

Their public statements notwithstanding, the insular government was open to any American enterprise that offered to invest in the Philippines, including sugar producers, which, along with lumber, was seen as the most potentially lucrative industry and the real key to the islands' economic development. Under the Organic Act, however, Congress had restricted the rights of corporations to purchase large amounts of public land, and this restriction made the establishment of plantation-style agriculture difficult. For years, the Commission had lobbied Congress to increase the maximum acreage corporations could own, and Roosevelt himself had made specific mention of this in both his 1904 and 1905 annual addresses. "In the proper desire to prevent the islands being exploited by speculators and to have them develop in the interests of their own people," the president declared, "an error has been made in refusing to grant sufficiently liberal terms to induce the investment of American capital in the Philippines and in Porto Rico."[82] Six years later, Forbes still considered these restrictions on land ownership at the root of the colonial state's revenue and development problems:

I think the interests of the Islands have been by far too well protected against exploitation. Where the country is developed and looking for land and where there is an abundance of capital, as in the United States, the conservation of great public tracts is very necessary . . . Here

---

[80] US Department of War, *Report of the Philippine Commission to the Secretary of War, 1910* (Washington, DC: Government Printing Office, 1911), 7.

[81] McIntyre to Edwards, July 12, 1910; Edwards Papers, Box 8, Folder 4.

[82] Theodore Roosevelt, Fifth Annual Message, December 5, 1905 in Richardson, ed., *Compilation of the Messages and Papers of the Presidents*, v. 11, 1177.

large tracts are held only under previous grants and tracts of not exceeding twenty five hundred acres may be held by corporations. Their limit of twenty five hundred acres was placed in order to prevent the development of the sugar industries and was undoubtedly made by representatives of the beet sugar industry of the United States, whose idea was not to develop the Islands but to check their development. Unfortunately they have succeeded too far and business has not sprung up here . . . [T]he laws are such as to make such development difficult if not impossible as the limit of acreage obtainable by one person is cut down to an amount which makes it hardly worth while fooling with, thus the industries of rubber, tobacco, sugar, cocoanut, silk and cacao are menaced.[83]

Yet on this issue, as insular officials recognized, Congress was unwilling to budge. Indeed, their success (albeit limited) in attracting capital also brought more scrutiny from Democratic members of Congress, who feared a land giveaway to American corporations – a repeat, they worried, of corporate avarice in the American West – and Republican representatives from sugar- and tobacco-producing states who feared more competition from the islands, particularly after they had been brought behind the American tariff wall.

Unlike free trade, however, the Commission had a way around Congress. They controlled the massive estates formerly owned by the Catholic Church – estates that could support plantation agriculture – and they began to look for buyers. Their attempts to sell these lands, and the resulting congressional investigation, reveal one of the rare instances when the actions of the colonial state left it embroiled in a domestic scandal, as well as its largely effective efforts to defend itself.

Selling the Friar Lands

The so-called "friar lands" consisted of approximately 403,000 acres previously held by three Catholic monastic orders – the Dominicans, Augustinians, and Augustinian Recollects – that had for centuries operated as a de facto arm of the Spanish colonial government. Following Spain's defeat, the Philippine Commission recommended that the lands be purchased, rather than seized along with the rest of public lands, both because they wished to maintain the sanctity of property rights and because they worried about Catholic opinion in the United States.[84] The idea of purchasing the friar lands evidently came quite early to the Commission, and was likely suggested by Archbishop John Ireland of St. Paul, Minnesota.[85] Taft visited Rome personally to conduct the negotiations with the Vatican, and the "friar lands" were eventually purchased for $7.2 million and financed through the first congressionally authorized bond sale by the insular authorities.[86] While this allowed the insular government to gain control over the estates without unduly offending American Catholics, it also saddled the insular government with a significant

[83] Forbes to Stimson, October 16, 1911; Forbes Papers, Confidential Letters, v. 1.
[84] Taft to Root, October 14, 1901; Root Papers, Box 164.
[85] See Root to Taft, September 5, 1901 and Taft to Root, September 26, 1901; Root Papers, Box 164.
[86] For more on the relationship between the colonial government and the Catholic Church, see Frank T. Reuter, *Catholic Influence on American Colonial Policies, 1898–1904* (Austin, TX: University of Texas Press, 1967).

debt burden, which required annual interest payments of more than $300,000.[87] Naturally, colonial officials were anxious to resell these lands as quickly as possible, both to relieve the state of this significant debt and, they hoped, to stimulate agricultural production.

Initially, there was some uncertainty about whether the friar lands could properly be considered "public lands," and subject to congressional restrictions – if not, then they would not fall under the Organic Act's restrictions. One colonial official thought they did not. Dean Worcester was the Commissioner for Interior, the colonial official with immediate administrative authority over the lands, and by 1908, he was also the longest-serving colonial administrator, having arrived in the Philippines with Taft as a member of the second Philippine Commission. In 1908 Worcester proposed removing the restrictions on land sales, a move he later justified on the grounds that limits "would have delayed for many years the sale of large tracts."[88] The newly inaugurated Philippine Assembly subsequently approved Worcester's proposal, although as historian Rodney Sullivan notes, "under circumstances suggesting that its most important effect, allowing the sale of vast tracts to American investors, was concealed from most assemblymen."[89] To be sure, there are good reasons to believe that this change in the law was not even understood by the BIA back in Washington, as several letters of confusion between Washington and Manila seem to indicate.[90]

Among the largest of these friar lands was the San José estate, an unoccupied 60,000 acre plot on the sparsely populated island of Mindoro.[91] Worcester had been aggressively advertising the availability of the friar estates for years, attempting unsuccessfully in 1906 to sell a small piece of it to the Philippine Products Company. It *was* a tough sell. Even after the landholding restrictions had been removed, most of the largest and undeveloped friar lands – those that would be most suited to plantation agriculture – were located in distant provinces with poor roads and ports. Anyone looking to turn the estate into a profitable plantation would not only need to purchase the land, but also need to expend significant capital to develop the infrastructure.

Worcester needed to find a group of investors with significant resources, and in 1909 he thought he had found just the right company. Edward L. Poole, a former sugar plantation manager in Hawai'i and Cuba, arrived to discuss the purchase of the property as an agent for the Mindoro Development Company (MDC), a previously unknown entity on the islands, but which was owned through equal stock shares by Horace Havemeyer, the director of the American Sugar Refining Company – the notorious Sugar Trust – and his associates, Charles Senf and

---

[87] Elliott, *Philippines to the End of Commission Government*, 52.

[88] Quoted in Rodney J. Sullivan, *Exemplar of Americanism: The Philippine Career of Dean C. Worcester* (Ann Arbor, MI: University of Michigan, Center for South and Southeast Asian Studies, 1991), 127.

[89] Sullivan, *Exemplar of Americanism*, 128.

[90] Forbes to McIntyre, October 18, 1909, in US Congress, *Hearings before the Committee on Insular Affairs* (Washington, DC: Government Printing Office, 1910), 22.

[91] There are conflicting accounts about whether the estate was truly unoccupied. This was the Commission's official position during the later investigation, but earlier colonial studies list 300 Filipinos living on the land. What happened to these people remains unknown. See Sullivan, *Exemplar of Americanism*, 136, for more on this controversy.

Charles Welch. The plan, it seems, was to establish a new sugar plantation to take advantage of the near-free trade available under the Payne–Aldrich tariff, and Poole thought that San José was the place to do it. After touring the estate with the assistant director of the Bureau of Lands, Charles Sleeper, Poole signed a preliminary agreement purchasing the full 60,000 acres for ₱734,000 (about $370,000).[92] The sale became final after it received President Taft's approval and US Attorney General G. W. Wickersham assured Poole that the Organic Act limitations on land sales did not apply to the friar lands. Taft himself later wrote that he "saw an opportunity to help the Government to $300,000 and to increase the agricultural investment in a backward island by double that sum."[93]

Initially, the news was greeted in Manila as a triumph – finally, the long-predicted infusion of American capital was beginning. Along with the purchase of the San José estate, Americans in Manila heard reports that investors were interested in the purchase of other former friar estates. As the unapologetically imperialist *Cablenews-American* reported in the summer of 1910, "There can be no doubt that the Payne Bill is responsible for the interest excited and that capital has only commenced to realize the possibilities for well directed investment here."[94] What initially had seemed a triumph of the colonial government's development strategy, however, would soon develop into one of its most notorious political scandals, and triggered what the colonial state most feared – a congressional investigation.

The Friar Lands Investigation and the Commission's Defense

Although the anti-imperialist faction in Congress had resigned itself to colonial occupation in the years since the Treaty of Paris, domestic American agriculture producers and their anti-imperialist allies remained deeply suspicious of efforts to stimulate sugar or tobacco production in the colonies. Havemeyer's purchase of the San José estate seemed to offer them the perfect opportunity to launch an investigation into Republican administration of the Philippines, particularly because the Sugar Trust was already mired in scandal after being fined $2.1 million for short-weighting its imports in Brooklyn.[95] The Anti-Imperialist League enlisted Congressman John A. Martin (D-CO) to look into the matter, and the deeper he dug, the more convinced Martin became that the San José plantation was sold under suspicious circumstances.

In a speech on the House floor in March of 1910, Martin fired the opening salvos of what would become a long and protracted investigation, declaring that "while the pretext of free trade was the beneficial development of the islands, the real underlying motive was their exploitation."[96] Martin then introduced a resolution directing the House Committee on Insular Affairs to investigate the Philippine

[92] Sullivan, *Exemplar of Americanism*, 129–30.
[93] Quoted in Stanley, *Nation in the Making*, 158.
[94] Ibid., 159.
[95] McCoy, *Policing America's Empire*, 257.
[96] C. Rec. 45 (March 25, 1910), 3784.

Department of Interior and its sale of the friar lands.[97] One of Martin's central criticisms was that congressional limits on public land applied to the friar lands as well, and that the Commission's (with Attorney General Wickersham's approval) decision to exclude them was illegal. Although the core of Martin's attack concerned the corporate exploitation of the islands, his condemnation of the insularity of the small coterie of colonial officials was central to his critique. One of his key accusations was that a conspiracy existed between President Taft and BIA chief Clarence Edwards to open the islands up to the Sugar Trust – a plan, he charged, made easier by their long tenure as colonial officials:

> Ever since 1900, first as President of the Philippine Commission, then as civil governor of the Philippine Islands, then as commissioner to Rome to negotiate for the purchase of the friar lands, and then as Secretary of War, Mr. William H. Taft has been the ruling figure in the Philippines.
> During all these years Gen. Clarence R. Edwards has been with Mr. Taft, in Washington, in the Philippines, and elsewhere. He is the President's close personal friend and companion, and as Chief of the Bureau of Insular Affairs, having immediate jurisdiction over the insular possessions, he may be said to be the viceroy of the Philippines.[98]

Although the attacks could be dismissed as anti-imperialist grandstanding, it was undeniable to even neutral members of Congress that the land purchases *were* suspicious. Worcester, of course, claimed that he had no knowledge that Poole was acting for Havemeyer. Whether or not this was true, it is clear that Havemeyer, Snef, and Welch had gone to extraordinary lengths to hide their full plans for the island, which included the development of a sugar mill and a railroad along the Mindoro coast. While working for the MDC, Poole was simultaneously engaged as an agent for three other legally independent California corporations whose stockholders were close personal friends of Welch, and which began to buy up land along the proposed railway route.[99] Yet Congress was severely hampered by its lack of information about the Philippines, and insular authorities – a number of whom were forced to testify – rallied to support their own. Because Martin was forced to rely almost entirely on government reports, the Commission's defense mainly consisted of ridiculing his lack of knowledge about conditions on the ground – a tactic Worcester used to great effect in his aggressive and sarcastic defense of the San José sale:

> The use made by Representative Martin of extracts from government reports and public documents reminds me very forcibly of the use made of Holy Scripture by the New England clergyman who, in the days when it was customary for a preacher to take a tot of rum before entering the pulpit on the Sabbath, got a drop too much and delivered an eloquent sermon on the text. "And Judas went and hanged himself. Go thou and do likewise!"
> In other words, Representative Martin, by the quotation and misinterpretation of passages which suited his purpose, and by the suppression of passages which if quoted would have made his contentions ridiculous, has succeeded in presenting an utterly misleading picture of the policy of the Philippine government relative to the disposal of friar lands.[100]

---

[97] Stanley, *Nation in the Making*, 159.
[98] *Hearings*, Committee on Insular Affairs (1910), 1076.
[99] Sullivan, *Exemplar of Americanism*, 129–30.
[100] *Hearings*, Committee on Insular Affairs (1910), 1072.

In the end, the Republican committee found the Commission innocent and the administration of the friar lands just, describing "charges and insinuations to the contrary" as "unwarranted and unjust." For supporters of the colonial state, this was a great vindication. "The result of this patriotic endeavor," one official sarcastically noted, "must have proven bitterly disappointing."[101]

Despite the favorable verdict, the investigation clearly rattled the Commission, and the new Secretary of War, J. M. Dickinson, after visiting the Philippines himself in 1910, ordered that the friar lands would now be governed by the standard limitations on the sale of public lands and would henceforth be sold only to Filipinos.[102] It is unlikely that he would have done so without the express approval of the president, who, it should be recalled, had earlier endorsed the sale of the estate. Taft was likely reacting to both the congressional investigation and the opportunity it offered to Filipino elites. Indeed, Speaker Osmeña and Quezon – now resident commissioner in Washington – had played their hand brilliantly.

Although neither Osmeña nor Quezon were particularly worried about the friar lands per se, they recognized an opportunity during this brief period of congressional attention to draw attention to the islands' political status, and to capitalize on American racism and fears of trade competition to win their nation's independence. By 1910, Osmeña and Quezon had developed a keen understanding of domestic American politics, and both recognized that the colonial state rested on a shaky political foundation. During Dickinson's visit, Osmeña delivered a memorial to the Secretary that both noted the "need for the aid of capital from without," but decried such investment, "which, once invested here, will when the time comes be opposed to any change of sovereignty, because it will not consider itself to be sufficiently safe and protected, except under its own."[103] This, of course, was precisely what Forbes had in mind. But with the 1912 presidential elections approaching, the Republicans had little interest in drawing attention to the Philippines, and so Dickinson – his hand now forced – conceded that he "would not be here to represent or further any plan which contemplated the denial of ultimate Philippine independence . . . It is a consummation devoutly to be prayed for."[104] As we will see, in the next two years, as the relations between the Commission and Filipino elites began to deteriorate, Osmeña and Quezon increasingly worked to bring unwanted congressional attention to the islands, threatening the colonial government's strategy of doing everything possible to reduce incentives for congressional oversight.

---

[101] Williams, *Odyssey of the Philippine Commission*, 359.

[102] Dickinson did not last long as Secretary of War, leaving the BIA with more responsibility over the islands. The frequent turnover of Secretaries of War did cause some problems, for they were increasingly reliant on the Bureau for their own information about the islands. Edwards joked to Dickinson after his departure about this: "Yes, I call myself the bear-leader to new Secretaries of War, but the thing I get more impatient of than anything else is that when they can do their own bear leading they pick up and leave." Edwards to J. M. Dickinson, August 24, 1911; Edwards Papers, Box 8, Folder 12.

[103] Quoted in Stanley, *Nation in the Making*, 160–1.

[104] Quoted in Ibid., 163.

EDUCATION FOR INDUSTRIAL DEVELOPMENT

The colonial state's education policies reveal a great deal about how American administrators perceived their mission in the Philippines – one dictated by their own ideological commitments rather than congressional instruction – and how "development" was seen as a larger process of Americanization. But the significant strides made in education were subject to the whims of the colonial education administrators, who vacillated from supporting a broad liberal curriculum for primary students to establishing industrial education programs that, they thought, would stimulate the colonial economy.

Free and compulsory education had been a goal of Aguinaldo's revolutionary state, and the American military government had begun to organize schools before the First Philippine Commission arrived in Manila. Indeed, it was in primary education where the colonial state excelled. Even before Taft left for the Philippines, he and Root agreed that education, "which shall tend to fit the people for the duties of citizenship," along with economic development, would be a cornerstone of American imperial policy.[105] No other Western colonial power devoted so many resources to schools.[106] Furthermore, the system of education envisioned was, in many respects, uniquely American. Breaking from past European practices, the American colonial state focused on primary education; indeed, the decision to educate the population widely was greeted with skepticism by Europeans. British poet Rudyard Kipling, despite his general approval of American colonial efforts in the islands – he had composed "The White Man's Burden" as a paean to American acquisition of the Philippines – had written to Forbes to express his concern:

I am grieved to notice your enthusiasm for education in the abstract, and your pride in the increase of educational facilities. In due time, say in two generations, you will reap the rewards of your beneficent policy – as we are already reaping the reward of ours in India – in the shape of prolonged and elaborate rebellion, sedition and treason: – this is almost axiomatic. The beauty of education is, that like drink, it awakes all the desires and at the same time inhibits (if this is the correct medical term?) most of the capacities. But these are things which I know I cannot persuade you of. The only things that matter in this fallen world are sanitation and transportation.[107]

A further break from European practice was to make English – the language of the metropole – the primary language of instruction.[108] This was a controversial decision, not the least because the Philippine *ilustrados* spoke Spanish. American insular authorities intended to focus on the mass education of children throughout

---

[105] Root quoted in May, *Social Engineering*, 80.
[106] May, *Social Engineering*, 181.
[107] Rudyard Kipling to Forbes, August 12, 1913; Edwards Papers, "Correspondence from Notable Persons," Box 3.
[108] Although it is true that native elites in British and French colonies often learned the colonial language, English and French were rarely the languages of instruction in common primary schools.

the Archipelago, the vast majority of whom had no knowledge of either language.[109] As Taft frankly explained the decision,

[English] is selected because it is the language of business in the Orient, because it is the language of free institutions, and because it is the language which the Filipino children who do not know Spanish are able more easily to learn than they are to learn Spanish, and it is the language of the present sovereign of the Islands.[110]

While it is hard to believe Taft's claim that English was easier for Filipino children to learn than Spanish, it was certainly easier for Americans to teach. Yet the emphasis on English also reveals the connection between economic development and colonial education. Indeed, as the Civil Service Board's 1901 report stated, "American progressive business methods, the genius and spirit of American civil government, and the ruggedness and strength of the American (English) language are inseparable."[111] As with civil service laws and the railroads, the English language was seen as a central component of economic development and as a way to cement the bond between colony and metropole. Much has been written on the so-called tutelary effects of American education, and, indeed, primary education was seen as an essential prerequisite for democracy.[112] Yet as the colonial government matured, and the colonial state began to play a more direct role in its economic development, the so-called industrial education began to replace the earlier liberal arts curriculum.

From Liberal to Industrial Education

The colonial state's emphasis on education raises some larger questions. Why all this investment? What did they hope to accomplish? Although colonial administrators never articulated a clear vision for their education program, their early efforts were premised on the assumption that education, particularly in English, would contribute to political stability and instill certain affection among Filipinos for American culture and the colonial project more generally. If the American colonial administers could not create any enthusiasm for colonialism among the US public, they would try to attract Filipinos to the United States. And they sought to achieve these goals, at first, by simply transplanting existing American educational practices to the Philippines – initially with almost no adjustments to the curriculum.

Fred Atkinson, for example, the director of the education bureau until 1902, submitted an education bill (Act. No. 74) that was essentially a copy of the current Massachusetts curriculum down to his decision to use the *Baldwin Readers*,

[109] Tagalog, the native Filipino tongue spoken widely in southern Luzon, was only one of the many native languages used throughout the islands. During the early period of American rule, government communication was done in Spanish and English, but this became less necessary as English quickly replaced Spanish as the language of the elite. Spanish was dropped as an official language in the 1930s prior to independence.

[110] US War Department, "Special Report of William H. Taft, Secretary of War, to the President on the Philippines" (Washington, DC: Government Printing Office, 1909), 27.

[111] "Report of the Civil Service Board to the Governor-General," *Report of the Philippine Commission*, 1901, v. II, 300, quoted in Hayden, *The Philippines*, 117.

[112] See, for example, May, *Social Engineering*.

which were then a common primary school textbook in the United States.[113] David Barrows, an anthropologist by training who would later serve as president of the University of California, soon replaced Atkinson. Barrows, too, was largely committed to traditional methods of liberal arts education, but he saw US educational efforts in the Philippines as part of a grander experiment in social engineering, and as an opportunity to radically restructure Filipino society along Jeffersonian lines. "I believe we should . . . seek to develop in the Philippines, not a proletariat, but everywhere the peasant proprietor," he wrote in his first annual report as director of the Bureau of Education.

Wherever we find the Filipino the possessor of his own small holding there we find him industrious and contributing largely to the productive industry of the islands . . . Now it is with this peasant–proprietor class particular in mind, and trusting in the outcome of our efforts to increase this class, that we must lay out our course of primary instruction.[114]

Barrows's new curriculum emphasized basic reading and writing in English, but it was also laced with morality lessons about the importance of thrift and landownership – lessons that were baldly supportive of American-led development. For example, one arithmetic exercise in a 1908 schoolbook posed the following problem to students:

Pedro is a tenant on Mr. Santos' farm. He has rented 4 hektars of rice land. After the cutting is paid for, Mr. Santos is to have for the use of the land one half of what rice is left, and Pedro will take the other half for himself. If 45 cavanes grow on each hektar, and one sixth is given for cutting, how many cavanes will the cutter get? How much will be left? What will be Mr. Santos' share? What will be Pedro's share?[115]

From this lesson, students were presumably supposed to understand that "Pedro" would be far better off establishing his own farm by homesteading some of the public land that the Commission was now attempting to sell. Indeed, after presenting this problem, teachers were instructed to "[e]xplain to the pupils carefully the right which the Filipinos have to take up land, and urge them to carry the information to their parents."[116] Along with these lessons, students were also given opportunities to participate in mock debating societies to practice the "machinery of politics." As one American teacher would later recall, "I recognized that my pupils did need the experience of a self-governing society, and practice in parliamentary usages, and so we organized our society from the three most advanced classes in the school." It was, she noted, "a pronounced success."[117]

Barrows remained committed to liberal primary education throughout the remainder of his tenure, but his vision was compromised by increased pressure on educational revenues, which left him to complain that infrastructure was being

[113] May, *Social Engineering*, 81.
[114] Barrows quoted in May, *Social Engineering*, 99.
[115] Mabel Bonsall and G. E. Mercer, *Primary Arithmetic: Part III* (Manila: World Book Company, 1908), 116.
[116] Bonsall and Mercer, *Primary Arithmetic*, 116.
[117] Mary H. Fee, *A Woman's Impressions of the Philippines* (Chicago: A.C. McClurg, 1910), 156–7.

pursued at the cost of municipal schools. In his annual report for 1908, he was perfectly frank:

The present municipal school revenue is barely half sufficient . . . By recent legislation the sum of ₱4,750,000 has been provided for rural roads and bridges during the present fiscal year; it ought to be possible to provide ₱3,000,000 annually for a system of primary instruction which is already thoroughly organized, able to economically apply every additional dollar provided, and thoroughly supported in all quarters by the Filipino people themselves.[118]

By 1908, however, the Commission was dominated by figures such as Forbes who had long emphasized that public works and economic development were far more important projects for the colonial state to pursue than liberal education. "The resources of the islands have not developed to a point where I feel that we are justified in largely increasing the appropriation for education," Forbes declared in his inaugural address. "The amount of education we shall be able to accomplish in ten years will be very much greater if we devote our first money to increasing the wealth of the people and later use the resulting increase of revenue for extending our educational facilities."[119] By 1909 a frustrated and disheartened Barrows returned to Berkeley, and the character of colonial education began to conform to the Forbes regime's focus on economic development.

Under Frank White, Forbes's handpicked replacement for Barrows, colonial schools were soon emphasizing practical or so-called industrial education. After taking office as Director of Education in 1909, he issued a statement that identified the "most important piece of work now before this office" as "the organization, promotion and proper supervision of industrial instruction." Every school would now be equipped with a garden to facilitate training in modern agricultural production. Woodworking and ironworking equipment would be provided for boys, while girls would henceforth receive "instruction for from two to five years in plain sewing and cooking." An even greater departure from Barrows's more traditional curriculum was White's insistence that schools be commercialized. "Instruction in hat-making, embroidery, pottery, and other minor industries, will have in view the training of the pupil to make always a serviceable and salable article," he wrote. "It will be our purpose to operate every trade school and every school farm on a business basis."[120]

In large measure, White was successful in implementing these changes, and by 1913 nearly every child was exposed to some form of industrial education.[121] Although similar theories of practical education were then in vogue in American education circles, the colonial government pushed them far more aggressively. The hope, as with state expenditures on infrastructure, was to stimulate economic development, in this case through the training of practical skills in weaving and woodworking, which would presumably translate into immediate jobs for the students.

Despite these questionable assumptions, American achievements in education were impressive, and they stand as the most significant achievement of their Progressive vision. As Figure 6.5 shows, primary school enrollment for children in the Philippines

[118] US War Department, "Report of the Director of Education," *Annual Report of the Secretary of War* (Washington, DC: Government Printing Office, 1908), 849.
[119] Quoted in Elliott, *Philippines to the End of Commission Government*, 273.
[120] December 13, 1909; Frank R. White, Director of Education–Bureau of Education, Circular No. 1909 – "Organization of Industrial Education"; Forbes Papers, Executive Data, v. 1.
[121] May, *Social Engineering*, 117–8.

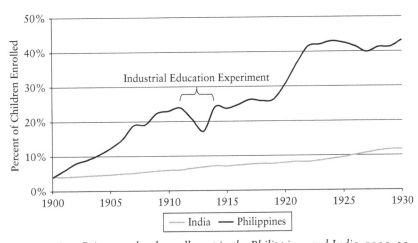

FIGURE 6.5. *Primary school enrollment in the Philippines and India, 1900–30.*
Source: Census of the Philippine Islands.
Note: Total children based on total "civilized population" of 5–15 years old in the Philippine census. India statistics from *Statistical abstract relating to British India*
(London: Her Majesty's Stationary Office, 1900–30).

outstripped enrollment in British India after just the first year of Commission government, and after the first decade of American rule, nearly one quarter of all children under 15 years attended primary school – at least for part of the year. Yet the shift during the Forbes regime to an emphasis on public works over education is also reflected in these statistics. Overall enrollment actually dropped from 610,000 in the 1910–11 school year to 440,000 in the final year of the Forbes regime. Much of this decline can be explained by White's decision to maintain his emphasis on industrial education in middle schools in the face of declining revenues by shuttering 1,000 primary schools.[122] And this shift to industrial education was due, in part, to the colonial state's continued inability to attract American capital to the Philippines. Its state-led development plans for the islands began to eclipse even a rhetorical commitment to a "tutelary" empire. These rather shocking declines in educational enrollment also reveal a signal weakness of the relative autonomy of Philippine colonial government. With few democratic checks, these Progressive experiments – even the most laudable among them – were vulnerable to the whims of American administrators.

Social Experiments in the Service of Progressivism

Schools were not the only educational institutions supported by the colonial government. A variety of other favored Progressive policies, from agricultural experimentation stations to large-scale public health campaigns, were conducted to teach the values of thrift and sanitation and to provide skills to stimulate the colonial export economy.[123] Yet much like education, these campaigns reveal colonial officials'

[122] Ibid., 121–2.
[123] Surely, the most unusual of these experiments was the Iwahig Penal Colony, a prison colony on the remote island of Palawan. Forbes had apparently got the idea from studying the George

fidelity to metropolitan Progressive polices, and provide strong evidence for the essential role that ideology played in the construction of American imperialism.

One of these more minor projects to stimulate the economy – one that adhered to current practices back in the metropole – was the development of a series of agricultural experimentation stations and seed distribution networks. The Bureau of Agriculture began a seed program in 1902, which by 1909 was annually distributing 500,000 seed packets to farmers.[124] These seed distribution projects were coupled with the construction of a series of agriculture experimentation stations, which concentrated on new varieties of sugar and tobacco.[125] To further stimulate agricultural research, the Commission developed a series of national laboratories with divisions of ethnology and fisheries, along with a library and museum.[126]

As with schools and agriculture experimentation stations, the colonial postal savings banks were designed to teach values and skills that would stimulate the economic output of the economy. In 1906, the Commission passed the Philippine Postal Savings Bank (Act. No. 1493), predating the creation of a similar institution in the United States by several years. Unlike the United States, of course, such policies could simply be enacted with few democratic checks – and often with little concrete rationale. As head of the Bureau of Commerce and Police, Forbes himself had prepared the law, which he developed from studying similar proposals by US Postmaster General, John Wanamaker.[127] According to Forbes, the bank would not only teach the importance of savings, but also result "in the deposit and use for income-bearing purposes of much of the hoarded savings which the people had been accustomed to keep buried in the ground or concealed about their premises."[128] In a long letter addressed to schoolteachers, he laid out his hopes for the banks, as well as his theory that children could be used to encourage their parents to invest in the new institution:

I wish to call to your attention, as the leaders of the future people of the city of Manila, the great opportunity which has been opened to them by the establishment of the Postal Savings Bank . . . Two-and one-half per cent, of the total value of all deposits over one peso and up to one thousand pesos will be paid each year by the Government to the depositors in the Postal Savings Bank and the investments are absolutely safe because practically guaranteed by the Government. It is believed that the children should be told of this opportunity and urged in every possible way to avail themselves of the privilege of depositing their money and receiving interest on the deposits. It is believed that all the details of the scheme should be so explained to them that they would not only be induced to place their own savings *but would become missionaries to tell their parents and relatives about it and induce them also to do the same.*[129]

Junior Republics. "It was believed," he later wrote, "that convicts not naturally depraved or criminal in their instincts, given a similar opportunity under favorable circumstances, would react in a similar way." That is, they would learn to reform their behavior. See Forbes, *Philippine Islands*, v. I, 504.

[124] Marcelino Constantino and Primo A. Honrado, "Seeds and Plants – From Propagation to Distribution," in *A Half-Century of Philippine Agriculture* (Manila: Graphic House, 1952), 220–1.

[125] Constantino and Honrado, "Seeds and Plants," 221.

[126] Forbes, *Philippine Islands*, v. I, 365.

[127] Forbes Journal, v. 2, May 1906, 12.

[128] Forbes, *Philippine Islands*, v. I, 285.

[129] November 13, 1906, Letter to School Teachers; Forbes Papers, US Philippine commission, 1900–16. Philippine commission railway records [my emphasis].

The time and attention that Forbes lavished on these banks was entirely out of proportion to any assistance they could have possibly provided to achieve the colonial government's development goals. Indeed, Forbes was so committed that he offered to personally contribute one peso to the first child in every class in the city of Manila who managed to save that amount himself.[130] Whatever their actual value to average Filipinos, programs such as these primarily reflect Forbes's commitment to an ideological vision for American imperialism, rather than a shrewd plan to increase colonial economic output.

Along with education, savings banks, and public works, improvements in public health were often held up as the most important thing the colonial government could achieve, both as a high-minded demonstration of American advances in science and as a way to increase economic output. To implement their hygiene and sanitation programs, the Commission appointed Dr. Victor G. Heiser, a surgeon from the US Public Health Service, as director of the Bureau of Health. Heiser, along with most colonial health officials, was a product of the new scientific medical schools then taking hold in the United States, and he saw in the Philippines an opportunity to apply new theories of public health in an environment with few political or institutional restrictions.[131] As historian Warwick Anderson writes in his detailed study of these policies, "Health authorities targeted toilet practices, food handling, dietary customs, housing design; they rebuilt the markets, using more hygienic concrete, and suppressed the unsanitary fiestas; they assumed the power to examine Filipinos at random and to disinfect, fumigate, and medicate at will."[132] During a 1908 cholera outbreak, for example, health officials employed more than 600 men in sanitation squads who, armed with 150,000 pounds of lime, were responsible for disinfecting houses and other unsanitary areas.[133]

Heiser's programs would be less interesting if they were merely confined to suppressing epidemics, but he also launched extensive educational campaigns to improve the health of Filipinos – a goal motivated both by the need to demonstrate the effectiveness of the new scientific approach to public health and as a reflection of the widely held belief that colonial development was hampered by the poor health of the population. Forbes would explicitly link health with productivity in the massive, two-volume defense of his administration published after he left office. "Perhaps," the governor-general wrote, "the most prevalent and serious of all the evils were the insidious intestinal parasites, causing a reduction in efficiency and an inability for sustained physical effort which had much to do with the prevalent unfavorable reputation of the Filipino as a laborer."[134]

To improve the "efficiency" of Filipinos by improving their health, the bureau built model sanitary houses to demonstrate proper hygiene, and published cartoons in English and Tagalog to warn about the dangers of spitting.[135] In a paper delivered to the American Philosophical Society, Heiser reported that "Manila now has

---

[130] Ibid.
[131] Warwick Anderson, *Colonial Pathologies: American Tropical Medicine, Race, and Hygiene in the Philippines* (Durham, NC: Duke University Pres, 2006), 7.
[132] Ibid., 99.
[133] Ibid., 119.
[134] Forbes, *Philippine Islands*, v. I, 330.
[135] Anderson, *Colonial Pathologies*, 116–7.

the most complete set of sanitary ordinances of any city in the world, and in many directions greater sanitary progress has been made than elsewhere," thus providing a model, Heiser claimed, for other nations and for the United States.[136] The colonial state made every effort to publicize the successes of their sanitation efforts, especially the dramatic reduction in the overall death rate from 27.46 per 1,000 in 1905 to 18.82 per 1,000 in 1913, which quickly became a favorite and often-cited fact for colonial officials.[137] Such ambitious health and educational projects were partially in the service of economic development – but that was not all. They were also enacted to demonstrate the value of Progressive policies to promote science, education, and thrift.

THE END OF THE REPUBLICAN ERA

By 1912, a small group of American officials had created a vast American colony with schools, banks, agricultural experimentation stations, and railroads even as Congress remained uninterested in its own colony and the American public largely indifferent. "Roads are built, being built and maintained; public buildings and other works are of durable materials," Forbes recorded in his journal. "Railroad work is being pushed to the limit of economic efficiency, and having tremendous effect in improving economic conditions . . . The revenues are better than ever, our credit is good, and trade each year sets a new highwater mark in the history of the Islands."[138]

In point of fact, the last years of Republican rule were years of relatively steady economic growth for the islands. In 1913, revenue from internal taxes had nearly doubled to more than ₱10 million from what it had been in 1908, and despite free trade with the United States, customs revenues exceeded ₱18 million in 1912.[139] The dramatic expansion of elementary schools, the seed distribution program, and the increasingly sanitary conditions in Manila were also frequently referenced by officials as tremendous successes. Yet from 1910 to 1912, a series of developments were already underway that would threaten the autonomy and the stability of the colonial government – and would eventually push it to financial collapse.

Among the most significant of these was the increasingly poor relationship between the Forbes administration and the Philippine Assembly. The Assembly had earlier quarreled with Forbes over the nomination of the resident commissioners to the United States, but in 1911 it began a far more threatening line of attack on the Commission's control over colonial revenues. The confrontation began when the Assembly amended the Commission's proposed appropriations bill, cutting the budgets of the Internal Revenue Bureau, the Bureau of Health, and other executive bureaus to the tune of ₱1.5 million.[140] Forbes rejected these changes, and, relying on a power granted to the governor-general by Congress, issued an executive order enacting the previous year's budget.[141] Osmeña's hostility to Forbes

[136] Victor G. Heiser, "American Sanitation in the Philippines and Its Influence on the Orient," *Proceedings of the American Philosophical Society* (1918): 57(1), 66.
[137] Forbes, *Philippine Islands*, v. I, 333.
[138] Forbes Papers, Journal, v. 5, March 23, 1912.
[139] Golay, "The Search for Revenues," 252–3.
[140] Jenista, "Conflict in the Philippine Legislature," 88.
[141] May, *Social Engineering*, 67.

was likely motivated both by his genuine frustration with the centralization of most significant powers by American-dominated bureaus, as well as by a more strategic calculation that his perceived support of the Forbes regime was beginning to become politically costly. In 1909, for example, he was forced to fend off attacks from the more radical wings of his own party, as well as the *Progresistas* who had accused the Speaker of lending "decisive support only to the desires of the American administration in these Islands."[142]

Consequently, by the 1911 legislative session, Assembly delegates were routinely passing bills that were designed to strip the Commission of its powers and place full administrative responsibility in the hands of Filipinos.[143] One of these measures (all vetoed by the Commission) proposed the establishment of the office of provincial engineer (Bill No. 505), which would have placed responsibility for public works in the hands of provincial officials (who were Filipino), and thus removed it from the American-controlled Bureau of Public Works. Another bill proposed new qualifications for the heads of central government departments (Bill No. 916), which would have made non-Filipinos ineligible.[144]

Forbes's characteristic response to these measures was to increase his own powers. After taking unilateral control over the budget process, he then proposed to establish a new state-run newspaper to counter the blistering criticism of his government in the local press. This, apparently, was too much even for Taft, who rejected it as un-American.[145] A more dramatic blow to Forbes's powers came with the Republicans' defeat in 1912. As we will see in Chapter 7, Forbes did not succeed in influencing Wilson's policies in the Philippines. Nevertheless, he did leave his Democratic successor a remarkable collection of resources to run the Philippines with significant independence from Congress and with little assistance from the domestic American state.

From 1907 to 1913, the colonial state shifted its focus from encouraging Congress to liberalize restrictions on colonial economic investment to finding ways around these restrictions. The cohesive set of insular state bureaucrats, administration officials, and economic advisors now had the expertise to project American power without the constraints of Congress or the need to rally the support of the American public. The lesson, in short, that insular state officials took from their experience in the Philippines was that Congress and the American public were impediments to achieving their vision for the Philippines, one that reflected their focus on economic development achieved through a technocratic Progressivism.

In a well-known 1907 letter to Taft, Roosevelt expressed his misgivings on the "Philippine question," which offers a revealing look at the lessons he had taken from the colonial experiment:

I wish our people were prepared permanently, in a duty-loving spirit, and looking forward to a couple of generations of continuous manifestation of this spirit, to assume the control of the Philippine Islands for the good of the Filipinos . . . In the excitement of the Spanish War people wanted to take the islands. They had an idea they would be a valuable possession.

---

[142] *La Democracia*, April 11, 1910, quoted in May, *Social Engineering*, 63.

[143] May, *Social Engineering*, 69.

[144] Bills from Second Philippine Assembly. Jenista, "Conflict in the Philippine Legislature," 95.

[145] Forbes, *Philippine Islands*, v. I, 183.

Now they think they are of no value, and I am bound to say that in a physical sense I don't see where they are of any value to us or where they are likely to be of any value. It has been everything for the island and everything for our own national character that we should have taken them and have administered them with the really lofty and disinterested efficiency that has been shown. But it is impossible, for instance, to awaken any public interest in favor of giving them tariff advantages; it is very difficult to awaken any public interest in providing any adequate defense of the islands.[146]

At no time, however, did Roosevelt, Root, or especially Taft consider abandoning their goal that the United States should expand its influence and join the ranks of the great world powers. If Congress and the American public would not support these goals, then they would simply need to be accomplished in ways that relied less on congressional and domestic support. They found common ground with Filipino elites, allowing them to advance their own political careers in exchange for championing some of the insular state's favoured development projects. They attracted American capitalists by guaranteeing and later subsidizing their investments through colonial revenue and monetary policy, and they attempted to sell off public lands to stimulate investment in plantation agriculture.

Yet as we will see in Chapter 7, the decision to invest colonial funds directly into the failing railroads would leave the colonial government further dependent on borrowing and currency manipulation to achieve its goals; the regime's autonomy would soon come at the expense of its own stability. Furthermore, despite its achievement of a remarkable degree of autonomy, the Commission was never able to cultivate a strong domestic American constituency for its policies. Without political legitimacy, the particular vision Republican authorities had for the Philippines was vulnerable to the arrival of officials who did not share their goals – indeed, to officials who were anxious to use the autonomy of the colonial state to reduce its economic ties to the metropole.

COMPARATIVE ASSESSMENT:

PUERTO RICO UNDER THE BIA

Puerto Rico's proven ability to attract capital investments and its clear link with metropolitan markets in the United States made its status as a permanent American possession far more certain than the Philippines's. As discussed in Chapter 4, this was due to the early reduction and eventual elimination of US tariff barriers, which contributed to the booming Puerto Rican sugar industry. Yet the Caribbean island's comparative economic success – at least in terms of American investment – did not lead to political stability or easy acquiescence to permanent US control. While Forbes struggled to manage Osmeña's *Nacionalista* Party in Manila, the governors of Puerto Rico were increasingly stymied by the dominance of Puerto Rico's Union Party (*El Partido Unión de Puerto Rico*) in San Juan.

Like the *Nacionalistas*, the Union Party was a cross-class alliance of professionals, intellectuals, and smaller landowners. Although it took no official position on the future status of Puerto Rico, the Unionists did demand full self-government through

---

[146] Roosevelt to Taft, August 21, 1907, in Morison, ed., *Letters of Theodore Roosevelt*, v. 5, 761–2.

the island's admission as a state or as an independent nation under US protection.[147] Such rhetoric did not find a welcome reception in Washington. Roosevelt, in his 1905 message to Congress, rejected self-government for San Juan, noting that the problems with Puerto Rico were "industrial and commercial rather than political."[148] Nevertheless, he did support granting Puerto Ricans American citizenship, which many in BIA circles thought would end talk of independence or increased autonomy. As Republicans were well aware, there was little immediate support in Congress for this action, but the proposal itself had the advantage of both embarrassing anti-imperial Democrats and shielding the colonial administration from the Unionist independence rhetoric.[149]

Despite clear disapproval from Washington, the Union Party proved to be immensely popular with the Puerto Rican electorate, commanding huge majorities in the elected House of Delegates until 1917. The Unionists demanded democratic reforms and economic assistance for smaller Puerto Rican-owned farms through a state-owned agricultural bank – proposals that were regularly blocked by the American-led Executive Council.[150] The situation became more troubling as the Unionists realized that the United States intended to keep Puerto Rico as a permanent colony. Although there was little they could do to pass polices over the objection of the American-dominated upper house, the Unionists (like their counterparts in the Philippines) could use their limited parliamentary authority in the lower elected house to embarrass the colonial government and to attract the attention of Congress and the domestic American press.

The disagreements between the Unionists and the Executive Council reached an impasse in 1909 when the Union Party refused to approve the governor's budget bill. This effectively denied the colonial government a legal operating budget and attracted the immediate attention of Washington.[151] Taft, now president, retaliated by bringing Puerto Rico under the BIA's control. He also mandated a new rule that if the lower house refused to approve a budget, the previous year's appropriation bill would be automatically enacted – the system that had long been in place in Hawai'i and the Philippines.[152] Given Taft's long experience with the BIA, it is not surprising that he considered the agency singularly equipped to manage the political troubles in the island. One executive agency would now manage the entire island, unlike the previous system, where each member of the executive council reported to different Washington departments. Although this was justified as a matter of efficiency, the BIA had the singular advantage of being relatively isolated from Congress, and it had a proven history of carefully curating information that came out of the colonies.[153] It would now be managed according to the same M-form organization as the Philippines.

---

[147] Trías Monge, *Puerto Rico*, 59.
[148] Theodore Roosevelt, Fifth Annual Message, December 5, 1905 in Richardson, ed., *Compilation of Messages and Papers of the Presidents*, v. 9, 1176.
[149] Ibid.
[150] Cabán, *Constructing a Colonial People*, 185.
[151] Ibid., 188.
[152] Trías Monge, *Puerto Rico*, 63.
[153] Cabán, *Constructing a Colonial People*, 189.

The Unionists had intended to force more liberal reforms by demonstrating how difficult governing would become without their support; the unfortunate result, however, was not liberalization, but even more centralized control through the BIA. The BIA with Taft's support would attempt to expand its control even further by supporting the Olmstead Bill, which was a barely veiled attempt to undermine the Union Party by placing literacy and economic restrictions on the electorate.[154] Even as it attempted to limit Puerto Rican participation, however, the BIA continued to support Roosevelt's plan to extend citizenship to all Puerto Ricans – the most practical solution, the agency claimed, for political unrest.[155]

George Colton, an old BIA hand who had served in the Philippines and as the head of the Dominican Receivership, was appointed as Governor in 1909. With Puerto Rico under BIA control, the colonial government began to follow the aggressive economic development strategy it had implemented in the Philippines. The BIA's plans in Puerto Rico were, in some respects, more straightforward. Two goals were paramount: (1) to increase American investment in Puerto Rican agriculture by improving road and irrigation infrastructure and (2) to bind Puerto Ricans to the United States permanently by supporting the extension of American citizenship.

As in the Philippines, road construction was the most important of the various infrastructure improvement programs. In the first eight years, the colonial government spent over $5 million on the construction of 788 km of roads. These roads, along with a massive irrigation system to provide water to 33,000 acres on the southern coast of the island, were designed to open up the island's interior for intensive sugar cultivation.[156] After 14 years, the government could take credit for substantial improvements in the quality of Puerto Rican infrastructure, with a system of roads, hydroelectric plants, improved ports, and telegraphs.[157] Yet this improved infrastructure, impressive as it was, primarily served the sugar industry that was dominated by American firms, and it was financed entirely by the Puerto Rican colonial government itself. In this way, the BIA's stewardship of the island was accompanied by its predilection for loading debt onto its colonies to finance its aggressive improvements plans.

Before the BIA took control of Puerto Rico, the total debt of the island was a modest $2 million.[158] Private capital found Puerto Rico to be a far more attractive investment than the Philippines, which meant that there was less immediate need to finance improvements through colonial bonds. Nevertheless, when control over Puerto Rico was transferred to the BIA in 1909, colonial officials dramatically increased the use of private bonds to finance development. Indeed, by 1913 Puerto Rico's debt stood at $5.8 million and would nearly double by 1918 to

---

[154] Ibid., 190.
[155] Ibid., 191.
[156] Ibid., 142.
[157] Ibid., 147.
[158] Clark, *Porto Rico and Its Problems*, 315–6.

$10.8 million.[159] Years later, an independent Brookings Institution audit of the Puerto Rican government would criticize it for such practices. "The chief result of much of the borrowing," the report would conclude, "has been a great waste of public revenue by diverting it to the payment of interest, while the piling up of debt charges is almost certain to cause embarrassment to the Treasury and hardships for the country during future periods of reduced prosperity."[160] At the time, however, the BIA remained committed to its position that such aggressive borrowing and lavish spending on improved infrastructure was the only way to attract investors. Unlike in the Philippines, at least, these improvements would lead to the development of a booming sugar industry, although much of that wealth would be repatriated to the United States.[161]

After regaining control of Puerto Rico in 1909, the BIA attempted to expand its control over the island through the 1910 Olmstead Bill. Although the act would have granted citizenship to Puerto Ricans, it would also have expanded the limits of corporate landowning to 3,000 acres and dramatically enhanced the powers of the BIA – powers that exceeded even what it had in the Philippines. Among other things, the bill would have granted the chief of the BIA authority over the Puerto Rican civil service, the power to approve and disapprove the banks in which the colony's funds were deposited, and, most dramatically, the power to deny the right of members of the Puerto Rican government to return to the United States on temporary business. As one historian of Puerto Rico notes, this could have prevented even the governor from returning to Washington to lobby for a bill that the BIA opposed.[162] Finally, it would have given control over Puerto Rican elections to a small commission, the purpose of which was obviously to reduce the power of the Union party.[163] Despite Congress's general deference to the BIA, this bill was clearly a step too far. William Jones (D-VA), who would later pass a citizenship bill under his own name for Puerto Rico, and other House Democrats refused to support the Olmstead Bill primarily because of the increased powers it would grant the Republican-dominated BIA.[164]

By the end of the Taft administration in 1912, American policy in Puerto Rico – now under the firm control of the BIA – remained uncompromising on the issue of self-determination, even as Taft continued to press for citizenship for Puerto Ricans. As he explained in his final message to Congress, citizenship was "just," but any discussion of citizenship would be "entirely disassociated from any thought

[159] Ibid., 316. A similar pattern of increased debt after the BIA took control would also occur in Cuba. When Charles Magoon, formerly General Counsel of the BIA, became the provisional governor during the second American occupation in 1909, he worked with Speyer & Co. to offer a $16.5 million loan to finance sewer improvements. Nearing and Freeman, *Dollar Diplomacy*, 180–1.

[160] Clark, *Porto Rico and Its Problems*, 326.

[161] Cabán, *Constructing a Colonial People*, 149

[162] Truman R. Clark, *Puerto Rico and the United States, 1917–1933* (Pittsburgh, PA: University of Pittsburgh Press, 1975), 20.

[163] Ibid., 20–1.

[164] Ibid., 20.

of statehood."[165] As we will see in Chapter 7, Congress would finally approve citizenship for Puerto Ricans in 1917 after 12 years of lobbying by the BIA.

From a comparative perspective, the Puerto Rican case illustrates the dynamics of BIA-directed colonial development even in a state that needed relatively little help attracting the interest of private capital or investment. Having developed relationships with banks from its work in the Philippines and the Dollar Diplomacy receiverships, the BIA turned to colony-backed bonds even in Puerto Rico – a colony that, unlike the Philippines, had little difficulty attracting private capital.

---

[165] Quoted in Trías Monge, *Puerto Rico*, 65.

7

Consequences and Collapse:
The Empire under Wilson

The government should own the railroad there. If, in this country a people as intelligent as ours find it difficult, if not impossible, to protect themselves from injustice at the hands of domestic railroad corporations, how can a people like the Filipinos hope to protect themselves from injustice at the hands of foreign railroad corporations?
—William Jennings Bryan (1916)[1]

News of Woodrow Wilson's victory in the election of 1912 must have been greeted with a sense of dread among most Americans in the Philippines. For the first time since the Spanish–American War, the Democrats – a party whose official platform condemned the colonial experiment as "an inexcusable blunder that has involved us in enormous expenses" – would take charge of the empire. Beginning in October 1913, and for the next eight years, Francis Burton Harrison would serve as governor-general. If Wilson had set out to choose an appointee more at odds with the largely Republican coterie of colonial bureaucrats, he could not have done better than to nominate this wealthy New York congressman with ties to Tammany Hall.[2] Not only was Harrison known to be among the strongest advocates of Philippine independence, but he also counted the resident commissioner, Manuel Quezon, as a personal friend. Within the first three years of his administration, Harrison and Quezon secured passage of the controversial Jones Law (a bill they had drafted), which provided for the first formal guarantee of eventual independence for the Philippines once a stable government was established.

Despite his clear support for an independent Philippines, however, Harrison's administration represented a less radical shift in administrative policy than is often assumed.[3] To be sure, Harrison had strong objections to the retentionist aims of the

[1] Bryan to Harrison, May 11, 1916; Harrison Papers, Box 18.
[2] As if his Tammany connections were not bad enough, Republicans were quick to note that Harrison's father had served as private secretary to Jefferson Davis!
[3] Recent works do not posit quite so sharp a break between the Forbes and Harrison administration. See Kramer, *Blood of Government*.

Republican administrators, but he did not disagree with the colonial state's promotion of economic development. Whereas the Forbes regime had been marked by aggressive efforts to recruit American capital to the islands, Harrison's tenure – partly as a result of necessity and partly as a result of his own ideological proclivities – would be marked by even more radical interventions into the colonial economy.

Like many members of the Progressive wing of his party, Harrison shared a certain suspicion of American industrialists. For Taft and Forbes, development and the attraction of capital had served as a way to tie the Philippines to the United States; for Harrison, it provided a way to demonstrate the islands' readiness for independence. Nevertheless, while the *goals* of the administration may have differed, the methods remained remarkably similar. Harrison, much like his Republican predecessors, relied upon a similar sort of legerdemain to keep colonial policies from attracting public and congressional attention and private money. Indeed, the level of congressional attention to their colonial possession did not improve with Democratic leadership. As one official wrote to Harrison in 1916, "[I]t is easy to see why Members of Congress feel almost annoyed when asked to consider questions affecting an alien people whom they do not understand, whose fate is in no sense essentially bound up with that of the United States, and who are separated by so many thousand miles both of ocean and interest."[4]

This chapter examines the transition to Democratic rule in the Philippines and the Caribbean. It begins with a look at the Democrats' efforts – as the governor himself put it – to "hustle the United States out of the Islands."[5] Ironically, the crux of Harrison's strategy depended on the very institutions and relationships developed by his Republican predecessors. The vague lines of authority and M-form organizational hierarchy that governed the colonial state's relationship to Washington – never fully fleshed out during the Republican regime – allowed the colonial government under Harrison to continue to operate with little congressional oversight. Moreover, Wilson did not share Taft's long experience and personal interest in the Philippines, which left even fewer checks on the governor's power.

With little guidance from Washington, but with the ready support of Filipino elites allied with Quezon, Harrison directed the colonial government to further a different ideological agenda, one that would make the colonial state itself the owner of major businesses in the islands. He purchased the MRC and created a bank (the PNB) that would lend vast sums of money from the gold reserve fund to promote increased agricultural production and manufacturing. He established a public utilities commission, a National Cement Company, a National Coal Company, and a National Development Company, which he later wrote, "really permits the Philippine Government to enter indirectly into almost any sort of business deemed to be in the interests of the people of the islands."[6] At the core of his project was an effort to develop a self-sustaining, independent economy in the colony that would undermine arguments for retaining the islands. Eventually, however, these aggressive lending and development efforts would result in a banking and inflation crisis that would nearly bankrupt the colonial government.

---

[4] Newton Baker to Harrison, September 1, 1916; Harrison Papers, Box 17.
[5] Quoted in Elliott, *Philippines to the End of Commission Government*, 393.
[6] Francis Burton Harrison, *The Corner-Stone of Philippine Independence: A Narrative of Seven Years* (New York: The Century Co., 1922), 261.

As with the Dollar Diplomacy receiverships, the radical autonomy of the colonial state would lead to increasingly unstable policies, which would prove embarrassing for Democrats, costly for Congress, and delay Philippine independence for more than a decade. A similar agenda in the Caribbean would end with the invasion of the Dominican Republic and Haiti. The administration may have changed, but the Democrats would embrace the methods developed by their rivals to manage the empire with little input from Congress.

PARTISAN CHANGE AND PHILIPPINE POLICY

The election of 1912 ended 14 years of Republican rule in the Philippines. Although American imperialism did not play a major role in the campaign, officials at the BIA were nervously tracking the election, especially as the Democrats appeared likely to win. "For the first time since the War with Spain," Frank McIntyre noted, "the Democratic Party is on the eve of becoming responsible, before the country and the world, for the government of the several possessions which came to us as a consequence of that war."[7] After serving through two presidential administrations that had provided vigorous and consistent support for the empire, there was considerable fear among the collection of bureaucrats who made up the American colonial state that a Democratic victory would result in disaster.

In the face of such looming threats, the BIA began a subtle campaign to soften the edges of the Democrats' more virulent anti-imperialist rhetoric. In July of 1912 McIntyre had drawn up a memo, apparently at the suggestion of a group of Democratic moderates, to outline the BIA's reasons for opposing the "radical plank" in the party's platform, an episode that provides a revealing glimpse into the mindset of the ostensibly nonpartisan BIA just before the Democrats took control. First, McIntyre noted, Democrats stood to gain little by featuring the Philippines in the election, reminding them that "the various platforms on which the Democratic party won the Congressional elections in 1910, omitted all reference to the Philippines." After this naked appeal to political logic, however, came the BIA's impassioned defense of the Commission's nation building efforts – one that emphasized both its ideological commitment to a very Progressive form of development and its financial independence from the metropole:

[W]e have improved them mentally by the establishment of the public school system which compares favorably with any system on earth; we have improved them physically by scientific and medical work, segregating lepers, vaccinating the people and improving in general sanitary conditions. We have improved the water supply by constructing waterworks in several cities and by boring artesian wells in villages throughout the Islands . . . We have constructed harbors, the finest in the Orient. We have built highways connecting peoples of different provinces and of the same provinces. We have constructed railroads. All these things have been done by the taxes collected in the Philippine Islands from the people of the archipelago. The United States does not appropriate today a dollar for any feature of the civil government to public improvements in the Philippine Islands.

---

[7] Frank McIntyre to Newton W. Gilbert (Acting Governor-General), July 23, 1912; RG 350, Box 610 (Serial 10418).

Yet, the BIA chief concluded, "that progress would continue or that the present advanced position would be maintained if the guiding hand should be withdrawn cannot for a moment be supposed."[8] Although the BIA officials were not ultimately successful in persuading leading Democrats to remove the more objectionable planks in their platform, they were able to moderate the policies of anti-imperialists.

Wilson himself was not known for holding strong views on the Philippines. To be sure, during the years following the Spanish–American War, he had vacillated between retention and independence, a fact that left some Republicans, including Forbes, feeling optimistic that he would endorse the status quo.[9] Such thoughts, however, were quickly put to rest after the election. "The Philippines are our frontier now," said the president-elect. "We don't know what is going on out there, and presently I hope to deprive ourselves of that frontier."[10] Nevertheless, during his first few months in office, a series of domestic battles over tariff and banking reform kept the Philippines off the president's agenda. With little indication of how Wilson might ultimately act, the older Republican guard and Quezon's Democratic allies began to fill this vacuum with their own attempts to shape elite opinion.

QUEZON, THE REPUBLICANS, AND INFORMATION

The push for Philippine independence was not led by American anti-imperialists or by radical revolutionaries, but by a Filipino official intimately familiar with the colonial government. Manuel Quezon, whose early rise from provincial lawyer to member of the Philippine Assembly was detailed in Chapter 6, had quickly emerged as a major force in Philippine politics. In 1909, he was elected as one of the two resident commissioners to Washington. Although he had been a voice of moderation during the early years of the colonial state, Quezon became a vocal advocate for independence when the Democrats won control of the House in 1910. Handsome, charismatic, and fluent in English, Quezon moved easily among officials in Washington and maintained close relationships with a number of Democratic members of Congress, including Francis Harrison, as well as the BIA chief, Frank McIntyre. From his official position in Washington, Quezon directed a lobby for Philippine independence that provided an alternative source for information about the islands – one that often sharply conflicted with the dominant narrative proclaimed by Forbes and Taft.[11]

Although much of Quezon's lobbying work took place behind closed doors, in September 1912 – just before Wilson's victory – he launched a new American periodical, *The Filipino People*, which would become the mouthpiece for the independence lobby. For years, the Republican administrators had forwarded the rather

---

[8] Frank McIntyre to Newton W. Gilbert (Acting Governor-General), Memo for Democratic Party, July 23, 1912; RG 350, Box 610 (Serial 10418).
[9] Roy Watson Curry, "Woodrow Wilson and Philippine Policy," *Mississippi Valley Historical Review* 41 (December 1954): 435. Even Quezon, in a candid conversation with McIntyre, confessed that he did not think Wilson would bring dramatic change to the colonial government. See Stanley, *Nation in the Making*, 180.
[10] *The Filipino People* (January 1913), 4.
[11] Stanley, *Nation in the Making*, 170.

consistent, if flawed, argument that the United States had a duty to bring economic prosperity to the Philippines, and that this prosperity would, in turn, undermine Filipino arguments for independence. Quezon understood the power of this line of reasoning, but he also knew that the coalition for retaining the Philippines was fragile. Indeed, he understood just how little most members of Congress cared about the islands, and how that contributed to the relative autonomy enjoyed by the Forbes regime in Manila.

Consequently, his newsletter provided a forum to criticize these arguments, but in a manner that would appeal to moderates in Congress. Rather than fiery denunciations of American rule, the newspaper would show, as Quezon himself wrote in the inaugural issue, "the practicability and desirability of setting up an independent Republic in the Archipelago."[12] His arguments by and large served to turn Taft's logic on its head.[13] In a direct attack of Taft's position, Quezon made the case for independence at a New York banquet (with Taft in attendance as the guest of honor) held in celebration of Republican achievements in the Philippines:

You boast yourselves, and rightfully so, with having done in the Philippines in a few years what has not been done in other countries in generations. But while this speaks of your energy and wisdom, it also speaks of ours and our advancement in civilization when you came to the Islands . . . Why should an American merchant need the presence of his flag to do business with us? Their opposition is ill-advised. The success of their respective undertakings requires the good will of the Filipino people, and they are rapidly alienating them with their well-known attitude.[14]

Although Quezon's own views on immediate independence were more ambivalent than this speech would suggest, his new campaign undermined the claims of understanding and expertise that the Republican colonial establishment had long used to silence opposition. Quezon was well aware of the near-monopoly on information exercised by the colonial government, and he now made an effort to correct the situation. In his newsletter, for example, he made several suggestions to "correct the abuse of misinformation concerning the Philippines." Among other things, he suggested that the War Department reports no longer contain the following:

1. Constant statements designed to show, upon doubtful or garbled statistical authority, the wonderful growth of prosperity and trade in the Islands.
2. Assertions concerning the remarkable spread of education in the Islands coupled with statements designed to show the abject illiteracy of the voters with due credit assigned to Americans for the education and due discredit assigned to Filipinos for the illiteracy.
3. Pleas for the expenditure of money and for the authorization of issues of bonds.[15]

Quezon also enlisted a variety of sympathetic American intellectuals to make the case that the information from Americans in Manila mischaracterized the situation.

---

[12] *The Filipino People* (September 1912), 12.
[13] Stanley, *Nation in the Making*, 181.
[14] Manuel Quezon, Address to the Philippine Society, June 12, 1913, printed in *The Filipino People* (June 1913), 5–9.
[15] *The Filipino People* (October 1913), 15.

As Parker Willis, a Columbia economist who had earlier written a critical account of the Taft-era colonial government, asked his readers, "Why should we believe Philippine administrators today when they tell us that the natives are reconciled to our rule and no longer care for the independent government for which they fought without weapons and for which they vainly sought to pay with their lives?"[16] Behind the scenes, Quezon continued to wield considerable influence – and it was Quezon himself who recommended the appointment of the new governor-general. After discussing the matter over with Harrison, Quezon had forwarded his name to Bryan who passed it on to Wilson. By mid-August 1913, Harrison's appointment as the new governor-general was secure.[17]

INDEPENDENCE AND THE JONES BILL

If the old Republican guard held out any hope that Harrison would prove more moderate than his reputation suggested, his inaugural speech quickly put such thoughts to rest. Arriving Manila in October of 1913, he explained that his administration would not remain wedded to past practices. "We regard ourselves as trustees," the new governor explained to the assembled crowd, "acting not for the advantage of the United States, but for the benefit of the people of the Philippines. Every step we take will be taken with a view to the ultimate independence of the Islands."[18]

Although Taft and Forbes had long attached such democratic flourishes to their speeches, Philippine independence, for them, always remained a lofty goal for the distant future. Harrison now indicated that it was something to be achieved in a matter of years. More significantly, at least for Republican observers, was Harrison's immediate decision to grant Filipinos a majority on the Commission – the upper house and executive branch of the colonial government – which had retained an American majority since its inception. Filipinos would now gain effective control of the entire domestic government.[19] As if these changes were not radical enough, Harrison and Quezon immediately moved to secure independence legislation from Congress. Merely three years later, they would succeed when the Jones Act of 1916 committed the United States to an official policy of Philippine independence. For a measure that represented such a stark change in America's relationship to its most important colony, it proved surprisingly easy to achieve.

As this section will show, the debate over Philippine independence quickly became more a question of *when* rather than *if*, and some congressional Democrats favored severing the connection far earlier than even nationalists like Quezon thought responsible. Nothing so demonstrates the political implications of the colonial state's lack of domestic support than the relative ease with which the Democrat-controlled colonial government was able to achieve a commitment on eventual independence from Congress. The colonial state's *in*ability to attract

---

[16] H. Parker Willis, "National Sincerity in Dealing with the Philippines," *The Filipino People* (November 1912), 24–5.

[17] Curry, "Woodrow Wilson and Philippine Policy," 439.

[18] Harrison quoted in *The Filipino People* (October 1913), 8.

[19] H. W. Brands, *Bound to Empire: The United States and the Philippines* (New York: Oxford University Press, 1992), 111.

substantial domestic investment to the Philippines meant that a robust coalition of interests in favor of retention had never materialized. Their carefully constructed reports and ties with private money had allowed them to manage the islands with a relatively free hand for over a decade, but neither Congress nor most domestic constituencies shared their vision for the Philippines. Ironically, Harrison and his new Filipino partners would take advantage of the relative autonomy that their Republican predecessors had created for the colonial state – in this case to demonstrate its viability as an independent nation.

"FILIPINIZATION" AND THE REPUBLICAN OPPOSITION

While the various measures to increase home rule were being debated in Congress, Harrison was quickly replacing Americans with Filipinos throughout the colonial state bureaucracy – a policy that would become known as "filipinization" and remain one of the most controversial reforms of the Democratic administration. McKinley's first Philippine commission had, of course, suggested that Filipinos receive preferential treatment for civil service positions, but the policy was rarely observed for the higher levels of colonial administration, a fact that had long been a major point of contention among Filipino leaders.[20] Harrison apparently agreed with these assessments. "The bureaus here are top heavy with Americans," he concluded in an early assessment to the Secretary of War.[21]

The new policy quickly earned Harrison the scorn of past administrators and many of the Manila Americans. Dean Worcester, perhaps the most recalcitrant member of the old guard, would later write that these filipinization campaigns were nothing more than an attempt by Harrison and Wilson "to snatch whatever temporary popularity might be gained by posing as friends of the Filipinos and to utilize it for their own political advancement."[22] Filipinization, in other words, was a barely veiled attempt to pack the well-established civil service with radical anti-imperialists. Naturally, Harrison dismissed these accusations as politically motivated attacks. "[I]n all questions affecting the civil service," he later wrote, "the spirit as well as the letter of the law and regulations in force, has been observed."[23]

This was not entirely true, of course. As Secretary of State, William Jennings Bryan had, in fact, requested appointments in the Philippines for some of his "deserving Democrats" with the dubious claim that it was necessary "to have Nebraska represented in the Philippines."[24] Nevertheless, Harrison's commitment to filipinization was not merely an effort to purge the colonial bureaucracy of Forbes loyalists. Although he did find some positions for the recommended Nebraskans, he noted that it "has been a hard thing to do for the reason that I have been giving the Filipinos almost all the offices as they became vacant in order to give them a chance to show their capacity for self-government."[25]

[20] Stanley, *Nation in the Making*, 205.
[21] Quoted in Brands, *Bound to Empire*, 109.
[22] Dean C. Worcester, *The Philippines Past and Present* (New York: Macmillan, 1930 [1914]), 696–7.
[23] Quoted in Hayden, *The Philippines*, 99.
[24] Bryan to Harrison, September 23, 1913; Harrison Papers, Box 18.
[25] Harrison to Bryan, December 6, 1913; Harrison Papers, Box 18.

In truth, the changes in personnel were somewhat less dramatic than the Republican denunciations suggested. Filipinos had long made up a majority of civil service positions in the colonial state, while the number of Americans employed had remained relatively constant at about 2,600 for a decade. Furthermore, the turnover for Americans employed in technical and teaching positions was always rather high; during the Forbes administration, for example, about 500 Americans per year left the colonial civil service. Although this rate remained roughly the same during the first three years of Harrison's administration, as Americans left the civil service they were slowly replaced with Filipinos, and by 1919 only 760 remained.[26]

The true outrage over Harrison's policies resulted less from the number of Americans dismissed than from his decision to purge top American officials whom he regarded as either "exceedingly disloyal to me or else violently opposed to the policies of President Wilson."[27] In practice, this policy led to the retirement of more than 200 former top officials, including the head of the customs service, Henry B. McCoy.[28] There were, of course, more purely political reasons for cleaning house. Change could hardly come to Manila if officials still loyal to Forbes dominated the highest reaches of the colonial bureaucracy.[29]

As in the Taft and Forbes administration, information about the Philippines was a jealously guarded prerogative of the colonial government, and Harrison, as well as his Filipino allies, was anxious to purge it of officials who might try to undermine the regime with unwelcome reports to Congress or domestic newspapers. Harrison was well aware that the colonial trust, so meticulously designed by Root, thrived through the shared ideological commitment of its members. As he later recalled,

> They stood together upon that issue, like the Old Guard at Waterloo, ready to die, but never surrender. If not in accord with the policy of the department heads and of the Legislature, they could block to a very large extent the working out of any reform. The new policy would be impossible if bureau chiefs were to perform political sabotage with the official machinery.[30]

Indeed, the centralized nature of the colonial government left the bureau chiefs with substantial autonomy within their various departments, and many were, as Harrison later wrote, "generally inspired with a disbelief in the ability of the Filipinos to carry on any important work of government."[31] Any changes to the Philippine colonial state required that the former department heads be purged.

The Philippine Society and the Campaign for Retention

The relatively anemic campaign to retain the islands was directed by the former Republican colonial state officials. Even before Harrison arrived to take control of

[26] Visitacion de la Torre, *History of the Philippine Civil Service* (Quezon City: New Day Publishers, 1986), 64.

[27] Quoted in Brands, *Bound to Empire*, 111.

[28] McCoy, *Policing America's Empire*, 261.

[29] Hayden, *The Philippines*, 97.

[30] Harrison, *Corner-Stone of Philippine Independence*, 77.

[31] Ibid.

the Philippines, the Republicans who had managed the American empire for the past decade saw the need for a new organization to defend the status quo. While he was still acting governor, Forbes, in a series of letters to his wealthy friends in American banking circles, proposed the establishment of a domestic lobbying group to influence Democratic policy on the islands. "I believe a campaign waged within the ranks of the Democrats just now would set them right on this important matter," he wrote to Thomas Lamont of J. P. Morgan. "I am inclined to think that only a small sum of money will be needed to handle the whole thing. My guess is about $25,000. I am willing to stand for a tenth of it and underwrite more. Can you help in this?"[32]

Forbes soon retained Martin Egan, the former publisher of *The Manila Times*, who had long been sympathetic to the Republican administration, and whose own writings reflected the belief of most colonial officials and American residents in the islands that their critics were woefully misinformed about the reality of American administration. As he wrote in a 1912 pamphlet,

One of the difficulties that bar the way to success in the Philippines is the failure of the American people to understand the problem and questions involved. Congress itself has rarely brought either understanding or sympathy to the question and by perversity that is exasperating those who are most active in the premises and talk the most on the subject often seem the least informed. There are in the United States several authorities on the Philippines who count themselves as profound who have never seen the islands. Newspapers and editorial comment on the islands is rarely well informed and seldom accurate.[33]

According to Forbes, his new lobbying organization – soon dubbed the Philippine Society – would present more "accurate" information to the public in a final attempt to win over moderate Democrats before Wilson had a chance to act. As he wrote to James Speyer, owner of the MRC, "If a campaign well conducted while the Democrats are in power just now could bring about a defeat of the present movement for a change in the Philippine status by the Democratic party itself – a defeat within their own ranks – it would settle the plan of a revolutionary change out here for quite a time to come."[34]

On the whole, major domestic American business interests remained indifferent to the islands, but the small American community in the Philippines was a vocal opponent of any possible independence measures. When the newly appointed Philippine Secretary of the Interior, Winfred Denison, openly advocated home rule and quick independence in a June 1914 speech at the City Club in Manila, he was quickly denounced by the local American press. According to *The Manila Times*, which had long served as the mouthpiece for conservative Manila Americans, "Careful reading of the speech in which the Secretary of the interior, Winfred Denison, developed his theories of colonial government – theories acquired in an arm-chair, and freshened by harmless adventures in a country where peace and order are legacies his predecessor left him – leaves the reader undecided whether impertinence or ignorance is

[32] Forbes to Thomas Lamont, January 26, 1913; Forbes Papers, Confidential Letters, v. 2.

[33] Martin Egan, *The Philippine Problem* (Manila: E. C. McCullough & Co., 1912), 6–7. Copy in Harrison Papers, Box 49.

[34] Forbes to James Speyer, January 26, 1916; Forbes Papers, Confidential Letters, v. 2. See also Forbes to Henry Higginson, January 26, 1916; Forbes Papers, Confidential Letters, v. 2.

its chief characteristic."[35] The small collection of American traders and exporters, however, likely had little influence on the new colonial government – even during the Republican era, they had been kept at arms length.

The most vociferous opponents of change in Philippine policy were the current and former officials of the colonial state. This came as no surprise to anti-imperialists. Moorfield Storey, head of the Anti-Imperialism League, had earlier written Harrison to warn him of opposition from "the bureaucracy which had grown to be such a dangerous and powerful element," as well as media interests in the Philippines.[36] Taft, in a January 1913 speech before the annual gala of the Ohio Society of New York, continued to march to the drumbeat of imperialism, calling the Philippines "the best colonies in the world," and urged that the Democrats "go on as we have."[37] By October of 1913, his tone had become even more strident. "We are seeking to *create* a national spirit – not, as under all previous systems, to suppress it," the former president wrote. "It is utter folly to suppose that in ten or eleven years all of this could be fully accomplished."[38]

For Taft and Forbes, an official policy of independence not only seemed unwise, but also undermined their nation building strategy. The former administrators had attempted to create an investment market in part by assuring American capitalists of the stability of colonial rule. Without this stability, they feared, economic development would prove impossible. "I feel perfectly sure of one thing, as sure as I can feel of anything in this world," Forbes wrote to the new Democratic Secretary of War, Lindley Garrison,

[A]nd that is that the present lessening of American control in any degree will prolong the necessity for it. Of course, there may be very different opinions as to what it is the duty of the American people to accomplish in the Islands; whether we are to turn them loose like Cuba before they are really ready, and let them worry along as best they can, or whether we are to really make something of them, make them rich, strong, progressive and self-reliant, complete in all their parts, capable of earning considerable wages and of accumulating wealth. To make their work really available takes capital and capital takes confidence, and so it all comes back to having a government out there that people have confidence in, and that confidence has just now been somewhat shaken.[39]

Whether or not the Philippine Society – which eventually included Taft, Wright, and Forbes, as well as various bankers and former administration officials – had any real influence on the Democrats' Philippine policy is difficult to determine. For the most part, Taft's older, more patrician Filipino allies had lost most of their political influence, and so could not be counted on to shape events in Manila. Martin Egan directly lobbied new officials in the Wilson administration and apparently convinced William McAdoo and William Redfield, the new secretaries of Treasury

---

[35] *The Manila Times*, July 1, 1914; clipping in Smith Papers, Box 2.

[36] Moorfield Storey to Harrison; Harrison Papers, Box 32. Incidentally, Storey was a close personal friend of Forbes's mother and a man whom Forbes continued to address as "Uncle Moorfield" even as he remained vehemently opposed to the League's efforts to undermine his administration.

[37] *New York Times* (January 19, 1913), 11.

[38] Taft, "Our Duty to the Philippines," *The Independent* (October 16, 1913). Copy in Harrison Papers, Box 49.

[39] Forbes to Garrison, November 5, 1914; Harrison Papers, Box 25.

and Commerce, respectively, of the wisdom of retention. Not surprisingly, business leaders with interests in the Islands, including J. G. White, the owner of the Philippine Railway and a member of the Society, were decidedly opposed to early independence, as were some major newspapers, particularly on the West Coast.[40]

But even from these supportive constituencies, arguments in favor of retention remained somewhat muted. A December 1912 editorial in the *San Francisco Chronicle*, for example, acknowledged that "[m]ost Americans would gladly be rid of the responsibility for the islanders if it could be done with honor."[41] The fact remained that the independence of the Philippines was never a particularly important issue for the American public, most of whom had never warmed to their nation's Asian colony. Quezon, always a close student of American politics, was well aware of this fact, noting to Governor Harrison,

I have not the slightest doubt but that the American people in general are favorable to Philippine independence. The trouble is that the people at large are not interested enough in this subject to write to their congressman, and the only voice that is being heard is the voice of those who are interested in retention, who are, naturally, actively working to defeat the bill.[42]

Moreover, Republicans in Congress were largely uninterested in expending political capital to defend a project that had generated, at best, indifferent support from the public. Such vague concerns were hardly the recipe for an impassioned defense of imperialism. Even Theodore Roosevelt, writing to Forbes in 1915, explained that he no longer saw the wisdom in keeping the colony if retention was not accompanied by a robust policy of imperialism. "It has been very bitter for me to have to grow to feel, as I have grown to feel," the former president wrote, "that the attitude of the American people was such as to make it unwise for us to retain [the Philippines]."[43] As Wilson entered office, then, support for American imperialism even among Republicans was sharply on the decline.

The Jones Act and American Capital

The ambiguity that characterized the early Philippine policy of the Wilson administration was quickly replaced with a clear commitment to home rule, although official independence would remain a more politically sensitive issue. Earlier in the year, Wilson had dispatched Henry Jones Ford, a friend and fellow political scientist at Princeton, to take stock of the situation.[44] While still governor, Forbes had written to Ford with his own suggestions – nearly all of which demonstrated

[40] Stanley, *Nation in the Making*, 189–90.
[41] *San Francisco Chronicle* (December 31, 1912), 6.
[42] Quezon quoted in Brands, *Bound to Empire*, 116.
[43] Roosevelt to Forbes, August 6, 1915; Forbes Papers, Box 5, Folder 248.
[44] Ford, however, was no rabid anti-imperialist. Although critical of American imperialism, he looked favorably on economic development. "Effective police control is the first duty," he had earlier written in the *Political Science Quarterly*. "But the opening of industrial opportunity is a correlated duty. When we prevent a people from living by rapine, we must enable them to live by industry." Henry Jones Ford, "The Ethics of Empire," *Political Science Quarterly* 22 (September 1907): 498–505. In the same article, Ford also forwarded a bizarre biological theory of empire based on "the universal tendency of organisms to extend into the media of one another."

his confidence that Wilson would leave his policies in place – including the establishment of "some government organ" which could mold "public opinion along the lines of the effort of the American people in the Philippine Islands," and an increase in the allowable debt for the colonial government. "We are trying to build a nation here," he wrote. "We can do it faster with money than without."[45] Forbes could hardly have been more out of step with the new administration's policies, and Ford pointedly ignored all of his recommendations. In fact, Ford's report recommended precisely the opposite course: He noted that Filipinos were ready to take on most of the tasks of self-government, and he advised Wilson to grant them effective autonomy in domestic affairs by installing a Filipino majority on the Commission.[46]

For his part, Quezon had been working to balance the increasingly strident demands for independence from a breakaway Philippine nationalist faction in Manila with the political realities in Washington. Two years earlier, he had worked with William Jones (D-VA), the aging chairman of the House Committee on Insular Affairs, to draft a bill that mandated elections for an upper house of the legislature with Philippine independence to follow eight years later.[47] In 1912, of course, with Taft still in office, the bill had no chance of becoming law. Quezon was well aware of this fact, and the act was designed in large part to shore up support for his *Nacionalista* party at home. Now, with Wilson in the White House, the opportunity to develop a comprehensive plan for independence presented itself.

Quezon's next proposal, which he first discussed with McIntyre at the BIA, delayed Philippine independence for at least 25 years and only after the country had achieved a 75 percent literacy rate for adult men.[48] This more conservative second attempt reflected his private fears that the Philippines was not ready for immediate independence, as well as his suspicion that southern Democrats in Congress, who had long seen the colony as an affront to American racial order, were simply looking for an excuse to be rid of it.[49] In the meantime, however, Jones had worked out a second bill, which provided for two elected branches in the colonial legislature and, more significantly, a guarantee of eventual independence. This bill, which Quezon supported in lieu of his own effort, passed the House in October of 1914 with a solid 212 to 60 vote, but soon became bogged down in the Senate over objections to the independence language in the bill's preamble.[50]

The prospects for the Second Jones Bill were revived when the 64th Congress convened in December 1915 with a larger Democratic majority. Yet American capitalists who had invested in the colonial government's bonds feared that a sovereign Philippine government would no longer honor them. J. G. White, whose company had played a major role in the development of Philippine railroads, vigorously opposed independence in the near term. "To withdraw from the Islands in from two to four years," he wrote to the chair of the Senate Committee on the Philippines,

Would be equivalent to ruthlessly destroying, to a large degree at least, the value of the investments which had been made at the invitation of the Philippine Government under

---

[45] Forbes to Ford, May 2, 1913; Forbes Papers, Confidential Letters, v. 2.
[46] Curry, "Woodrow Wilson and Philippine Policy," 437; Stanley, *Nation in the Making*, 198.
[47] Stanley, *Nation in the Making*, 173.
[48] Brands, *Bound to Empire*, 113.
[49] Curry, "Woodrow Wilson and Philippine Policy," 442.
[50] Ibid., 444.

the authority of the Government of the United States, and would consequently be treating unfairly the citizens who had responded to this invitation by investing their funds to meet these requests.[51]

Quezon himself played a large role in appeasing the American investors. As he later reported to Governor Harrison, "I have seen many people in New York especially those who have money invested in the Philippines, and by using all kind[s] of arguments to suit their particular view, I am succeeding in getting them not to fight . . . the bill."[52] Another attempt to reduce such opposition was championed by the Secretary of War, Newton Baker, who asked the Senate Committee on Appropriations to guarantee the bonds – an effort that was ultimately unsuccessful.[53]

Back in Manila, Harrison applied equal pressure to American businesses. The dependence of business investors on the colonial state – a situation created by Harrison's Republican predecessors – gave the new governor some powerful tools to keep them in line. Although major investors such as the White syndicate – owners of the Philippine Railway Company – had initially greeted the new Democratic administration with caution and, in some cases, outright hostility, the dependence of the American business community on the colonial state made such opposition difficult to sustain. The most significant American investments, after all, were dependent on government contracts or loan guarantees for their survival, a fact that was emphasized by Harrison's promise that his opponents "would be made to suffer."[54] To silence Manila lawyer Charles Cohn, for example, one of his most vehement critics, the new governor-general sent word to San Francisco investors that they would be wise to move their interests from Cohn's Manila law firm to a more cooperative one. More commonly, however, he worked to assuage the colonial state's private partners through favorable financial arrangements, including the controversial San José friar estate owners who were given access to ₱600,000 worth of government loans to prop up their struggling business.[55]

Quezon's lobbying and Harrison's financial inducements to toe the line seem to have paid off. During a series of hearings before the Senate Committee on the Philippines, representatives of both American sugar interests and the colonial railroads gave measured support for the bill. "I am in favor of this bill," George Fairchild of the Mindoro Sugar Company testified. "I believe the initiative in a great many matters should be granted to the Filipinos, for, while I am not in favor of immediate independence, I believe that we should not withhold from them, or we should not break, I should say, the promise we have made to them."[56] Or, as he had written earlier in a trade publication, "Home rule for the Philippine Islands, in the opinion of a very large majority of the American business men in the islands, under this bill, with its safeguards and with some amendments is looked upon

---

[51] J. G. White to Gilbert Hitchcock, February 1, 1916; RG 46, Senate Committee on the Philippines, Box 66.
[52] Quezon to Harrison in September 14, 1914; Quoted in Stanley, Nation in the Making, 220.
[53] Newton Baker to Thomas S. Martin, March 24, 1916; RG 46, Senate Committee on the Philippines, Box 66.
[54] McCoy, Policing America's Empire, 261.
[55] Stanley, Nation in the Making, 211.
[56] US Senate, Hearings before the Committee on the Philippines (Washington, DC: Government Printing Office, 1915), 439.

with favor."[57] Charles Swift, the president of the Philippine Railway Company and the Manila Electric Railway, expressed similar support: "The only interests I have anywhere are in these two properties, so I consider that I am something like the Filipino. Whatever helps the Filipino will help me," he told the Senate.[58]

The flexibility of American business interests in the face of the shifting preferences of the colonial regime is less surprising than it may seem. American investors were never directly committed to the ideological goals of the Taft and Forbes regime, but they *were* committed to the financial subsidies that had long supported their businesses. The railroads – easily the largest American investments in the islands – were, by the end of the Forbes era, surviving primarily through the generous loan terms and direct investments by the colonial government itself. In fact, the owners of both railroads had plans to sell their unprofitable companies to the colonial government – the purchase of which would be financed through further bond offerings. Swift's only real concern seemed to be the status of his company's bonds if and when the archipelago should become independent. Yet his assertion that the United States would remain responsible for these debts seemed to surprise the Committee:

The CHAIRMAN. Do you mean . . . that the Government of the United States is responsible for the bonded debt of the Philippine Islands?

Mr. SWIFT. Yes, sir; morally responsible, at any rate. I suppose a bondholder buying the bonds, if he were a foreigner, would undoubtedly make a claim that the United States was responsible; and why should it not be? What did the Filipino have to do with issuing those bonds? The amount of the bonds was fixed in Washington; the form of the bonds was fixed in Washington; the price was fixed in Washington; and the sale was made in Washington.

The CHAIRMAN. Then the United States would be responsible for the interest on the railroads' bonds in the Philippine Islands?

Mr. SWIFT. I think so, myself . . . A large number of those bonds . . . were sold at one time, and bids for those bonds were received in the office of the Insular Bureau in Washington.

Senator LIPPITT. Do you mean that if the United States Government abandoned the Philippine Islands, and turned them over to the Filipino people, the United States Government would be responsible for those bonds in case the Filipino government did not pay them?

Mr. SWIFT. Yes, sir; that is my position.[59]

Having thrown their lot in with the success of the colony, the private investors had little recourse but to cooperate with the new regime and to distance themselves from the former administrators. In a little less than two years, Harrison was able to remove his opponents from office and to co-opt the private interests with investments in the islands. Ironically, the very autonomy of the colonial state was used to defeat its architects. Indeed, the *inability* of the colony to attract much domestic political or economic interest left it with relatively few domestic political opponents in its quest for independence.

In August of 1916, after defeating a new bill to grant independence within five years, the Jones Bill was adopted nearly as it had been introduced in 1914. When Wilson signed the Jones Act on August 29, 1916, he ushered in a new era of Philippine–American relations, giving the Filipinos far greater control over their

---

[57] George Fairchild, Letter to the Editor, *Journal of Commerce and Commercial Bulletin* (September 2, 1914); reprinted in US Senate, *Hearings before the Committee on the Philippines*, 461.

[58] US Senate, *Hearings before the Committee*, 584.

[59] Ibid., 587–8.

domestic affairs. The Philippine Commission was abolished; a new bicameral legis-lature was adopted; and for the first time, the United States officially acknowledged that the Philippines would eventually be granted independence.[60] The date of its official independence, however, would remain unknown, along with the status of the capitalists' loans. This ambiguity would usher in a new era. Harrison, Quezon, and their allies would now try to use the resources of the colonial state to bootstrap its development and show that it was ready for full sovereignty sooner rather than later.

NATIONALIZATION AND DEVELOPMENT

Just prior to leaving the Philippines for the last time as governor-general in August 1913, Cameron Forbes wrote a long letter to his Democratic successor. Among other things, Forbes advised him that "no matter what the future holds for the Philippine Islands, the present need is an increase in the purchasing power of the people. Even if they want to purchase independence they have got to have more money to do it with. Therefore our present concern is to make them more wealthy."[61] Initially, there was some uncertainty about whether Forbes's focus on economic development would survive the change in administration. As Winfred Denison, one of the newly appointed Democratic members of the Commission, asked in a public address not long after his arrival, "Why should we insist upon hustling the East against its will and at its expense if the East itself wishes to lie placid murmuring *mañana*?"[62]

Within weeks of his arrival in the Philippines, however, it became clear that Harrison, along with his Filipino allies, had no intention of abandoning economic development. The development of the islands was one policy that the former Republican administrators, the new Democratic administration, and Filipino elites could readily agree upon. Yet the relative scarcity of capital remained a key prob-lem during Harrison's administration, as it had been during the Taft and Forbes eras. Indeed, the always-tenuous financial condition of the colonial government had become increasingly precarious by the time Harrison took office in 1914. Customs revenues, for example, which remained the most important source of income for the colonial state, fell by 39 percent between 1912 and 1913, and by 1914 total revenues were down by ₱5.7 million from 1913.[63]

In large part, the revenue situation was settled by the imposition of new taxes in 1915, which raised rates for merchants and manufacturers, and consequently stabilized the government's revenues.[64] Furthermore, the start of World War I dra-matically increased the demand for Philippine exports and led to a corresponding increase in government revenues (see Figure 4.2). The stabilization and increase in colonial revenue, however, did not translate into a significant increase in American investments. As Table 7.1 demonstrates, even after two decades of US occupation, British investors had invested almost twice as much capital in the Philippines. Despite this lack of manufacturing interest and direct investment, the colonial

[60] Hayden, *The Philippines*, 167.
[61] Forbes to Executive Secretary Frank Carpenter, August 25, 1913; Harrison Papers, Box 21.
[62] Cited in Elliott, *The Philippines to the End of Commission Government*, 274.
[63] Golay, "Search for Revenues," 254.
[64] Ibid., 254–5.

TABLE 7.1. *Foreign capital invested in the Philippines by country, 1919 (thousands of pesos)*

Britain	968,607
United States	553,022
Germany (seized during World War I)	174,486
Japan	131,500
The Netherlands	23,919

Source: O. D. Corpuz, *An Economic History of the Philippines* (Quezon City: University of the Philippines Press, 1997), 246.

state, through its quasi-autonomous status, retained control over its tax revenue and currency reserves – resources they would soon use to begin a radical experiment in state-led development.

As this section will demonstrate, colonial economic policy during the Harrison administration relied ever more on government direction of the colonial economy. In part, these direct interventions into the economy were driven by the continued failure of the colonial state to attract private investments. As Harrison would later write in an autobiographical account of his administration, "the growth of the idea [nationalization] in the Philippines was not due to a desire to preempt the field for investments, but arose simply and solely from the refusal of sufficient American and foreign capital to enter the country."[65]

In part, too, the policies were driven by Harrison's ideological commitment to the public ownership of utilities. Unlike the Forbes administration, which had used colonial resources to guarantee loans, Harrison attempted to use the resources of the colonial government itself to ease access to capital markets and to directly manage colonial development. Most significant was his decision to establish a government-run bank to give Philippine manufacturers and local governments access to relatively cheap government loans. Through this institution, the government gained access to New York capital, enabling it to pump money into the colonial economy by operating – without congressional approval – as a quasi-official arm of the US government on Wall Street. As we will see, the consequences of this policy were nearly catastrophic.

Creating a Colonial Development Bank

The idea for a government-run colonial bank did not originate with Harrison. Americans had long been critical of the usurious practices of local moneylenders – often the only source of capital for Filipino farmers – and the large English banks that financed the import–export trade but provided little capital for local manufacturers.[66] As early as 1901, Charles Conant had suggested the creation of an

[65] Harrison, *Corner-Stone of Philippine Independence*, 253.
[66] H. Parker Willis, "The Philippine National Bank," *Journal of Political Economy* 25 (May 1917): 409–42. For more general histories of Philippine banking, see Paul D. Hutchcroft, *Booty Capitalism: The Politics of Banking in the Philippines* (Ithaca, NY: Cornell University Press, 1998); Yoshiko Nagano, *State and Finance in the Philippines, 1898–1941: The Mismanagement of an American Colony* (Singapore: National University of Singapore Press, 2015).

FIGURE 7.1. *The Philippine Society banquet. Taft is seated beneath the flags at the main table.*
Photo source: The Filipino People (June 1913).

agricultural bank, and in 1907 the colonial government gained congressional approval for a modest bank to make small agricultural loans of no more than $5,000, which the Philippine Legislature later allocated ₱1 million from the general fund for start-up capital.[67] Although the bank did provide a welcome new source of financing for farmers, access to loans was restricted to those who could demonstrate formal ownership of their property, a requirement that most small-scale Filipino farmers could not meet.

A greater problem, however, was the bank's difficulty in attracting capital. Both European and American bankers demurred when asked by the colonial government to invest in the bank, citing administrative difficulties or lack of experience in agricultural banking. Consequently, by the close of the Forbes administration, the bank's start-up capital was virtually depleted. To provide some temporary relief, in February 1913 the Philippine Legislature authorized the bank to become the primary depository for municipal and provincial funds, and at the end of 1914 – the first year of Harrison's administration – the bank had more than ₱4,000,000 in outstanding agricultural loans.[68]

By 1915, the modest successes experienced by the agricultural bank seemed to offer a solution to one of the central objectives of Harrison and his *Nacionalista* allies: a way to achieve economic development without relying on the very sort of

---

[67] Charles A. Conant, *A Special Report on Coinage and Banking in the Philippine Islands* (Washington, DC: Government Printing Office, 1901). For a description of local lending practices see Willis, "The Philippine National Bank," 412; Yoshiko Nagano, "The Agricultural Bank of the Philippine Government, 1908–1916," *Journal of Southeast Asian Studies* 28 (September 1997): 301–23.

[68] Stanley, *Nation in the Making*, 235.

foreign investments that would jeopardize Philippine independence. That summer, Vice Governor Henderson Martin proposed increasing the bank's capital by transferring ₱10 million from the insular treasury and expanding its mandate to make commercial and industrial, as well as agricultural, loans. Months later, this fairly measured proposal had evolved into something more radical when Harrison used his speech at the opening of the new legislative session to call for a government-run bank to stimulate national development.[69]

The most significant objection to this proposal came from Frank McIntyre at the BIA who opposed further government intrusion into the colonial economy. During this period, the National City Bank of New York had acquired the International Banking Corporation – one of the major branch banks in Manila – and McIntyre argued that the colonial government should hand over its financial responsibilities to National City, which had also proved helpful in financing some of the dollar diplomacy interventions.[70] Harrison, it seems, was not entirely opposed to working with the new American bank, going so far as to acknowledge that "the new ownership of the International Banking Corporation may enthuse vitality and enterprise into the operations of their branch here and be more helpful to general commerce and agriculture in the Islands."[71] Nevertheless, the governor-general moved ahead with his proposal, retaining H. Parker Willis, a Columbia economist who had earlier written a critical account of Republican stewardship of the Archipelago, to study the possibility of a government bank. After suggesting a variety of safeguards to prevent abuse, Willis came out in favor of the new policy.

More than anything, these disagreements reveal the ideological divide that was emerging between the colonial government and the ostensibly nonpartisan BIA. As Quezon wrote from Washington, "We should make Philippines financially independent of any outside corporation."[72] Both Harrison and the Filipino nationalists were anxious to decouple the colonial economy from private American interests without sacrificing economic expansion; a goal, they thought, that could only be accomplished with a government-owned development bank. McIntyre was hardly opposed to colonial economic development, but the creation of a national bank struck him as a dangerous and radical proposal. Even Professor Willis admitted that it was a significant departure from traditional American economic policy. "It is for the United States," he acknowledged, "a new form of government activity in the business field, an attempt to dispose of certain pressing economic problems through organized effort."[73] In the end, however, the power a national bank offered Harrison and his Filipino allies to shape the colonial economy trumped McIntyre's concerns. Rather than facilitating Philippine independence, however, the bank would soon become one of the colonial state's biggest liabilities.

In February 1916 Harrison signed into law a bill creating the PNB – arguably the world's first government-run development bank – with an initial capitalization of ₱20 million.[74] The bank opened in July of 1916 and quickly experienced massive

[69] Ibid., 235.
[70] Newton Baker to Harrison, October 25, 1916; Harrison Papers, Box 17.
[71] Harrison to McIntyre, March 13, 1916; Harrison Papers, Box 26.
[72] Quezon to Osmeña, December 9, 1915; Harrison Papers, Box 28.
[73] Willis, "The Philippine National Bank," 409.
[74] George F. Luthringer, *The Gold-Exchange Standard in the Philippines* (Princeton, NJ: Princeton University Press, 1934), 88.

growth. Its resources, which amounted to ₱29 million on opening day, had grown to almost ₱250 million by the end of 1918, giving it a 62 percent share of all banking resources in the islands.[75] The PNB also had control over nearly all the insular government's resources. The Insular Treasurer reported that 76.6 percent of the currency reserves, along with ₱65 million of the insular government's own funds, were on deposit with the PNB's New York Branch, while only ₱17 million – over half of which actually belonged to the currency fund – was on deposit with the Treasury itself. In short, the vast majority of the insular government's cash and currency reserves were under the control of the PNB by 1918. As long as the bank remained sound, none of this would have been cause for concern, but if the PNB became insolvent, the results would be catastrophic for the colonial government, which kept less than ₱9 million in its own vaults.[76]

This situation was made even more perilous by the broad powers given to the bank. Not only did it serve as the central depository for all colonial funds – national, provincial, and municipal – but it also operated as a commercial bank.[77] Indeed, the final bill, unlike Willis's proposal, lacked a number of the safeguards, such as separate divisions for long-term development loans and short-term commercial securities and paper operations. Rather than a government-supported development bank or a bankers' bank, in other words, the PNB became a combination of the two: a central bank that simultaneously operated as a commercial bank on the open market. Moreover, the president and vice president of the bank were given unilateral authority to issue commercial loans. Under such conditions, even Willis, who would serve as the PNB's first director, questioned "whether the Bank can maintain itself absolutely free of political interference or control. It is this rock of 'politics,'" he ominously concluded, "upon which many financial institutions in the Latin–American countries have split."[78]

The Gold Standard Fund and the PNB

The PNB's spectacular growth, as well as its subsequent collapse, can only be understood through a careful reconstruction of its control over the Philippine Gold Reserve Fund. During the Harrison administration the Fund grew to play a more and more central role in colonial finance, although its use as a tool to drive development actually emerged with the governor's Republican predecessors. As discussed in Chapter 6, Forbes had redirected millions of pesos from the Fund when colonial revenue collections fell during final years of his administration in order to maintain expenditures on his cherished public works projects. In 1911, the Commission adopted Act 2083, which fixed the Fund at 35% of the currency in circulation and authorized the insular treasurer to transfer money from the Fund in excess of that amount to the colonial treasury. The amounts involved were not small. By the end of 1912 these transfers amounted to ₱3.3 million and by 1917 came to over ₱10 million.[79]

---

[75] Ibid., 94.
[76] Ibid., 95.
[77] Ibid., 90.
[78] Willis, "The Philippine National Bank," 439–40.
[79] Luthringer, *The Gold-Exchange Standard*, 21.

A more significant departure from traditional banking practices, however, was a provision in Act 2083 to lend up to 50 percent of the remaining Fund to local governments for the construction of municipal markets and other local improvements, a practice that amounted to over $3.6 million in local loans by 1913.[80] Although initially critical of this practice, Harrison's own plans for colonial economic development required significant capital investments, too. As he confessed to Charles Conant, "I share your doubt about the advisability of the lending of half of the Gold Standard Fund for local improvements here, but that system is at present in vogue."[81]

In truth, the Fund proved equally beguiling to Harrison. This was particularly true because Congress had consistently refused to act on the insular government's repeated requests to increase its debt ceiling. With this decree, Congress presumably thought it restricted the colonial state's ability to take on new loans. Yet as we have seen, congressional oversight was hampered since the earliest days of colonial administration by its relative lack of interest in its largest colony – a fact that was often compounded by the carefully curated facts presented by the colonial government. Although insular authorities were forced to respect the debt limit, they could, through some creative interpretations of the law, use their gold reserve fund as collateral for further loans – financial transactions that Congress was unlikely to carefully scrutinize.

Following Forbes's lead, then, Harrison and the Philippine legislature began to use the Fund to pump money into local governments. In 1912, only 12 percent of the fund had been invested in this way, but by 1914 nearly 45.7 percent was tied up in loans. Harrison had earlier been in negotiations with Congress for a large loan, but with these negotiations going nowhere and with the 50 percent threshold quickly approaching, the governor requested access to the remaining gold.[82] Consequently, in February 1915 the threshold was increased to 80 percent. As in earlier actions, the colonial state retained a relatively free hand to manage its own resources, and continued to do so, even as Congress regularly restricted its ability to engage in practices that might affect the metropole's finances or credit.

When the PNB opened its New York office in 1917, the opportunities to leverage the colonial state's resources dramatically expanded. Initially, there was some hope that it would become a branch of the newly created Federal Reserve System – a move that, if acceptable to Washington, would have dramatically expanded its influence and access to capital.[83] It was, however, quickly decided that as a technically foreign bank this would be in violation of the Federal Reserve Act. An additional complication arose because New York banking laws prevented the PNB from holding its own currency reserves. Consequently, the gold was deposited in a variety of private banks and stored to the credit of the PNB.[84] Colonial authorities, however, were quick to see that this necessity could prove beneficial as well. Thus, New York banks that were friendly to the colonial government could expect deposits, as could banks in politically important states.

[80] Forbes, *Philippine Islands*, I, 401–2.
[81] Harrison to Conant, November 5, 1914; Harrison Papers, Box 19.
[82] Luthringer, *The Gold-Exchange Standard*, 22.
[83] Ibid., 92.
[84] Ibid., 102.

Not long after the PNB's creation, for example, the insular treasurer wrote to Gilbert Hitchcock (D-NE), Chairman of the Senate Committee on the Philippines, with a generous proposal. "[W]e have some quite large deposits in the New York banks," the treasurer reported. "It is our intention to distribute them to other banks outside of New York in the United States. And thinking that you possibly have some banks in Omaha which you would like to name as depositories, I would like to transfer possibly six hundred thousand dollars gold from New York to your state."[85] Naturally, this was an offer that Hitchcock and two Nebraska banks were happy to accept.[86]

The real difficulty, however, arose as a result of the bank's inability to separate its currency trading operations from the PNB's own funds. In its zeal to increase the PNB's resources, the insular government paid little attention to the intermingling of the bank's commercial funds and those of the government's currency reserves – an oversight with predictably disastrous consequences. Through a variety of complex accounting missteps, gold that was supposed to be held to the credit of the Gold Reserve Fund was eventually credited to the PNB's open account and subsequently used to finance more loans – a violation of both banking regulations and common sense.[87] In short, the gold was being counted twice: first on the PNB's own books to finance development loans in the Philippines and second by the insular treasurer as hard currency reserves. The result, although nobody seems to have recognized it at the time, was tremendous inflation and a completely inadequate gold reserve fund. It did, however, allow the PNB access to a substantial amount of capital, which it promptly provided for development loans.

The situation could perhaps have been salvaged if these loans remained sound, but this was not to be the case. These very loans became increasingly toxic as borrowers began to default on their debts following the end of World War I, leaving the colonial government with a currency that was, in essence, backed by a series of increasingly worthless securities. Prior to the reckoning, however, the Gold Reserve Fund provided Harrison's colonial government with vast amounts of capital to engage in its own, ever more fantastic development schemes – and, because such capital was presumably used to back the colonial state's own currency, such practices raised no objections from Congress.

INVESTMENTS: RAILROADS, NATIONAL INDUSTRIES, AND EXPORT AGRICULTURE

Notwithstanding the eventual outcome of Harrison's development policies, for a time they seemed to promise sustained prosperity in the Philippines. In the seven years following his inauguration as governor, the colonial government would purchase

---

[85] A. P. Fitzsimmons to Gilbert Hitchcock, December 14, 1916; RG 350, Box 711 (Serial 14221). See also RG 46, Senate Committee on the Philippines, Box 66. A. P. Fitzsimmons to Gilbert Hitchcock, February 13, 1917; RG 46, Senate Committee on the Philippines, Box 66.

[86] A. P. Fitzsimmons to P. L. Hall, Central National Bank, December 15, 1916. RG 46, Senate Committee on the Philippines, Box 66. A. P. Fitzsimmons to P. L. Hall, Central National Bank, December 15, 1916. RG 46, Senate Committee on the Philippines, Box 66.

[87] For the most detailed account of the banking crisis in the Philippines, see Luthringer, *The Gold-Exchange Standard* and Nagano, *State and Finance in the Philippines*.

the MRC. It would establish a Public Utilities Board and create a series of state enterprises, including a National Coal Company, a National Cement Company, and a National Development Company, and, through the PNB, it would provide generous loans to fuel the industrialization of sugar processing.[88] Much of this development, as in the earlier Republican period, was driven by Harrison's own ideological commitment to ideas that were then in vogue in Democratic circles in the United States, and he would marshal the colonial government's own resources to shape the colony according to these theories.

Railroad Nationalization

Among the most radical interventions into the colonial economy during the Democratic administration was the nationalization of the MRC, the largest industrial interest in the archipelago. Despite the fact that the railroads were supposed to spur American investment in the Philippines, both the MRC and the PRC had struggled to maintain financial viability even with the generous loan terms provided by the colonial government. As discussed in Chapter 6, construction costs on both railroads had far exceeded their original estimates. Indeed, the owners of the PRC had long been willing to sell their shares to the government, and White & Co. had approached the government as early as 1909 about the matter. The MRC was in better shape, but by 1914 its directors refused to proceed with further construction unless the colonial government provided even more guaranteed loans.

Unlike his predecessor, however, Harrison was unwilling to provide more subsidies. Although he suspected that corruption was responsible for a significant proportion of the railroads' inflated costs, the MRC's desperate financial straits also seemed to offer an opportunity to gain direct state control over one of the major engines for colonial economic growth.[89] As he wrote to Secretary of War, Lindley Garrison, in January 1914, just months after his arrival, "My own desire would be to see the Government take over the management of all the Philippine railroads since we are already involved . . . in an annual expenditure of about ₱600,000 to meet interest on their bonds."[90]

As with the plan for a national bank, the most concerted opposition to the nationalization of the colonial railroads came from Washington. For a time, the BIA, Secretary of War Garrison, and even Quezon believed that any such plan would seriously jeopardize the Jones Bill, since the railroads had for so long been presented as an unqualified triumph of colonial development. "I am firmly of the opinion that to allow now the railroad to go into hands of a receiver would seriously hurt Philippine policies of the administration," Quezon wrote to Harrison, "because the opposition would at once make much capital out of the failure of the railroad to prove that the new policies are ruining the country."[91] McIntyre and Garrison entirely concurred with this assessment. Both recommended that Harrison prepare an additional ₱2.5 million loan to provide further financial assistance to the MRC, reasoning that "the avoidance of any appearances of the failure

[88] Stanley, *A Nation in the Making.*
[89] Harrison to Garrison, October 24, 1913; Harrison Papers, Box 42.
[90] Harrison to Garrison, January 11, 1914; Harrison Papers, Box 42.
[91] Quezon to Harrison, November 11, 1914; Harrison Papers, Box 25.

of this great enterprise in the Islands are of controlling importance."[92] Harrison reluctantly complied with these orders, providing the MRC with small loans to keep it afloat throughout the Jones Bill negotiations.

At the same time, however, through his Public Utilities Board, the governor was hastening the MRC's decline. He had never abandoned his plans to nationalize the MRC – a move that would give him control of the colony's most significant corporation and simultaneously remove some of his most vehement critics (the beleaguered PRC was far more cooperative). Although the colonial government had a brief scare when it appeared that an immediate independence bill might pass – a situation Harrison feared would make bonds for the purchase of the MRC impossible to sell – the adoption of the more conservative Jones Bill put such fears to rest.[93] In truth, the nationalization of the railroad proved surprisingly easy. After all, Speyer and the remaining investors had every reason to sell their interest in the railroad to the government. The MRC had long been dependent on the colonial state for subsidies, and if the government no longer wished to provide such support, it made sense to get out of the business altogether. In 1916, Speyer & Co. quickly settled for the rather generous terms that Harrison offered: $4 million (financed with another bond sale) in payment for the railroad's stock and the assumption of $10.5 million of the MRC's bonded debt.[94]

Harrison's decision to proceed with the nationalization of the MRC would prove to be among his most controversial policies. While former Republican administrators – Forbes and Taft chief among them – criticized this apparently un-American decision to involve the government so directly in industry, more sympathetic observers focused on the generosity of the purchase price.[95] After all, $4 million in cash seemed to be a rather favorable offer for a company with over $10 million in debt and nearly worthless stock. In his 1917 history of the Philippines – one that, for the most part, is an admirably balanced account of the early Harrison years – Charles Elliot described it as "unjust to the Filipino people" and "disastrous to the treasury."[96] Even Harrison later acknowledged this as a rather unusual move, he took care to remind his readers that "railroads are generally owned and operated by the governments in all near-by countries and colonies."[97] It did not hurt that control over the islands' major railroad would also allow the governor to direct its development without the need to negotiate with private interests.[98]

In most respects, however, government ownership of the railway did not lead to a dramatic change in policies. As Arturo Corpuz notes in his careful study of the colonial railway system, a longstanding goal of the railroad's American directors

[92] McIntyre to Harrison, November 11, 1914; Harrison Papers, Box 25.
[93] Harrison to McIntyre, March 31, 1916; Harrison Papers, Box 26. Indeed, Harrison was so worried that the independence bill might affect the sale of the railroad that in 1916, when the original bill appeared likely pass, he requested that Jones include provisions that would simultaneously authorize the government to purchase the railroad. McIntyre to Jones, February 23, 1916; Harrison Papers, Box 26.
[94] Elliott, *Philippines to the End of Commission Government*, 312.
[95] See Forbes, *Philippine Islands* for a supportive view.
[96] Elliot, *Philippines to the End of Commission Government*, 311.
[97] Harrison, *The Corner-Stone of Philippine Independence*, 255.
[98] Stanley, *Nation in the Making*, 226.

was to transform the MRC from a passenger railroad into a freight railroad.[99] Only freight revenue, it was thought, would provide enough business to make it a viable operation, while simultaneously reducing the cost for sugar processing and export. American railroad policy in both administrations was shaped by efforts to open up new sections of the archipelago for development through expanded service to agriculturally productive regions.[100] While the railroad directors had to report to the government after 1917, the administration was far from hostile to Filipino or American firms that were investing in sugar; indeed, the development of the Philippine sugar industry as a major export crop remained at the heart of the government's policies.

To serve the growing sugar industry in Pampanga, for example, a new branch line to Floridablanca (about 55 miles northwest of Manila) had earlier been constructed off the major north–south MRC line. In 1918, a group of American investors proposed that the MRC extend this branch a few miles farther from Floridablanca to the village of Carmen, where they proposed to build a sugar processing plant, commonly known as a "central." This request was not uncommon, but the debate that it generated is particularly illustrative of the pro-sugar policies pursued by the government-owned railroad. At a meeting to debate this proposal – with Governor-General Harrison in attendance – James Rafferty, an American and the director of the Bureau of Commerce and Industry, condemned the proposed extension as wasteful and unnecessary. In his memo to the board, he noted that the construction was "exclusively for the benefit of a corporation which is well able to supply its railroad extension."[101] The MRC general manager, however, came out strongly in favor of the extension, which, he argued, would benefit the villagers of Carmen and provide much-needed freight revenue to the line. In the end, the arguments for the line extension carried the day.[102]

What requires explanation, then, is not change in the government's railroad policy, but consensus that it should use the MRC to promote export agriculture. Certainly the role of wealthy Filipino and American sugar-processing interests played a role in soliciting this support from the government. As many scholars have noted, the larger shift from exclusive American control of the colonial government to an active Filipino-led legislature did little to stop the march to a cash-crop economy based on sugar, hemp, and copra.[103] Yet the role of Harrison's beliefs in theories that government-owned railroads and utilities could better direct development should not be obscured. "I am and have for some years been a strong believer in government ownership of railroads wherever that policy is feasible," he had written to the Secretary of War not long after his arrival in the Philippines. "The long series of scandals and frauds connected with the construction of the Manila Railroad Company certainly afford us an object lesson in how private ownership

[99] Arturo G. Corpuz, *The Colonial Iron Horse: Railroads and Regional Development in the Philippines, 1875–1935* (Quezon City: University of the Philippines Press, 1999), 184.

[100] Ibid., 172.

[101] Ibid., 181.

[102] The new line was finished in 1919, leading to a dramatic increase in the Floridablanca branch's receipts, which increased from ₱94,806 in 1918 to ₱368,696 in 1920. Corpuz, *Colonial Iron Horse*, 180.

[103] O. D. Corpuz, *An Economic History of the Philippines* (Quezon City: University of the Philippines Press, 1997).

of railroads may not be ideal."[104] No less an authority than William Jennings Bryan considered it an eminently sensible policy. "You are entirely right," he wrote to Harrison. "The government should own the railroad there. If, in this country a people as intelligent as ours find it difficult, if not impossible, to protect themselves from injustice at the hands of domestic railroad corporations, how can a people like the Filipinos hope to protect themselves from injustice at the hands of foreign railroad corporations?"[105] As Bryan's hearty endorsement suggests, at the root of Harrison's decision to nationalize the railways was a belief, popular among some liberal Progressives, that public utilities and railroads ought to be owned by the state. Unable to accomplish such reform in the United States, they applied this policy to their largest colony – initially with great success – and saw railroad revenues increase from ₱4.4 million in 1916 to ₱10.8 million in 1919.[106]

Agricultural Industrialization and Government Corporations

Along with the nationalization of the MRC came the creation of a variety of national industrial corporations. In 1917, the National Coal Company was established to offset the price of coal and received ₱3.1 million in government funds over the next three years.[107] The National Petroleum Company, National Iron Company, National Cement Company, and the Coconuts Product Company followed in 1918. The most powerful of these – and the longest lasting – was the National Development Company, which Harrison later reported, "really permits the Philippine Government to enter indirectly into almost any sort of business deemed to be in the interests of the people of the islands."[108] For the most part, however, the business of all of these government corporations was export agriculture – specifically the production of sugar, hemp, and coconut oil.

With the passage of the Payne–Aldrich Act in 1909 and the Underwood Tariff of 1913, the Philippines effectively gained the right to export sugar duty free to the United States. Yet local sugar producers lacked the centrifugal sugar processing plants (known as sugar centrals) that would allow them to manufacture the high-grade refined sugar that was commonly sold in the American market. Without these industrial plants, only low-grade *muscovado* sugar could be produced, which commanded a much lower price, leaving the Filipino producers heavily in debt.[109] Although US investors had developed two modern centrals by 1910, the congressionally imposed restrictions that prevented Americans from owning large tracts of land limited the interest of American firms in Philippine sugar production. Moreover, the relative lack of investment capital available in the islands meant that even enterprising Filipino producers had difficulty upgrading their facilities. "What is undoubtedly needed in the sugar region of the Philippines is the investment of substantial amount of new capital in the erection of modern 'centrals' or mills,"

[104] Stanley, *Nation in the Making*, 231.
[105] Bryan to Harrison, May 11, 1916; Harrison Papers, Box 18.
[106] Charles Edward Russell, *The Outlook for the Philippines* (New York: The Century Co., 1922), 148.
[107] Harrison, *Corner-Stone of Philippine Independence*, 259.
[108] Ibid., 261.
[109] Willis, "The Philippine National Bank," 435.

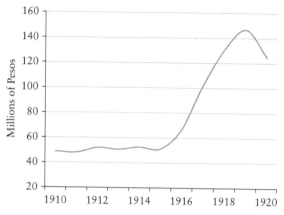

FIGURE 7.2. *Philippine currency in circulation.*
Source: Adapted from Luthringer, *The Gold-Exchange Standard.*

explained Parker Willis.[110] Indeed, the development of these modern methods was precisely what the colonial government intended to finance.

In the last four years of Harrison's administration, the government cooperatives – flush with cash from the PNB – would support an enormous bubble of speculative investment to expand Philippine agricultural exports. With ₱26 million of financing, 18 modern centrals were in operation by 1919, as well as 41 new coconut oil mills. Although it was unknown at that time, Figures 7.2 and 7.3 demonstrate the shocking decline of the colonial gold reserve fund, and the accompanying spike in currency in circulation caused by the PNB's generous loans.

As is often the case, easy access to credit was the central cause of this economic bubble. Parker Willis, who designed the bank and took a leave of absence from the Federal Reserve to serve as its first director, shared many of the goals of the administration. He, too, saw the bank as a way to dramatically increase Philippine exports and to expand the economy. Yet Willis, whose approached banking was conservative and academic, quickly became unpopular with *Nacionalista* leaders who hoped to use the bank as a promotional tool for the economy and their own political goals.

The aggressive lending policy that soon became a hallmark of PNB business was largely the work of General Venancio Concepción, a veteran of the revolution and friend of Speaker Osmeña, who served as PNB president beginning in 1918. Some combination of crony capitalism and a genuine desire to promote Philippine development and stabilize export prices led Concepción to make a number of ill-advised loans during the next two years. The government had ample warning that many of the bank's practices were unsound. Even Harrison's own brother, Archibald Harrison, who served as a director of the PNB, had warned that the bank was granting development loans for land that could never be economically cultivated.[111]

[110] Ibid., 436.
[111] Stanley, *Nation in the Making*, 241.

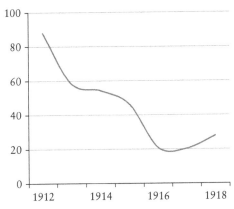

FIGURE 7.3. *Percent of Gold Standard Fund held in reserve.*
Source: Adapted from Luthringer, *The Gold-Exchange Standard.*

The government had, for example, received fair warning from its advisors in New York as early as the summer of 1918 to expect a contraction of the sugar market, yet it continued to finance the development of more centrals. In addition, Philippine hemp producers were given generous access to financing. The Philippine Fiber and Produce Company, which had secured a ₱1.6 million line of credit, was later authorized by Concepción for a total of ₱4.6 million in loans. When the hemp market declined in the latter half of 1918, the bank authorized more loans to hemp exporters in a misguided effort to buy hemp and stabilize the price.[112]

Nevertheless, this new infusion of capital, coupled with a dramatic increase in commodity prices during World War I, fueled an unprecedented boom in sugar and coconut oil throughout the Philippines. Between 1919 and 1920, sugar became the most valuable product of the islands, and coconut oil, which was not even commercially manufactured in 1917, became a leading export.[113] Although much of this wealth would later prove illusory, for a time it seemed that Harrison's state-led development strategy was marvelously successful. "Can any one who was in Manila in 1918 and 1919 forget the financial boom of those years?," the governor would later wistfully ask in a book about his administration. "Men were 'getting rich quick' through oil, hemp, coal, and shipping."[114]

Economic Collapse and Republicanism

Sadly, this prosperity would be short-lived – and with it, the proof that the Philippines was ready for independence. With the end of World War I, the bubble in agricultural commodities that fueled so much development in the islands burst.[115] Corporate and agricultural borrowers who had received loans far in excess of their

[112] Ibid., 242–3.
[113] Corpuz, *Economic History of the Philippines*, 247.
[114] Harrison, *Corner-Stone of Philippine Independence*, 259.
[115] Corpuz, *Economic History of the Philippines*, 248.

collateral now began to default. In the case of the sugar industry, for example, the PNB had lent ₱21 million *more* than it was authorized to do – a fact that became catastrophic as a variety of sugar-refining companies began to collapse. This would have been bad enough, yet the currency reserve itself had been slowly depleted to make these very loans. By 1920, as the Philippine peso began to trade unofficially at 12 cents to the dollar, even the governor became concerned.[116] "I find your various cablegrams and letters about the bank," he wrote to the BIA, "and am seriously concerned about the continued depletion of the reserve fund."[117] By the end of December 1920, with ₱24.2 million notes in circulation and ₱134.7 million of deposits, the PNB and Insular Treasury had only ₱3.7 million between them.[118]

As one economist later wrote, "A run seems to have been prevented by the knowledge that the Insular Government owned ninety-four per cent of the capital stock of the Bank, and that back of the immediate responsibility of the Insular Government was the moral responsibility of the Government of the United States."[119] In the final accounting, the total losses amounted to more than ₱72 million. The bank's capital had been completely wiped out.[120] "Our examination thus far reveals the fact that the bank has operated during almost the entire period of its existence . . . in violation of every principle which prudence, intelligence, and even honesty could dictate," the accounting firm Haskins and Sells later reported in its audit of the bank.[121]

This dire situation at first led the US Treasury through the BIA to demand an immediate reduction of the currency in circulation and an end to further loans by the PNB. Initially, Concepción, the PNB's director, refused: "We must not lose sight of the fact," he wrote, "that this bank, unlike the others, on account of its being national, is in some way subordinated to the policy pursued by the Government in the way of economic plans."[122] By late 1920, however, the news of the PNB's instability had become so severe that most banks were refusing to accept its drafts; a situation that became even more desperate after it was revealed a few months later that the manager of the PNB's Shanghai branch had lost nearly ₱10 million in illegal currency speculation.[123] In 1922, the colonial government was forced to issue a ₱23 million bond just to stabilize the currency – and even this was not enough. Much of the ₱12 million Manila Port Works bonds as well as the ₱20 million Public Improvement bonds were also used to prop up the currency.[124] In the end, the PNB debacle increased the bonded debt of the Philippine government by nearly ₱40 million.[125] More damaging, however, was the support this banking collapse gave to the Harrison administration's Republican critics – most notably Cameron Forbes. Harrison and Quezon's efforts to use the financial and political autonomy

---

[116] Russell, *Outlook for the Philippines*, 150.
[117] Harrison to McIntyre, July 11, 1920; Harrison Papers, Box 26.
[118] Luthringer, *The Gold-Exchange Standard*, 157.
[119] Ibid., 157.
[120] Quoted in Luthringer, *The Gold-Exchange Standard*, 156.
[121] Ibid., 155.
[122] Stanley, *Nation in the Making*, 247.
[123] Ibid., 247.
[124] Luthringer, *The Gold-Exchange Standard*, 209.
[125] Ibid., 209.

of the colonial state to bootstrap the Philippines into stability and development had backfired in a spectacular way.

With the election of Warren Harding, the Republicans returned to Manila in 1921. Cameron Forbes and the new governor-general, Leonard Wood, were dispatched to assess the Philippines's readiness for independence. Although they made a thorough tour of the islands, their conclusion was preordained: the Philippines was not ready for independence.[126] The PNB was marked out for special opprobrium, with their lengthy report describing it as "one of the most unfortunate and darkest pages in Philippine history."[127] Now, they concluded, with the currency reserves depleted and the peso "practically a fiat currency," only the colony's status as a possession of the United States was preventing total financial collapse. As Dean Worcester would write later, in an attack on Wilson and Harrison that seems to capture the blinding fury of the former Republican-era colonial officials,

For seven years after 1913 authority to direct and control the actual government of the Philippine Islands was vested in two Virginians. One had followed an academic career until it led him to the White House. The other had become a Tammany Congressman. Both, however, were blood and bone of the Old Dominion, and of Jeffersonian Democracy. Principal and agent, these two southerners translated their philosophy of politics and of life into law and administration in a distant dependency where they were practically uncontrolled either by the immediate consequences of their acts, or by any effective public opinion at home. Only because the American Congress exercises final authority over the Philippine Islands did they fail to carry their policy to its logical conclusion, the complete separation of the Philippines from the United States.[128]

In many ways, Worcester's assessment was right. Harrison's power in the islands was largely unchecked by public opinion or congressional oversight, but he had only built upon the tools of autonomous colonial government left to him by his Republican predecessors, of whom Worcester was one. If the Taft and Forbes-era Republicans had used a variety of creative arrangements to draw the Philippines in closer to the United States, Harrison had relied on a similarly autonomous capacity in his attempt to move it quickly along the road to independence. Few of his initiatives – the purchase of the railways, the establishment of a national bank, and the use of that bank's capital to issue millions of pesos worth of bad loans – would have been possible without the colonial state's long relationship to American capital, and its network of BIA officials who had learned how to operate while attracting little notice from Congress.

Although such autonomy was put in the service of a decidedly different ideological agenda, Harrison, if anything, was even more aggressive in developing the colonial government's autonomy within the restrictions set forth by Congress. Quezon and the Filipino elite were equally aware that the tools of autonomy could be leveraged to demonstrate Manila's fitness for independent rule. The consequence of their zeal was, of course, the banking collapse, but their *ability* to engage in such experiments was due to earlier efforts to bind the Philippines to the United States.

[126] Stanley, *Nation in the Making*, 262.
[127] *Report of the Governor General of the Philippine Islands* (Washington, DC: Government Printing Office, 1922), 37.
[128] Worcester, *Philippines*, 725–6.

Perhaps the chief result of the banking collapse was the support it gave conservative forces to delay commonwealth status for the Philippines. The colonial government's finances would recover with the economic boom of the 1920s, but the legacy of the PNB failure lent credence to conservative voices for years. Indeed, Wood would spend most of his term in office engaged in internecine battles with Quezon and the Filipino elites in an attempt to slow this process.[129] After Harrison and Quezon's reforms, however, there was no question that the islands were headed for full home rule, but with the Republicans back in control, Quezon and his allies in Manila would need to wait for more than a decade until the Tydings–McDuffie Act of 1934 set the terms for full separation.

PUERTO RICO UNDER WILSON: COMPARATIVE ASSESSMENT

Unlike the Philippines, there was little question that Puerto Rico would remain a permanent colony after the success of American plantation agriculture. Considering the dramatic changes in the Philippines, perhaps the most surprising development in Puerto Rico was that Wilson largely followed the policies of the previous administration. As discussed in Chapter 6, the BIA had resumed control of the island at the beginning of the Taft administration, and it now moved to present citizenship as a panacea for political unrest in the colony. Only citizenship, the agency claimed, would end the calls for independence from the Union Party and retain Puerto Rico permanently as a territory of the United States.[130] Consequently, Wilson's appointees worked to speed the Philippines along on the path to independence; in Puerto Rico, they worked to quell unrest and bind the island closer to the United States while permitting a small number of liberal reforms.

The new governor, Arthur Yager – a former classmate of Wilson's at Johns Hopkins – appointed more Puerto Ricans to the Executive Council and maintained a cordial relationship with the Unionists. He also worked with William Jones of the House Insular Affairs Committee and Resident Commissioner Muñoz Rivera to draw up the new organic act. The administration's proposal was certainly more liberal than the BIA's preferred legislation, but it still left the American governor firmly in charge of the island. Moreover, citizenship was offered to guarantee permanent colonialism, and neither Congress nor Wilson had any interest in providing Puerto Rico with a path to statehood. As Jones himself declared, "If Porto Rico were admitted to statehood there would be two senators and at least half a dozen Porto Rican representatives; and the fear exists that they might exercise a decisive influence in the United States Congress and practically enact laws for the government of the United States."[131] Such a possibility, it seems, left statehood with almost no support in Washington.

The Jones–Shafroth Act of 1917 – passed one year after the Philippines's Jones Act – did provide citizenship for all Puerto Ricans, except to those who affirmatively objected. The Jones Act provided Puerto Rico with an elected Senate, but it also allowed the colonial governor a veto and provided Congress with the

[129] Corpuz, *Economic History of the Philippines*, 248.
[130] Cabán, *Constructing a Colonial People*, 199.
[131] Quoted in Cabán, *Constructing a Colonial People*, 201.

right to annul any laws passed by the two Puerto Rican assemblies.[132] Despite the bill's importance to Puerto Ricans, it received scant attention from the Senate, which was primarily concerned with the war in Europe. Only a dozen senators showed much interest in the debate, and even John D. Shafroth (D-CO), Chairman of the Senate Committee on Pacific Islands and Puerto Rico, remained woefully uniformed about basic details of colonial policy.[133]

Although only 288 people refused American citizenship, most understood that the Jones Act was designed to keep Puerto Rico in permanent colonial status. It would not be pushed to independence like the Philippines, but it would also not be considered for statehood like Hawai'i or other territories with significant white populations.[134] In large part, the Jones Act was a victory for the BIA. It retained control over Puerto Rico, but collective naturalization did little to achieve the BIA's goal of creating a contented colonial population. Those who favored independence felt trapped as it seemed that the island was doomed to remain a colony with limited self-government; those who favored statehood were left to hope that the United States would eventually permit it to enter as a state – but few Puerto Ricans favored permanent colonial status.[135]

The Philippines and Puerto Rico, of course, were not the only places where the supposedly internationalist Wilson administration would make use of its Republican predecessors' tools for greater executive autonomy in foreign policy. In the Caribbean, the failure of Dollar Diplomacy would trigger two formal invasions of the Dominican Republic and Haiti, as Wilson and Bryan attempted to "discipline" their quasi-colonies on the island of Hispaniola.

WILSONIAN DOLLAR DIPLOMACY

Soon after taking office, Woodrow Wilson made his objections to the Taft administration's Dollar Diplomacy arrangements perfectly clear. In a 1913 address at the Southern Commercial Congress in Mobile, he noted that Latin American nations "have had harder bargains driven with them in the manner of loans than any other peoples in the world. Interest had been exacted of them, that was not exacted of anybody else, because the risk was said to be greater; and then securities were taken that destroyed that risk – an admirable arrangement for those who were forcing the terms!"[136] If this did not suggest the new direction Wilson planned to take, the appointment of William Jennings Bryan as his Secretary of State certainly did. Dollar Diplomacy, according to Bryan, was nothing more than "a repudiation of the fundamental principles of morality."[137]

The threat that the Great Commoner posed to the receivership system was hardly lost on American bankers. Brown Brothers and J. W. Seligman, which had

---

[132] Trías Monge, *Puerto Rico*, 75.
[133] Ibid., 74.
[134] Ibid., 76.
[135] Ibid.
[136] Albert B. Hart, ed., *Selected Addresses and Public Papers of Woodrow Wilson* (New York: Boni & Liveright, 1918), 18.
[137] Quoted in Lars Schoultz, *Beneath the United States: A History of U.S. Policy Toward Latin America* (Cambridge, MA: Harvard University Press, 1998), 220.

so recently been persuaded by Knox to extend a loan to Nicaragua, threatened to pull out. At the very least, as one State Department official wrote to Assistant Secretary of State Huntington Wilson, they would extend no more credit "in the absence of any knowledge of what the attitude of the incoming administration might be."[138] These, of course, were the exact fears that J. P. Morgan had expressed in 1905. Without a formal contract, how could bankers have any guarantee that their investments would be safe in a new administration? For his part, Huntington Wilson tried to smooth the transition and helpfully summarized the policy for the new Secretary as "intelligent team work."[139]

Yet as the bankers would soon discover, they had little reason to worry. Both Wilson and Bryan embraced Dollar Diplomacy as a central tool in their own Caribbean policy, especially after the outbreak of the war in Europe seemed to make American dominance of the Caribbean all the more important. Bryan himself, it seems, did not have any serious objections to the idea of using loans to stabilize countries in Latin American and the Caribbean. Rather, much like Governor-General Harrison in the Philippines, he objected to the appearance that the state was doing the work of bankers. Soon after assuming office, he had proposed to Wilson that the United States should *directly* lend money to the Caribbean nations. "If, for instance, in the stating of your policy, you propose, with the approval of Congress, that the Government lend its credit . . . we will offer what no one else is in a position to offer, and show that our friendship is practical and sufficient, as well as disinterested."[140] Wilson, however, quickly rejected this idea "as a novel and radical proposal."[141]

Rather than repudiate the partnership with the bankers or question the wisdom of the receiverships, the Wilson administration recommended yet more loans and increased American control in the Caribbean. Indeed, even as evidence of the policy's spectacular failure presented itself in the Dominican Republic, the secretary would recommend that Haiti, too, should be controlled through a receivership. "The success of this Government's efforts in Santo Domingo," he wrote to Wilson "would it seems to me, suggest the application of the same methods to Hayti [sic] whenever the time is ripe."[142] His fellow Democrats met Bryan's curious support for Dollar Diplomacy with surprise and indignation. Despite a personal appeal from the Commoner himself, the Senate refused to support a more comprehensive receivership agreement with Nicaragua, according to *New York Times*, "on the ground that it is a return to the imperialism against which Secretary Bryan declaimed so vigorously in 1900."[143]

Undeterred, Bryan pressed on, eventually arranging a tighter receivership agreement with Nicaragua and extending American control to Haiti. Even these modified arrangements, however, soon proved too unstable to be sustained. Wilson

---

[138] Ibid., 220.

[139] Ibid., 209.

[140] Bryan to Wilson, October 28, 1913; Bryan to Wilson, July 17, 1913; Bryan Papers, Box 29. See also Bryan to Wilson, August 6, 1913; Bryan Papers, Box 45; Bryan to Wilson, February 21, 1914; Bryan Papers, Box 45.

[141] Wilson to Bryan, March 20, 1914; Bryan Papers, Box 45.

[142] Bryan to Wilson, January 7, 1915; Bryan Papers, Box 45.

[143] *New York Times*, June 19, 1914; Selig Adler, "Bryan and Wilsonian Caribbean Penetration," *Hispanic American Historical Review* 20 (May 1940): 216.

ordered the marines to occupy Haiti, and, a year later, extended military control to the Dominican Republic and Nicaragua. In an irony that became so familiar in later decades, the United States now needed to erect a formal colonial state to defend – with bullets – a policy designed to achieve hegemony through peaceful and informal means. Yet how this came about owes much to the convenience Bryan and Wilson found in the Dollar Diplomacy relationships established by their predecessors.

Haiti under American Occupation

A move to bring Haiti under a Dollar Diplomacy protectorate was underway well before Wilson took office. As the Dollar Diplomacy partnerships became an increasingly common practice, bankers became more willing to invest in less stable markets. Nowhere was this more evident than in Haiti. For decades, French banks had served Haiti's financial needs and France remained the republic's principal trading partner. This began to change in 1909, when National City and Speyer agreed to buy $800,000 worth of bonds from the German-owned Plaine du Cul-de-Sac (P.C.S.) railroad. In November of that same year, Speyer and National City had also attempted to secure control of the Haitian Banque Nationale, but lost out to a consortium of German investors who proceeded to float a new Haitian loan of 65 million francs.[144]

By 1909, however, both Speyer and National City had longstanding relationships with officials in the American foreign policy state, which they could now draw on to challenge their European rivals. Roger L. Farnham, a vice president at National City and the new president of the Haitian National Railroad, brought the Americans' objections to the State Department, where he skillfully invoked the specter of French and German influence in the Caribbean.[145] Politics more than economics was at the heart of the State Department's concerns: American investment in Haiti was negligible, amounting to less than ½ of 1 percent at this point.[146] Consequently, the State Department let it be known that it would object to any bank reorganization that did not give Americans at least a 50 percent share and control of the new Haitian bank. In January 1911, the Europeans agreed to these new terms, and Americans soon replaced the French as the directors of the newly recapitalized Banque Nationale. Farnham's plan, it seems, was to close a loan to refinance Haitian debts, while guaranteeing collection through the establishment of a Dominican-style receivership. Although the Taft administration had opposed such arrangements, the situation changed dramatically when Farnham himself became Bryan's chief advisor on Haiti.[147]

Bryan feared that a Haitian default would lead to European intervention in the Caribbean – and he now found the earlier Dollar Diplomacy arrangements an attractive tool to secure Haiti without involving Congress, while professing to the American legation in Haiti that "this Government was actuated wholly by a

---

[144] Hans Schmidt, *The United States Occupation of Haiti 1915–1934* (New Brunswick, NJ: Rutgers University Press, 1995 [1971]), 35–9.
[145] Munro, *Intervention and Dollar Diplomacy*, 331–2.
[146] Schmidt, *Occupation of Haiti*, 41.
[147] Ibid., 50.

disinterested desire to render assistance."[148] Of course, part of the reason for Haiti's instability was due to the fact that its payments on its foreign debt took up nearly 80 percent of its revenue.[149] By 1914, further political instability in Haiti and the intransigence of its leader, Davilmar Théodore, left Bryan open to suggestions by Farnham that an economic collapse in Haiti would give the French and German governments a reason to intervene. In December of that year, the secretary quickly approved a request from the National City Bank to remove $500,000 of the bank's gold reserve funds and to transport them to New York on an American gunboat. Farnham, however, was not satisfied, and he continued to draw attention to possible French and German interests in Haiti. Bryan, for reasons that remain entirely inexplicable, seems to have bought Farnham's agitprop and began to fear that France and Germany – two countries then at war! – would combine forces to take the Haitian harbor of Môle St. Nicolas.[150]

To be sure, Bryan's motivation was less about advancing American banking interests than in achieving order, stability, and American supremacy in the Caribbean – particularly because Haiti shared the island of Hispaniola with the Dominican Republic, which was already under American control. Wilson and Bryan were anxious to gain control of Môle-Saint-Nicolas, if not for the American Navy which already had Guantanamo Bay in Cuba, then to prevent foreign powers from securing it. He now wrote to Wilson to propose "a plan similar to that adopted in Santo Domingo – namely, send a Commission down there to bring the leaders together into agreement upon a provisional President, with a view of holding an election to be supervised by us – the choice of the people to be recognized and supported, as in Santo Domingo."[151]

Although Robert Lansing, who assumed the position of Secretary of State in June 1915, was less trusting of Farnham, he was, in the words of historian Hans Schmidt, "an ardent Germanophobe in his own right," which did nothing to put the United States off the path to intervention.[152] The situation deteriorated even further when a gruesome civil war tore Haiti apart, and resulted in the overthrow of Haitian President Vilbrun Guillaume Sam in July 1915 – the pretext used for intervention.[153] On July 28, 1915, Rear Admiral William B. Caperton landed in Port-au-Prince with over 300 marines. The Haitian government was forced to sign a treaty accepting an American financial advisor and customs receiver who would now be given control over its revenues and expenditures – a treaty that was approved by the US Senate, which believed that German interests were waiting in the wings.[154] This decision ushered in an American military occupation that would last until 1934.

Within a few weeks of Caperton's landing, the Americans had secured control of the Haitian government's revenues and customs houses in Port-au-Prince and

---

[148] Bryan to American Legation, Haiti, December 11, 1914; Bryan Papers, Box 45.
[149] Schmidt, *Occupation of Haiti*, 43.
[150] Ibid., 53.
[151] Bryan to Wilson, January 7, 1915; Bryan Papers, Box 45; Bryan to Wilson, April 2, 1915; Bryan Papers, Box 45.
[152] Schmidt, *Occupation of Haiti*, 57.
[153] Rosenberg, *Financial Missionaries*, 82–3.
[154] Ibid., 82–3.

other coastal towns.[155] Wilson and Secretary of State Lansing had few concrete plans, aside from protecting Haiti from the (almost certainly fictional) threat of a German invasion, and stabilizing the Haitian state until a friendly president could be elected.[156] After being refused by several prominent Haitians, Philippe Sudre Dartiguenave, the president of Haitian Senate, was persuaded to serve under US "protection," and assumed the office in August 1915 while the entire country was placed under martial law.

The terms of the treaty soon followed the basic blueprint for American occupations and were dictated to Dartiguenave and the Haitian government: financial control through a customs receivership, a local constabulary with America officers, and American management of public works.[157] As in the Dominican Republic, the occupation government labored to maintain the fiction that Haiti remained a sovereign nation – a political necessity to avoid congressional scrutiny. The Haitian police force or *Gendarmerie d'Haiti*, for example, remained officially part of the Haitian government. In fact, even the US Marine Corps officers in charge of the units were officially given commissions by Haiti.[158] As the tortured language of the Gendarmerie Agreement explained, "All American officers of the Gendarmerie shall be appointed by the President of Haiti upon nomination by the President of the United States, and will be replaced by Haitians when they have shown by examination that they are fit for command."[159]

These marine officers in the Gendarmerie were given a unit of Haitian soldiers and ruled over their assigned jurisdictions with nearly unlimited power. One American civilian would later recall that the marine officers in the Gendarmerie became judge, paymaster, director of schools, and tax collector to towns throughout Haiti.[160] Yet American military officials, from the most junior marine to senior officers in the Navy, rarely received clear instructions from Washington. In the early months of the occupation, for example, Admiral Caperton himself seemed utterly bewildered by the state of the occupation. Writing from his flagship in June 1916 to the American customs receiver in Port-au-Prince, Caperton confessed that he had heard little from Washington and felt "entirely in the dark."[161] Even by December 1917, the situation had not improved. As Brigadier Commander Eli K. Cole wrote, "It is very unfortunate, from my point of view, that I have absolutely no knowledge as to the policy that our Government desires to follow in regard to Haiti."[162]

With Haiti under US control, the State Department next moved to refund its debt. The National City Bank made the rather extraordinary demand that these new Haitian bonds be designated by the Treasury Department as security for

[155] Schmidt, *Occupation of Haiti*, 70.
[156] Ibid., 71.
[157] Ibid., 75.
[158] For a careful study of American marines during the Haitian occupation, see Mary A. Renda, *Taking Haiti: Military Occupation and the Culture of U.S. Imperialism, 1915–1940* (Chapel Hill, NC: University of North Carolina Press, 2001).
[159] Gendarmerie Agreement; Butler Papers, Accession 1, Box 6.
[160] Dr. S. G. Inman quoted in Schmidt, *Occupation of Haiti*, 90.
[161] Caperton to Charles Conard, June 8, 1916; Caperton Papers.
[162] Quoted in Schmidt, *Occupation of Haiti*, 109.

public bank deposits and that the US receivership remain in Haiti during the entire life of the bonds.[163] Although the United States did not make a formal commitment to remain in Haiti for that long, the flyer advertising the bonds sale (as had frequently been done in the Philippines) emphasized the structure of the receivership and the moral commitment of the United States to supervise repayment.[164]

With the focus on the war in Europe, however, the creation of a new Occupation government in Haiti occurred almost without notice from Washington or the press. As one historian writes, "Following the 1921–22 reorganization, the Occupation emerged as a static, internally disciplined institution capable of efficiently sitting on Haiti. There were few spectacular developments or changes in American policy until the strikes and riots of 1929."[165] Left alone, the Occupation adopted what had now become a blueprint for American quasi-colonies, and emerged with a nearly obsessive focus on road building, eventually constructing a 170-mile road from Port-au-Prince to Cap Haïtien, in the hope that Haiti would become attractive for American investment. The little development that was achieved, however, was always in service to Haiti's debts – the bonds that were sold by National City to refinance its former debt. Political uprisings in 1929 would eventual lead to US withdrawal in 1934, but for over a decade, Haiti would remain under American control and make faithful payments on the new debts it had accepted at gunpoint.

The occupation of Haiti was motivated by strategic concerns, but the model embraced by Bryan and Wilson was the one developed by their Republican predecessors in the Philippines and the Dominican Republic. It was attractive precisely because it asked Congress for so little. Although the Senate did approve the 1915 treaty, American obligations in this case were relatively minor – even the bond itself was not technically guaranteed by the US Treasury, as was the case with other colonial bonds. The use of this private money, however, left the United States supporting a military government that even its own marine officers found exploitative. Smedley Butler, who served as the first commander of the Occupation government, would later describe the US Occupation government as a "glorified bill-collecting agency."[166] Haitians themselves would finally make this Dollar Diplomacy policy expensive and politically embarrassing for the United States, and a series of uprisings in 1929 and a vicious crackdown by the Occupation government led the United States to look for a quick exit by the 1930s. For well over a decade, however, the receivership model pioneered by Roosevelt and Root kept Haiti under American control, and would poison United States–Haitian relations for the remainder of the twentieth century.

---

[163] Schmidt, *Occupation of Haiti*, 132.

[164] Ibid., 165.

[165] Ibid., 109.

[166] Hans Schmidt, *Maverick Marine: General Smedley Butler and the Contradictions of American Military History* (Lexington, KY: University Press of Kentucky, 1987), 232. Nevertheless, Butler's later objections are curious given that he maintained friendly relations with Farnham at the National City Bank throughout much of the occupation, and he asked for his help to obtain a posting in France during World War I. See Farnham to Butler, January 21, 1918; Butler Papers, Accession 2, Box 2.

THE DOMINICAN INTERVENTION

The fragility of the Dominican receivership model was apparent well before Wilson took office. Dominican President Ramón Cáceres was assassinated in November of 1911, prompting a scramble for the presidency by regional leaders throughout the island and leaving the Dominican Receivership insecure.[167] Although President Taft and his Republican administrators downplayed these tensions, it was clear by the beginning of the Wilson administration that the situation had become untenable. The United States initially responded to this instability by orchestrating the dismissal of one Dominican president and pressed his successor, Juan Jiménez, to agree to enhanced powers for the American financial advisor and the appointment of a second American as director of public works. Such reforms were, according to officials in the Wilson administration, intended to stabilize the Dominican government and allow it to continue to faithfully service its debt. When the Dominican Congress balked at this plan, the State Department responded by demanding even further power for its American representatives, including a command that the Dominican armed forces be disbanded and replaced, as had been done in the Philippines, with an American-controlled constabulary force.[168] Such demands did not receive a welcome reception in the Caribbean, although President Jiménez was more receptive than the Dominican Congress. Jiménez's Minister of War, General Desiderio Arias, eventually moved against the president and took effective control of Santo Domingo – a state of affairs entirely unacceptable to the American-controlled Receivership.[169]

In November of 1916, the commander of the Navy's Atlantic Cruiser Force, Captain Harry Knapp, was ordered to Santo Domingo. On arrival, Knapp declared a military government and effectively seized control of the Dominican state, declaring that he had arrived to return the Dominican Republic "to a condition of internal order that will enable it to observe the terms of the treaty [of 1907]."[170] Although the final push for formal intervention was due to a number of factors, fears of possible German influence during World War I and the need to protect the receivership and American bonds played a major role. As in Haiti, the military government received little attention from Washington. The goals of this intervention, however, aside from maintaining timely payments to the Dominican Republic's creditors, were never spelled out, leaving most decisions to the American administrators on the ground. The fact that the BIA recruited the vast majority of the local American officials from the Philippines meant that policies pioneered in Manila were quickly adopted in Santo Domingo.

Along with the usual focus on road construction and the training of a constabulary force, the military government attempted to improve trade with the United States by convincing the Dominican Congress to lower tariff rates an average of 38 percent, and removing all duties on a number of products, such as agricultural

[167] Healy, *Drive to Hegemony*, 161. The rising conflict between the Receivership and the Dominican government can be traced in RG 139 (SD-1-261-351), Box 4.
[168] Bruce J. Calder, *The Impact of Intervention: The Dominican Republic during the U.S. Occupation of 1916–1924* (Princeton, NJ: Markus Wiener, 2006 [1984]), 7.
[169] Calder, *Impact of Intervention*, 8.
[170] Ibid., 17.

and industrial machinery.[171] This was intended to provoke a reciprocal agreement from the United States – one that would never arrive.

Another thing that would not arrive was the economic prosperity long promised by the American government as a reward for Santo Domingo's punctilious payment of its debts. A dramatic fall in commodity prices in the early 1920s left Dominican sugar and tobacco growers facing major losses. As government revenues collapsed, the American military officials were now forced to ask Washington to authorize another series of loans simply to continue paying its bills. Millions more were authorized, with a hefty percentage going to the American bankers who originated the loans, putting the D.R. in further debt. But even with this new infusion of cash, the military government continued to operate in the red until its dissolution in 1924.[172]

The cause of the final withdrawal and the return of Dominican sovereignty was due primarily to Dominican nationalists who wasted no opportunity to bring attention to the incompetence of the American military government. The nationalists and their American allies were well aware that making the military government a national political issue was the surest way to guarantee a swift American departure. During 1920, Dominican writers and journalists continued to protest American rule, leading to domestic crackdowns by the military government, which only inflamed Dominican nationalism. By 1922, even Washington was looking for a swift exit from Santo Domingo.[173]

WILSONIAN EMPIRE

In 1921, the Senate launched an investigation into the occupations of Haiti and the Dominican Republic, as well as the role of bankers and foreign policy bureaucrats in developing the policies that led to the invasions.[174] Ironically, a policy designed to extend American hegemony "on the cheap" and to avoid congressional scrutiny became both expensive and highly politically visible. Yet Congress's actions came well after the damage had been done.

Although both Republican and Democratic Congresses had opposed any suggestion that bankers' bonds were guaranteed by the state (even in the Philippines), insular bureaucrats were able to develop creative institutional arrangements that effectively provided the same assurances. Congress's attempts to limit further extensions of the American Empire by refusing to approve even moderate treaties, however, only motivated foreign policy bureaucrats to rely on their private partners all the more. In the Philippines, the financial autonomy established by earlier Republican officials was embraced by the new Democratic administrators to push the Philippines along a path to development – a situation that nearly ended with the collapse of colonial finances. Such "progressivism by the sword" would end as

[171] Ibid., 75–6.
[172] Ibid., 81.
[173] Ibid., 237.
[174] 67th Congress, Senate Select Committee on Haiti and Santo Domingo, *Inquiry into Occupation and Administration of Haiti and Santo Domingo* (Washington, DC: Government Printing Office, 1922).

politically costly and counterproductive failures – a collective achievement of the Roosevelt, Taft, and Wilson administrations.[175]

For bankers, however, the collapse of the receivership system did little to temper their enthusiasm for securities in Latin America. In the 1920s, as the speculative fever in financial circles spread, they sold hundreds of millions of dollars of sovereign bonds to American investors.[176] The increased stability of the Latin American bond market that was due, in part, to Dollar Diplomacy contributed to this speculation, which itself would contribute to the onset of the Great Depression as the investor confidence in sovereign bond offerings began to evaporate at the close of the decade.

By the 1920s, the dream that formal colonialism would advertise the power and success of American institutions was dead. As the empire became a political liability for both Republicans and Democrats, even many of its early architects – Elihu Root chief among them – had reconsidered their position. The occupation of the Dominican Republic came to an abrupt end in 1924. Financial difficulties, combined with the efforts of Dominican nationalists to embarrass and obstruct the military government, led the Harding administration to support a quick exit, and on September 18, 1924, the last marines left Santo Domingo.

Haiti would face a longer occupation than the Dominican Republic, primarily because there seemed to be no clear way to guarantee the debt of American bondholders without a military presence. After a 1922 reorganization, the occupying marines continued to implement the legacy policies of American imperialism – road building and the punctilious payment of debts – with little instruction or interest from Washington. By 1929, however, strikes and riots had made the situation untenable, and by 1930 President Herbert Hoover began to push for an American departure.

Any exit hinged on the transfer of the Banque Nationale back to Haiti. Yet the advent of the Great Depression left the National City Bank – the Haitian Banque Nationale's American owner – with few options as it became increasingly clear that, as one State Department official reported, President Hoover wished "to withdraw from Haiti bag and baggage immediately if possible."[177] When the sale of the Banque Nationale to Haiti was finalized in 1935, the marines promptly withdrew. Although the exit from Haiti was due to Depression-era fatigue more than to a change in policy, it was celebrated by American officials as a positive example of President Hoover's new Good Neighbor policy.[178]

As the Caribbean occupations came to an end, the question of Philippine independence took center stage. By the 1930s, there was little question that the Philippines would gain its commonwealth status soon – and even the anti-independence groups were only working to delay the inevitable. The Depression, more than any gesture of good will, was the primary factor in finally pushing Congress to grant independence. The Hoover and later the Roosevelt administrations were eager to end

[175] Schmidt, *Occupation of Haiti*, 132.
[176] Barbara Stallings, *Banker to the Third World: U.S. Portfolio Investment in Latin America, 1900–1986* (Berkeley, CA: University of California Press, 1987).
[177] Quoted in Schmidt, *Occupation of Haiti*, 222.
[178] Ibid., 18.

criticism from American farmers that they were competing with Philippine agricultural producers, or from laborers who worried that Filipino immigration would take jobs from white Americans.

Roosevelt expressed the sentiment of many in Congress and his administration in a confidential meeting as the final details of the Philippine independence bill were being hammered out. "Let's get rid of the Philippines," the president said, "that's the most important thing. Let's be frank about it."[179] For its part, Congress, in the words of one historian, "now desired independence *from* the Philippines, complete and absolute, by a certain date; it was incapable of imagining the process of decolonization as taking more time, or requiring more care, than that which it had already prescribed."[180] Although the exact terms of the independence bill took some time to work out, few in Congress had any interest in retaining control over the islands. Finally, in 1934, the Tydings–McDuffie Act was passed. It granted the Philippines commonwealth status and total independence from the United States within 10 years. The age of American formal empire, which had been advertised as a great triumph of the American system, would end less than 40 years later in a series of military withdrawals and hastily considered legislation.

[179] Brands, *Bound to Empire*, 163.
[180] Theodore Friend, *Between Two Empires: The Ordeal of the Philippines, 1929–1946* (New Haven, CT: Yale University Press, 1965), 157.

8

Conclusion

The trouble is people in the United States don't care anything about the Philippines. After the war excitement subsided, people sank back into indifference. Wilson was inclined to do the opposite of what the Republicans had done. Harrison was sent there with the Democratic theory of immediate return of the Islands to their people. This theory was not reached by consideration but by prejudice against the Republicans . . . When a democracy undertakes to govern a colony or undertakes to carry on foreign affairs they do it damned badly.

—*Elihu Root* (1930)[1]

By the end of their lives, Elihu Root and Theodore Roosevelt would both reach the same conclusion about formal imperialism: It was incompatible with American democracy. Yet they arrived at this belief not because they considered their theories of Progressive, tutelary empire to be flawed, or because they found imperialism to be incompatible with the American liberal tradition. As Root explained, the structure of American mass democracy with its system of competing political parties, the provincial focus of most members of Congress, and the general indifference of the public made a rational, centralized colonial policy impossible. Democracy, to borrow a favorite phrase of Theodore Roosevelt's, was always the empire's heel of Achilles. Roosevelt's eldest son, Theodore Roosevelt Jr., who served as governor of Puerto Rico and the Philippines in the 1930s, eventually reached the same conclusion as his father. Walter Lippman, in his preface to Roosevelt Jr.'s memoir, described it as "a confession that the imperialistic dream of 1898 has proved to be unrealizable, that the management of an empire by a democracy is impossible."[2]

If there was anything exceptional about American imperialism, it did not come from the metropole's liberal culture or democratic traditions. Although American administrators frequently wrapped themselves in the mantle of Jeffersonian democracy, the empire they created was designed to limit democratic checks and to operate with limited input from colonized peoples and from their own duly elected

---

[1] Root to Jessup, September 20, 1930, quoted in Jessup, *Elihu Root*, v. 1, 369.
[2] Theodore Roosevelt, *Colonial Policies of the United States* (New York: Doubleday, Doran & Co., 1937), xiii.

representatives in Congress. Empire, of course, was not new to the United States, but the acquisition of overseas colonies that were never intended for white settlement demanded new systems of state authority. Unlike the American settler empire created on the North American continent, the imperialism that would take root after the Spanish–American War developed, in part, as an interinstitutional battle between Congress and the executive. In the end, it was this struggle within the structure of the constitutional system that most directly shaped the American empire.

A central claim of this book is that we must understand the "imperial experiment" as a formative moment in American state development. The American empire created a new political space that was seen by some officials as an abundant opportunity to increase the relative power of the executive in foreign affairs. Scholars traditionally think of institutions as sources of stability, but new responsibilities in governance can also present opportunities for new systems of authority to form. As Karen Orren and Stephen Skowronek write, such moments may create "a new distribution of authority among persons or organizations within the polity at large or between them and their counterparts outside."[3] And as we have seen, past actions by Congress and the bureaucracy changed the options available to the president and executive bureaucracies in the projection of American power and the governance of overseas colonies. Each new expansion required a renegotiation among Congress, the president, and the relevant bureaucracies, but the temporal dimension dictated what options were available at each time – past fights changed the future rules and strategies.

This book has explained key moments in the development of American empire as strategic moves by the president and executive officials to maximize their discretion over American foreign affairs, while minimizing congressional supervision. A series of strong presidents – Theodore Roosevelt in particular – certainly played a role in this outcome. Roosevelt himself was famously boastful about his convictions in support of an expansive executive, remarking to one British statesman in 1908 about his actions in expanding the reach of US empire, "in all these cases I have felt not merely that my action was right in itself, but that in showing the strength of, or in giving strength to, the executive, I was establishing a precedent of value."[4]

Yet these changes were not due to force of personality alone. Had American insular state bureaucrats remained passive actors, the empire might have taken a very different form. There were, after all, few congressional pressures to do much more than maintain order. Ironically, Congress's restrictions on the power of colonial officials gave rise to new institutions that limited its oversight and proved difficult to control. As Roosevelt explained in 1906,

Some of the things the Senate does really work to increase the power of the Executive. In this nation, as in any nation which amounts to anything, those in the end must govern who are willing actually to do the work of governing; and in so far as the Senate becomes a merely obstructionist body it will run the risk of seeing its power pass into other hands.[5]

[3] Karren Orren and Stephen Skowronek, *The Search for American Political Development* (New York: Cambridge University Press, 2004), 123.
[4] Roosevelt to George Otto Trevelyan, June 19, 1908, in Morison, ed., *The Letters of Theodore Roosevelt*, v. 6, 1085.
[5] Roosevelt to John St. Loe Strachey, February 12, 1906, in Morison, ed., *The Letters of Theodore Roosevelt*, v. 5, 151.

Now Congress, which had dominated American foreign relations for the second half of the nineteenth century, was left with few tools and limited capacity to direct the American external state. By 1917, merely two decades after the Spanish–American War, a French social scientist observed that Roosevelt's successor, Woodrow Wilson, "exercises a virtual dictatorship in foreign policy."[6]

In an age of congressional power, the executive's dominance of foreign affairs could not be assumed – it had to be built. By delegating most responsibility for overseas colonial administration, but restricting access to domestic state resources, Congress motivated colonial state officials to seek out new sources of power. Most members of Congress had little direct interest in America's overseas empire and were concerned, first and foremost, with protecting domestic constituencies. Although similar public–private partnerships were central to an earlier period of overland expansion, their proximate cause in this era was the inability of colonial bureaucrats to secure sufficient domestic state support for their ambitious agenda.

Faced with such limited support, insular state bureaucrats formed partnerships with bankers that were based on an implied, if not legal, guarantee of their investments. Through their own organizational efforts, resulting mainly from their belief that the United States should become a great power, insular state bureaucrats developed an independent civil service, a separate revenue base, an independent currency, and the ability to raise funds through Wall Street bond sales. The development of this institutional capacity allowed executive officials to continue to expand the American empire even in the face of public indifference and congressional obstructionism. In the Philippines and Puerto Rico, colonial state officials gained access to private American capital through bond sales to finance infrastructure improvements. In the Dominican Republic and Haiti, private money was used to refinance sovereign debt and to bring these nations under informal American control. Yet the order that the receivership system promised proved illusory. This fragile autonomy, with its reliance on information control, private funds, and a set of ideas about the goals of empire, would eventually collapse. Indeed, stability would come not from attentive financial management by colonial state bureaucrats, but from the marines ordered in by Woodrow Wilson.

This story, then, shows how truly autonomous action is possible in the American constitutional system by a group of committed executive officials, but it also demonstrates that autonomy achieved through these means is unlikely to be sustainable over the long term. If there is anything hopeful to come out of this study, it is that colonized people recognized this, too. The financial collapse in the Philippines and the independence movements in Haiti and the Dominican Republic embarrassed the insular state, drew unwanted attention from Congress, and suggested that there was no easy path to imperial power. The soft underbelly of the American empire was not in Manila, Santo Domingo, or Port-au-Prince. It was in Washington.

---

[6] Joseph Barthélemy quoted in Robert A. Dahl, *Congress and Foreign Policy* (New York: Harcourt, Brace, 1950), 96.

MECHANISMS OF RULE

The theories advanced here show how the expansion and governance of the empire was shaped by the American system of separated powers, and how the empire was constructed with low administrative capacity and little public support. In this way, the development of American empire might be thought of as the negative image of Carpenter's (2001) theory of bureaucratic autonomy – one that suggests a sinister, but more tenuous, path to autonomous state action through the three mechanisms discussed in this book:

- Inconspicuous Action: *Executive officials exploit Congress's limited electoral incentives to invest in oversight by pursuing strategies to reduce attention and remain politically inconspicuous.*
- State-Building through Collaboration: *Bureaucrats may pursue independent goals through the formation of collaborative partnerships to "borrow" the capacity of non-state actors.*
- Ideas as Goals: *Shared policy paradigms serve as focal points and road maps for bureaucrats by clarifying goals, defining means-end relationships, and holding coalitions together.*

One common thread that runs through the first two mechanisms is that they were motivated by congressional constraints on the power of executive officials to achieve an expansive empire. As the narratives in this book demonstrate, congressional opposition to imperial expansion profoundly shaped the development of empire, primarily through *ex ante* adjustments by the president and colonial bureaucrats to avoid congressional scrutiny. In the final analysis, it is clear that these restraints were strong – the bureaucrats were not willing to flout Congress's will directly – and congressional opposition made the creation of an enduring American empire significantly more difficult.

This fear of congressional sanction, however, led presidents and executive officials to construct a foreign policy state by exploiting Congress's short-time horizons and by manipulating the salience of the "empire question" at home. Prevented from achieving their more ambitious goals by Congress, they pursued it through other means: by holding a monopoly on information about affairs in the colonies, by acting to minimize public attention and to avoid congressional scrutiny, and by raising private capital when Congress proved unwilling to provide public funding. To continue to increase American influence in international affairs in the face of a hostile and intransigent Congress, in other words, insular officials took advantage of Congress's focus on domestic concerns by controlling information and by asking for few domestic state resources. The result was that the BIA was able to achieve many of its goals for an expansive American empire – at least in the short term.

Although presidential power was enhanced through this experience of imperialism, none of the presidents in this period (with the exception of Taft, of course) paid particularly careful attention to colonial policy. Roosevelt, for example, largely deferred to Root and Taft in all matters relating to the empire, and Wilson seems to have left the Philippines entirely in the hands of Harrison. Much of this story, then, is a story of the response of bureaucrats to these congressional constraints.

The actions of state elites were, initially, driven by their unfruitful interactions with Congress, and in this sense they were – at least in the early days of the empire – "forced to be free."[7] The result of this, however, was the creation of new forms of capacity (such as access to Wall Street capital) that allowed them to begin implementing their own imperial policies. Yet as the narratives here have shown, these new forms of capacity rested on fragile foundations (both political and financial) that would soon collapse. In the end, it was not American cultural traditions but American institutions that shaped the empire's development.

Although the dream of long-lasting formal empire would, of course, collapse in the 1920s, these decades of colonial rule laid the foundations for an executive-dominated national security state that would emerge after World War II. After all, the lessons of formal imperialism could have hardly been lost on officials such as Sumner Welles, who served as special commissioner to the Dominican Republic's occupation government and later served as Under Secretary of State for Franklin D. Roosevelt; or Henry Stimson, who served as Secretary of War under Taft and Governor of the Philippines under Herbert Hoover before he became Secretary of War during World War II.

AMERICAN EMPIRE AND PROGRESSIVISM

In light of the importance placed on ideas in this study – the last of the explanatory mechanisms – it seems right to conclude with a reflection on the role of Progressivism in the creation of American imperialism. As intellectual historians have long pointed out, Progressive ideas and social policies traveled easily between Europe and the United States, and reforms in one place often influenced those in the other.[8] As the narratives presented here suggest, these ideas also traveled to the colonial periphery and shaped the empire in powerful ways. The architects of American imperialism found in these Progressive ideas a justification for a vision of imperialism that would demonstrate to the world the genius of American administration and the benevolence of American culture.

One can only understand their antithetical goals of bringing democracy to colonized societies and implementing programs of social control if one understands that these were also goals of domestic Progressives. Participation was valued so long as complex decisions were reserved for experts. To be sure, they wanted the United States to become a great power, but these strategic motivations were no less dear to them than their ambitious plans to remake their colonies and protectorates in the image of the United States itself. It was crucial that domestic and international audiences see America's approach to imperialism as more enlightened and

---

[7] I thank an anonymous reviewer for suggesting this phrase.
[8] For some excellent examples, see Daniel T. Rodgers, *Atlantic Crossings: Social Politics in a Progressive Age* (Cambridge, MA: Harvard University Press, 1998); Alan Dawley, *Changing the World: American Progressives in War and Revolution* (Princeton, NJ: Princeton University Press, 2003); James T. Kloppenberg, *Uncertain Victory: Social Democracy and Progressivism in European and American Thought, 1870–1920* (New York: Oxford University Press, 1986). See also Andrew Bacevich, *American Empire: The Realities and Consequences of U.S. Diplomacy* (Cambridge, MA: Harvard University Press, 2004).

far more democratic than its European rivals. As journalist and historian Carleton Beals wrote in his 1932 classic *Banana Gold*,

The credo of the Imperialist is simple; he believes that the United States represents the final word in human perfection; that all Americans are always honest, and that nearly all foreigners are devious and dishonest; that all Americans are brave and most foreigners cowards. He believes in good roads, sanitation, the strict enforcement of the law, stability, work, machinery, efficiency, the punctilious payment of debts, and democracy . . . The Imperialist at work abroad is muddle-headed but he is fantastically honest; the shining aura of the crusade always mantles all his acts.[9]

The result was their obsessive focus on infrastructure, sound money, public health, and elementary education. That some of these programs were beneficial to colonized people cannot be denied. Yet whatever the benefits gained from American investments in education and health, these reforms were *imposed* on people to demonstrate the genius of American culture. Indeed, many of them – from elementary education to the construction of roads and railroads – were developed in the hope that the colonies would emerge as desirable places for American investment. The truth, as Mark Twain understood in 1901, is that there never was anything particularly benevolent or tutelary about America's system of imperialism. This "Blessings-of-Civilization Trust," like its rival European regimes, ultimately survived through violence and existed for the benefit of a small number of metropolitan elites.[10]

[9] Carleton Beals, *Banana Gold* (Philadelphia, PA: Lippincott, 1932), 294.
[10] Mark Twain, "To the Person Sitting in Darkness," *North American Review* 172 (February 1901): 161–76.

Index

Printed in the USA
CPSIA information can be obtained
at www.ICGtesting.com
CBHW032316010424
6237CB00003B/197